David Irving is the son of a Royal Navy commander. Educated at Imperial College of Science and Technology and at University College, London, he subsequently spent a year in Germany working in a steel mill and perfecting his fluency in the language. His best-known works include *The Destruction of Dresden, Accident – The Death of General Sikorski, The Rise and Fall of the Luftwaffe* and *The Trail of the Fox: The Life of Field Marshal Erwin Rommel.* He has translated *The Memoirs of Field Marshal Keitel* and *The Memoirs of General Reinhard Gehlen. Hitler's War,* his famous 'sequel' to *The War Path,* is also published by Papermac in a two-volume edition.

THE
WAR PATH
Hitler's Germany
1933-1939

David Irving

MACMILLAN LONDON

First published in Great Britain 1978 by Michael Joseph Limited

First published in paperback 1983 by
PAPERMAC
a division of Macmillan Publishers Limited
4 Little Essex Street London WC2R 3LF
and Basingstoke

Associated companies in Auckland, Dallas, Delhi, Dublin,
Hong Kong, Johannesburg, Lagos, Manzini, Melbourne, Nairobi,
New York, Singapore, Tokyo, Washington and Zaria

ISBN 0 333 35790 6

Printed in Hong Kong

The cover illustration of Adolf Hitler at Bückeberg, 1934, is
reproduced by kind permission of Ullstein Bilderdienst, West Berlin.

Contents

Author's Foreword

This book narrates one man's path to war – Adolf Hitler's. The narrative ends at the precise moment when the companion volume, *Hitler's War**, begins: the evening of 3 September 1939, as he leaves his Berlin Chancellery for the Polish war-front. Like that volume, which aroused controversy, *The War Path* also tries to describe events from behind the Führer's desk, and to see and understand each episode through his eyes. The technique necessarily narrows the viewpoint, but it does help to explain otherwise inexplicable decisions. Nobody that I know of has attempted this before, but to me it seemed worth all the effort: after all, Hitler's war sucked in one country after another, left forty million dead and caused all Europe and half Asia to be wasted by fire and explosives; it destroyed Hitler's Third Reich, bankrupted Britain and lost her her Empire, and brought lasting disorder to the world's affairs; it saw the entrenchment of Communism in one continent, and its emergence in another.

I have approached the main narrative in logical chronological sequence. How Hitler actually came to power in 1933 is merely outlined here – the topic has been proficiently covered by others, particularly Karl Dietrich Bracher and Wolfgang Sauer. The focus of my research fell on his years of power; and from 3 February 1933, when Hitler tells his generals in secret of his ambition to launch a war of imperial conquest in the east as soon as Germany is able, the detail thickens and the colour becomes enriched.

As in the writing of *Hitler's War*, I have avoided as far as possible the use of all published literature in favour of the available primary sources of the day. Many works that I have read do adhere to the strictest rules of historical evidence. But too many do not, too many post-war books contain pitfalls for the historian. Quite apart from the doctored diaries mentioned in my Introduction to *Hitler's War* – like Ciano's diaries – some sources on the pre-war years are no less

* *Hitler's War*, published in 1977 by The Viking Press Inc (New York), Hodder & Stoughton Ltd (London) and in other countries.

tainted: the late Konrad Heiden's early biography *Der Führer* is largely worthless; Carl-Jakob Burckhardt's "diary" quoted in his memoir, *Meine Danziger Mission 1937–1939*, is impossible to reconcile with Hitler's actual movements as recorded in the diaries of his staff; while *Conversations with Hitler* (Zürich, 1940), the oft-quoted book by the former Danzig politician Hermann Rauschning who emigrated to the United States, has bedevilled analyses of Hitler's policies ever since. An internal Nazi investigation showed that Rauschning met Hitler only a couple of times on formal occasions. The republication of Rauschning's book in Vienna in 1973 includes a final chapter deleted from the original 1940 edition entitled "Hitler Privat"; it was revealing in more senses than one, as it purported to describe how Hitler regularly woke up at night screaming, "It's Him – Him!", meaning the Devil. As the noted West German historian Professor Eberhard Jäckel has emphasized in *Geschichte in Wissenschaft und Unterricht* (No 11, 1977) this disposes of Rauschning's credibility once and for all. The published "memoirs" of one of Hitler's personal secretaries, also entitled *Hitler Privat*, published by Albert Zoller in Düsseldorf in 1949, are equally unreliable; the secretary concerned, Christa Schroeder, had had to write a manuscript in Allied captivity, and vehemently disowns the authorship of much of what was, without her knowledge or consent, published in the book.

In this list of spurious "primary sources" belong, in my view, Martin Bormann's alleged notes on Hitler's final bunker conversations in 1945, published in 1961 as *The Testament of Adolf Hitler*: the plans of the respectable German firm Hoffmann & Campe to publish these intriguing notes in German were abandoned three years ago.

Of course, field-work is expensive and often unrewarding. It is an acquired taste. It means bargaining for years with governments like that of East Germany for permission to search for buried documents; it means long separations from wife and family, sleeping on overnight trains, and haggling with crabby retired generals and politicians or their widows, to part them temporarily from their carefully-guarded caches of diaries or letters. It means leafing through hundreds of thousands of pages of filthy paper in remote and chilly archives, intuitively registering egregious facts in the hope that some of them may, perhaps, click with facts found years later in another file five thousand miles away.

Years have passed since I began. I remember, in 1965, driving to Tilbury docks to collect a crate of microfilm ordered from the US government for this book; the liner that brought the crate has long been scrapped. I never anticipated that thirteen years would pass before publication. I suppose I have taken it all at a far too leisurely pace. Other writers have overtaken me; I have been scooped more than once, and in more than one country – but I hope that this biography will outlast its rivals, and that more and more future writers will find themselves compelled to consult it for materials that are contained in none of the others.

I make no apology for having revised the existing picture of Adolf Hitler. The post-war world's view of him has been so conditioned by our own propaganda against him, that only the cartoon caricature of him prevails; hence any account based on authentic records of the era is bound to enhance history's view of him in some respects – although it will detract from it in many others. I have tried to accord him the kind of hearing that he would have got in an English court of law – where the normal rules of evidence apply, but also where a measure of insight is appropriate.

Yet it is ironic that diplomatic historians never once bothered in thirty years to visit the widow of Joachim von Ribbentrop's state secretary, von Weizsäcker; they would have found out that she still had all her husband's papers and diaries.* Had they looked for the widow of Walther Hewel, Ribbentrop's liaison officer to Hitler, they would have learned about his diaries too. And what kind of historian offers us a book on the origins of the Second World War without consulting the German foreign ministry file entitled: "Documents on the Outbreak of the War"? (It contains for instance the wiretap reports on the British and French embassies in Berlin, 1938–9, and decoding results on their secret telegrams.) And who are these emotional historians of the Jewish holocaust who rely only on the printed Nuremberg exhibits, and have never troubled themselves even to open a file of the SS chief Heinrich Himmler's own handwritten telephone notes, or to read his memoranda for his secret meetings with Adolf Hitler? Some people allude to Hitler's *Mein Kampf* or, more specifically, to the "Wannsee Conference" called in January 1942 by Reinhard Heydrich as proof of Hitler's evil intentions against the Jews; but Hitler never indicated in his book any intention to liquidate these enemies of his, and nor was any such intention referred to in the various transcripts of the Wannsee Conference (which was, in any case, called by Heydrich at state-secretary level – the conference was neither convened nor attended by Hitler and I do not think he even knew of it).

History since 1945 has been plagued by the effects of the Nuremberg Trials – by the prosecution teams' methods of selection of exhibits, by the subsequent publication of the selected documents in neatly printed and indexed volumes, and by the incineration in a Bavarian forest pit of documents that, it was felt, would hinder the Allied prosecution effort. Exhibits were chosen less for their representative nature than because they displayed Axis criminality, or tended

---

*They have now been published by a Canadian, Leonidas E. Hill: *Die Weizsäcker Papiere 1933–1950* (Berlin, 1974).

to bolster the various propaganda hypotheses employed prior to 1945 to justify western intervention in Hitler's war – they were calculated to prove that Hitler *had*, all along, harboured aggressive designs against Britain and her Empire, that he *had* plotted war against the United States, and that the systematic liquidation of the millions of European Jews *was* all part of the Nazi grand design, to which every one of the defendants was privy. It was all so much more emotive for western appetites than Hitler's mundane territorial ambitions in Central Europe and the east.

At Nuremberg, everything was simplified in the first trials (though rather more truth began to emerge in the Subsequent Proceedings that commenced in late 1946). The Nuremberg prosecutors produced records of only three key secret Hitler speeches to his commanders – those on 5 November 1937, 23 May 1939 and 22 August 1939 – and they based much of their speculation on them: a kind of leaping from peak to peak. But, as Trevor-Roper has rightly observed, the central purpose of Hitler's foreign policy remained consistent throughout his career: a campaign of conquest in the east. And when all Hitler's secret speeches are analysed, using reliable source materials, this is quite clear: he stated this objective in his speech of 3 February 1933 (pages 28–9), and on numerous subsequent occasions. I have located without much difficulty the records of many more secret "programme" speeches by Hitler, proving this consistency of aim: on 21 January 1938, on page 67 ("One day, the entire world . . ."); on 28 May 1938 (page 101); on 15 August 1938 (pages 123–4); and of particular interest, several speeches delivered by Hitler in secret to senior officers during January, February and March 1939 – and recorded on discs – during which he made it quite plain that Nazi Germany was inevitably steering towards war (pages 173–6). These speeches, of pivotal importance, have been neglected by Hitler's biographers – either because they had not been identified and listed in convenient archive catalogues; or because the biographer did not set foot in foreign archives anyway; or because the speeches have not yet been translated into English. German writers have even lamented – e.g. in the annotations to *Tagebücher eines Abwehroffiziers* (Stuttgart, 1970) – that no transcripts of the speeches exist: well, they do, and I have quoted some of their most important lines.

In writing this volume I have obtained a number of little known but authentic diaries of people in Hitler's entourage, including an unpublished segment of Alfred Jodl's diary; the official diary kept for OKW chief Wilhelm Keitel by his adjutant Wolf Eberhard, and Eberhard's own diary, 1936–9; the diary of Nikolaus von Vormann, army liaison officer to Hitler during August and September 1939; and diaries kept by Martin Bormann and by Hitler's personal adjutant, Max Wünsche, relating to the Führer's movements. In addition I have used the unpublished diaries of Fedor von Bock, Erhard Milch, Wilhelm Leeb,

Ernst von Weizsäcker, Erwin Lahousen and Eduard Wagner. Many of these men wrote revealing private letters too – Frau Elisabeth Wagner gave me some 2,000 pages of Eduard Wagner's letters, significant sections of which turned out to have been omitted from their published version. Christa Schroeder, Hitler's secretary, also made available to me important contemporary papers, while Julius Schaub's family let me copy all his manuscripts and writings about his twenty years as Hitler's senior aide. I believe I am the first biographer to have used the papers of Herbert Backe, a state-secretary in the Nazi government; I am certainly the first to have exploited the diaries, notebooks and papers of Fritz Todt, builder of Hitler's autobahns and his first munitions minister, through the kindness of his daughter, Ilsebill Todt.

Some of the most revealing documents used exclusively here in *The War Path* are the private manuscripts written by General von Fritsch, which I obtained from a Soviet source; they relate the entire Blomberg/Fritsch crisis of 1938 through Fritsch's own eyes. No former Hitler employee whom I approached declined to grant me interviews; from the various government archives I obtained detailed interrogation reports on many of them, too. All these records are now part of the Irving Collection in the Institute of Contemporary History in Munich, available with some exceptions to other researchers. There, too, researchers will find the line-by-line annotations originally prepared for this book (some 1,500 pages of source-notes!); these were dispensed with in this volume for reasons of space, but where I anticipate that the reader will definitely want to know more, I do point – at the back of the book, from page 267 – to some of the more noteworthy sources that I have tapped. Second World War researchers will find that many of the special microfilms of materials that I prepared while researching this book are now available through E. P. Microforms Ltd., East Ardsley, Wakefield, Yorkshire, England.

There have been sceptics who questioned whether the heavy reliance on – inevitably angled – private sources is any better as a method of investigating Hitler's career than the more traditional quarries of information. My reply is that it would, equally, be wrong to deny the value of such private sources altogether. I certainly have not, and the result is, I hope, the closest possible approximation to the truth about Hitler's approach to war. As the authoritative *Washington Post* noted in its review of *Hitler's War*: "British historians have always been more objective towards Hitler than either German or American writers." American writers have certainly used high-key palettes when painting recent portraits of him. Walter C. Langer's study, *The Mind of Adolf Hitler: The Secret Wartime Report* (New York, 1972), contained some speculative psychiatry too obscene for reproduction here. And what are we to make of the amazing language used by the American psycho-historian Professor Robert Waite, in linking Hitler to the liquidation of the Jews: "Even the method of the murders", wrote Waite, "was in line with Hitler's personal infatuation with hygiene, filth, stench, putrefaction and strangulation."

My Adolf Hitler was a different man from Waite's. There is, in the chapters that follow, further evidence in support of my contention that Hitler was a less omnipotent Führer than has been believed, and that his grip on his subordinates weakened with each passing year: three episodes – the aftermath of the Ernst Röhm affair of 30 June 1934, the Dollfuss assassination a month later and the anti-Jewish pogrom of November 1938 – show how his powers were pre-empted by men to whom he felt himself in one way or another indebted, by Himmler, the SS and Goebbels. Perhaps the Blomberg/Fritsch scandal itself belongs in this category as well.

While my Hitler's central and guiding ambition always remains constant, his methods and tactics were profoundly opportunistic. Like Winston Churchill, who often referred to hearing the "fluttering wings" of Fate, Hitler firmly believed in grabbing fleeting opportunities. "There is but one moment when the Goddess of Fortune wafts by," he lectured his adjutants in 1938, "and if you don't grasp her by the hem you won't get a second chance!" The manner in which he seized on the double scandal in January 1938 to divest himself of the over-conservative Army C-in-C, Fritsch, and to become his own Supreme Commander too, is a good example: he had no *need* to engineer such a situation, because one word from Hitler would have sufficed for both men to resign dutifully anyway; but when the scandal broke, he knew how to exploit it.

To British readers it is of no small interest to see how desperately Hitler tried to impress on the British his lack of aggressive ambitions in the west. He was probably sincere in this – he had certainly built the wrong air force and the wrong navy for a sustained campaign against the British Isles; while subtle indications, like his instructions to Fritz Todt in 1936 (page 31) to erect huge monuments on the Reich's western frontiers, suggest that for Hitler these frontiers were of a lasting nature.

There is commensurate proof of Hitler's plans to invade the east – his February 1933 secret speech, his August 1936 memorandum (page 50), his June 1937 instructions for the expansion of Pillau as a Baltic naval base (page 64), and his remarks to Mussolini in May 1938 (page 97), that "Germany will step out along the ancient Teutonic path, towards the East." Not until later that month did Hitler finally resign himself to the likelihood that Britain and France would probably not stand aside (page 102). There is no evidence that Hitler regarded the Nazi-Soviet Pact of August 1939 as anything but a cynical measure of convenience.

These last pre-war years saw Hitler's intensive reliance on strategic deception and psychological warfare techniques. The principle was not new: Napoleon himself had defined it as, "In a war all is mental, and opinion makes up more than half of reality"; and Napoleon had pointed out too, "The reputation of one's arms in war is everything and equivalent to real forces." By using the records of the Propaganda Ministry and various editorial offices, I have tried to illustrate how advanced the Nazis were in these techniques, from the remilitarization of the German Rhineland in 1936 to their biggest triumph, the Munich Agreement of 1938.

Related to this theme is my emphasis on Hitler's startlingly efficient foreign Intelligence sources. Other writers seem to have ignored this factor, readily ascribing Hitler's surefootedness to his alleged "intuition", his *Fingerspitzengefühl*. As in *Hitler's War*, we find in this book too that the Nazis' wiretapping and decoding agency, the Forschungsamt, holds the key to many of Hitler's successes, both internally and in foreign affairs: the agency provided him with instructive and sometimes hilarious wiretaps on people like Pastor Martin Niemöller (page 221), it eavesdropped on foreign diplomats in Berlin and – even more significantly – it fed to Hitler hour-by-hour transcripts of the lurid and incautious teleophone conversations conducted between an embattled Prague and the Czech diplomats in London and Paris in September 1938 (pages 136–46). These are used here for the first time. From the time of Munich until the outbreak of war with Britain, the agency fed similar wiretap information to Hitler on the conversations between the British and French governments and their embassies in Berlin: thus he could follow hourly how his enemies were reacting to each Nazi ploy, and he rightly deduced by 22 August 1939 that while the western powers might well formally declare war, they would not actually fight – not at first, that is.

Those critics who took exception to my treatment, in *Hitler's War*, of his attitude to the "Jewish question" – and there were many, particularly in North America – will find that his actions in the years before the war were wholly consistent with my central hypothesis: that Hitler grasped quite early on that anti-Semitism would be a powerful vote-catching force in Germany (see pages xx–xxii) and that he had no compunction against riding that evil horse right up to the portals of the Chancellery in 1933; but that once inside and in power, he "dismounted" and paid only lip-service to that part of his creed. The Nazi gangsters under him continued to ride to hounds, however, even when Hitler dictated differently, e.g. in November 1938 (pages 165–6). As for the concentration camps, of which that at Dachau was the most notorious during the period covered by this book, Hitler comfortably left that dark side of the Nazi rule to his executive henchmen, notably Heinrich Himmler. He never visited one, and expressed no desire to; those senior non-SS officials who did obtain privileged access to the camps, like Ernst Udet or General Erhard Milch in 1933, were favourably impressed (as indeed were selected foreign guests accorded the same privilege); but those were early days. The liquidation programmes had not yet begun, and there is clear enough evidence that Hitler's wishes frequently did not coincide with the clumsy and mindless brutality of his cronies. Himmler is known to have visited Auschwitz liquidation camp twice, in 1941 and 1942; Hitler never did. Führer though he was in name, he rarely intervened in the Nazi Party's persecution of the Jews, one way or the other. Documents that actually link Hitler with the treatment of the Jews invariably take the form of embargoes. Thus we find a senior Reich law officer minuting in the winter of 1941–2: "Reich Minister Lammers" – Hitler's top civil servant – "informed me that the Führer has repeatedly pronounced that he wants the solution of the Jewish Question put off until after the war is over." Whatever way one looks at this document, whatever way we interpret that phrase, "solution of the Jewish Question", it is incompatible with the notion that Hitler wished, ordered or even knew of the liquidation programme that was in fact already under way. (The document, believed destroyed in 1946, has only recently surfaced in a Justice ministry file, R22/52, in the archives in Koblenz.) Hermann Göring is on record as stressing, at a meeting of the Reich research council on 6 July 1942 in Berlin, how much the doctrinaire harassment of Jewish scientists, for example, was deprecated by the Führer and himself:

> I have discussed this with the Führer himself now; we have been able to use one Jew two years longer in Vienna, and another in photographic research, because they have certain things that we need and that can be of the utmost benefit to us at the present. It would be utter madness for us to say now: "He'll have to go. He was a magnificent researcher, a fantastic brain, but his wife is Jewish, and he can't be allowed to stay at the University," etc.
>
> The Führer has made similar exceptions in the arts all the way down to operetta level; he is all the more likely to make exceptions where really great projects or researchers are concerned.*

The critics act as though anti-Semitism was a purely Nazi phenomenon, and not a curse that has plagued civilization for millenia. But wartime London saw many instances, as did the United States: there was violent anti-Jewish rioting in Boston, Massachusetts, in November 1943. Anti-Semitism was endemic in North America: Roosevelt conducted empirical experiments to find out what Jewish concentration a local community could tolerate, and found that the average township would not stand for more than four or five such families. Every modern US president complained of Jewish pressure-groups, often in the most undiplomatic language. Harry S. Truman said in one Cabinet meeting in July 1946, "Jesus Christ could not please them when he was here on earth, so how could anyone expect that I would have any luck!"† These typify the kind of

---

* I first published this revealing quotation in my history of German atomic research, *The Virus House* (London, 1967).

† John Morton Blum (ed.), *The Price of Vision – The Diary of Henry A. Wallace, 1942–1946* (Boston, 1973).

latent anti-Semitic feelings to which even educated and "upper middle-class" British and Americans were prone between the wars – the kind of sentiments on which the Nazi phenomenon was able to prey. But it was the Nazi Party fanatics who took their anti-Semitism to such cruel extremes.

For readers conditioned to blame all the miseries of Poland's Jews on Hitler, it will perhaps be a jolt to read a secret note by the Polish ambassador Josef Lipski on a meeting with Hitler in September 1938 (page 162): Lipski wrote that Hitler had mentioned the idea of solving the Jewish problem in unison with Poland, Hungary and perhaps Romania too, by obliging the Jews to emigrate ("to the colonies"). Lipski wrote enthusiastically to his foreign minister in Warsaw: "I replied that we would erect a fine statue to him in Warsaw if he found a Solution." (The Russians published the letter after the war.)

And if Hitler *was* an incorrigible anti-Semite, what are we to make of the urgent edict issued by Rudolf Hess, deputy Führer, during the infamous Night of the Broken Glass – the first, Goebbels-inspired, nationwide anti-Jewish pogrom in November 1938 – ordering an immediate stop to all such outrages "on orders from the very highest level". Every other historian, even if he found this document (which is in Berlin files), has shut his eyes to it and documents like it, and hoped that when he opened his eyes the horrid, inconvenient item would have somehow gone away.

They have resorted to postulating the existence of Führer orders even if there was not the slightest written evidence of their existence. John Toland, author of a recent Hitler biography published in the United States, appealed emotionally in the magazine *Der Spiegel* for German historians to refute my statement that Hitler did not order the systematic liquidation of the European Jews, and was probably not even aware that it was going on; but so far the German historians have been unable to help him, apart from suggesting that "of course" the whole project was so secret that only oral orders were issued, so as not to implicate the Führer. But why should Hitler have become so circumspect in this instance, since in contrast he had shown no compunction about personally signing a blanket order for the liquidation of tens of thousands of *fellow-Germans* (the Euthanasia Programme); and his comparable orders for the liquidation of enemy prisoners (the Commando Order), of Allied airmen (the Lynch Order) and Russian functionaries (the Commissar Order) are documented all the way from Führer's headquarters right down the line to the executioners? Jews did not rank higher than any of these in popularity in Nazi Germany.

To buttress such hostile arguments, other writers have relied on weak and unprofessional evidence. I am quite sure that they do so in the sincere belief that their evidence is adequate, but closer analysis does not bear this view out. For example, they offer shrewd alternative translations of words in Hitler's speeches – apparently the liquidation was too secret for him to sign an order, but not so secret that he could not brag about it in his public speeches! – and seemingly damning quotations from documents that have, however, long been discarded by serious historians as fakes, like the Gerstein Report or the Bunker conversations. They have not infrequently relied on false logic, assuming for the purposes of their argument the very things that they are supposed to be proving: but of explicit, written, wartime evidence, the kind of evidence that could hang a man, not one line has been produced.

I suspect that part of the reason for the powerful feelings generated by *Hitler's War* is this: the critics have attacked it not for what is in it, but for what they had expected to find in it. Rumours about what I was writing circulated for many years – long before I even set pen to paper! I hope that with the completion of this two-volume biography, some of these rumours at least have been laid, and that History will find something to learn from Hitler's rise and fall. What I most regret is that in the commotion staged over the biography's revelations about Hitler's real attitude to the Jews, far more serious questions in the body of the biography are being overlooked: the discovery, for instance, that at no time did this man pose or intend a real threat to Britain or the Empire. Could Britain have acted more rationally in 1939 and 1940? Should she have? These are questions that ought not to be ignored.

DAVID IRVING
LONDON, DECEMBER 1977

Prologue: The Nugget

How can we ever learn what Hitler's real ambitions were?

No doubt an unrefined black nugget of ambition did nestle deep within him, but it was well hidden beneath a thousand shrouds, and repressed by his own personal fears of baring his innermost intentions even to the most intimate of his friends.

One of the men closest to him, who served him as airforce adjutant from 1937 to the very end, has emphasized that even when we read of some startling outburst by Hitler to his henchmen, and we feel we are getting closer to the truth, we must always ask ourselves: was that the real Hitler, or was it still just an image that he wished to impose on that particular audience of the moment? Were those his authentic aims, or was he just seeking to jolt his complacent satraps out of a dangerous lethargy?

So we must go prospecting deep down into the bedrock of his history before we can trace to its origins that consistent seam of secret, consuming ambition of which the last six years of his life were just the violent expression. *Mein Kampf*, written in prison in 1924 and afterwards, certainly reveals some of these secrets, and in later years he regretted having published it for just that reason; because the Hitler of the Chancellery in Berlin was more circumspect than the Hitler of the barricades, and the Hitler in the first foothills of power was more subtle of tongue than the demobilized foot-soldier and agitator of the beerhalls of Bavaria.

Excellent sources survive, even before *Mein Kampf*. The confidential police reports on twenty of Hitler's early speeches, delivered in smoky, crowded halls in the revolutionary Soviet Munich of 1919 and 1920, provide a series of glimpses at the outer shell of his beliefs, which he was still adapting to accommodate whichever views he found to be most loudly acclaimed by the two or three thousand listeners he attracted on each occasion. Here Adolf Hitler, just turned thirty years of age, expressed no grand geopolitical ideas, no dreams of eastern empire: evidently these ambitions must have grown within him soon after. His agitation pivoted on the terms dictated to Berlin's "craven and corrupt" representatives at Versailles; he tried to convince his audience that defeat in the World War had been inflicted on them not by their enemies abroad, but by the revolutionaries within – the Jew-ridden politicians in Berlin. This, 1920, was the year in which the National Socialist German Workers' Party launched its programme, donned its swastika armbands and organized its own squads to keep order – the later Sturmabteilung (SA) brownshirt bullies.

Stripped of their demagogic element, the speeches are significant only for Hitler's ceaseless reiteration that a Germany disarmed was prey to the lawless demands of her predatory neighbours. After the victory of 1871, Germany had been a nation of purpose, order, incorruptibility and exactitude – mighty, magnificent and respected, healthy within and powerful without, her engineers and merchants gradually displacing the British from their accustomed place astride the world markets by their diligence, uprightness and profundity. This, indicated Hitler, was the real reason why Britain had fought the war; this was the reason for the Treaty of Versailles. It was the victory of naked force over justice – the same lawless means that Britain had used against China in the opium war of 1840, and the means that had gained for Britain practically one-fifth of the earth's surface. In these outpourings Hitler's envy of Britain became plain – his envy of the national spirit, master-race qualities and genius whereby the British had won their colonial empire.

Other themes emerged in these early, beerhall speeches. He demanded that Germany become a nation without class differences, in which manual labourer and intellectual each respected the contribution of the other. On one occasion, in April 1920, he even proclaimed, "We need a dictator who is a genius, if we are to arise again."

His sentiments were ultra-nationalist. The new Party had "German" in its title, he said, "because we want to be German, and we are going to make war on the Polish-Jewish vermin". His targets were not modest even then: he was going to establish a new German Reich, extending from Memel in the east to Strasbourg in the west, and from Königsberg to Bratislava. In another secret speech, delivered to an audience in Salzburg – evidently on 7 or 8 August 1920 – Hitler roused his Austrian compatriots with the same two ideals: "Firstly, Deutschland über alles in der Welt. And secondly, our German domain extends as far as the German tongue is spoken."

This Salzburg speech, of which only one, faded, fragile and hitherto unpublished shorthand transcript has survived, comes closest to revealing his early mind and attitudes. He made the bursting of the "chains of Versailles" the prerequisite for any reforms in Germany – and foremost among those reforms he called for the eradication of the "Jewish bacillus" from their midst:

This is the first demand we must raise and do raise: that our people be set free, that these chains be burst asunder, that Germany be once again captain of her soul and master of her destinies, together with all those who want to join Germany. (*Applause*).

And the fulfilment of this first demand will then open up the way for all the other reforms. And here is one thing that perhaps distinguishes us from you [Austrians] as far as our programme is concerned, although it is very much in the spirit of things: our attitude to the Jewish problem.

For us, this is not a problem you can turn a blind eye to – one to be solved by small concessions. For us, it is a problem of whether our nation can ever recover its health, whether the Jewish spirit can ever really be eradicated. Don't be misled into thinking you can fight a disease without killing the carrier, without destroying the bacillus. Don't think you can fight racial tuberculosis without taking care to rid the nation of the carrier of that racial tuberculosis. This Jewish contamination will not subside, this poisoning of the nation will not end, until the carrier himself, the Jew, has been banished from our midst. (*Applause*).

Language like that went down well. Hitler had laced his earlier speeches with more abstract topics like the relationship between national strength and international justice; but he soon found that that was not the language that the mobs wanted to hear. In successive speeches in 1920 he called for the hanging of war profiteers and racketeers; he identified them as the Jews; and then he began to concentrate his venom on the Jews as a whole, on the Ostjuden from Russia, and on the "Polish-Jewish vermin" who had flooded into Vienna and Germany.

On 13 August 1920, the police reports show, Hitler for the first time devoted his speech solely to the Jews. First he developed abstruse racial theories, far above the head of his beer-swilling listeners. But then he accused the Jews of responsibility for the war, of having governed Germany criminally badly and of profiteering. Moreover, he warned, it was the "oriental wideboys" in the German press who were even now systematically undermining Germany's national soul – dividing and subverting her. Of friendly Vienna they had made a second Jerusalem; and while Austria's soldiers returned to slums, almost half a million Jews – mostly from Galicia – had flooded in and were now living in palatial apartments.

These slanderous claims aroused his unruly audiences. Hitler was encouraged to propose the solution. The Nazi Party must open a crusade against the Jews. "We do not want to whip up a pogrom atmosphere. But we must be fired with a remorseless determination to grasp this evil at its roots and exterminate it, root and branch." This was greeted by storms of applause; so was his recommendation: "All means are proper to that end – even if we have to agree terms with the Devil!" A few weeks later he boasted, "When we come to power, we will charge in like buffaloes." And on another occasion he repeated, "We cannot skirt round the Jewish problem. It has got to be solved."

Between 1920 and his seizure of power in 1933, the events need only be sketched in. Adolf Hitler launched an abortive revolution in Munich in November 1923, was tried, imprisoned in Landsberg fortress and eventually released. He published *Mein Kampf* and rebuilt the Party, riven in his absence by disssension, over the next years into a disciplined and authoritarian force with its own Party courts, its brownshirt SA guards and its black-uniformed "Pretorian Guard", the SS, until at the head of a swollen army of a million Party members he arrived at the Chancellery in Berlin in January 1933, after thirteen years of warfare against his self-defined targets – Marxist class-struggle, Jewish cultural and economic domination and the fetters of Versailles. It was no mean feat for an unknown, gas-blinded, penniless acting-corporal to achieve by no other means than his power of speech and a driving ambition to fulfil a still-concealed and dark ambition.

The private letters of Walther Hewel, a nineteen-year-old student imprisoned in Landsberg with him, show graphically the extraordinary hold that Hitler already exerted on his followers – a hold that lasted until 1945, when the writer committed suicide with Hitler. On 9 November 1924, first anniversary of the putsch, he wrote:

At 8 P.M. yesterday, to the strains of the Hohenfriedberg March played by the prison band, Hitler, Lieutenant-Colonel Kriebel, Dr Weber and Rudolf Hess came over to us. – 8:34 P.M.: the historical moment when the trucks of "Storm Troop Hitler" went into action on the eighth. Then Hitler made a short speech which it is simply impossible to convey in writing. It left us numb. In a few words he moved us so much that every one of these often rough and unruly men went back mutely and tamely to their cells. For half an hour none of us could speak. – What would many men have given to hear this man this evening! As though surrounded by seven thousand people in a circus, so Hitler stood in our midst in the little room. – Today, Sunday, he came over at 1 P.M. and briefly said: "Young men, one year ago at this moment your comrades were lying dead amongst you." Then he thanked us for having been so loyal to him, then and now, and gave us each his hand. And when Hitler takes your hand and looks into your eyes something like an electric shock strikes through you, a pu'se of power and energy and *Deutschtum* [Germandom] and everything that is strong and beautiful in the world. When he had done the round, he stepped shortly back: "And now – a Heil to our dead comrades. Heil!" The *way* that man said those few words, it was all over for us. . . . Perhaps you can't imagine what it's like when men honour their dead comrades, who died for something they wanted all their lives, for something of beauty, purity and majesty. Perhaps you can't, in your milieu of people who have long forgotten what Germany is, and imagine they are serving her by their speechmaking or politicking or pawning all German property abroad. But what is so beautiful and reassuring for me is that Hitler is not the visionary, the utopian, the blind patriot that people take him for, but a really great politician, thinker and realist. . . . The terrible thing is that Hitler's enemies know him better than anybody, and the Press – which is of course wholly in Jewish hands – has defamed and ridiculed the man. An old trick: first a deathly silence, then scorn, then all-out war – and then annexation. (There are Jewish firms that manufacture swastikas.)

On 14 December 1924 the student wrote once more from Landsberg:

Hitler just joined us again and had tea with the four of us. He told us about all sorts of people, and about his friend Scheubner-Richter who was killed on the ninth. Then he talked about the Mother and Woman as such. . . . And then you lie for hours on your bunk dreaming of a Germany that has regained her honour, and is not bogged down in lying, cowardly and petty Parliamentarianism – dreaming of Germans who are real men, clever and brave and not riddled with selfishness, and of German women who are mothers and not whores; dreaming of a people that love their Fatherland fanatically, and of leaders of superior intellect that will fashion this mighty populace into a sword, and will know how to wield it with cold premeditation. You ask who can lead us out of this distress. The Leader is Hitler. A short time after his release from prison, he will have millions of men around him again. . . . Because there is only one salvation left for Germany, and that is Hitler.

During those years before 1933, Hitler had fashioned his plans into their final form. He had set them out in *Mein Kampf*, and repeated them more coherently in a 1928 manuscript which he never published. He was as confident that he would see these ambitions fulfilled as that the buildings, bridges and monuments that he had neatly sketched – on postcards in black ink at his desk in Bavaria – would one day grace the reconstructed cities of Germany and Austria.

In Hitler's view, Germany's present statesmen had put domestic strength too low in their priorities. He would reverse that: a process of national consolidation would come before any ambitious foreign policies. And so indeed he acted as Chancellor, from 1933 to about 1937, adhering closely to the theories that he had laid down in the twenties in his writings and speeches, whether to mass audiences or private groups of wealthy industrialists. First he restored Germany's psychological unity; on this stable foundation he rebuilt her economic strength; and on that base in turn he built up the military might with which to enforce an active foreign policy.

It was in Hitler's 1928 manuscript that he had set out his foreign policies most cogently. Of brutal simplicity, these involved enlarging Germany's dominion from her present 216,000 square miles to over half a million, at

Russia's and Poland's expense. His contemporaries were more modest, desiring only to restore Germany's 1914 frontiers. For these men Hitler expressed nothing but contempt; this was the "dumbest foreign aim imaginable", it was "inadequate from the patriotic, and unsatisfactory from the military point of view". No, Germany must renounce her obsolete aspirations to overseas colonial markets, and revert instead to "a clear, unambiguous Raumpolitik", grasping enough Lebensraum to last the next hundred years. First Germany must "create a powerful land force", so that foreigners took her seriously. Then, he wrote in 1928, there must be an alliance with Britain and her empire, so that "together we may dictate the rest of world history".

His oratory during these years had developed most powerfully, as even his most sceptical followers admitted. His speeches were long and *ex tempore*, but logical. Each sentence was intelligible to the dullest listener without insulting the more demanding intellects. The quasi-religious idea he championed, the suggestive force emanating from him, gripped each man in his audience. As Robespierre once said of Marat, "The man was dangerous: he believed in what he said."

Hitler's resilience in power after 1933 was founded, as David Lloyd George wrote in 1936, on having kept his promises. He abolished the class war of the nineteenth century (some said he had replaced it by race war instead). He created a Germany of equal opportunity for manual and intellectual workers, for rich and poor. He made no attempt to curry favour with the intelligentsia. "He doesn't care a straw for the intelligentsia," wrote Hewel, his prison companion, on 14 December 1924. "They always raise a thousand objections to every decision. The intellectuals he needs will come to him of their own accord, and they will become his leaders." Twenty years later, in a secret speech to his generals on 27 January 1944, Hitler himself outlined the pseudo-Darwinian process he had hit upon to select Germany's new ruling class: he had used the Party itself as a deliberate vehicle for singling out the future leadership material – men of the requisite ruthlessness, whose knees would not fold when the real struggle began.

That was why his Party's manifesto had been deliberately pugnacious and aggressive.

I laid down the line to take, although there were those who warned me, "You won't win many supporters like that." But I didn't want them all, I wanted to win over a particular nucleus from the public, the nucleus that is hard as nails. I didn't want the others. . . .

That is why I set up my fighting manifesto and tailored it deliberately to attract only the toughest and most determined minority of the German people at first. When we were quite small and unimportant I often told my followers that if this manifesto is preached year after year, in thousands of speeches across the nation, it is bound to act like a magnet: gradually one steel-filing after another will detach itself from the public and cling to this magnet, and then the moment will come when there'll be this minority on the one side and the majority on the other – but this minority will be the one that makes history, because the majority will always follow where there's a tough minority to lead the way.

In power after 1933, Hitler adopted the same basic methods to restructure the German nation and toughen his eighty million subjects for the coming ordeal. His confidence in them was well placed: the Germans were industrious, inventive and artistic, they had produced great craftsmen, composers, philosophers and scientists. Hitler once said that their national character had not changed since the Roman historian Tacitus had described the German tribes who had roamed north-west Europe, nearly two thousand years before – a "wild, brave and generous blue-eyed people". Hitler asserted that if, nonetheless, history had witnessed the Germans repeatedly engulfed by the tide of human affairs, then it was because their feckless leaders had failed them.

The National Socialist movement, he was determined, would not fail Germany. Just as Moscow's leaders were re-educating the Russians to their creed, the Nazis would educate each German along the same lines, and inject a new ideological hormone to strengthen him. The German citizen was the basic molecule of the *Volk*. Into that Volk an authoritarian order must first be brought, before the great crystalline lattice of a monolithic and unshatterable Reich could be created. Just as the soldier must unquestioningly accept orders, so the citizen of the new Germany would be trained to obey.

It is hard to define in advance the success of Hitler's rule in strengthening the character of his people. But its effects can be demonstrated by comparison, for example, with fascist Italy. Mussolini swept into power there with only a few thousand followers, and never succeeded in educating or converting the broad mass of the Italian people, even in twenty years of fascist rule. In 1943, the flabby structure of Italian fascism evaporated in a puff of smoke, after a few air raids and the noiseless overthrow of Mussolini. In Germany, however, after only ten years of Nazi indoctrination and education, Hitler's subjects were able to withstand enemy air attacks – in which fifty- or a hundred-thousand people were killed overnight – with a stoicism that exasperated their enemies. At the end, when Germany was again defeated, those enemies had to resort to the most draconian and punitive methods, of mass trials, confiscation and expropriation, internment and re-education, before the seeds that Hitler had sown could be eradicated.

Hitler had built the National Socialist movement in Germany not on capricious electoral votes, but on *people*, and they gave him – in the vast majority – their unconditional support to the end.

PART 1

APPROACH TO ABSOLUTE POWER

First Lady

Here is where Hitler's path began to lead to war – here in Munich's Ludwig Strasse. It is a broad boulevard choked with the Mercedes, Opels and Volkswagens of the opulent West Germans; electric streetcars silently glide between endless rush-hour crowds waiting in the crisp winter air, surrounded by the clamour of a provincial metropolis. At one end of the boulevard is the Victory Arch; at the other, the grimy stone Feldherrnhalle mausoleum. Once, in 1914, a wan young man set up his easel outside it and painstakingly sketched its gloomy, cavernous porticoes in water-colours to eke out a meagre living. This Feldherrnhalle had seen that same young man again in November 1923, as he and a handful of his followers trudged obstinately towards the carbines pointed at them by the cordon of Bavarian police.

Even now the boulevard is little changed. The buildings are the same. So are most of the people.

It was here in Ludwig Strasse that – unsuspected by the silent crowds lining the icy pavements as dawn rose on 22 December 1937 – Nazi Germany jolted imperceptibly on to the course that was to lead it to ruination. General Erich Ludendorff, Hindenburg's chief of staff in the Great War, had just died, and his simple oak coffin was lying in the shadow of the Victory Arch, draped with the Kaiser's colours. Tall black-shrouded pylons flanked the coffin, topped with bowls of lingering fire. High-ranking officers of the new Wehrmacht – the Nazi armed services – froze all night at each corner of the bier, carrying on silken cushions the eighty medals of the departed warrior. Special trains were bearing Hitler and his government through a snowstorm towards Munich.

The preparations for the state funeral were complete.

Just before 10 A.M. Hitler himself arrived, clad in his familiar leather greatcoat, peaked cap and leather jackboots. Field-Marshal Werner von Blomberg, the erect, greying war minister – the first field-marshal to have been created by Hitler – put up his right arm in salute. General Hermann Göring, the

Luftwaffe's commander and most powerful man after Hitler and Blomberg, followed suit; Göring had marched with Hitler and Ludendorff that blood-stained day here in 1923. The German army's commander, Baron Werner von Fritsch, was overseas, so an infantry general stood in for him.

To the thud of muffled drums, six officers hoisted the coffin on to a gun-carriage and Ludendorff's last journey began.

The photographs show Hitler walking alone and ahead of his commanders and ministers, bare-headed, his face a mask, his eyes set on the Feldherrnhalle – conscious that one hundred thousand eyes were trained on him. Moments like these, he once said, were a supreme and silent ecstasy for him. This, he knew, was what his people wanted to see: their Führer, followed by his faithful henchmen, surrounded by his subjects, united in a common act of spectacle and grandeur. Probably his mind went back to 1923: here, abreast the royal palace, the hail of police bullets had met them. Ulrich Graf had screamed, "Don't shoot!" But six or seven bullets had cut him down. Scheubner-Richter, shot through the heart, had staggered back and clutched Hitler to the ground. Another bullet had struck Göring. Altogether a dozen of his followers had been killed, but Ludendorff had marched on, furious that the Bavarian police should be firing on him – Ludendorff, hero of the Great War.

The smoke of the ten pylons flanking the Feldherrnhalle curled languidly up into the windless morning air. Hitler's hands were solemnly clasped in front of him. The coffin was shouldered on to the pedestal. Blomberg stepped to the waiting microphone, and the ceremony began.

As the last melancholy strains of "The Faithful Comrade" died away, a nineteen-gun salute began from the battery in the Hofgarten, scattering indignant pigeons into the misty air. Munich went back about its business. Hitler left with his adjutants for the courtyard where the cars were waiting.

Here Blomberg approached him: "Mein Führer, can I speak somewhere with you in private?"

Hitler invited him round to his private apartment. Within five minutes he was in the lift at Number 16, Prinzregenten Platz, going up to his unpretentious second-floor residence.

Blomberg did not beat about the bush. He informed Hitler – as his superior – that he would like to marry again (his wife had died five years ago), and he asked Hitler's permission as a formality. Hitler had known for some time that his war minister was having an affair. In fact Blomberg had come straight from the young female's side, at a resort hotel in Oberhof, to attend the funeral. Blomberg warned him that she was of modest background – a secretary working for a government agency – but was this not what National Socialism was all about? Hitler gave his consent without hesitation. Far better, he reflected, for Blomberg to take a simple wife than to err like so many other top generals. Ludendorff's second wife had dabbled in black magic; Wilhelm Groener had been obliged to marry his trained nurse shortly before the birth of their child; Hans von Seeckt had married a Jewess, and the final breach between Seeckt and Kurt von Schleicher had been a row over a mistress.

With Blomberg, Hitler had established close rapport. This explains why both he and Göring agreed to act as witnesses at the wedding, although it was shrouded in something like secrecy. The bride was twenty-four, while Blomberg was nearly sixty. The little ceremony took place behind closed doors at the War Ministry in Berlin on 12 January 1938. Göring even left his own grandiose birthday luncheon to attend. Otherwise, Hitler found only the minister's adjutants and Blomberg's family present. The bride was undoubtedly attractive: she was slim, with fair hair, a broad forehead, grey-blue eyes, a petite nose and a generous mouth. The couple departed immediately on their honeymoon, not knowing that their marriage would later be construed as having set Adolf Hitler on the final approach to absolute power in Germany.

The minute-by-minute sequence of the next few days can be reconstructed from the diaries of the adjutant of Blomberg's chief of staff – General Wilhelm Keitel – and the police file on the girl that Blomberg had married. Their honeymoon was soon interrupted by the unexpected death of Blomberg's mother. Blomberg took Keitel to her funeral on 20 January at Eberswalde, thirty miles from Berlin. He remained there for four days, putting her affairs in order. When he returned on the twenty-fourth, some disturbing news must have awaited him because he immediately applied for an urgent audience of Hitler. But the Führer was away from Berlin until evening, and in the event it was Hermann Göring who got to Hitler with the news first.

Hitler had returned to Munich briefly to open the great arts and craft exhibition.

When his car now drew up outside the Berlin Chancellery late on 24 January 1938, he found that the crisis was upon him. Göring was waiting, with a buff folder in his hands. So was Colonel Friedrich Hossbach, the Führer's military adjutant. Hitler motioned the latter to wait and took Göring into the privacy of his study. Göring announced: "Blomberg has married a whore! Our new first lady has a police record. He tricked us into acting as witnesses."

What had happened in Blomberg's absence was this: three days earlier, the police president of Berlin, Count Wolf von Helldorf, had called to see Blomberg – but could not, as he was still at Eberswalde. So at 4:15 P.M. he had shown Keitel an innocuous police-file card – a change-of-address record – and asked if Keitel could confirm that the lady in the photograph was the new Frau von Blomberg. Keitel however had only seen her at the funeral, heavily veiled. He suggested Göring, as he had been at the wedding. Helldorf then explained to Keitel that something of the woman's past had just come to light now that she had registered her change of address to Blomberg's apartment in the war ministry building. He visited Göring next morning, 22 January, and gave him the complete police dossier on Fräulein Eva Gruhn – as she had been before.

As Hitler opened the buff folder now, on 24 January, a collection of file cards, photographs and printed forms met his eyes. There were fingerprint records, and photographs of the full-face and profile type associated with Wanted notices. There were also half a dozen loose glossy photographs showing a woman in various sexual poses with an unidentified man and a wax candle.

It is too much to expect that Hitler read the folder closely enough to grasp the human story it conveyed. The initial impression was overwhelming. The police statements were a stark mirror image of a Berlin society in the grips of economic crisis. Fräulein Gruhn's father had been killed in the war when she was five. She was a problem child. Her mother was a registered masseuse, specializing in treating women and cripples (the eager police investigation conducted that very day had found no indication whatever that it was the kind of "massage parlour" that later prurient minds were to make of it). In 1932 Eva had left home at eighteen, and moved into a rented Wilhelm-Strasse apartment with her lover, a Czech Jew of forty-one, one Heinrich Löwinger. Later that year he had been offered pornographic photographs, and it struck him that this was an easy way to make money. He had hired a Polish photographer, Ernst Mikler, and the pictures were taken one Christmas afternoon. Löwinger promised the girl a percentage, and swore not to sell the pictures in Berlin. He had sold only eight, at eighty pfennigs apiece – in Berlin – when he was pulled in with his accomplices. The misguided Eva Gruhn was released almost immediately. The only other items in the dossier were search notices relating to her having left home while under-age, and a 1934 police data card which clearly states that she had "no criminal record".* According to the dossier, she was now a stenotypist, and had last visited her mother on 9 January with her future husband: "And we all know who *that* is," somebody had scribbled in the margin.

All this was very old hat. But for Hitler – eagerly prompted by Göring – there was only one conclusion. Blomberg had knowingly married a woman who was not fit to be an officer's wife, and had inveigled them both into giving their blessing and approval. As he turned page after page, he became visibly angry. Handing it back to Göring, he exclaimed: "Is there nothing I can be spared?"

---

* Researches in the police files of major German cities have produced no substantiation for the legend that she was a "police-registered prostitute"; this is not to say that Hitler was not given that impression at the time.

Hitler accompanied Göring silently back to the entrance hall, then withdrew to his private quarters. His mind was in turmoil, he later said. He was stunned that Blomberg could have done this to him – Blomberg, who had done most to reconcile the Wehrmacht to the Nazi Party. Now he had brought shame on the whole Wehrmacht.

Clearly, as Göring had said, the field-marshal would have to resign; but who could succeed him as war minister? Heinrich Himmler, the all-powerful Reichs-führer of the black-uniformed SS, was one candidate. So, of course, was Göring. First in line was General von Fritsch, the army's commander; but his old-fashioned outlook on modern war technology militated against him. He had not grasped the significance of the tank. Hitler had a deep respect for Fritsch – but he had one distasteful skeleton in the cupboard, a skeleton of which Göring had probably just reminded Hitler.*

If Fritsch was now to become war minister, then it could be ignored no longer: two years earlier, during the 1936 crisis of Hitler's remilitarization of the Rhineland, the SS chief Heinrich Himmler had shown him a police dossier linking Fritsch with a homosexual blackmailer. At that time Hitler had refused to look into it, to avoid burdening the military command at such a time of crisis. As recently as December 1937 – though here the evidence is weaker – Himmler had again brought the dossier, and stressed the security risk involved if Fritsch *was* a homosexual. Hitler suspected that the Party was just settling scores against Fritsch, as one of their harshest critics; he demanded the destruction of the dossier, and written confirmation to that effect. But the Party persisted; the SS had shadowed Fritsch on his recent winter cruise to Egypt, and Blomberg was persuaded to ask Hitler to replace the anti-Party adjutant of both Fritsch and Hitler, Colonel Hossbach, by a less hostile officer.

Hitler had not seen Fritsch since 15 January 1938, when they had had a two-hour argument. Fritsch described it thus:

> When I came to the replacement of Hossbach, the Führer angrily began talking about his worries at the spread of anarchist propaganda in the army. I tried in vain to calm him down. I asked for concrete evidence, for me to look into. The Führer said that he did have such material, but he could not give it to me, only to Blomberg. In other words, an open vote of No Confidence in me. I had no intention of leaving it at that. I planned to ask the Führer for his open confidence in me, failing which I would resign. But it never came to that, because I couldn't reach the Führer any more until 26 January.

Hitler decided to have it all out with Fritsch. At 2:15 A.M. on 25 January, he told an aide to summon the adjutant Hossbach by telephone to the Chan-

---

* In his confidential handwritten notes of these dramatic weeks, which were removed to Moscow from Potsdam in 1945 and were released to me by a Soviet source, Fritsch surprisingly denied any ambition to succeed Blomberg or stand in Göring's way: "I would have refused such an appointment since, in view of the Party's attitude to me, the obstacles would have been insuperable."

cellery. But the colonel was in bed, and stubbornly declined to come round before next morning.

Hitler had no choice but to brood all night on the dilemma. He lay awake until dawn, staring at the ceiling and worrying how to avoid tarnishing his own prestige.

Several times next day, 25 January 1938, Göring eagerly came back to see him. At 11 A.M. he reported that he had seen Keitel and instructed him to have a talk with the unfortunate war minister. By early afternoon, he had been to see Blomberg himself – he reported – and told him he must resign; the Führer had advised Blomberg to go abroad for a year, to avoid a public scandal. Göring related to Hitler that the minister had admitted everything – he was a broken man. It is unlikely that Göring admitted his own part in the marriage – how Blomberg had persuaded him to remove the main rival to Fräulein Gruhn's affections, by securing a well-paid job for the man in South America.

This again left the matter of a successor. In Hossbach's presence, Göring now furnished to Hitler the Gestapo dossier on the homosexual linked to Fritsch's name in 1936. It was the second time in twenty-four hours that Göring had pressed such dynamite into Hitler's unwilling hands. The folder was evidently a recent reconstruction, containing several carbon copies of interrogations, affidavits and photostats, all unsigned. A certain blackmailer, Otto Schmidt, had been arrested in 1936 and had then recounted in sickening detail the homosexual exploits of one "General von Fritsch", as witnessed by himself in Berlin in November 1933. He had accosted the general, introduced himself as "Detective Inspector Kröger" and threatened to arrest him. The general had produced an army ID card and blustered, "I am General von Fritsch." He had bribed Schmidt with 2,500 marks collected from his bank in the Berlin suburb of Lichterfelde. An accomplice bore Schmidt's story out. Shown photographs of Fritsch, the blackmailer had identified him as the general. As Göring pointed out to Hitler, Schmidt's evidence had proved true in sixty other cases. The dossier, in short, was damning.

Even so, Hitler was uncertain. He ordered Göring to question Schmidt in detail; and he forbade Hossbach to mention the matter to Fritsch, as he wanted to confront the general in person and study his reactions. Unfortunately Hossbach that same evening confided, rather incoherently, to Fritsch that allegations had been made about improper behaviour with a young man in November 1933; and this incomplete prior knowledge was to have fateful consequences for Fritsch. He concluded that a certain member of the Hitler Youth was behind the complaint: in 1933, in response to the Party's appeal for winter welfare assistance, he had agreed to feed one Berliner; subsequently he had arranged for the youth – Fritz Wermelskirch – an apprenticeship at

Mercedes-Benz's factory at Marienfelde. The youth had then turned to crime, and when he bragged to underworld friends that he had a high-ranking benefactor Fritsch severed all connections with him. That had been three years ago.

Hitler was unaware of that. The blackmailer in his dossier was called Schmidt; the accomplice was Bücker, and the homosexual male prostitute involved was one Weingärtner.

Next morning, to his credit, Hossbach frankly admitted to Hitler that he had warned Fritsch. But he described how the general had hotly rejected the allegation as "a stinking lie", and had added: "If the Führer wants to get rid of me, one word will suffice and I will resign." At this, Hitler announced with evident relief, "Then everything is all right. General von Fritsch can become minister after all."

During the day, however, other counsels prevailed.

Blomberg played his part in them. He was ushered into Hitler's library in plain clothes, to take formal leave of the Führer. At first Blomberg angrily criticized the manner in which he had been dismissed, and Hitler responded with equal acrimony. Then ire gave way to sorrow and Hitler – who genuinely feared that Blomberg might take his own life – tried to console him. He hinted that when Germany's hour came he would like to see Blomberg at his side again, and then bygones could be bygones.

The discussion turned to a successor. Blomberg remarked that Göring was next in line. Hitler retorted, "Göring has neither the necessary perseverance nor the application." As for Fritsch, said Hitler, there was now some belief that he was a secret homosexual. To this Blomberg evenly replied that he could quite believe it. (Hitler was not alone in having accepted the blackmailer's evidence, prima facie: even Hossbach went down into the adjutants' smoking-room that day, slumped into the red leather sofa and drew "§175" – the penal code clause on homosexuality – with his forefinger in the air, adding, "Von Fritsch!" to his fellow adjutants.)

Thus the word of the C-in-C of the German army, his monocle firmly screwed into his eye, ramrod stiff as a Prussian soldier should be, came to be tested against the utterances of a convict – the general nine years Hitler's senior, his accuser Otto Schmidt by now aged thirty-one, pale, puffy from years of incarceration.

Late on 26 January, Fritsch was summoned to the library of the Chancellery. Göring and Hitler awaited him. Fritsch himself wrote this hitherto unpublished account of the famous scene:

I was eventually called in at about 8:30 P.M. The Führer immediately announced to me that I had been accused of homosexual activities. He said he could understand everything, but he wanted to hear the truth. If I admitted the charges against me, I was to go on a long journey and nothing further would happen to me. Göring also addressed me in the same vein.

I emphatically denied any kind of homosexual activities and asked who had accused me of them. The Führer replied that it made no difference who the accuser was. He wished to know whether there was the slightest ground for these allegations.

Fritsch remembered Wermelskirch. "Mein Führer," he replied, "this can only be a reference to that affair with a Hitler Youth!"

This was not the heated denial Hitler had expected. Distracted beyond all measure already by the Blomberg scandal, he was dumbfounded by Fritsch's answer. Otto Schmidt, the man in the Gestapo dossier, was no Hitler Youth. Hitler thrust the folder into Fritsch's hands. The general rapidly scanned it, purpled, and dismissed it all as a complete fabrication. But now the fat was in the fire. Hitler was suspicious, and Göring "acted", as Fritsch was to recall in puzzlement next day, "as though there was a mass of other things in the files as well".

At a signal from Hitler the convicted blackmailer was himself led in to the library. Schmidt pointed unerringly at the general and exclaimed, "That's the one."

From that moment on, Hitler lost much of his awe of the army's generals, he afterwards confessed. "Homosexuals big and small – they'll always lie on principle," he argued.

When Hossbach urged him at least to give a hearing to General Ludwig Beck, the Chief of the General Staff, the very telephone call to Beck's home at Lichterfelde stirred fresh suspicions in Hitler's tortured mind: had not the blackmail money been collected from a bank at Lichterfelde? He interrogated Beck about when he had last lent money to his C-in-C. The puzzled general could only reply that he had never done so.

The Minister of Justice, Dr Franz Gürtner, read the dossier too, and duly reported that prima facie there was enough evidence to indict the general.

Fritsch's own pathetic story continues,

I gave the Führer my word of honour that I had nothing to do with this affair whatever. Confronted with the allegations of a habitual crook, my word was brushed aside as of no consequence. I was ordered to report to the Gestapo next morning, where I would be told more details. I demanded a thorough investigation to clear it all up beyond a shadow of doubt. Deeply shaken at the abruptness displayed by the Führer and Göring towards me, I went home and informed Major [Curt] Siewert [*personal chief of staff*] in brief about the allegations. Soon afterwards I also informed General Beck. I mentioned to both that it might be best for me to shoot myself, in view of the unheard-of-insult from the Führer. Both these gentlemen argued against such a step, and I had to agree with them: the Führer and the people influencing him would have seen in my suicide the final and welcome proof that I was guilty.

Fritsch saw no alternative but to stand and fight: he demanded a full court martial to clear his name. Several weeks passed before the inquiry was convened, and before then the investigation would take a most unexpected turn. Only now, with the help of the previously unknown Fritsch manuscripts from Moscow and the diary of Keitel's adjutant, Wolf Eberhard, can the intricate sequence of events be fully pieced together.

Meanwhile, the damage had been done. Through this extraordinary chain of events – it cannot safely be called coincidence – Hitler's control over the German armed forces, the Wehrmacht, became absolute.

When he sent next morning, 27 January 1938, for Blomberg again to discuss a successor, the field-marshal reminded Hitler – probably more out of anger at the hidebound General Staff than from any personal conviction – that since President Hindenburg's death the Führer was constitutionally Supreme Commander of the Wehrmacht already. If he appointed no new war minister, then he would have direct control of the armed forces.

"I'll think that over," replied Hitler. "But if I do that, then I'll be needing a good Wehrmacht chief of staff."

"General Keitel," suggested Blomberg. "He's done that job for me. He's a hard worker and he knows his stuff."

As Blomberg left the Chancellery for the last time, he noticed that the sentries did not present arms to him.

Hitler received Keitel at 1 P.M. Wilhelm Keitel was a tall, handsome general of unmistakably soldierly bearing although he had been ordered to come in plain clothes. Six years older than the Führer, Keitel had headed the army's organization branch during the recent expansion. He was a champion of a unified Wehrmacht command – to Hitler this was important. Hitler asked him who ought to succeed Blomberg, and Keitel too offered Göring's name.

"No, that is out of the question," replied Hitler. "I don't think Göring has the ability. I will probably take on Blomberg's job myself."

He also asked Keitel to find him a new adjutant. Colonel Hossbach's loyalty evidently lay towards his C-in-C, rather than to his Führer. Keitel picked Major Rudolf Schmundt. Forty-two, big-eared and capable, the new Wehrmacht adjutant was to wield a psychological influence over Hitler that has passed largely unobserved by military historians.

Hitler – Keitel – Schmundt: the links of the chain of command were coming together. But over Fritsch's position – the next link – hung a question mark.

As Hitler had ordered, General von Fritsch submitted to Gestapo interrogation that morning, 27 January. Concealed microphones recorded every word on discs. The 83-page transcript has survived, revealing the drama as the baron was again confronted with the blackmailer: Otto Schmidt still stuck to his story despite the sternest warnings from Dr Werner Best of the Gestapo on the consequences of lying. Schmidt described how the general he had seen in 1933 wore a monocle, a fur-collared coat and a stiff dark hat. He had smoked at least one cigar during the blackmail bargaining. The alleged homosexual act was again described by Schmidt: "This Bavarian twerp", referring to the male prostitute Weingärtner, "was standing up and the man knelt down in front of him and was sucking at it . . ." to which Fritsch could only expostulate, "How dare he suggest such a thing! That is supposed to have been *me*?"

He conducted part of the questioning himself. More than once he commented bitterly, "It's strange that my word should count for less than the word of this scoundrel." None of Schmidt's details fitted him. For example, he had not smoked even a cigarette since 1925. But he frankly admitted that Schmidt's evidence appeared damning. "I must admit that if pressure has been brought to bear on him from some source or other to tell a lie, then he's doing it damnably cleverly."

Perhaps no utterance reveals his own uprightness better than one sad reflection: "One thing does seem clear – that it was at least an *officer* involved."

Unknown to him the two other "witnesses" had been posted unobstrusively in the Gestapo HQ where they could see him. Weingärtner was emphatic that this was *not* his client of 1933. Bücker detected a certain resemblance, but would not swear to it. Hitler was not informed of this ambivalent outcome. "If the Führer had only been told of these two facts," Fritsch later wrote, "then his decision would surely have been very different, in view of the word of honour I had given him."

Hitler however had already written off Fritsch. On 28 January he was already discussing a short-list of successors as C-in-C, army.

His first choice was General Walter von Reichenau – Keitel's predecessor at the war ministry. Keitel advised against him, as he was too closely identified with the Nazi Party to meet with army approval. His own candidate was General Walther von Brauchitsch, a stolid, widely respected officer whose reputation was founded on his period as army commander in the isolated province of East Prussia. In fact Keitel had already telephoned him urgently to take the next train from Dresden; he arrived at a quarter to nine that evening.

At first sight Brauchitsch did appear the ideal choice. Next morning Keitel repeated to Hitler the answers given by the general under close questioning; in particular Brauchitsch was willing to tie the army closer to the Nazi state and its ideals, and he was not averse to getting rid of General Viktor von Schwedler as chief of army personnel – the major obstacle to Hitler's exercising complete control over senior army appointments – but Brauchitsch was only lukewarm on the issue of a unified Wehrmacht command.

Hitler sent for Brauchitsch. But now the general mentioned that he too had delicate personal difficulties: he wanted a divorce to marry a Frau Charlotte Rüffer, herself a divorcee. Hitler saw no problem, but Brauchitsch explained that his first wife must be settled financially – and this, he hinted, he could not afford. All in all the last week of January 1938 must have left in Hitler's prim and prudish mind a remarkable impression of the private lives of his generals.

Brauchitsch's nomination by Keitel thus appeared to have foundered. The jostling for Fritsch's office resumed. Reichenau was seen haunting the war ministry building. Göring sent his loyal aide Colonel Karl Bodenschatz to drop hints amongst Hitler's adjutants that Göring might take over the army too. Admiral Ercih Raeder, the navy's C-in-C, sent an adjutant to propose the revered but cantankerous General Gerd von Rundstedt as an interim tenant for the job. The adjutant found Hitler brooding in his private rooms at the Chancellery. Hitler rejected Rundstedt as too old. He heaved the weighty Army List volume across the desk to the navy captain and challenged him: "You suggest one! Do you know of anybody? Which should I take!"

The harsh truth was that, *faute de mieux*, Brauchitsch was the only realistic choice. He had the support of Blomberg, Keitel and Rundstedt; even Fritsch let it be known that he was not averse to him; and Göring, fearful lest the dynamic Reichenau should land the job, eventually threw his weight behind the rival.

On 3 February Hitler agreed, declared himself satisfied with Brauchitsch's attitude on the Church, the Party and military problems, and formally shook hands with him as Fritsch's successor. The unfortunate General von Fritsch – whose landlady, chauffeurs and valets were being pulled in from all over Germany by the Gestapo for questioning – was asked that same afternoon by Hitler to submit his resignation. Fritsch wrote later, "I accepted this demand, as I could never have worked with this man again."

In retrospect, it must be said that it is clear that Hitler believed him guilty. Even Fritsch accepted this, writing many weeks later that he was certain that he was the victim of an SS plot: "I don't think the Führer knew of Himmler's foul trick in advance, or sanctioned it – he made a far too frantic impression on the evening of 26 January [*the library confrontation with Otto Schmidt*] for that."

On 4 February, Hitler accordingly signed an icy letter to him, formally accepting his resignation "in view of your depleted health". He added a few brief words of commendation for the general's service in rebuilding the German army. The letter was published in full – thus driving the last nail into Fritsch's coffin, as it turned out.

Meanwhile, Hitler had charged Dr Hans Lammers, head of his civil service, to negotiate the terms of a financial settlement for the first Frau von Brauchitsch to agree to a noiseless divorce. Eventually the Reich settled an allowance of about 1,500 marks a month on her; the general transferred a further 20,000 marks to her, and the divorce took effect in April. Hitler thereby purchased complete moral sway over the army's new C-in-C – and for a relatively paltry sum.

Hitler – Keitel – Schmundt – Brauchitsch: the chain of command had gained another link. Brauchitsch was a slow-speaking, introverted, quiet army general of the best pedigree (he had been page to the Empress Augusta Viktoria). Hitler decided that Brauchitsch, Göring and Raeder as the three service C-in-Cs would take their orders from a new supreme command authority, the Oberkommando der Wehrmacht (OKW), with Wilhelm Keitel as its *Chef*, or chief of staff. Hitler himself would be Supreme Commander, with the new OKW as his military secretariat. This OKW would also exercise Blomberg's former ministerial functions. His old National Defence division, the Abteilung Landesverteidigung, would transfer to the OKW as an operations staff, commanded by Colonel Max von Viebahn, a staff officer of the older generation.

Thus Keitel himself became Hitler's principal military secretary. Hitler never regretted the choice; the general came from a long line of landed gentry and officers, and he was neither obstinate nor independent in his ways. His *métier* was a willingness to obey – to pass on orders efficiently and without question. After all, Hitler proposed to decide his own military policies. At most he needed an industrious and efficient machine to put them into effect.

By the end of January 1938 he was confident that he had ridden out the Blomberg/Fritsch crisis. He confided to Keitel that he was planning to do something that would make Europe "catch its breath". It would also serve to distract attention from the Wehrmacht's problems. Now he could pull public triumph out of the jaws of this private scandal. He would carry out a general top-level reshuffle, to give the impression not of a momentary weakness but of a gathering of strength. He hinted that the theatre for his first European diversion would be Austria.

It was indeed a minor landslide that now engulfed military and diplomatic Berlin. Hitler changed his foreign minister and minister of economics; inconvenient diplomats like Ambassador Ulrich von Hassell in Rome were forcibly retired; Göring was promoted to field-marshal, three score army and Luftwaffe generals who were too old, conservative or obstinate were axed or transferred, and Keitel's younger brother Bodewin became chief of army personnel.

All these changes were decreed on 4 February. Most of the dumbfounded victims first learned of it when they opened their newspapers next morning. From the intercepted telegrams of the foreign diplomats in Berlin, Hitler knew that the last days had been rife with speculation. By the fifth he knew that his spectacular upheaval had largely succeeded. The British press lord, Rothermere, telegraphed him, "May I add, my dear Führer, my congratulation on the salutary changes you have made. Your star rises higher and higher."

The German army could not be so easily fobbed off. Ugly rumours spread. Fritsch's deposal was seen as vivid evidence of the hold that the Party was gaining over the armed forces. So at 4 P.M. on 5 February Hitler delivered to his leading army and Luftwaffe generals, standing around him in a semi-circle in the war ministry, a two-hour speech in which he mercilessly described the allegations that had resulted in the resignations of both Blomberg and Fritsch. He read out the formal legal opinion of the minister of justice, and quoted choice extracts from the Otto Schmidt dossier. He does not appear to have mentioned Fritsch's denial. But he did announce that a special tribunal would try the general's innocence, with Göring, Brauchitsch and Raeder themselves as judges, aided by two presidents of the Reichskriegsgericht (the Reich Court Martial). He forbade anybody present to discuss the matter beyond these four walls.

The speech was received in embarrassed silence. Hitler had spoken with such conviction that no voice was raised in protest. But evidently some army officers were not wholly satisfied with this outcome, because some weeks later Wilhelm Canaris, the director of military intelligence, admonished his regional officers in these words: "For the time being we have just got to accept this explanation of events. At present it is quite impossible to discuss them."

At eight o'clock that evening, Hitler presided over what was, it turned out, the last Cabinet meeting ever called. He briefly introduced Keitel and Brauchitsch to them – the former would faithfully administer the Wehrmacht High Command (OKW) until the end of the coming war in 1945, while the latter proved a complaisant army C-in-C only until December 1941 when he and Hitler parted. After the Cabinet meeting, Hitler set out for his mountainside home in Bavaria – as Führer, Reich Chancellor and now supreme commander of the armed forces in fact as well as name.

Yet if these January 1938 scandals had proven anything, it was this: that Adolf Hitler was more deeply in the thrall of his devious henchmen and cronies than even he suspected.

By early March, when he was back in Berlin, the first whispers were reaching him that he had been misled – that Himmler, the SS and the Gestapo had deceived him and that even Göring was not entirely above blame. Hitler evidently took a merciless line: Fritsch was lost beyond retrieval; while Himmler, the SS and Göring were indispensable. (Of the SS he shortly defined: "They must be political state troopers, blindly loyal to State and Führer. If troubles break out, these troopers must crush them ruthlessly.") He was still confident that the army tribunal would prove that Fritsch was guilty.

The army investigators had begun their inquiries in February. Fritsch had engaged a gifted barrister, Count Rüdiger von der Goltz, whose clients had included Goebbels in a pre-1933 libel action, the "Holstein saboteur" and various political assassins. Triumphantly the Gestapo now claimed that this barrister had also been blackmailed by Otto Schmidt. Goltz indignantly demanded to see the file. Now it was found to refer to a different lawyer, Herbert Goltz, since deceased.

This was an interesting discovery. Fritsch wondered whether he too was the victim of a mix-up. And indeed, on 1 March, Goltz succeeded in establishing that the blackmailer had witnessed only a cavalry captain of similar name, Achim von *Frisch*; the army investigators traced this man and he very commendably admitted the felony. To clinch it, he even produced Otto Schmidt's signed receipt for the 2,500 marks he had been paid. Disturbingly, he also revealed that the Gestapo had investigated his bank account at Lichterfelde *on 15 January*. Was it pure coincidence that this was only three days after the Blomberg wedding? What was certain was that some Gestapo official had known the real identity of Schmidt's victim all along!

General Walter Heitz, representing the tribunal, took this startling evidence to Hitler on 3 March 1938. Hitler's first impulse was to call off the impending trial. But Heinrich Himmler was present, and he interjected: "The Fritsch and the Frisch cases are two entirely different matters. The blackmailer Schmidt has himself identified the general!" To underline this particular point, Achim von Frisch was now also arrested, since he had confessed to homosexual offences.

Hitler ordered the trial to begin on 10 March, hoping no doubt that his intuition about the general might still prove right – or that Providence would provide him with some means of mastering this internal crisis too. In a way, Providence did: because on the eleventh, the three judges (Göring, Raeder and Brauchitsch) were suddenly needed elsewhere: Hitler was about to annex Austria. The trial was adjourned to the seventeenth, and by that date Hitler had amassed such popular acclaim that his position was impregnable to criticism from the army.

The trial began. A few days later, Fritsch himself wrote,

> Initially my impression was that Göring [*who presided*] was working towards an open verdict – in other words that my guilt had not been established, but that it was still possible.
>
> But the weight of evidence was so great that even Göring had to announce that no reasonable person could fail to be convinced of my innocence. Finally

the key witness, the blackmailer, confessed that everything he had said about me was a lie.

It was Göring's angry cross-examination that elicited Otto Schmidt's confession. During the hearings it came out that on the very eve of the trial the head of the Gestapo's homosexual investigations branch, Kriminalrat Josef Meisinger, had threatened Schmidt with a sticky end should he recant on his sworn testimony. Fritsch was honourably acquitted.

There is no evidence that Hitler concerned himself in the least with the slimy background of this Gestapo intrigue. The facts were however these: Reinhard Heydrich, chief of Reich security, had established the Meisinger section, Section IIH, four years before. In 1936, Otto Schmidt had named the general during interrogation, in the vain hope that the charges against him would be quietly hushed up. Meisinger willingly believed him, but Heydrich and the Gestapo chief Heinrich Müller had both considered it an inadequate basis for action. The statements stayed on file. When Müller fell ill, Meisinger showed the dossier to Himmler, who showed it to Hitler—with the results already related. It was one of Meisinger's officials who had checked the Lichterfelde bank account in January, so Meisinger at least realized the error he had made. Shortly after the trial began, Himmler sent him out of harm's way to Vienna; his career was unimpaired by the blunder.

Not so General von Fritsch's career. On the day after his acquittal, he wrote to his lawyer: "Whether and to what extent the Führer will allow me to be rehabilitated still remains to be seen. I fear he will resist it with all his might. Göring's closing remarks would seem to indicate this in part."

In his private notes, Fritsch recollected:

Both before the end of the examination of the witnesses and while reading the tribunal's verdict, Göring took pains to justify the Gestapo's actions. . . . Göring repudiated the fine words spoken by Count von der Goltz about the army and myself. He admittedly spoke of the tragedy of my position, but said that under the circumstances it could not be helped. Throughout it all you could hear the leitmotif, "Thank God we've got rid of him and he can't come back." Göring kept referring to me with emphasis as "Colonel-General von Fritsch (*retired*)".

In Fritsch's view, it all indicated that Göring had a guilty conscience.

Not until Sunday, 20 March, could General von Brauchitsch obtain an interview of Hitler to demand Fritsch's rehabilitation. "The Führer was apparently not entirely opposed to rehabilitating me," wrote Fritsch later, "but he has postponed a decision. Meantime the other side will have their chance to get to work on him."

As a man of honour and an officer, Fritsch refused to take it any longer. He drafted a twelve-point list of the facts proving the Gestapo's intrigue. At the end of March he incorporated them in a letter to Himmler. It ended with the extraordinary words, "The entire attitude of the Gestapo throughout this affair has proven that its sole concern was to brand me as the guilty party," and, "I therefore challenge you to a duel with pistols."

His notes record that he asked first Beck and then Rundstedt to convey the letter to Himmler as his seconds. Both politely declined. Fritsch had no option but to await his public rehabilitation by the Führer.

Under pressure from Brauchitsch, Hitler did take a sheet of his private gold-embossed notepaper and write sympathetically to Fritsch. But the letter contained no real apology.* The general replied with a pathetic homily about the bond of confidence he had mistakenly believed to exist between them. He would not be satisfied, he said, until the Gestapo culprits had been punished. Hitler let him know that at the next Reichstag session he would personally speak words of praise for Fritsch: but Easter, then the end of May and finally 2 June 1938 – all dates when a Reichstag session had been rumoured – passed without event.

By early June, Germany was just recovering from a new crisis over Czecho-slovakia. Hitler refused to convene the Reichstag yet, to avoid having to report in public on the crisis. But Brauchitsch warned him that the army's generals were already in ugly mood; Fritsch had now gone so far as to draft an open letter to every senior general revealing the facts of his acquittal, and this may have come to Hitler's ears.

All the army and Luftwaffe generals who had heard his secret Berlin speech on 5 February were therefore ordered to a remote Pomeranian airfield on 13 June 1938, ostensibly to witness a Luftwaffe equipment display. It was a stiflingly hot day. At noon Hitler arrived, and then withdrew while the three-hour judgment and findings in the Fritsch trial were read out by the tribunal's president.

With visible embarrassment Hitler now began to speak: "Gentlemen, I was the victim of a very regrettable error over General von Fritsch." He asked them to picture his "mental agony", caused by the Blomberg affair. In 1936, he said, he had not taken the Schmidt dossier seriously; but after the Blomberg scandal he believed anything possible – particularly when Fritsch had astounded him by mentioning that wholly unconnected Hitler Youth incident. The trouble was, he explained, that now he could hardly disavow himself as Führer before the whole German nation: he had announced that Fritsch had resigned through "ill health" – a *terminus technicus* which, he threatened, he would not hesitate to use in future too.

"The allegations against General von Fritsch were not malicious fab-

* Published as a facsimile, page 19.

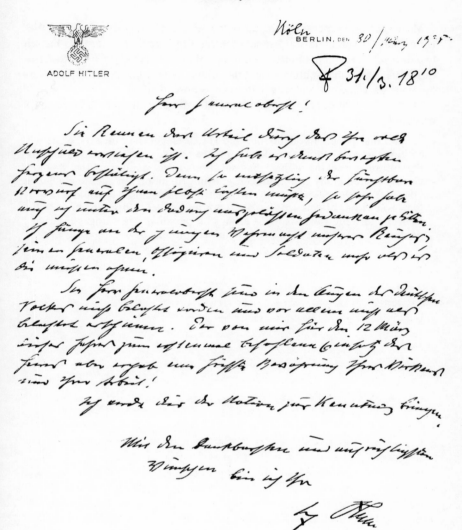

rications," he insisted. "A minor official blundered – that's all." He had ordered the blackmailer to be shot, he announced; and he appealed for their confidence. He concluded by assuring them that the Wehrmacht would always remain sacrosanct from Party interference. "There is no question of outside influences acting, as in Russia." (Stalin had just purged his senior generals.)

More than one general left that airfield with the momentary conviction that Hitler had spoken honestly. Brauchitsch reported the day's events to Fritsch two days later. Hitler appointed him to be colonel of his old regiment too. But this ancient honour did little to heal the injury. Fritsch saw it as a sop to army opinion, since the real culprits had escaped unscathed.

"Either the Führer sees to it that law and order prevail again in Germany," he wrote,

> . . . and that people like Himmler and Heydrich get their deserts, or he will continue to cover for the misdeeds of these people – in which case I fear for the future. Since the Führer has sanctioned and condoned the way the Gestapo acted in my case, I must regretfully abandon my plan to challenge Himmler to a duel. Besides, after so much time has elapsed it would probably look somewhat affected. What I cannot and never will understand is the Führer's attitude towards me. Perhaps he personally begrudges me that I dented his aura of infallibility by being acquitted.

Dictator by Consent

When Hitler became Chancellor on 30 January 1933, Germany was in an hour of extreme national crisis, an international bankrupt in an insolvent world, and on the verge of civil war between the six million Communists and the Nazis. There were millions unemployed and on half-time working. On 5 March 1933 his Party increased its strength in the elections to 288 of the Reichstag's 647 seats. The Communist Party was banned – a step Hitler had advised against in his first Cabinet of 30 January, fearing a general strike ("You can't ban six million men") – and the Communist deputies were expelled from the Reichstag. An alliance with Alfred Hugenberg's German National Party gave him a majority, which Hitler used to obtain four years' special powers with an Enabling Act. Now he could issue such laws as he saw fit.

At once he began to enact the laws he had promised, including the uglier decrees designed to force the Jews out of Germany's professions, Germany's trades and eventually Germany.

He had a sounder appreciation of economics than people believed. Count Lutz Schwerin von Krosigk, whom he inherited in 1933 as finance minister, wrote privately after the war: "He dismissed warnings of inflation with the – not altogether inaccurate – comment that under a strong government inflation was impossible. In which connection he had an absolutely healthy instinct on the necessity of keeping expenditure in line with income." Over the first few months Schacht and the Reich Cabinet came to regard Hitler as a genius. He restored national confidence in the future, which was the basis for any economic recovery. Strikes and lock-outs were made illegal, there were strict price and wage controls, and money gained purchasing power again. Meanwhile, Dr Hjalmar Schacht, the autocratic chairman of the Reichsbank, moved to restore Germany's solvency, by shielding the frail home economy against the bleak winds of the foreign depression and introducing strictly bilateral trade agreements, and then devising ingenious means of raising credit for Hitler's ambitious programmes.

The workers were no longer social outcasts. All the cancerous symptoms of industrial unrest – strikes, absenteeism, malingering – became phantoms of the past. As Hitler's brief successor, Karl Dönitz, was to put it in 1945: "What did the workers care about the Jewish problem and all that? At last they had food and work again, and they were respected human beings."

In the New Germany, the regimentation of labour had high priority. In April 1933 the government closed down the free trades unions and transferred their staff, five million members and assets, one year later to a monolithic German Labour Front, the DAF. It was the biggest trades union in the world, and one of the most successful. Dr Robert Ley, the stuttering, thickset Party official who controlled the DAF for the next twelve years, certainly deserves a better appraisal from history. An ex-Great War pilot, he had been lured by a 1925 Hitler speech into resigning a well-paid job as an IG Farben chemist, and worked solely for Hitler's cause. In November 1932, Hitler had appointed Ley the Party's "Reich Organizations Leader".

The DAF eventually embraced thirty million members, of whom all but the six million collective members joined voluntarily; the union regularly received 95 per cent of the subscriptions due – an unparalleled expression of the German workers' confidence in the DAF. With this vast wealth the DAF built for them holiday cruise vessels, housing, shops, hotels and convalescent homes; it financed the Volkswagen factory, the Vulkan shipyards, factories in the food industry and the Bank of German Labour. The DAF amassed assets of ten billion marks. Hitler respected Ley's ability, and was willingly photographed in the company of Ley's blonde and beautiful first wife. Nor had he misjudged Ley's loyalty, for the labour leader was to stand by him beyond the end.

Hitler's first power base in 1933 was, therefore, the workers. No history can safely overlook this fact. Among the papers of Walther Hewel – the nineteen-year-old student who shared his Landsberg imprisonment – I found this doctrine written in Hitler's own spiky hand:

They must learn to respect each other and be respected again – the intellectual must respect the manual labourer and vice versa. Neither can exist without the other. From them both will emerge the new man: the man of the coming German Reich!

Adolf Hitler,
Landsberg, 18 December 1924
(Fortress Arrest).

There was one particular dream that Hitler also mentioned at Landsberg, and put into effect immediately he came into power – the construction of a network of super highways covering all Germany. Göring recalled him raising the matter at his very first Cabinet. And Schwerin von Krosigk also wrote,

Hitler used to describe how the city folk returned from their Sunday outings in overflowing trains getting their buttons torn off, their hats crushed, their good mood ruined and every benefit of the relaxation wasted, and how different it would be if the city workers could afford their own cars to go on real Sunday outings without all that. . . . Road-building had always been the sign of powerful governments, he said, from the Romans and the Incas down to Napoleon.

On 11 February 1933, Hitler announced the autobahn construction programme; on 28 June the Cabinet passed the law, and a few days later he sent for Dr Fritz Todt, an engineer who had written a 48-page study of the problems of road-building in 1932, and asked him if he would like the job of Inspector-General of German Road Construction. He said he had always preferred travel by road to rail, as the contact with the people was closer: "I must have driven half a million miles in my fourteen years of struggle for power." Todt accepted the job: the interview lasted barely three minutes. On 5 July, at 9 P.M., Hitler again sent for Todt, strolled for ninety minutes with him, spoke vehemently of the autobahns of the future, told Todt what routes the first network would take, laid down the minimum width of the traffic lanes and sent Todt to begin work at once. (All this emerges from Todt's own private papers.)

The military importance of the autobahns has been exaggerated. The German railroad system was of far greater significance. But Hitler was interested in the political impact of the autobahns: more than railroads, he saw them as the future instrument of colonization in the east. For the present they were the means whereby Germany's national unity could be enhanced, because he ·realized that the fight against provincialism and separatist trends even within Germany would last for many years yet. An office was set up under Todt, employing expert supervisors to control the individual private construction firms that would work on these huge building projects – the radical principle of self-responsibility that Albert Speer was later to apply with such effect to the entire arms industry.

To win the rest of the German people, Hitler appointed a Minister of Propaganda and Public Enlightenment, Dr Josef Goebbels, a 35-year-old Rhinelander with a club foot. To this fiery agitator of the Berlin barricades fell the task of forcing the media to speak with one voice – the voice of National Socialism.

To his Cabinet on 11 March 1933 Hitler explained the need for the Goebbels ministry with disarming frankness:

> One of the chief jobs of the ministry will be to prepare [the nation] for important government moves. For instance in the oil and fats affair occupying this Cabinet now, the public would have to be educated that the farmers would face ruin if nothing were done to improve sales of their products. They must draw attention to the importance of this measure in wartime. Factory

workers must be made to understand the need for aid to the farmers, with statistics. Radio talks must serve the same end.

The government's measures would not begin until there had been a certain period of public enlightenment.

Hitler saw the random bickering of the newspapers of the democratic countries as an inexcusable frittering-away of a vital national resource. He considered that the press could become a powerful instrument of national policy. To establish a virtual Nazi Party press monopoly Hitler used the sprawling Franz Eher publishing house, which he had purchased in 1920 with a 60,000-mark loan from the Reichswehr general Baron Franz von Epp. At the time, it was publishing an insolvent Munich daily, the *Völkischer Beobachter*, with barely 7,000 subscribers. He changed the newspaper's format from tabloid to large Berlin size, and made Alfred Rosemberg editor in 1923.

Meanwhile he had appointed Max Amann, his sergeant-major in the World War, to manage Eher's in April 1922. Amann was a dwarf-like, one-armed Bavarian who had managed the Party's business affairs well. The *Völkischer Beobachter* began a steady circulation climb, cushioned from the economic depression by the publishing house's phenomenal sales of *Mein Kampf*. Even so, by 1932 Hitler's fifty-nine daily newspapers were reaching only 780,000 readers. The real press monopoly did not begin until the seizure of power in 1933.

Within a year, the Nazi Party controlled eighty-six newspapers with 3,200,000 readers. Laws were passed closing down 120 socialist and Communist printing plants. They were sold to the Party at knock-down prices. The *Völkischer Beobachter* gained a circulation of one and a half million. Amann soon controlled seven hundred newspapers. The Ruhr industrialists like Hugo Stinnes and Alfred Hugenberg, who had owned large blocks of newspapers, were forced to sell out to Amann. The freedom of editors had already been seriously curtailed by emergency laws passed by the pre-Hitler governments of Heinrich Brüning and Franz von Papen. But Goebbels and Amann surpassed them both in tackling the dissident voices, cleansing the publishing houses, bringing them into line or simply confiscating them.

Jews and Marxists were forbidden in any case to practise journalism in Nazi Germany. In October 1933, Hitler enacted an editors' law modelled on the regimentation of journalists in fascist Italy. From mid-1935 the Catholic-owned press was also purged of all divisive religious trends. Sinning newspapers were sniffed out and closed down. As Goebbels publicly emphasized: "I reject the standpoint that there is in Germany a Catholic and a Protestant press; or a workers' press; or a farmers' press; or a city press or a proletariat press. There exists only a *German* press."

To Goebbels' new monolithic organization Hitler assigned three tasks: to illuminate to the world the urgency of the problems he was about to tackle; to warn that he would not be trifled with; and to show the world the solidarity of the German people.

At the same time Hitler established his police state – the stick to supplement the carrots Goebbels offered. Control of the Reich's police authorities passed progressively into the hands of Heinrich Himmler, Reichsführer of the SS. Aged thirty-two in 1933, Himmler initially controlled the police force in Munich after Hitler came to power; then followed all Bavaria, and by 1935 he controlled all Reich police forces except Prussia, where Göring kept him at bay.

Hitler thought highly of Himmler. He readily accepted that Himmler's "concentration camps" were indispensable for the political re-education of the dissident – and indeed of the dissolute as well, because by 1935 the camps contained more than one hapless inmate whom Hitler had ordered incarcerated as a drastic cure for alcoholism or some other less savoury human failing. ("The punishment was not ordered by the Führer to hurt you," Himmler wrote to one alcoholic in Dachau on 18 May 1937, "but to retrieve you from a path that has clearly led you and your family to ruin.")

Chief of the Reich's security police was one Reinhard Heydrich. In March 1933 Himmler had appointed him, then twenty-nine, and a former naval officer – discharged for misbehaving with the daughter of a Schleswig-Holsten civic dignitary and subsequently lying to a naval Court of Honour – to head the political section at Munich police HQ. Heydrich soon excelled in Himmler's security service, the Sicherheitsdienst (SD). In April 1934, Göring gave him control over Prussia's Gestapo, the secret state police. A tall, blond officer with classic Aryan features, Heydrich – renowned in later years for his cold-bloodedness – must have had some humour in his dusky soul, because in 1939 he dared write to the Reichsführer SS that a witch had been identified amongst Himmler's ancestors, burnt at the stake in 1629: or perhaps it was meant seriously after all.

On the nature of Hitler's contacts with Himmler and Heydrich there is little that can be said with certainty. Their talks were always in private, without any adjutants in attendance. Himmler, in his pedantic manner, listed in spiky pencil handwriting the topics he intended to discuss with the Führer, and he sometimes added Hitler's decisions on each case. I transcribed the entire collection of these notes, but the gaps they reveal are so astounding that – if they are complete – we must assume either that Himmler kept Hitler in the dark about whole areas of his nefarious activities, or that Himmler knew how to act to please his Führer without any need for explicit discussion between them.

One of the most important weapons in Hitler's police state was controlled however by Hermann Göring, not Himmler. This was the Forschungsamt, or

"Research Office", set up in 1933 with a monopoly of all wiretapping operations. By 1935 it had moved into a large but discreet compound in Berlin's
Charlottenburg district, heavily guarded inside and out. It had also developed
an efficient decoding section with 240 cryptanalysts aided by Hollerith
punched-card computers, capable of decoding three thousand intercepted
foreign messages per month.

In the years of his great diplomatic triumphs, it was Hitler's furtive knowledge of foreign reports from Moscow, London, Paris or Ankara that permitted
his dazzling flashes of "intuition". But the FA was also a high-grade and rapid
source of police, economic and political Intelligence. By pneumatic post from
Berlin's telephone exchanges, and by courier from the other cities, the wiretap
transcripts poured into the FA building for analysis. Printed on the characteristic brown paper that gave them their famous name – the "Brown Pages" –
they were distributed to Hitler's ministers in locked despatch boxes on the
strictest "need-to-know" basis.

Tragically, the entire FA archives were destroyed in 1945. The scattered
items that have survived demonstrate its sinister efficiency, whether putting
routine wiretaps on the fringe actors of the coming chapters like Gauleiter
Julius Streicher, Miss Unity Mitford, Princess Stephanie Hohenlohe, Goebbels' mistresses and even Hitler's adjutant Fritz Wiedemann, or screening the
telephone lines between the outside world and foreign embassies or the mis-
siles laboratory at Peenemünde.

The FA cryptanalysts tested the Nazis' own codes for vulnerability too. Their
findings were not often welcome. The foreign ministry stubbornly refused to
believe that its codes could be broken. The FA also devised special codes of
such perfection that when one was taken to London in 1935 for the Anglo-
German naval talks, a burglary attempt was made on the London embassy by
British agents trying to obtain it.

The first reference to the FA's work is in a Cabinet meeting of 29 March
1933, when Hitler was told of allegedly exaggerated reports being filed on
anti-Jewish atrocities in Germany. "The atrocity reports were principally
cabled to America by the Hearst Press representative here, Deuss. This has
been established beyond doubt by tapping his telephone conversations."
(Hitler agreed that Deuss should be deported.) But German opposition
elements were also wiretapped. One Brown Page relates a phone call by the
wife of General Kurt von Schleicher to a woman friend, with a riddle: "What is
it? – Without an *i*, nobody wants to be it; with an *i*, everybody." The answer was
arisch, Aryan (*Arsch* is not a word of great endearment!). Göring roared with
laughter when he read it; later the wiretap on Schleicher's phone was to cause
him some embarrassment.

Hitler prudently cultivated Germany's venerable president, Field-Marshal von Hindenburg. Hindenburg was supreme commander, and he could also block any of Hitler's proposals to which he objected. Hitler wooed him by appointing Dr Hans Lammers, an expert on constitutional law and ten years Hitler's senior, as Head of the Reich Chancellery; Lammers in turn schooled Hitler on how to get on with Hindenburg, and in particular how to moderate his voice and language. Hitler also promised Hindenburg to retain Dr Otto Meissner as Chief of the President's Chancellery, and Franz Seldte as Minister of Labour – promises that he honoured until his death twelve years later.

Hindenburg at first had reservations about Hitler. But he was moved by the solemnity of the new government, and by its successes. Hitler's accession to power had been followed not by civil war, but by torchlight parades and ceremonies like the pseudo-religious "Day of Potsdam", a spectacle which had moved him and even the most hard-boiled generals to recognize that a new era was dawning for Germany.

Hitler also worked hard to win over the Reichswehr, the armed forces. His main thesis had always been that in foreign affairs the weight of arms speaks louder than moral rectitude. But Germany was permitted only a Hundred Thousand Man army – smaller than most comparable countries' fire brigades. Italy by comparison had 600,000 soldiers; and France's army was the most powerful on earth. To match Poland alone would probably take Germany five years. The Versailles treaty – which Hitler was determined to violate – forbade Germany to manufacture heavy artillery, military aircraft, tanks or anti-aircraft guns; her navy was quiescent; she had no air force.

The army which General Hans von Seeckt had created in 1919 was however no ordinary army: it was an officer cadre, merely waiting for the right time for expansion. No government could exist without its support. There is an aphorism about Prussian militarism, coined by Mirabeau, which aptly fits the pre-Hitler Reichswehr: "Prussia isn't a country with an army – it's an army with a country!" Thus, prior to 1933, Hitler approached the Reichswehr with all the blandishments and posturing of a stateman courting a neighbouring power that he needed as an ally. He swore before the Reich court in Leipzig not to subvert the Reichswehr; and when he later learned that the former chief of staff of the SA, Captain Franz von Pfeffer, had during his term of office clandestinely contacted Reichswehr officers, he ejected him from the Nazi Party.

His own early contacts with the Reichswehr had disappointed him. He had revered the retired General von Seeckt, until in November 1932 he met him privately in Göring's Berlin apartment. Here Seeckt described his own relations with the German People's Party. Hitler abruptly stood up and interrupted: "Herr Generaloberst! I had thought I was speaking with one of our great army commanders from the World War. That you are having relations with a political party has surprised me. That will be all." He explained afterwards to Göring, "I cannot start building up a new military power with a political general."

Relations with the current C-in-C of the army, the foppish General Kurt von Hammerstein-Equord, were cool. He once drawled to Hitler, "Herr Hitler, if you come to power legally, all well and good. If you do not, I shall open fire."

With all the generals, however, Hitler had a powerful argument: he was going to put them back in business – he was going to restore to Germany her striking power, regardless of the restrictions of Versailles.

The new war minister whom Hindenburg had appointed, General Werner von Blomberg, was the main instrument that Hitler could wield in his fight for the armed forces' loyalty. Blomberg had commanded the enclave of East Prussia, and he had come to respect the Nazi Party organization there as a valuable supplement to the province's defences against the constant threat of Polish attack. He was the first Cabinet minister to declare his unconditional loyalty to Hitler. Hitler saw in him a fine, upright Prussian soldier. At his Obersalzberg home, the Berghof, a large bedroom was set aside above the Great Hall for Blomberg's visits there, and no other general used it after his resignation in 1938. Blomberg schooled the army to unquestioning subservience to Hitler; in this he was assisted by his chief of staff Reichenau, who had also come from East Prussia – an active, ambitious general by no means deaf to the Nazi ideology (he had in fact already put out feelers to Hitler in 1932).

Very shortly after seizing power, Hitler asked to meet the generals. Blomberg still had no Berlin apartment, so he "borrowed" Kurt von Hammerstein's at No. 14 Bendlerstrasse for the reception. It was 3 February 1933. Hitler arrived with Lammers and Wilhelm Brückner, his towering adjutant. Hammerstein announced to the assembled generals and admirals, standing in a semi-circle: "Gentlemen, our Reich Chancellor!" Hitler was nervous, and showed it until the dinner-party ended, when he tapped his glass for silence and began to address them.

The speech lasted over two hours and was of immense historical importance. Hammerstein's adjutant, Major Horst von Mellenthin, concealed behind a curtain, wrote notes. They read in part:

> . . . There are two possible ways of overcoming our desperate situation: firstly, seizing by force new markets for our production; secondly, obtaining new Lebensraum* for our population surplus.
> A peaceloving public cannot stomach objectives like these. Thus it must be

---

* Another general present noted his words thus: "We might fight for new export markets; or we might – and this would be better – conquer new Lebensraum in the east and Germanize it ruthlessly."

prepared for them. Germany must recapture the complete freedom of decision. This will not be feasible unless political power is won first. That is why my aim is to restore our political power. My [Nazi Party] organization is necessary to get the citizens back into shape.

Democracy is a utopia, it's impossible. You won't find it in either industry or the armed forces, so it's not likely to be much use in such a complicated institution as a state. Democracy is the worst of all possible evils. Only one man can and should give the orders This is the ideal I've been working towards since 1918, and when I think that my Movement – which has swollen from seven men to twelve millions – has raised me aloft from simple soldier to Reich Chancellor, it seems to show that there's still a large part of the public waiting to be won over to this ideal.

The public has got to learn to think as a nation. This will weld it together. This cannot be done by persuasion alone, but only by force. Those who won't agree must get their arms twisted. Our supreme commandment is to maintain our unity. This process is today well under way. This is why I built up my organization and dedicated it to the state. Our target is the restoration of German might. That's what I'm fighting for with every means. To restore our might we'll need the Wehrmacht, the armed forces.

The public must be educated on a uniform basis. Marxism must be eliminated root and branch. . . . What matters above all is our defence policy, as one thing's certain: that our last battles will have to be fought by force. The [Nazi Party] organization was not created by me to bear arms, but for the moral education of the individual; this I achieve by combatting Marxism. . . . National Socialism will not emulate Fascism: in Italy a militia had to be created as they were on the very threshold of a Bolshevik menace. My organization will solely confine itself to the ideological education of the masses, in order to satisfy the army's domestic and foreign-policy needs. I am committed to the introduction of conscription [*forbidden by the Versailles treaty*].

This path I have set out to you will take many years to tread. If France has real statesmen, she will set about us during the preparatory period – not herself, but probably using her vassals in the east. So it will be wrong to commit ourselves too much to the idea of equal armaments. We must make all our economic and military preparations in secret, and only come out into the open when they are 100 per cent complete. Then we will have regained the freedom of decision. . . .

Then we must decide: foreign markets, or colonies? I'm for colonies. . . . One day the time will come when we can raise a mighty army (and let me emphasize that I will never use the armed forces to fight an internal enemy: I have other means of doing that.*) So I ask you to understand my aims and accept my political aid. With my Movement, a miracle has happened for the Fatherland. But this miracle will not recur, so we must use it.

He could hardly have made himself clearer. Even so, his audience were

* The SS. At his first Cabinet meeting on 30 January 1933, Hitler ruled that even if the Communists called a general strike he would not permit the armed forces to put it down.

unimpressed. One muttered, "Is that man supposed to be the Führer of the German people?" But by then Hitler's revolution was only four days old, and they all had much to learn.

Four days later the Cabinet discussed various ways of reducing unemployment. Hitler interrupted, "Every publicly-supported project for creating employment must be judged by one criterion alone: is it or is it not requisite for the restoration of the German nation's fighting capability." He laid down that for the next five years, until 1938, there would be only one guiding aim: "Everything for the Wehrmacht. Germany's world position will be a factor of its Wehrmacht's position, and of that alone." A few days later, Hitler forced through Göring's big "civil aviation" budget. The Cabinet record related: "The Reich Chancellor [Hitler] explained that . . . it is a matter of providing the German nation in camouflaged form with a new air force, which is at present forbidden under the terms of the Versailles treaty."

The raising and training of this new Luftwaffe were carried out surreptitiously, cloaked by army and SA units, under the broad supervision of the labour minister, Seldte. Flying training was provided by the Lufthansa airline and the various amateur flying and gliding clubs. Lufthansa's director, Erhard Milch, was conscripted to build the secret air force; Hitler had discussed the plans with him secretly in 1932. Milch recommended the rapid creation of a makeshift bomber force, rather than of fighters or reconnaissance planes – not large enough initially to provoke the dreaded foreign intervention, but still powerful enough to burn the fingers of any power that did intervene: a "risk Luftwaffe", rather like von Tirpitz's "risk navy" before 1914.

During the next two years Milch built aircraft factories, requisitioned the Junkers aircraft company for the state, and arranged for Lufthansa to start flying special night routes as training for bomber pilots. Hitler told Blomberg that the embryo panzer and Luftwaffe troops would be favoured as an élite for the next few years. He particularly wanted the Luftwaffe officer corps to be imbued with a "turbulent spirit of attack". The initial "risk Luftwaffe" was to be ready by late 1935; thereafter the air force would be expanded to one commensurate with Germany's new world position by 1 October 1938 – a date on which, by chance, Hitler did indeed make history.

Of deeper interest are the instructions that Hitler issued to the German navy on coming to power. The Commander-in-Chief, Admiral Erich Raeder, had attended the dinner-party on 3 February 1933, but Hitler called him to a separate briefing soon after. The main purpose was probably to decide on the configuration of the new battleship class *D*. In fact the navy had already discussed with Blomberg's predecessor, General Kurt von Schleicher, in November 1932, an extensive naval construction programme – including a Fleet Air Arm and submarines. But capital warships take as long to design and build as small cities, and cannot be adapted to suit each passing whim of a dictator. So navies unlike armies must be firmly modelled on those of the most likely enemy. Hitler instructed Reader on this occasion to base his calculations on the French and Russian navies. Raeder warned that France had begun building new warships, the *Dunkerque* class, of a truly formidable size. Raeder's adjutant, Captain Erich Schulte-Mönting, recalls:

> Hitler told Raeder it would be the tentpole of his future foreign policy to coexist peacefully with Britain, and he proposed to give this practical expression by trying to sign a Naval Agreement with her. He would like to keep the German navy relatively small, as he wanted to recognize Britain's right to naval supremacy on account of her status as a world power. He proposed to recommend the balance of forces accordingly.

Before their eyes, the Germans now saw Hitler's promises coming true.

On 23 September 1933 he ceremonially dug the first spadeful of Fritz Todt's autobahn network at Frankfurt – a city where eight thousand men were unemployed in 1932. At 7 A.M. the first seven hundred men, equipped with tools handed out to them by the local Party gauleiter, marched out across the River Main to the sound of bands playing and crowds cheering. At 10 A.M. Hitler spoke to them: "I know that this festival day will soon be over – that times will come when rain or frost or snow embitters you and makes the work much harder. But nobody will help us if we don't help ourselves."

After he had gone, the workers stormed the little heap of earth he had shovelled, and took it home as souvenirs. "Even the women and children are coming for it," the foremen complained. Such was the almost religious fervour Hitler had generated already. Gradually the network of highways spread. Fritz Todt was a constant visitor. He wrote to another professor on 30 September 1933, "The most beautiful thing about my work is the close proximity to the Führer. I'm absolutely convinced that any man coming together with the Führer for just ten minutes a week is capable of ten times his normal output."

The autobahns followed routes that engineers had previously claimed impassable, for example across broad moors like the south shore of Lake Chiemsee in Bavaria. Long viaducts like the Mangfall bridge, 200 feet high, were personally selected by Hitler from seventy competing designs, for their clear and simple but solid lines: "What we're building will still be standing long after we've passed on." He toured the sites and spoke with the workers. "When I'm as old as you," he flattered one seventy-year-old labourer at Darmstadt, "I'd like to be able to work like you now."

In November 1936, Hitler gave orders that the Reich's frontiers were to be marked on the autobahns by monuments 130 feet high, a politically symbolic gesture noted especially in Holland.

With his rearmament programme already under way, Hitler's logical next step was to disrupt the League of Nations. He told Hindenburg that it was so firmly anchored in the Diktat of Versailles, that it resembled nothing if not a ganging-up by the victors to ensure that the spoils and booty of the World War were exacted from the vanquished. He would have co-operated with the League if they had accepted Germany as an equal; but as they would not, he proposed to withdraw on 14 October 1933.

It was a risky decision, because it invited armed sanctions against Germany at a time when her defences were still hopeless. But President Hindenburg welcomed the decision. Hitler sent Walther Funk, Goebbels' state-secretary, to East Prussia to fetch the field-marshal to sign the documents. Hindenburg boomed his approval: "At last a man with the courage of his convictions!" At the Cabinet meeting on 13 October, Hitler announced that he would dissolve the Reichstag next day too, to give the public a chance to vote their approval of his "peace policies" in a general election coupled with a plebiscite. The plebiscite resulted in a mighty roar of approval – 40.5 million Germans voted in his favour, or over 95 per cent of all votes cast.

Two days later, on 14 November, the deputy Chancellor, von Papen, congratulated Hitler before the assembled Cabinet:

> We, your nearest and dearest colleagues, stand here today under the impact of the most extraordinary and overwhelming votes of support ever accorded by a nation to its Führer. Through the genius of your leadership and through the ideals you re-created before us, you have succeeded in just nine months in creating from a nation torn by internal strife and bereft of hope, one united Reich with hope and faith in the future. . . .

The concealed but urgent rearmament continued. Blomberg reassured his generals early in 1934 that Hitler was planning to keep the peace "for a number of years", to enable the reconstitution of the Reich and its new Wehrmacht to proceed unhindered: "And even then he is not planning to lay about anybody. But then the Reich will be better able to try its arm at grand strategy," Blomberg explained.

In 1933, Hitler's powers were still closely circumscribed by Hindenburg's prerogatives as president. He had no influence over the senior army appointments, for example. And General von Schwedler's army personnel branch was a "hotbed of reaction" in his eyes. But in February 1934 the army's C-in-C, Hammerstein, was replaced by Baron Werner von Fritsch, and Hitler's influence slowly grew over the army.

He and Fritsch were poles apart in temperament. Fritsch used an outsize monocle, which he switched from eye to eye; he had a grating academic voice, a demanding attitude towards his inferiors – among whom Hitler inferred he was included – and a manner of sitting bolt upright with his hands on his knees, as though this were so prescribed in some army manual. But for all this Fritsch was a fervent nationalist, and he shared with Hitler a hatred of the Jews, the "Jewish press", and a belief that "the pacifists, Jews, democrats, black-red-and-gold and the French are all one and the same, namely people bent on Germany's perdition". He had a soft spot for Hitler, and his views did not alter before his untimely death in 1939.

It was General von Fritsch who ordained in February 1934 that the army should include the Nazi swastika in its insignia, to help Hitler defend the regular army against the growing menace presented by Ernst Röhm's brown-shirted SA "army".

Fritsch came to like working for Hitler.* He was grateful for the Chancellor's trust in him, but he could find as little respect for the "hotheads" surrounding him as could they for this conservative, hesitant and cautious general. On the day Fritsch first reported to him, Hitler told him: "Create an army that will be as powerful as possible, of inner homogeneity and uniformity and of the highest possible standard of training." But Fritsch found the army – as he later wrote – "in ruins", wide open to the jealous intrigues of General von Reichenau and the Party factions warring against it, upon which his predecessor had turned only an indolent and inactive eye.

The success of Hitler's January 1933 "revolution" had moreover rendered Röhm's street army of brownshirt brawlers and bullies largely superfluous. The SA had swollen to two-and-a-half million men. Encouraged initially by Blomberg and Reichenau it had been given rudimentary military training by the regular army as a sop to Party feelings. But by early 1934, the SA wanted more: it became a real threat not only to the puny regular army, but to Hitler too. Röhm considered that Hitler was betraying the "socialist" character of his programme, and he demanded the creation of a People's Army based on the SA.

Hitler was already apprehensive of any false move that might provoke fatal foreign intervention. He had seen this storm brewing since the summer of 1933, when he addressed a joint meeting of SA and Reichswehr officers at Bad Godesberg on the Rhine. There he had explained that every revolution must be followed by a period of evolution. This play on words left the SA unsatisfied. Friction increased, despite an appeal by Blomberg to Röhm in mid-January 1934 not to rock the boat. On 1 February – the day Fritsch took over the army – Röhm responded with a memorandum demanding nothing less than a merger of the regular army into the SA, with himself, Röhm, as C-in-C.

Hitler supported the sole legitimacy of the army's claim to bear arms. But the Nazi Party could not so easily exorcize the monster it had conjured up, and the

* This is amply borne out by Fritsch's private letters (now in Oxford University files) and by his 1938–9 manuscripts (at present in Soviet hands).

rift could not be papered over. To Röhm, "revolutionary spirit" was all-important. Not to Fritsch. "The army is founded on discipline," he argued at a worried conference with Blomberg on 3 February 1934, "and not on any 'revolutionary spirit'." Together they resolved to defeat Röhm.

For diplomatic reasons, Hitler tried to postpone a showdown. But when the British foreign minister, Anthony Eden, visited Berlin to complain about the secret Luftwaffe and the violations of the spirit of Versailles, Hitler pledged that the huge SA would be demilitarized. And this underlay a series of proposals drawn up by the war ministry on 27 February. In future, the SA would be limited to para-military training and youth-toughening courses. Blomberg would have the right to inspect the SA. These unpalatable proposals were forced on the SA by Hitler in person. He summoned the SA leaders and Reichswehr generals to the war ministry building on 28 February, and rudely dispelled Ernst Röhm's aspirations to an SA "People's Army". He implored the SA to abandon its claim, before serious damage was done to Germany's hard-fought national unity. One army general, Kurt Liebmann, noted that day:

> H[itler] said this: "When I took over the government in January 1933, I felt I was marching forward along a broad, well-paved road. But then that road got narrower, and the surface worse. It turned into a narrow footpath – and today I have a feeling that I am inching my way forward, along a tightrope, while every day fresh burdens are thrust on me, now on the right, now on the left."

Hitler had already committed himself secretly to the reintroduction of conscription, so the SA was approaching the end of its usefulness. In any case, only the existing Reichswehr – with its professional officers and well-trained cadres – could meet his main need; because according to another general, Maximilian von Weichs, who took shorthand notes of the speech, Hitler added: "The new army must be capable of all manner of defence within five years; and of all manner of attack within eight." Since the western powers would probably not permit Germany to win Lebensraum, short sharp wars might be necessary in the west, "and after them, wars in the east".

Hitler formally commanded both Blomberg and Röhm to sign the new proposals. Röhm did so, and afterwards shook hands with Blomberg on the document; but Hitler later learned that Röhm had that same day issued orders to his commanders at his Berlin SA headquarters in Standarten Strasse which flagrantly violated it. Röhm had moreover also ridiculed him as "that ignorant World War corporal".

The Forschungsamt put a wiretap on the principal SA telephones. Röhm's movements were watched. He was seen in contact with the former war minister Schleicher, and with foreign diplomats like France's ambassador, André François-Poncet. One diplomat encouraged him with the reminder that he might become the "Bonaparte of the Third Reich". The SA was observed to be stockpiling weapons – evidently for a "second revolution", in which Hitler would be deposed.

Hitler decided to make an example of Ernst Röhm – albeit one of his former closest friends, one of the privileged few with whom he had ever used the familiar *du*. He was going to make an example of him that would deter all future dissidents. In this, Hitler had many allies as the homosexual SA chief had mighty enemies: Himmler, Göring and Reichenau had all joined forces against him. The army's General Fritsch, who was to write ingenuously four years later that he suspected that Himmler and Reichenau had "a large hand" in these events, was according to his own adjutant Mellenthin one of the first to incite Blomberg and Reichenau against Röhm.

Only once, in September 1939, is Hitler known to have discussed privately what he knew of Röhm's machinations, and by that time he was already probably rationalizing rather than recalling:

Ever since 1933 it was crystal clear to me that a showdown was inevitable – that it was him or me. I knew of all the crimes this man and his gang had committed, but I could not touch him if I was not to put at risk all I had by then accomplished. Our real power was still very slight, there was nothing like the present unity of Party and State; our rearmament was just beginning, and the slightest push from abroad would have brought the whole structure down like a house of cards.

I knew too that in France particularly there were powerful forces urging intervention – the terms of the Versailles Diktat provided justification enough. I have to thank the French ambassador [François-Poncet] alone that it did not come to that. I was reading all his despatches [*intercepted by the FA*]. I knew that Röhm was mixed up in treasonable talks with him and the French. But I could see that Poncet was confidentially advising Paris against any intervention – the French should wait until civil war broke out here, which would make things easy for them.* It was only knowing this that kept me going throughout 1933 and 1934. It was a terrible load on my mind, but with each day we were growing stronger. So I kept my nerve and waited until the last moment before the [SA] uprising began. Then I had to strike fast. . . .

The bloody purge of the SA on 30 June 1934 presents the historian with difficulties. It is now impossible to state with certainty how far Hitler was himself behind it, and how far he was unwittingly duped by the army and the SS, acting in a brief and unholy alliance.

Certain facts are clear. The SA was planning to supplant Hitler's government at some future date. Shadow ministers had already been nominated by Röhm –

---

* The Forschungsamt was continuously deciphering the French diplomatic cables; but the French diplomatic archives do not now appear to contain any reports indicating that Röhm was conspiring with Monsieur François-Poncet, and in correspondence with me the latter has denied it.

himself as war minister, Schleicher as chancellor, and the Messerschmitt director Theo Croneiss as aviation minister. Fritsch ordered all army commands to gather incriminating material on Röhm's purposes. Blomberg showed to Hitler an order apparently signed by Röhm on 23 May, for the SA to procure arms where it could so as to "put muscle into the SA's dealings with the Wehrmacht". The language could hardly have been plainer – *if* it was a genuine document and not one fabricated by the army, the Abwehr (military Intelligence agency), Papen or any of Röhm's other multifarious enemies. Hitler anyway was convinced. He told his Cabinet later, "This completed the evidence of high treason." He argued that if mutiny broke out on the high seas, it was the captain's duty to quell it.

Soon his agents indicated that the SA group Berlin-Brandenburg, under the notorious Karl Ernst, was stockpiling illegal arms for an operation "at the end of June". This gave him something of a deadline, but Hitler allowed the plot to thicken first: he was due to meet Mussolini in mid-June, and he wanted nothing to corrupt his image before then. Croneiss meanwhile switched horses, and confessed to Göring the whole conspiracy. Göring challenged the SA chief to come clean, but Röhm hotly denied everything. Göring was convinced of his guilt, and told Hitler so. Hitler – as Göring later described – put both hands on his shoulders and solemnly assured him: "Göring, you are not mistaken."

At the beginning of June 1934, Hitler had a four-hour session with Röhm; Röhm gave his word of honour to stop the intrigues. He agreed to go on leave to Bavaria from 7 June, and to send the SA on thirty days' leave in July. When Röhm departed from Berlin he publicly warned his enemies not to hope that the SA would not be returning from its July furlough. But the army knew better. One colonel – Eduard Wagner – wrote to his wife on the eleventh, "Rumour has it that Röhm won't be coming back."

Someone selected the last day of June 1934, a Saturday, for the purge. It may have been Hitler – Saturday was, later, certainly his favourite day for staging *coups de théâtre*. He evidently tipped off Admiral Raeder that the balloon would go up then, as the admiral in turn cryptically recommended his senior staff to postpone a week-long study cruise they were planning for that week, without giving any cogent reason.* One factor bringing everything to a head was the visible decline in President Hindenburg's health (Hitler saw him on 21 June, to report on his visit to Italy). Rumours multiplied. On the twenty-third,

---

* Hitler saw Raeder on 18 and 22 June 1934. On the eighteenth he instructed Raeder to conceal Germany's submarine-building orders placed in Holland and Spain, and not to divulge that the new German battleships would be over 25,000 tons: the navy was to speak of "improved 10,000–tonners". Raeder mentioned that from 1936 onward Germany's big ships must have 14-inch guns like the British *King George V* class.

Their discussion on 22 June centred on Germany's participation in the coming international naval conference.

General Fritsch began issuing orders alerting army units to possible uprisings. Machine-gun nests appeared in the corridors of the war ministry. The army discussed with the SS how far it could abet anti-SA operations by supplying weapons, ammunition and motor transport to the SS.

In the files of Army District VII, Munich, there is a somewhat cryptic note dated 28 June 1934: "Reich war ministry advises: . . . Chancellor's attitude is, am convinced of army's loyalty. Reichenau in buoyant mood. Röhm's order." Hitler and Göring left Berlin that day for the Ruhr, to attend a local gauleiter's wedding. Under enemy interrogation in July 1945, Göring testified: "There we were informed that Röhm had given the SA orders to stand by and had summoned all SA commanders to meet him at Wiessee." Hitler sent Göring back to Berlin at once, with instructions to strike against the SA as soon as a certain code-word reached him. In Berlin, Göring instructed his deputy, Colonel Milch, to put an armed guard on the city's airfields at Staaken, Gatow and Tempelhof on the thirtieth. (This is in Milch's diary.)

Röhm was still at Bad Wiessee near Munich. Late on 28 June, Hitler telephoned Röhm's adjutant to collect the main SA commanders there to meet him on the thirtieth. Throughout the next day, telephone reports from Himmler and Göring spoke of a mounting crisis. At midnight on 29 June, Hitler startled his staff with a decision to fly to Bavaria in person. Brückner later speculated that a courier had brought crucial information from Berlin. Milch's papers in fact show that Göring's state-secretary Paul Koerner – the titular head of the FA – was sent by Göring to Hitler with a number of wiretaps proving Röhm's guilt. Word certainly reached Hitler, before he took off, that incidents had broken out in Bavaria and that the Berlin SA had been alerted for an operation at 4 P.M. next day, the thirtieth. How far Hitler believed these messages and how far they were genuine, we can no longer ascertain.

In Bavaria some SA units had mysteriously clashed with regular army soldiers. But the two leading local SA commanders, August Schneidhuber and Wilhelm Schmid, at once hastened to Munich and assured Gauleiter Adolf Wagner – who was also Minister of the Interior there – of their loyalty to Hitler! So somebody's dirty-tricks department had obviously been busy.

When Hitler's plane landed at Munich early on 30 June, army officers were waiting on the airfield to greet him. According to General Adam's adjutant, Hitler barked at him: "Tell your general that I'm going to drive out to Wiessee now and shoot Röhm with my own hands!" But he did not – he called at Wagner's ministry, tore the insignia from the two bemused SA generals Schneidhuber and Schmid and packed them off to Stadelheim prison, where they were joined later by Röhm and a busload of other SA worthies whom Hitler had personally – and not without personal risk – rooted out of their hotel at Wiessee, allegedly in the midst of a sordid homosexual orgy. By

8 A.M. he was back at the ministry in Munich. The code-word was sent to Göring to begin the purge in Berlin too.

Of great interest is the record of Hitler's utterances filed that day by Adam's HQ, after Hitler's return from Wiessee:

> All the SA commanders are now under lock and key except Gruppenführer [Karl] Ernst. I was aware of his [Röhm's?] weaknesses, but I hoped for a long time to be able to channel this affair along the right lines. It's all over now. It's been infinitely hard for me to part from comrades that have fought in this struggle of ours for years on end. These people would have ruined the entire SA. I had to put a stop to it some time.
>
> The scenes during our swoop on Wiessee were scandalous and shameful – more disgusting than I would ever have thought possible.
>
> Now I have laid down a clear line: the army is the only bearer of arms. Every man, whether SA or not, is in future at the army's disposal. Any man to whom the Wehrmacht beckons, belongs to it. I have maximum faith in the Wehrmacht and the Reich war minister [Blomberg]. A line has had to be drawn. You can rest assured that I will now establish order.

At Party HQ in Munich, behind protective Reichswehr cordons, Hitler drafted a press communiqué, spoke to loyal SA officers and appointed a harmless successor to the doomed Ernst Röhm – the SA-General Viktor Lutze, who had accompanied him on the night's adventures. In Berlin, meanwhile, Göring, Himmler and Reichenau had closeted themselves in Göring's villa and were issuing arrest and execution orders of their own. (Milch witnessed this grisly scene.)

There were, admittedly, some facts that did not fit in with Hitler's version of events. Early that morning he had informed Adam's staff in Munich that individual SA leaders had planned a revolt, but that it was the Party's private concern, not the regular army's except inasmuch as Generals Schleicher and Ferdinand von Bredow appeared involved. But the Berlin SA commander Karl Ernst was half-way to Bremen harbour, setting out on a honeymoon cruise with his young bride. At Potsdam, a gang of men burst into Schleicher's house, asked if he was the general, and gunned him down at his desk; his wife was also shot. This was Göring's doing. His Forschungsamt was still tapping Schleicher's phone; when homicide detectives from the Potsdam prosecutor's office telephoned the justice ministry from the house, to report that Schleicher was evidently the victim of "a political assassination", Göring angrily contradicted them – the official version would, he said, be quite different.

Bredow also met a sticky end, as did some of Papen's staff, including the controversial Dr Edgar Jung.* When the thirteen hundred men of the SS

---

* Jung, who had written Papen's notorious Marburg speech of 17 June 1934, has sometimes been termed a martyr. In the Secret State Archives in Munich are police and tax files which reveal that he

Leibstandarte (Lifeguards) Regiment arrived in Munich that afternoon, Hitler handed a list of seven names to their stocky commander, Sepp Dietrich, and instructed him to see their execution at Stadelheim prison. At 8 P.M., he flew back to Berlin. At Tempelhof Airport, Milch had drawn up a guard of honour in the uniforms of the new secret Luftwaffe – the first time that Hitler set eyes on them.

Fräulein Christa Schroeder – his private secretary – recalls sitting alone that evening in the Chancellery, eating her vegetarian meal, when Hitler unexpectedly joined her, and exclaimed: "So! Now I have taken a bath, and feel clean as a new-born babe again."

Much had in fact happened that unsettled Hitler. Göring had wantonly liquidated Gregor Strasser, Hitler's rival; and there had been a rash of arbitrary murders in Bavaria – often clearly mistakes of identity. He learned that somebody had killed his old friend Pastor Bernhard Stempfle, an almost daily acquaintance of earlier years, who had helped edit *Mein Kampf* for publication.

Hitler's adjutant Wilhelm Brückner described in private papers how Hitler vented his annoyance on Himmler when the Reichsführer SS appeared at the Chancellery with a final list of the victims – eighty-two all told. In later months Viktor Lutze, Röhm's successor, told anybody who would listen – when his tongue had been loosened by drink – that the Führer had originally listed only seven men; he had offered Röhm suicide, and when Röhm declined this "offer" Hitler had had him shot too.* Despite Hitler's instructions, the seven had become seventeen, and then eighty-two. "The Führer was thus put in the embarrassing position of having to sanction all eighty-two killings afterwards," complained Lutze. Lutze put the blame squarely on Himmler and Göring. A report of Lutze's drunken meanderings was sent to Himmler, and he showed it to Hitler – who characteristically took no action either way: Lutze was not disciplined, but nor were the highly-placed murderers. One curious fact suggests that Lutze was right, however: in an act of ironic magnanimity that he was to repeat in 1944 after the failed Bomb Plot, Hitler ordered state pensions provided for the next-of-kin of the people murdered in the Night of the Long Knives, as 30 June 1934 came to be known.

Afterwards, Hitler began to suffer nightmares and could not sleep. His medical records reveal that stomach ailments began to plague him: but the guilty conscience seemed worth it – he had purchased the undivided loyalty of the Reichswehr generals, a "blood-brotherhood," one might say. On 3 July 1934, Blomberg as war minister thanked him on behalf of the assembled

was a hired assassin of the Bavarian government, who liquidated among others the separatist leader Heinz-Orbis in 1924.
* Martin Bormann's diary lists seven names on 30 June 1934: "Röhm plot uncovered: Schneidhuber, Count Spreti, Heines, Hayn, Schmid, Heydebreck, Ernst all shot."

Cabinet. The Cabinet retrospectively legalized most of the killings as "acts of state emergency".*

The official version put about by Hitler, and by Blomberg on 5 July to his generals, is interesting. It harps on the dangers the Röhm uprising had posed. Röhm, they said, had planned a wave of terror during July, to prove that the Reich was powerless when his SA went on leave. He had put out feelers to Schleicher, and through Bredow to certain neighbouring countries (by implication, France). Hitler had instructed Röhm to meet him with the SA commanders at Wiessee, planning to arrest them. The SA had however got wind of this, he claimed, and had brought its nefarious plans forward – hence the rash of incidents in Bavaria that Friday night. The rest was history. To those who noticed the inconsistencies, Blomberg promised an official "blue book" with all the proof they needed. It never materialized.

After the Cabinet meeting, Hitler flew to East Prussia and reported to the fast-fading president. Hindenburg was sympathetic. "My dear Chancellor," he said, "those who make history must be able to shed blood. . . ."

* Not all the killings were so legalized. The Cabinet minutes of 2 August 1934 refer to a number of people convicted for having settled private scores: in one case a litigant had shot a man on 30 June, simply for having testified unfavourably against him during a civil action.

Triumph of the Will

Before July 1934 was over, there was further damage to Hitler's image abroad. In an impatient attempt at overthrowing the dictatorial Austrian regime, panicky SS gunmen had shot dead the Chancellor, Engelbert Dollfuss, in his own office on 25 July.

In later years Hitler loudly protested his ignorance, and, by implication, innocence of the plot. But the recently available private papers of General Wilhelm Adam, military commander of Bavaria's Military District VII at the time, give the lie to this. He was ordered that morning to report to Hitler in Bayreuth where he was attending the annual Wagner festival. Hitler boasted, "Today the Austrian army is going to overthrow the government!" He revealed that Dr Anton Rintelen, a prominent right-wing Austrian politician, was going to take Dollfuss' place; and that Rintelen would authorize the return of all Austrian refugees, i.e. the Austrian Nazis who had fled into Germany. Adam's job would be to equip these Austrian "legionaries" with weapons from Germany army stocks before they returned across the frontier to Austria.

Adam was frankly sceptical. So Hitler assured him, "The moment I get word from Vienna I'll inform you, then you will believe me." At 3 P.M. Hitler telephoned. "Everything is going according to plan in Vienna. The government building is in our hands. Dollfuss has been injured – the rest of the news is confused as yet. I'll phone again." But he never did, because Dollfuss was dead; the SS gangsters in Vienna had been routed, and Europe's capitals were in uproar.

The background of this half-baked and tragic plot was this: ever since coming to power, the total union of Germany and Austria had been one of Hitler's aims – for the distant future. As Foreign Minister von Neurath explained in Cabinet on 7 April 1933, "Union with Austria cannot be actively campaigned for, for the time being, on account of Italy's opposition." The Nazi Party had, however, long extended into Austria, finding broad sympathy amongst its impoverished population for its anti-Communist and anti-Jewish platform. Unemployed Austrians cast envious eyes on Hitler's, success in curing German unemployment. The Austrian section of the Party was controlled from Bavaria by a German, Theo Habicht; the autocratic Dollfuss regime had adopted uncompromising stands against both the Nazis and the Social Democratic movement in Austria, and Dollfuss used the machine-gun and gallows in a way which indicated that the lessons of his more successful neighbour in Berlin were not lost on him. In the spring of 1934 he banned the Austrian Nazi Party, and introduced the death penalty for offences like the illegal possession of explosives – a law of which Habicht's outlawed followers increasingly fell foul.

Were it not for the support that Dollfuss enjoyed from Mussolini, and from the powerful Italian army on the Brenner frontier, Hitler would have been less embarrassed by the unexpected miscarriage of the SS plot in Vienna. The plot had failed for three reasons. First, Habicht had exaggerated the size of his following in Austria – particularly the support from the Austrian army. Second, the plot had been leaked to Dollfuss' cabinet, and some ministers had betaken themselves to safety. And third, the illegal Austrian SA movement, disgruntled by the events of 30 June in Germany, wilfully withheld the support they had promised: they were supposed to disarm any loyal Austrian army and police units. As a result, the SS gang involved found themselves out on a limb, and made matters worse for Hitler by appealing in a panic to the German legation for assistance. Hitler disowned them. He closed the frontier, sent a telegram of sympathy to Dollfuss' widow and dismissed Habicht. The assassins were publicly hanged in Vienna.

Hitler also sent Franz von Papen, his vice-chancellor, to Vienna as "special ambassador"; and immediately statements appeared in the German press announcing investigations as to whether any German officials were implicated in the plot!

There was one lesson which was signally ignored by Hitler's opponents in July 1944: that the assassination of the dictator alone is no guarantee that a regime will collapse.

Hitler had sent Dr Hans Lammers up to East Prussia to notify President Hindenburg of the circumstances of Dollfuss' murder. Lammers returned with word that the aged president had already slipped so far that he doubted whether he had grasped the portent of this message. On 1 August 1934, Hitler himself flew to Neudeck to take leave of the field-marshal. It was difficult for the dying man to speak – he kept addressing Hitler as "your Majesty".

That evening Hitler told his Cabinet that the doctors gave Hindenburg less than twenty-four hours to live. The Cabinet enacted the following law, to take effect from Hindenburg's death:

The office of Reich President is combined with that of Reich Chancellor. In consequence, the previous powers of the Reich President will devolve on the Führer and Reich Chancellor, Adolf Hitler. He will nominate his own deputy.

Hindenburg died next day, his last words being to convey his best wishes to Herr Hitler. Hitler decided to get the Cabinet's (barely constitutional) new law confirmed by the public; in a plebiscite on 19 August, 90 per cent of the German people voted in favour.

"Thus," Hitler triumphed to Blomberg, "I have conquered Germany."

The oath of allegiance of the Wehrmacht was now transferred to the Führer. But only Blomberg as war minister could actually issue orders, a formal obstacle which was not removed until 1938.

Meantime, Himmler's own SS regiments began to appear, the spectacular parades of his well-drilled, tall and muscular troops being the highlight of the Party Rally in 1934. Nobody can now watch Leni Riefenstahl's chilling film of this festival, *Triumph of the Will*, without shuddering at the sight of the SS troops breaking into the parade-step as they stomped into sight of the Führer. The SS uniform was black and elegant, and there was no shortage of candidates for this élite that Himmler had created.

Himmler was an ambitious, sinister, idealistic creature of devious ways. His ideas on human behaviour had been gleaned from animal-breeding lectures at agricultural college years before. The SS had certain affinities to the Jesuit monastic orders, an enforced mysticism which even Hitler found slightly ludicrous: in 1940, witnessing the pagan Yule celebration of the SS Leib-standarte at Christmas, he quietly commented to an adjutant that this would never take the place of "Silent Night".

He announced to Blomberg that he would allow the SS to raise one armed division, the Verfügungstruppe – forerunner of the Waffen SS. When war came in 1939, Himmler's army expanded far beyond that, but to Hitler the Waffen SS was a fourth armed service, a trustworthy élite, and as late as 1942 he ruled that the peacetime ratio of Waffen SS to regular army should be pegged at one to ten.

The army, however, envied and mistrusted the SS. Himmler's first SS officer training school was far more lavishly equipped than anything the army could afford. General von Fritsch, the C-in-C of the army, suspected that Himmler was intriguing against him. Generals claimed that the SS was assembling dossiers on them. Hidden microphones were actually discovered in Wehrmacht offices like the military district HQ in Munich. In 1938, when the safe in Blomberg's office – which he had vacated – would not shut properly, it was found to be jammed by a wire which was traced to an amplifier beneath the floorboards; Wilhelm Canaris, the Abwehr chief, investigated and traced the wiring to the Gestapo HQ (or so he claimed). The SS was suspected of infiltrating agents into the army. Smaller SS formations were quietly mushrooming throughout Germany, like the "death's head" guard units in the concentration camps, and various armed police formations. The SS swamped the cavalry, in which the increasingly mechanized army took little interest, and it moved in on the Kyffhäuser League, the large non-political ex-servicemen's association, so that one day all its leading officials also appeared in the black garb of the SS.

The second half of 1934 was marked by the open hostility between the Party and the new Wehrmacht. An internecine struggle between the forces of tradition and those of revolution threatened. The army believed a witchhunt by the SS was beginning. The Party in turn suspected that Fritsch was plotting an army coup against Hitler in January 1935. Colonel Karl Bodenschatz heard his boss Göring discuss this with Hitler. Milch also mentions these rumours, in his unpublished memoirs, identifying the sources as within the Party. Hitler may have anticipated an assassination attempt. In December 1934 he twice busied Lammers and the Cabinet with secret decrees appointing Blomberg and Hess his executors in affairs of Wehrmacht and Party, and Göring as his successor, in the event of his death. Outwardly, however, he played it cool. When Dr Robert Ley – the Party's organization chief – complained that an army general had insulted the Party and Hitler, Hitler angrily retorted: "Ley, I don't want to hear about it. I trust my officers and they trust me."

A noisy campaign began, fed by foreign newspapers and émigré organizations abroad, designed to set the Wehrmacht and Party at each other's throats. There was talk of a blood-bath once Hitler had been eliminated. Eventually Hitler's nerves were so frayed that he summoned Party and Wehrmacht leaders to the Prussian state opera-house on Unter den Linden at short notice on 3 January 1935, and in a dramatic two-hour speech again stated his loyalty to the Wehrmacht. He described it as a pillar of state as vital for Germany's future as the Nazi Party – "both of equal importance and invincible as long as they remain united". An SS official present, Werner Best, later recalled: "Hitler was in a state of extreme nervousness, almost pathological depression. His speech was a mixture of threats and exhortations. Its climax was his despairing pronouncement that he would put a bullet through his brains if the various Reich agencies refused to work in harmony."

Admiral Hermann Boehm recalled Hitler as saying, "Suppose some Party official comes up to me and says, 'That's all well and good, mein Führer, but General So-and-so is talking and working against you.' Then I reply, 'I won't believe it.' And if he then says, 'Here is the written proof, mein Führer,' I tear the rubbish up, because my faith in the Wehrmacht is unshakeable."

This speech clearly re-established Hitler's authority. "After the Führer's speech," Fritsch himself laconically observed, "The witchhunt by the SS died down for a time."

Hitler attended to the Wehrmacht body and soul. He documented his interest in military technology by listening avidly to the complex technical briefings by Milch and by the navy's General-Admiral Karl Witzell, his unusually receptive brain soaking up the data and dimensions thrown out to him so well that he could regurgitate them years later without an error.

On 6 February 1935 he toured the army's research station at Kummersdorf – the first chancellor to do so since Otto von Bismarck in 1890. General Heinz Guderian demonstrated his prototype tanks and armoured cars – provoking exclamations of delight from Hitler. Blomberg and Reichenau actively supported this modern technology, but neither Fritsch nor his chief of staff, Ludwig Beck, looked favourably on it. Beck was a calm, dedicated staff officer appointed in October 1933 for his right-wing views in place of the more hostile General Wilhelm Adam. Beck had connived in the events of 30 June 1934, but he had no greater ambitions for the General Staff than to remould it along the lines of his idol, Count Helmuth von Moltke. Beck saw tanks only as an infantry support weapon; these beasts were too fast for his liking. He mistrusted radio and all other newfangled gadgets. He scorned the idea that divisional commanders should go into battle in the front line; he could only challenge Guderian, "How do you propose to command without map-table or telephone? Haven't you ever read Alfred von Schlieffen?"

Hitler decided he could flex the new Wehrmacht muscles. On 9 March – a Saturday – he formally announced that Germany had created a secret air force. This violation of Versailles evoked no serious response, so Hitler reintroduced conscription on 16 March, also a Saturday. His secret target was to multiply the army's seven divisions to twenty-four, and then by 1939 to thirty-six. This provoked some friction with Fritsch, who objected that the new divisions would not be of the usual high standard. Mussolini protested uneasily at the conscription move, and joined with France to repeat, at a mid-April 1935 meeting at Stresa, that any German violation of the demilitarized zone along the Rhine would call forth British and Italian intervention as well as French, under the terms of the Locarno treaty. This indeed was Hitler's next planned move, but he was not, in 1935, prepared to risk it before 1937.

The French did start massing troops on the German frontier, so he had no alternative but to wait. In April 1935, Fritsch informed army generals that any German violation of the Rhineland's status that year would with certainty be "the drop that overflows the barrel".

On 30 March 1935 the war ministry invited Göring, Raeder and Fritsch to investigate what defence was possible if France and Italy should surprise Germany with a pre-emptive attack. Worse, in April Hitler learned that France was preparing an alliance with the Soviet Union, and that it was to be extended to Czechoslovakia. Twenty-five big airfields were already under construction – far in excess of any legitimate Czech needs. It was obvious that Czechoslovakia would be used as the air-base for an assault on Germany. On 2 May, Blomberg therefore circulated a secret provisional directive for Operation Training (*Schulung*), a surprise attack on Czechoslovakia to eliminate that risk in the event of war in the west. Beck immediately threatened resignation if this contingency plan were ever carried out. On 24 April, Fritsch had assured his generals, "The Führer is determined to avoid war, and will leave no stone unturned to that end. Whether he succeeds in this depends on us alone."

The nervousness about France's intentions persisted that summer. On 10 July, Blomberg issued a further important directive. Its verbatim text has not been found, but it can be constructed from related documents. It provided that any French invasion of the Rhineland would be used as a *casus belli* by Hitler: he would order the German para-military units there – Landespolizei, frontier defence units and the like – to stage a holding action until the Rhine bridges could be blown and all boats removed, to make the river impassable. The Wehrmacht would then defend Germany on the Rhine.

By the autumn of 1935, the anti-German "Stresa Front", as it was called, collapsed: in May, Britain had reached a bipartite naval agreement with Germany; and in October, Italy's invasion of Abyssinia set Europe by the ears.

Immediately after reintroducing conscription, Hitler had begun his overtures to Britain. He conducted the negotiations himself; later, he sent Joachim von Ribbentrop, his unofficial envoy on disarmament questions, to London. As Hitler elucidated to his appreciative generals, speaking in Munich on 17 March, "My foreign ministry doesn't influence foreign policy – it just registers political occurrences." His view was: "The British will come running to us sooner or later." Later that month Sir John Simon, the British foreign secretary, and Mr Anthony Eden appeared in Berlin to try to secure some limitations on German rearmament. Hitler received them in the Congress Room of the Chancellery – where Hindenburg had first received him as Chancellor two years earlier with the sonorous injunction, "Walk as close to the walls as you can, Herr Hitler, the floor won't last much longer!" – and bragged that his army was expanding to thirty-six divisions, which was true, and that the Luftwaffe was already as big as the RAF, which was not.

Hitler had his own priorities clear. When Sir John talked of a German colonial empire, and drew his hand across the map of Africa from the French Congo to Italian Somaliland, the Führer interrupted him: "I am not interested in colonies at present." He proposed that the British government agree to an expansion of the German navy to a mere 35 per cent of the British tonnage, and the construction of a small German submarine force. Eventually Britain agreed. The Anglo-German naval agreement was signed by Ribbentrop in London in June 1935, a connivance in yet a third violation by Hitler of the terms of Versailles that certainly inspired him to believe that a far-reaching alliance would be possible with Britain later on.

Earlier, on 25 May 1935, he was with Raeder at Hamburg. When he heard the naval agreement was to be signed, Hitler rejoiced: "Today's the happiest day of my life. This morning I was informed by my doctor that my throat infection is not serious; and this afternoon I get this tremendous political news."

Hitler was still far from healthy, however. He confided to doctors that he could not sleep, and suffered bad stomach spasms – in fact since 30 June 1934, the Night of the Long Knives.

He had a morbid terror of cancer, having seen his mother die of it. When he contracted a polyp on his vocal chords in 1935 he had feared for some time that it was a cancerous growth. On 5 May the polyp was removed by Professor Carl von Eicken – who was to repeat the same operation in November 1944. Hitler was forbidden to speak for three days; he had to write down his instructions, even to Göring who was bound for an important conference in Rome.

When Hitler's throat or stomach pains recurred in later years, Hitler furtively leafed through various medical dictionaries. His staff found them opened at references to cancer diagnoses.

At their last meeting in August 1934, Hindenburg had warned Hitler against the Italians. The dying field-marshal had painfully levered himself upright in bed and croaked, "Now, Herr Hitler: don't trust the Italians!" Hitler had reported this to his Cabinet, and added – according to Schwerin von Krosigk – that his dream was to unite Germany, Italy *and* Britain in one alliance. If Japan would join in, then world peace would be assured. But he had made it plain in the same Cabinet session that if ever he had to choose between Britain and Italy, Hindenburg's words would form the basis of his choice. Mussolini's attack on Abyssinia on 3 October 1935 brought matters to a head. Hitler himself termed it a real turning-point. Fritz Wiedemann quoted him soon after as always having said, "If I have to choose between Britain and Mussolini, the choice is clear: Italy is obviously closer ideologically, but *politically* I see a future only in alliance with the British." Hitler knew and admired the British soldier from his own experience in the World War. Besides, he considered Mussolini's invasion of Abyssinia premature, however reasonable the Italian desire for a colonial empire. "The time for struggle between the static and the dynamic nations is still some way off," he declared.

However, Britain and France announced sanctions against Italy. Hitler had to choose, and he chose Italy after all. He could not afford to see fascist Italy destroyed. To his leading generals and ministers – as Keitel recalled – Hitler explained why he must assist Mussolini to circumvent the sanctions. "The day may come", he said, "when Germany too has to stand up against outside intervention – the day when we also begin to stake our rightful claims."

Wiedemann, his adjutant, recalls, "When Hitler was preoccupied with some plans or other, he often shut himself up alone in his room. You could hear him pacing restlessly up and down. He always took the really big decisions like rearmament, occupation of the Rhineland, etc., alone – mostly against the counsels of his staff and advisers. He knew full well that he alone had to bear the responsibility."

Powerfully influenced by Dr Goebbels, Hitler now abandoned the path of statesmanlike and responsible policies, and embarked on the slippery ascent towards European hegemony. The parallel to the French Revolution is striking. That too had been born of the faith of a suffering multitude and carried to triumph by a few idealists. That too had been consumed by quarrelling within its own ranks and a growing terrorization of the minority. That too had degenerated into a vulgar struggle for the elimination of whole classes of enemies – just as at Nuremberg now, in September 1935, the Nazis had promulgated their notorious state laws excluding the Jews from all professions and prospects of advancement in Germany.

By mid-February 1936, Hitler had resolved to bolster up his regime by a fresh spectacular coup: he would remilitarize Germany's Rhineland now – again in violation of Versailles – one year ahead of his secret schedule. As a pretext he would take France's imminent ratification of her pact with Russia. He secured Mussolini's secret guarantee not to honour his obligations under the Locarno treaty, because Hitler could argue that the new French-Russian pact would be irreconcilable with Locarno.

On 2 March, Blomberg issued a preliminary directive. Next day Fritsch sent instructions for three infantry battalions to cross the Rhine to Aachen, Trier and Saarbrücken on a given date; but Fritsch, referring to the (now lost) July 1935 directive, made it clear that should the French counter-attack, the German forces might have to withdraw to the Rhine. On the fourth the French ratified the Russian pact. On the fifth Blomberg ordered the occupation of the Rhineland to begin two days later – again a Saturday. The Cabinet approved. The infantry marched in.

Hitler's step was greeted by a chorus of protest from the west, and by noisy sabre-rattling from the French. Blomberg lost his nerve and begged Hitler to withdraw before shooting broke out. Their infantry battalion at Saarbrücken was exercising in the market square under the very guns of the French frontier. The three German attachés in London sent a joint telegram of warning to Blomberg, But Hitler's nerves stood the test better, and neither Britain nor France actually moved against him; he attributed this in part to the intervention of Britain's new monarch, Edward VIII. "What would have happened on 13 March 1936," he bragged in January 1942,

> . . . if anybody other than myself had been at the head of the Reich! Anyone you care to mention would have lost his nerve. I was obliged to lie, and what saved us was my unshakeable obstinacy and my amazing aplomb. I threatened, unless the situation ceased in twenty-four hours, to send six extra divisions into the Rhineland. The fact was, I only had four brigades. . . . I must agree that Ribbentrop is not a particularly likeable companion, but he's a sturdy and obstinate man. Neurath displayed the same qualities on this occasion. A retreat on our part would have spelt collapse.

The German public was demonstrably impressed by Hitler's methods. At the end of March 1936 he attracted an overwhelming vote of popular support – the vote was over ninety to one in his favour. This was as close as he ever came to democracy, – a massive and intimidating publicity campaign launched after some successful Nazi *fait accompli*, followed by a (genuinely secret) ballot to confirm the Führer's actions. It was a logical extension of Hitler's method of dictatorship-by-consent.

"At the end of March or early in April [1936]", General von Fritsch was to write in 1939, "I invited the Führer to do the army the honour of becoming Honorary Colonel of the 9th Infantry Regiment at Potsdam. The Führer accepted, and the regiment was to march to Berlin for the purpose on 20 April [*Hitler's birthday*]. Shortly before that date I took a tumble with my horse at Achterberg, so I could not be in Berlin on the twentieth. On 19 April, Hossbach [*Hitler's adjutant*] phoned me that the Führer had withdrawn his agreement to become Colonel of IR9." At the time this was a baffling mystery to Fritsch. On Hitler's birthday next day, he sent him a telegram from his sickbed at Achterberg: "The army and I follow you in proud confidence and willing faith along the path you are marking out ahead into the future of Germany." (On 18 January 1939, Fritsch commented: "That was absolutely true at that time. Today I haven't any faith at all in the man. How far the army's officer corps has faith in him, I cannot surmise.") By 1939, of course, Fritsch suspected the reason why Hitler had withdrawn his acceptance: "It was in the spring of 1936," he wrote,

> . . . that Himmler furnished to the Führer the dossier claiming I had been blackmailed. Perhaps that's why the Führer withdrew his agreement to

become Colonel. His later explanation that the Party would never understand his becoming Colonel of a regiment wasn't very likely, or at least not acceptable. The following is also possible: Himmler finds out that the Führer wants to become Colonel of IR9; he fears this may strengthen the army's influence even more. This he wants to thwart. When he hears of the case of the cavalry captain, [Achim] von Frisch, he alters it to my name and pressures the blackmailer to testify accordingly. That rascal Himmler is absolutely capable of such a deed.

By 9 April 1939, when Fritsch sombrely wrote down these reflections, the whole face of Central Europe would have changed.

Contemplating Germany's economic position in August 1936, Hitler chafed that so little had still been accomplished by the new Nazi government to make the country self-sufficient – a prerequisite for war. Late in April he had put Hermann Göring in charge of raw materials and foreign currency questions. Schacht was indignant, but Hitler had set aside his criticisms. Impatient at the slow progress, in August 1936 Hitler dictated to his secretary a long, rambling and ill-styled memorandum on the economy and handed it to Göring. "Four precious years have passed," he dictated:

> Without doubt, we could by today already have been wholly independent of fuel, rubber, and even (in part) iron-ore imports from abroad. We are presently producing seven or eight hundred thousand tons of gasoline; we could be producing a million tons. We are manufacturing several thousand tons of rubber a year – it could be seventy or eighty thousand tons. We are expanding iron-ore output from two-and-a-half to seven million tons, but it could be twenty, twenty-five or even thirty million tons.

Göring was delighted at the new job. His state-secretary, Paul Koerner, wrote on 7 September to a colleague in the food ministry: "Today was our finest hour as far as the economy is concerned. Göring came back from the Obersalzberg bringing us the new guidelines for our work over the next years. Unfortunately I can't tell you more . . . but when you get back to Berlin, you'll find a clear way mapped out ahead."

Hitler had certainly nailed some of his secret military ambitions to the mast: Germany must be "capable of waging a worthwhile war against the Soviet Union", because "a victory over Germany by Bolshevism would lead not to a new Versailles treaty but to the final annihilation, indeed the extermination, of the German nation". Hitler announced that he as Führer had to resolve once for all Germany's economic problems by enlarging her Lebensraum and thus her sources of raw materials and food. Industry, meanwhile, was to prepare for synthetic gasoline and rubber production before further time was lost. In detail, Hitler stated these two demands: "First: in four years the German army must be ready for action; and second, in four years the German economy must be ready for war."

Hermann Göring himself was appointed head of this new "Four Year Plan". He read out Hitler's memorandum to the Cabinet on 4 September 1936, making one thing clear: "It is based on the assumption that war with Russia is inevitable. What the Russians have accomplished so can we." Wiedemann, writing in March 1939, recalled Göring as remarking to Hitler late in 1936: "Mein Führer, if I am not mistaken in my views, a major war is inevitable within the next five years. You are presumably agreed to my dealing with every proposal on that assumption."

fascism!

By then, Hitler was already involved deeply in the Spanish Civil War.

On 25 July 1936, in the interval of an opera at Bayreuth, emissaries from an obscure Spanish general, Francisco Franco, were introduced to the Führer by Canaris. They brought an appeal from Franco for aid in overthrowing the Republican government in Madrid – he wanted German transport planes to ferry his loyal Moroccan troops from Tetuan in North Africa to the Spanish mainland. Hitler agreed and within twenty-four hours the first Luftwaffe transport planes had already left Tempelhof for Morocco. On 31 July, Milch took leave of the first eighty-six Luftwaffe volunteers: they would fly the transports and fighter escorts – six Heinkel 51s being shipped from Hamburg for that purpose. Mussolini also sent an Italian contingent, under General Mario Roatta. By October a full-scale civil war was raging; Britain and France were committed with volunteers on the Republican side, and the first Russian tanks and bombs were detected. After discussing it with Göring, Milch and Albert Kesselring – the Luftwaffe's new chief of staff – the Führer authorized full-scale Luftwaffe intervention. Göring sent a bomber squadron to Spain on 6 November; thus the Condor Legion was born.

Hitler welcomed this war for various reasons. He could test the new German equipment under combat conditions, and train successive waves of officers and men. Göring also welcomed it as a means of obtaining from Spain raw materials like tungsten, copper and tannin for the Four Year Plan. Besides, the war distracted attention from Germany's rearmament; this led Hitler to reject an anxious suggestion by his envoy to Franco, General Wilhelm Faupel, for the despatch of a regular army division to bring the war to a rapid end.

But the foreign ministry were alarmed at the prospect that Germany might find herself by accident in open conflict with Russia, Britain or France. A day or two after Hitler delivered a "major political speech" to his Cabinet on 1 December – of which no note survives – Göring commented to his department heads: "Russia wants war, Britain is rearming strongly." He ordered the Luftwaffe to be ready for instant action, regardless of the cost. Germany wanted peace until 1941, Göring told them: "But we can never be sure that there won't be complications before then. We are in a sense already at war, even if not yet a shooting war."

By early 1937, the Nazi state could be likened to an atomic structure. The nucleus was Hitler, surrounded by successive rings of henchmen. The innermost ring was Göring, Himmler and Goebbels, privy to his less secret ambitions and the means he was proposing to employ to realize them. In the outer rings were the ministers, commanders-in-chief and diplomats, each aware of only a small sector of the plans radiating from the nucleus. Beyond them was the German people. The whole structure was bound by the forces of the police state – by the fear of the wiretap, the letter censors, the Gestapo and ultimately the short-sharp corrective spells provided by Himmler's renowned establishments at Dachau and elsewhere. The outer shell of Nazi "electrons" was the most unstable – obscure Party hacks, who might equally achieve a spectacular promotion like Alfred Rosenberg in 1941, or whirl away suddenly into oblivion. One of these was Dr Ernst "Putzi" Hanfstaengl, a long-time intimate of Hitler, who valued his wit and proficiency as a piano accompanist. The farcical manner of Putzi's going casts more light on the nervous, suspicion-charged atmosphere of 1937 Nazi Berlin than a chapter of other incidents.

Hanfstaengl lunched one day early in February at the Chancellery. The conversation turned to the Spanish war and the soldier's lot. Hitler's flabby friend – by now "foreign press adviser" to the Party – had been at Harvard in 1909, and passed the World War in US internment. He interjected tactlessly that the courage of an internee far exceeded any demands made on a soldier in battle. Everybody choked. Göring, who had commanded the Richthofen fighter squadron, and Goebbels loudly disagreed. This was the last time Hitler saw Hanfstaengl. After Hanfstaengl left the table, the others ominously remained behind, and hatched a cruel plan to deflate him. Hitler happily approved it. A few days later, Hanfstaengl was "selected" for a hazardous mission and handed an envelope to be taken personally to General Franco; a plane was already waiting. Bodenschatz – our main source on this – escorted the palpitating Hanfstaengl to the waiting Junkers 52, and bid him God speed. As film cameras whirred, a parachute was strapped on. The purpose of this became apparent when Hanfstaengl opened the sealed orders from Hitler, which the pilot now handed him: these briefed him that since Franco was in the Alcazar at Toledo – a canard that should at once have raised suspicions! – the brave emissary was to parachute directly into the besieged fortress to reach him.

The Junkers took off, and flew "towards Spain" – in reality, on Hitler's orders, merely circling for hours over the now dark Berlin countryside. Then it made an "emergency landing on an enemy airfield" – in fact at Klein Posen, twenty miles from Berlin. Hitler waited in Berlin for his friend's rueful return – but in vain, for his plot had hilariously misfired. As the plane rolled to a halt, Hanfstaengl jumped out of the door and vanished into the darkness, convinced that the Führer had ordered his secret liquidation! He surfaced in neutral Switzerland, then "escaped" to London, from which foreign capital he guiltily refused to return. Göring sent Bodenschatz three times to try and persuade him. In vain: Hitler's former crony quivered quietly in West Kensington until it was too late to return.

In Hanfstaengl's home the Gestapo found an unflattering manuscript about Hitler's youth, which probably explained Hanfstaengl's guilty reaction to the Führer's clumsy prank.

It is unlikely that Hitler would have cared much about Hanfstaengl's manuscript. He cared nothing for his public image either – although he did resist every attempt made by well-meaning friends to change his "postman's cap", his crinkly boots and his outmoded moustache for styles more suited to the Thirties. He desired neither present publicity nor the acclaim of posterity. He wrote to Hans Lammers directing that if the British *Who's Who* really insisted on having details of his life, they were to be given only the barest outline. As he explained years later, in a secret speech to his generals in 1944 when they protested at his harsh decisions on the Russian front: "It is a matter of supreme indifference to me what posterity may think."

"One Day, the World"

Hitler's foreign policy – aside from his central ambition to march east – was often guided by irrational and emotional instincts. His intervention in Spain was only one example, inspired by fellow-feeling more than logic. Early in November 1937 he confidentially told his staff that a total Franco victory was not desirable for Germany: "Our interest is in spinning the war out, and maintaining existing tensions in the Mediterranean." That Franco was fighting the Communist-backed Republicans was of only secondary importance. In April 1938, Hitler mused out loud to Reinhard Spitzy, Ribbentrop's private secretary: "You know, we have backed the wrong horse in Spain. We would have done better to back the Republicans. They represent the people. We could always have converted these socialists into good National Socialists later. The people around Franco are all reactionary clerics, aristocrats and money-bags – they've nothing in common with us Nazis at all!" (By the summer of 1940, when Hitler was allied to Stalin and he urgently desired permission to march through Spain, he must have regretted even more deeply that he had connived in the Republican defeat; because Franco denied him the per-mission.)

His relations with Mussolini were equally illogical, springing from nothing more substantial than what he termed in *Mein Kampf* his "intense admiration of this great man south of the Alps". He lavished gifts on the Italian dictator. Henriette Hoffmann – daughter of Hitler's court photographer – has described how Hitler was to be seen in his favourite Munich café with a bookbinder, inspecting leather samples for a presentation set of the philosopher Nietzsche's works for Mussolini: Hitler rubbed and stroked the leather skins, sniffed them and finally rejected them all with the pronouncement, "The leather must be glacier-green," – meaning the bleak blue-green of the glaciers from which Nietzsche's Zarathustra contemplated the world. (Hitler was a Nietzsche fan: in his Munich apartment he kept the silver-knobbed black walking-cane with which Nietzsche had strolled the banks of Lake Geneva with Richard Wagner.)

Despite Hitler's official visit to Venice in June 1934, Mussolini had gone his own way, unimpressed by his Nazi imitator. Austria remained a bone of contention between them, particularly after Dollfuss' murder. Hitler's aid during the Abyssinia crisis had mollified the fascist leader, however, and now they were allies in Spain the Duce began to refer to an "Axis" between Rome and Berlin. In September 1937 the Duce was Hitler's guest for a week of the biggest military manoeuvres in Germany since 1918. His Italian visitors toured the Krupp steelworks in Essen; Hitler showed them Germany's new weapons and machinery – like the high-pressure steam turbines being built for the new battlecruiser *Scharnhorst*. After showing them the blast furnaces, rolling mills and armour-plate works, Hitler and Ribbentrop took Mussolini alone into a hall where Krupp engineers took the tarpaulins off Hitler's proudest possession – a gun barrel so huge that it had to be transported on two parallel railroad tracks. Mussolini stroked it and congratulated the Führer, clearly astonished at the weapon's size.

In Berlin the Duce addressed a crowd of 750,000. His German was fluent, enabling him later to confer in private with Hitler without any interpreters present. Afterwards, a cloudburst brought Berlin's traffic to a standstill. Mussolini was soaked to the skin. At the President's Palace, where he was staying, the Duce encountered German officialdom at its most mulish, for a house rule dating back to the mists of Prussian history prohibited residents from drawing hot water for baths after 7 P.M. Hitler never forgave Hindenburg's ancient secretary, Otto Meissner, for this, and afterwards used Chateau Bellevue in Berlin as the official guest-house instead.

According to his new Luftwaffe adjutant, Major Nicolaus von Below, Hitler kept harking back over the weeks that followed to the Mussolini visit and the Wehrmacht manoeuvres that had accompanied it. They stirred deep within him a train of thought which was to come to the surface early in November.

The German public found Hitler's interest in Mussolini as incomprehensible as his shift from a pro-Chinese to a pro-Japanese policy in the Far East. Until 1937 Blomberg, the army and the foreign ministry had persuaded him to maintain an influential mission in China, headed first by Seeckt himself and more lately by General Alexander von Falkenhausen. The expectation was that the Chinese leader, Chiang Kai-shek, would exchange raw materials for German guns, ammunition and arms factories. But now Hitler's self-confident interference in Germany's traditional foreign policies began. He saw Chiang as corrupt and wife-dominated, and predicted that Chiang's lack of contact with the people would drive the Chinese into the arms of the Bolsheviks.

The Nazis mistakenly identified with the Samurai tradition of Japan; whereas the foreign ministry's Far East experts saw much closer ideological affinities to Chiang and the Kuomintang. In 1936 German-Japanese staff talks began in Berlin through the efforts of the Japanese military attaché, General Hirosho Oshima, and Ribbentrop's bureau. They were followed by the signature of the largely valueless "Anti-Comintern Pact". Again the horrified Neurath was left in the dark until the last moment. After the Japanese declaration of war on China in June 1937, Hitler cancelled German aid to China and turned a deaf ear on all advice that the chaos of war would advance Bolshevism in the Far East. Ribbentrop now openly demanded a military Tripartite Pact between Germany, Japan and Italy, "in anticipation of the inevitable conflict with the western powers". The pact was signed in Rome on 6 November 1937. It was concrete evidence of Hitler's growing disenchantment with the British – a trend which Neurath had first noted after Mussolini's visit to Germany in September.

Ever since 1922 Hitler had looked on Britain as a future partner to dominate the world. He frankly admired the ruthlessness with which the British had grasped their empire, and the hardness in adversity with which they had preserved it since. He had devoured volumes of English folklore. He knew that the three white rings on sailors' collars denoted Admiral Horatio Nelson's great victories. He had repeatedly defined, "The collapse of the British Empire would be a great misfortune for Germany and all Europe." He sketched vague plans for putting Germany's new army at Britain's disposal if ever her colonies in the Far East should be attacked.

Ribbentrop shared these improbable sentiments. He claimed personal acquaintance with influential Englishmen (when Hitler pointed this out to Göring, the uncharitable reply was: "Yes, but the trouble is that they know Ribbentrop"). Hitler had wanted to make him Neurath's state-secretary, but since their ambassador in London had just died, Ribbentrop begged that posting instead – promising to win for Hitler the British alliance he coveted. He had already introduced numerous influential Englishmen to the Führer. In 1945 the Americans captured the transcripts of some of these interviews – with Lord Beaverbrook, proprietor of the *Daily Express*, on 22 November 1935; with Stanley Baldwin's private secretary, T. E. Jones, on 17 May 1936; with the conductor Sir Thomas Beecham on 13 November 1936, and with numerous others: unhappily these documents have since vanished, as have several others relating to Ribbentrop's dealings with the British. In 1941, Ribbentrop explained to the Turkish diplomat Acikalin: "I know I'm regarded in many quarters as the Führer's 'evil genius' in regard to foreign affairs. But the fact is I always advised the Führer to do his utmost to bring about Britain's friendship. . . . I warned the Führer in 1935 that in my view Britain was steering towards war." Now, as ambassador in London, Ribbentrop secretly offered Baldwin an "offensive and defensive alliance": he told his staff two years later it had been refused.

Ribbentrop had been cordially received in London, but his position was soon weakened in his other capacity as the German delegate on the Non-Intervention Committee on Spain. He became the butt of mounting criticism in London (in justice, it must be added that his successor in 1938 and 1939 faired no better). An unprecedented and counter-productive newspaper campaign began against Hitler and Ribbentrop, which the embarrassed Whitehall officials explained they were powerless, in a democracy, to curb. It was a tragedy that Hitler knew so few Englishmen: he had met the Mitfords, Sir Oswald Mosley, Lord Rothermere, the journalist Ward Price; and Major-General J. F. C. Fuller, the acknowledged British tank expert, had also confidentially seen him. In September 1936, Britain's former prime minister, David Lloyd George, spent two weeks in Germany as his guest. He admiringly wrote in the *Daily Express* how Hitler had united Catholic and Protestant, employer and artisan, rich and poor into one people – *Ein Volk*, in fact. (The British press magnate Cecil King wrote in his diary four years later, "Lloyd George mentioned meeting Hitler and spoke of him as the greatest figure in Europe since Napoleon and possibly greater than him. He said we had not had to deal with an austere ascetic like Hitler since the days of Attila and his Huns.") They reminisced about the World War, and Hitler ventured an immodest estimate of how it would have ended had he been Chancellor then. Lloyd George revealed that in 1918 the British were on the point of throwing in the sponge, since Field-Marshal Earl Haig had indicated that the Allied offensive could not continue much longer. This was a flattering exaggeration, but Hitler did not tire of repeating the point to his weary generals when their own war entered its bleaker years.

At the end of May 1937, Blomberg reported back to Hitler on the coronation ceremonies in London. The widow of King George V, he said, had implored him to avoid a repetition of 1914. Hitler could only manage a sceptical reply. In June, there was another contact with the Anglo-Saxon world when Mr Mackenzie King, the somewhat eccentric Canadian premier, had a confidential two-hour talk with him (he wrote in his voluminous diary his favourable impressions of the Nazis' "constructive" work). But to Hitler the flavour of all the reports from London was that Britain had resumed a barely concealed rearmament effort, particularly of the RAF; and there was therefore a real time-limit on achieving his secret strategic ambitions. His military attaché, Baron Geyr von Schweppenburg, reported from London on 19 February 1937: "In any war, time will work *for* Britain, but only if she can survive initial defeats which would make it impossible for her to fight on." Geyr's further despatches in 1937 repeated the warnings about Britain's growing strength. Hitler's bitterness at this was obvious. Hjalmar Schacht ascribed it to Hitler's annoyance that the British had merely "pocketed" the naval agreement – whereby Germany had voluntarily limited her own warship and submarine construction – and had not made any equal contribution to Anglo-American relations. Hitler had explained to Ribbentrop in 1935 that he was not proposing to repeat Admiral von Tirpitz's earlier error in getting involved in an arms race; he was going to concede naval supremacy to the British, and hope that they would make him a similar concession with regard to Germany's future land armies. Over the next years, however, it was clear that the British were not offering any such quid pro quo, and in September 1938 the German naval staff was sadly to summarize: "The realization has dawned on the navy and the Führer over the last one-and-a-half years that, in contrast to what the Führer had hoped for at the time of the signing of the naval agreement, Britain cannot be excluded as a possible future enemy."

Hitler had certainly not anticipated this "estrangement" between Britain and Germany. In April 1935 the then German ambassador in London, Leopold von Hoesch, had convincingly reported the pro-German, indeed pro-Nazi inclinations of Britain's Prince of Wales: the 41-year-old heir to the throne dramatically disapproved of the anti-German policies of the Foreign Office, and "fully understood that Germany wished to face the other nations squarely, with her head held high . . ."; in June 1935 he made such an emphatic declaration of friendship to Germany in a public speech that his father, King George V, had to rebuke him and remind him of the constitutional restraints placed on the British throne. Upon his assumption of the throne a few months later, King Edward VIII made no secret of his belief that only an Anglo-German alliance would preserve Europe from fresh warfare and ruin. In January 1936 a fellow-Etonian, the Duke of Saxe-Coburg Gotha, asked him confidentially whether a discussion between Prime Minister Baldwin and Hitler might be desirable; as the Duke reported to Hitler, the new monarch replied, "Who is King here? Baldwin or I? I myself wish to talk to Hitler, and will do so here or in Germany. Tell him that, please." The Duke's illuminating report continues,

> The King is resolved to concentrate the business of government on himself. For England, not too easy. The general political situation, especially the situation of England herself, will perhaps give him a chance. His sincere resolve to bring Germany and England together would be made more difficult if it were made public too early. For this reason I regard it as most important to respect the King's wish that the non-official policy of Germany towards England should be firmly concentrated in one hand and at the same time brought into relations of confidence with the official policy. The, in this

respect, peculiar mentality of the Englishman must be taken into account if we want to achieve success – which undoubtedly is attainable.

The King asked me to visit him frequently in order that confidential matters might be more speedily clarified in this way. I promised – subject to the Führer's approval – to fly to London at any time he wished.

Not much is known of the secret contacts that followed between Hitler and King Edward VIII. Hitler was to claim on 13 May 1942 that the King had offered to meet Germany's colonial needs by allowing Germans to settle Northern Australia, thereby creating a powerful shield for British interests against Japan. Hitler regarded the abdication crisis of 1936 as a pretext by the King's enemies to remove him on account of his pro-German feelings. The British Cabinet records of those weeks are closed until the twenty-first century, but they probably throw little light on the real background of the abdication anyway: the British government, records Edward VIII's biographer, were anxious to confine the issue to the simple one of his marriage "and there is no doubt that they succeeded".* But Hitler was in no doubt, and told Julius Schaub and others on his staff that the estrangement would not have occurred had Edward VIII remained on the throne. His successor, King George VI, was weak and vacillating, said Hitler, and wholly in the grip of his "evil and anti-German advisers". When Edward, now Duke of Windsor, visited Berchtesgaden in October 1937 he told Hitler much that confirmed this view. Ribbentrop found in the Duke "something akin to a British National Socialist". Unfortunately, the record of their meeting has vanished from the captured files.

A less tangible reason for Hitler's restlessness was the realization that the years were slipping by, while his grand design was remaining unfulfilled.

The same uninspiring faces assembled – with diminishing regularity – in the Cabinet room; the agenda laboured under the same suffocating minutiae of state. A civil servant, the Gestapo official Werner Best, who sat in on one such meeting in 1937, found Hitler had become "increasingly nervous, bad-tempered, impatient, gloomy, abrupt, distrustful, unjust, dogmatic and intractable". Was this the fiery prophet of the years of struggle? "With glowering mien," wrote Best, "he listened to the submissions of the various Reich ministers and retorted in a surly voice. His aversion to the topics, to the wrangling and even to the people present was obvious." He felt himself succumbing to the inertia of government bureaucracy: these faces, these procedures, these very buildings were those of the regimes he had displaced and despised. His contempt of Neurath's foreign ministry was one example of this,

---

* Frances Donaldson, *Edward VIII* (London, 1974).

as was his hatred of red-tape and lawyers. ("I will not rest until every decent German sees it is an infamy to be a lawyer!")*

Hitler wanted new environs, new men and new methods. He began appointing special plenipotentiaries to perform certain tasks parallel to the fossilizing government agencies – it was less exhausting than trying to revive the latter. The Ribbentrop bureau was one example. Cabinet meetings as such virtually ceased late in 1937. Instead Hitler dealt directly – through Lammers – with affairs of state, while he transmitted his will directly to the ministers and generals without discussion.

Now things moved faster. Thus the end of Cabinet government in Germany coincided with the beginning of his aggressive designs to annex Lebensraum in the east. For this ambition the subjugation of Austria and Czechoslovakia was a geographic prerequisite, as any map could show. A psychological requisite was the proper processing of public opinion. He was to explain in November 1938, with remarkable frankness, after accomplishing the first phase (Austria and Czechoslovakia):

> Circumstances forced me to speak almost entirely of peace these last ten years and more. It was only by harping on Germany's desire and search for peace that I managed, little by little, to secure the freedom of action and the armaments that we needed to take each successive step.

The time had arrived, he continued in that secret speech, to prepare the German public psychologically for each foreign crisis, until the people themselves cried out for a violent solution.

The first target would be Austria. He proposed to win here by peaceful means if possible. Not that this precluded a bloodbath afterwards: "If and when the Austrian problem is solved," Hitler said in one adjutant's hearing in May 1937, "there will be nothing else for it: hundreds of thousands of Austrians will have to go to the wall. We can't create order there otherwise!" In Austria there was a vociferous organized campaign for solidarity with the Reich. In July 1937, Hitler was deeply moved by the participation at the big Breslau song festival of contingents from the German-speaking areas outside the Reich's frontiers – in Austria and Czechoslovakia – and he had incited them by his reference in a speech to "95 million Germans", of whom only 68 millions were at present part of his Reich. This showed the size of his appetite. The Austrian contingent, in bright national costumes, stormed his tribune; the women wept uncontrollably – a scene to which Hitler frequently referred in private during the coming months. Earlier in July he had appointed an SS-Gruppenführer, Dr Wilhelm Keppler, to act as the Nazi Party's special agent for Austrian affairs;

---

* An admirable sentiment: twelve of the fifteen Watergate criminals were lawyers; Reinhard Heydrich's entire staff were lawyers, too.

but he warned Keppler that he would not contemplate a revolutionary solution. (He could not afford another Dollfuss-type incident.)

In Czechoslovakia too there was a large ethnic German minority. Quite apart from the 150,000 counted in 1930 in Slovakia, there were 3½ million Germans "trapped" on the wrong side of the frontier, in Bohemia and Moravia, by the artificial frontiers which had created Czechoslovakia in 1919. To Hitler, the Czechs had no right to be in Bohemia and Moravia at all: they had not moved in until the sixth and seventh centuries, when they had infiltrated everything. "The Czechs are past masters at infiltration," he was to state in October 1941. "Take Vienna: before the World War, only about 170 of the 1,800 Imperial court officials were of German origin – all the rest, right up to the top, were Czechs." Memories of the Czechs, as Pan-Slav fanatics, still lingered within him from his school years: during the Russo-Japanese War, his Czech schoolfellows had sympathized with the Russians, and the Germans with the Japanese. 'When we learnt of the fall of Port Arthur the little Czechs in my class at school wept, while the rest of us exulted," he recalled in September 1941.

To these emotional motives Hitler's own strategy added other reasons to destroy Czechoslovakia. "He who has Czechoslovakia", he preached to his inner circle, "holds the whip hand in Central Europe." Czechoslovakia's alliances with France and Russia offended and alarmed him. On 19 January 1937, General Geyr had reported from London concrete evidence that the Russian and Czech staffs had agreed on the details of Russian air operations from Czech airfields against Germany; Soviet liaison officers were already in Prague. Conversely, Czechoslovakia would be a useful springboard for Hitler to invade the Ukraine.

Most of the ethnic Germans lived in the border "Sudeten territories" of Bohemia and Moravia, where Czech and French engineers had laboured for years to erect fortifications similar to the Maginot Line on the French frontier. The Czech president, Dr Eduard Beneš, had chosen to enforce the "Czechification" of the local administration of these territories, leaving the ethnic German population there both unemployed and aggrieved. Baron von Neurath had tried to induce Beneš to mollify these policies, without success. Germany's relations with Czechoslovakia relied formally on a 1925 treaty of arbitration built into the Locarno treaty. For tactical reasons Hitler had not actually renounced this when reoccupying the German Rhineland in 1936. When his foreign ministry now suggested a useful technicality which would permit him to side-step the treaty, Hitler would not agree. He wanted, he said, to avoid any suspicion that he was plotting against Czechoslovakia – as indeed he was. The question was: when should he strike. Spitzy recalls one scene at this time, of Hitler scanning the latest agency reports through gold-rimmed spectacles, while Ribbentrop peered over his shoulder. "Mein Führer," said Ribbentrop, "I think we shall soon have to draw our sword from its scabbard!"

"No, Ribbentrop," responded Hitler. "Not yet."

He doubted, in November 1937, whether his commanders were ready for war. Twice Göring asked Blomberg whether the generals would follow Hitler unconditionally. Evidently the Party doubted the Wehrmacht's loyalty. Blomberg's last directive to the Wehrmacht, in June 1937, had been primarily defensive, not offensive. It had mentioned only two minor attack contingencies: "Otto," an attack on Austria should she restore the hated Habsburg monarchy; and "Green," a surprise attack on Czechoslovakia if France or Russia invaded Germany (because the Russian air force must be prevented from using the now-complete airfields in Czechoslovakia). Fritsch had dutifully ordered the army to study ways of breaching the Czech fortifications. But to Hitler it seemed that his army lacked enthusiasm. It certainly lacked ammunition and arms for a long conflict.

This was a problem that the Wehrmacht had not encountered before. The records show that from the autumn of 1936, Germany was gripped by an increasingly severe iron and steel shortage. Early in 1937 the three services were ordered to cut back their arms budgets. This was met by a storm of protest. The navy argued emphatically against any reduction of warship construction, now that Britain, a naval power, was emerging as a possible enemy too. In particular, more submarines would have to be built. But the gap could not be bridged. The navy demanded 88,400 tons of steel for each of the months June, July and August 1937, and 77,400 tons a month thereafter. They were promised only 45,000 tons – but even this seemed unlikely, as in April the navy had received only 23,600 tons. Raeder informed Hitler that in consequence, of the launchings planned in 1938 – two battleships (*Bismarck* and *Tirpitz*), two heavy cruisers and two aircraft carriers – all would have to be postponed except for one cruiser and one carrier. Shipyard construction would also be affected. A furious inter-service row broke out. The Luftwaffe pointed out that it was getting 70,000 tons of steel a month, but this permitted only 75 per cent of their arms production and no work on civil defence; if they could not get at least 48,825 tons per month *more* the Luftwaffe programme would remain incomplete until 1947. At Blomberg's suggestion Hitler called the bickering C-in-Cs to the Chancellery to settle the dispute.

Such was the background of one of Hitler's most portentous secret conferences – the so-called "Hossbach Conference" of 5 November 1937. Because Hitler decided to use this opportunity of revealing to them his true secret goals – if only to impart to all of them a real sense of urgency, or as he put it to Göring, "to put some steam up Fritsch's pants". Colonel Fritz Hossbach, his

Hossbach Memorandum – be ready for war in 4 years ~5/11/37

Wehrmacht adjutant, wrote a summary five days later of the proceedings. Part of this has survived: so has a telegram sent by the French ambassador to Paris in code at 7 P.M. next day, reporting what he had – with dramatic accuracy – learned of Hitler's exceptionally long meeting, and the astonishingly large number of generals and admirals summoned to the Chancellery. Ironically, Göring's Forschungsamt decoded François-Poncet's telegram, and Blomberg ordered the closest investigation to trace the ambassador's source (which is still unknown): the testimonies in German admiralty files therefore provide much background material on the "Hossbach Conference".

It was not a Cabinet meeting. The subject was far too important for such an audience, Hitler explained. But to lend solemnity to the proceedings (as he told Göring) he did invite the foreign minister besides Blomberg, Göring, Raeder and Fritsch. Even Hitler's five other adjutants were excluded. He told them to wait in the glass-walled conservatory of his "official residence", a wing of the Chancellery. The glass doors were closed behind him, and a thick curtain drawn across. The dozen or so munitions and economics experts whom Blomberg had also rounded up, fruitlessly as it turned out, had to kick their heels for the next four hours in the smoking-room next door. After the first half, Neurath swept out without talking to them. When the rest of the conference ended at 8:30 P.M., the word passed round: "The navy has won!" and, "Only the navy gets twenty thousand tons."

The reason for Neurath's sealed lips is clear. Speaking from a sheaf of loose notes, Hitler had reiterated his determination to launch a war to solve Germany's Lebensraum "problems" within the next five or six years, since Germany could not hope to become self-sufficient in food production, and the countries enjoying excess food-production capacity would hardly part with it voluntarily. Indeed, as a first stage in solving this Lebensraum problem, Hitler might, under certain circumstances, order a "lightning attack" on neighbouring Czechoslovakia during 1938 – e.g. if civil war broke out in France between the Left and Right, or if Italy's operations in the Mediterranean should lead to a full-scale war between her and Britain and France next summer.

Hitler was so emphatic that Fritsch proposed cancelling his projected leave, due to start in ten days' time. Göring suggested they should dismantle their operations in Spain. Both Blomberg and Fritsch urged Hitler to prevent a war on two fronts – that is, to prevent Britain or France from declaring war on Germany. But Hitler's view was that Britain had already tacitly written off Czechoslovakia, and France would follow suit.

They raised no other objections to Hitler, either then or later. Göring efficiently issued immediate fresh instructions to the Luftwaffe; and in December, Blomberg drafted a new directive to the armed forces, shifting the planning focus with immediate effect to "Operation Green", the lightning attack on Czechoslovakia. The section relating to "Green" was issued by Blomberg's ministry on 21 December: once Germany was ready she could attack Czechoslovakia, thus solving the Lebensraum problem – an intriguing oversimplification – "even if one or more major powers are ranged against us"; of course, the western frontier defences would have to be improved, as Germany was outnumbered there; but Hitler would try to avoid war on two fronts or any other fatal military or economic risks. Should the political situation not develop well, the directive continued, "Green" might have to be postponed for some years; on the other hand a situation might arise depriving Czechoslovakia of all her potential allies except Russia: "Then 'Green' will take effect even *before* Germany is fully prepared for war."

The Blomberg directive defined the objective of "Green" as the rapid occupation of Bohemia and Moravia – the largest, westernmost provinces of Czechoslovakia – coupled with a simultaneous political union with Austria, which latter would require military force only if "other means" proved unsuccessful before then. War minister Blomberg had approved this document in draft, but had then left on 15 December for a week at Oberhof with his ill-starred lady friend. The army C-in-C, Fritsch, had left for Egypt on two months' leave – with the Gestapo tailing him. By the end of January 1938, neither would still be in office.

One significant misconception in Blomberg's directive shows how little he appreciated the scope of Hitler's ambitions – the notion that the success of "Green" would solve the "Lebensraum problem".

As anyone who had read Chapter 14 of *Mein Kampf* knew, Hitler had set his sights much further afield. Throughout these years his eyes had remained fixed on Russia. In his first speeches he had drawn attention to her open spaces; and if we apply the only proper yardstick to gauge his inner aims over the years that followed, if we examine his long-term material preparations, only one conclusion remains – that his "dream land", his new empire, awaited him in the east.

One such material clue is in German admiralty files, a letter from the naval commandant at Pillau in East Prussia reporting a conversation between Hitler and the local gauleiter, Oberpräsident Erich Koch, in June 1937: Hitler had, he said, warned of Pillau's coming importance as a naval base "even more powerful than Kiel or Wilhelmshaven", to accommodate a bigger fleet in future years: "In the Führer's view the time will come – in say six or seven years – when Germany can progress from her present defensive posture to an offensive policy. Within Europe, this kind of development will only be possible towards the east."

It was characteristic that Hitler's own naval C-in-C, Raeder, had to learn of this by roundabout Party channels. Hitler consistently kept the German public in ignorance of his true aims, because there were few who ventured far into the forbidding jungle of *Mein Kampf*. But he also kept his Wehrmacht C-in-Cs in blinkers until the very eve of each new military phase. Only Party loyals were given early warning. It is regrettable that no records have been found of most of Hitler's important secret speeches to his gauleiters, like that on 2 June 1937 to which Erich Koch was probably referring. One speech to lower-level Party leaders survives as a sound recording on discs, delivered on 23 November 1937. In this he proclaimed, "The British purchased their entire empire with less blood than we Germans lost in the World War alone." He lamented that once already Germany had had Europe in the palm of her hand, only to see it slip through the fingers of feckless monarchs. "Monarchies are at most capable of hanging on to what has been conquered. World empires are won only by revolutionary movements." He is heard adding later, "Today the German nation has at last acquired what it lacked for centuries – an organized leadership of the people."

Hitler was not interested in overseas conquests, as he had made plain in the "Hossbach Conference" on 5 November. Such colonies could always be cut off from Germany by British naval blockade. "The only succour – and it may still seem a dream to us – lies in winning larger Lebensraum." This he defined as follows: "It will be more pertinent to look for raw material areas right next door to the Reich, in Europe, and not overseas." Therefore when Lord Halifax, the British statesman, visited him in Bavaria on 19 November to discuss Hitler's views on obtaining colonies in Africa – at some other European power's expense, not Britain's – he failed to excite the Führer's interest. Halifax linked the deal with a demand for unilateral German arms limitations, which was quite unacceptable; and besides, Hitler's view was that Germany's former East African colonies were hers by right, and not pawns for political bargaining.

By the end of 1937 it was clear that the coming year would be dominated by two factors – by Hitler's ardent resolve to begin his fight for Lebensraum and empire in the east; and by the growing certainty that in the west, Britain would do all she could to thwart him.

Late in December 1937 his London ambassador, Ribbentrop, submitted to Hitler a summary* of Britain's attitude to Germany: she regarded Germany as her most deadly potential enemy, as Hitler alone could threaten the heart of the British Empire, Britain herself. Chamberlain was, Ribbentrop intimated, cur-

---

* This document clearly proves that Ribbentrop did warn Hitler that Britain would fight – contrary to the legend established at the Nuremberg trials in 1946. I quote it at length, as the document was "not found" by the editors of the Allied document publication, *Documents on German Foreign Policy*.

rently formulating a new initiative with the hope of purchasing peace in Europe; in return, the British would offer colonies and certain concessions on Austria and Czechoslovakia. But, he warned, while the British public was largely in favour of a lasting agreement with Germany, there was a hostile ruling class that could always swing the public round to support war, for example by atrocity-mongering against the Nazis. There was, wrote Ribbentrop, a "heroic" ruling class that would not shrink from war to protect their material interests as a world power. "When Britain sees the odds improve, she will fight."

Ribbentrop reported that many people anticipated that Britain would adopt a stronger line in 1939; he himself would put it later, because of their backward naval construction programme. For the present, he believed, Britain and France were mulling over what offer of colonies they should make. He correctly predicted that Britain would come forward with a secret offer in February or March 1938. He did not advise Hitler to accept the inevitable strings, namely German arms limitations and a guarantee for Czechoslovakia, unless the colonies offered made it really worthwhile. He himself smelt a rat – that probably the British, knowing Hitler would never accept, were just preparing an alibi to demonstrate Germany's intractability. His conclusion therefore was this:

If Britain continues even in future to block Germany at every turn, then there can be no doubt but that the two nations will ultimately drift apart. Nonetheless, it seems proper to me that our future policies should remain anchored to striving for agreement with Britain. The embassy will therefore work consistently towards an Anglo-German entente.

On 2 January 1938, Ribbentrop significantly amended this view. He concluded in a despatch to Hitler that while they should continue to seek agreement with Britain, they must secretly build up their own system of alliances too. "Today," he wrote to the Führer, "I no longer believe in a rapprochement. Britain does not want a Germany of superior strength in the offing as a permanent threat to her islands. That is why she will fight."

The upshot was a sudden demand by Hitler in January for more battleships. A document in naval construction files reads, "Arms policy: in a conference with the C-in-C of the navy [Raeder] at the beginning of 1938 the Führer ordered a considerable strengthening of the fleet and, in this connection, an acceleration of the construction effort. By the end of 1944, for instance, there are to be four, and not six as previously planned, battleships of the H-Class [Bismarck] complete." Raeder agreed, provided he was given the skilled labour and raw materials his shipyards needed.

Ribbentrop's warning imparted urgency to Hitler's programme. On 21

January 1938 he delivered the first of many speeches to his generals, assembled after a Nazi indoctrination course in Berlin. According to Colonel Alfred Jodl's diary, it lasted two-and-a-half hours. An anonymous three-page typed summary exists, showing that Hitler began with an illuminating description of the Roman Empire, and how thereafter Christianity had given western civilization the inner unity it needed to stave off eastern invasions. He contrasted Bolshevism and National Socialism, parliamentary democracy and the unitarian state. "Only one man can lead, but that man shoulders the entire burden of responsibility. It is a heavy burden. Believe me, generals, I have had sleepless nights over my grave decisions, and now my nerves have gone to pieces and I just cannot sleep any longer for worry about Germany." He explained that Germany's food situation was particularly grim.

A good harvest provides just enough food for our present population for one year. If the harvest is only mediocre, we lose several months' food supplies. If the harvest is poor – and this will certainly happen one day – the German people will only get enough food for quarter or half a year – on the basis of the *present* population, that is. But Germany's population growth is 600,000 new heads every year. That's six million in ten years. How can Germany continue to feed her people? That is only possible if we acquire new territory – and we must get that by brute force.

That was the point Hitler had been working up to. He ended,

Germany's position is really bleak, and day and night I battle with the problem. But one fact leads me to believe that there may be hope for the German nation yet: if we look closely at the ruling nations of this earth – the British, French and Americans – the statistics show that only a vanishingly small component of them, perhaps 40 or 50 million pure-blooded citizens of the ruling country, are controlling millions of other human beings and gigantic areas of the world. There is only one nation on earth, living in the heart of Europe in great compactness, of uniform race and language, tightly concentrated together: and that is the German nation, with 110 million Germans in Central Europe. This comparison gives us cause to hope. One day the entire world must and shall belong to this united block of Central Europe.

Goddess of Fortune

A chalk-grey scar across the dark-green mountain landscape is all that remains of the Berghof, Hitler's villa built high above the little Alpine town of Berchtesgaden, to which he returned early on 6 February 1938. Blasted in a British bombing-raid in 1945, the remains were dynamited by the American occupation forces some years later. It was here that Hitler came to seek serenity and time to ponder the path ahead. Munich or Lake Chiemsee might sulk in mist or fog, but this corner of Bavaria seemed to bask in perpetual sunshine. Ever since he had first been driven at breakneck speed up the rough mountain paths on the pillion seat of a motorbike, he had fallen in love with this Obersalzberg mountainside, a green ridge straddling lakes and pine forests, velvet meadows and dairy herds. He had been introduced to the mountain by Dietrich Eckart, a wealthy poet and one of Hitler's first benefactors, who gave the Nazi Party its battlecry, "Germany Awake". Here in the late 1920s Hitler had purchased a cottage, Wachenfeld, in about one-and-a-half acres, with the royalties earned by *Mein Kampf* and articles published under a pseudonym by the Hearst Press and the *New York Times* in America. Around this cottage he had built the Berghof. The air was clean and fresh: "Fresh air is the finest form of nourishment," he would say. Eventually he appointed Martin Bormann, Hess's chief of staff, to manage the Berghof – a position that gradually gave him control over Hitler's household too.

Bormann, a former estate-manager from Mecklenburg, had worked his way up by cunning and by an almost offensive friendliness towards equal and subordinate alike. In 1932 still only head of the SA insurance branch – paying out claims for brownshirts injured in the street-fighting – by 1945 he was one of the most powerful men in German domestic politics. He was a hard worker, and took care that Hitler knew it: he would telephone for a routine invitation to Hitler's lunch table, which he would then conspicuously cancel "because of the pressure of work"; or he would arrive late, making the same excuse. To the slothful and pleasure-loving soldiers and bureaucracy, his love of hard work made Bormann a thoroughly loathsome creature. He worked day and night, seven days a week. "Since 1933 I've worked like a horse," he wrote to Party officials after Hess's strange defection in 1941. "Nay, more than a horse – because a horse gets its Sunday and rests at night, while I've had never a Sunday and scarcely a night off these last few years."

Hitler's word was Bormann's command. Bormann bought up the adjacent land-plots to preserve the Berghof's privacy. He pulled down the old Platterhof inn some way above the Berghof and rebuilt it as a spacious hotel – after all, the Obersalzberg was to be a place of pilgrimage. Once Hitler mentioned that a farmstead spoilt his view: when he next looked, it had vanished and the site was levelled and freshly turfed. On 13 June 1937 – a Sunday – Bormann noted in his diary, "Because of the heat of high summer, the Führer wished there were a tree where the daily 'march-past' occurs. I have ordered a tree from Munich." The lime-tree was erected four days later! (On 1 July 1937, Bormann feverishly scribbled in his notebook, "I must inspect the building-sites every day: drive 'em, drive 'em!")

The daily march-past ritual was part of the Hitler legend. Thousands flocked to the Berghof to see him in the flesh. These were his subjects, he was their leader. "The Führer is up here at the Obersalzberg now," wrote his autobahn architect Fritz Todt to a friend. "On days when he has nothing particular to do he permits anybody who wants to, to come past his garden after lunch at about 2 or 3 P.M., and he waves to them. It's always a very gay procession up here on the Obersalzberg. . . . The folks walk past quietly saluting, and they mustn't shout or anything. Only the children are allowed to jump over to the Führer."

Bormann had laid out new roads up the mountain and built barracks and anti-aircraft gun-sites too. The rooftops of a new SS guard barracks could be seen in a hollow behind the Berghof, and more barracks straddled the only approach roads from the town. The main feature of the rebuilt Berghof was the Great Hall, a room over sixty feet long. One entire wall was a panorama window – Hitler proudly told his visitors, "Really I've built a house around a window." It looked out across the valley to distant pine-clad slopes, so that unprepared visitors walking into the Great Hall gained the momentary, eerie notion that they were looking at an unusually vivid green drapery, until their eyes could refocus to infinity and the distant shapes of the trees of the Untersberg mountain were seen.

From the quarries of the Untersberg would later be hewn the red marble slabs with which Hitler would rebuild his Berlin Chancellery. Legend has it that in that mountain is the medieval emperor Barbarossa – that he never died but has sat there for a thousand years, until his beard has grown right through his table, and that one day he will return when Germany most needs him to re-establish her power and tranquillity.

In the Great Hall of Hitler's Berghof there was an overlong heavy table, surfaced with a red marble slab from across the valley. On it each morning the adjutants spread out the mail, newspapers and latest despatches from Berlin. On this same marble slab were later unfolded the maps of Europe and charts of the world's oceans. One 1940 photograph* shows the Führer leaning on the maps, surrounded by generals and adjutants: there is Walther von Brauchitsch, Fritsch's complaisant successor as army C-in-C, and the chief of the General Staff, with Rudolf Schmundt – chief Wehrmacht adjutant – and Wilhelm Keitel characteristically one pace behind the Führer. The potted plants have been pushed to the far end of the table, and Schmundt has casually laid his leather document pouch amongst them. Alfred Jodl, Wehrmacht chief of operations, is standing expressionlessly with folded arms in front of a rich tapesty. On the back of the snapshot Jodl himself has pencilled, "31 July 1940: Up at the Berghof. The Führer is enlarging on a decision taken shortly before – and it's a good thing that the maps can't be recognized."

The maps are of the Soviet Union. It is in this Great Hall that Hitler haṣ secretly announced to the watching gererals his decision to invade Russia.

Nazi romantics would visualize the Berghof as the pulsating dynamo at the hub of the Reich, loud with the clamour of secret messengers, uniformed orderlies and adjutants. Hitler's coterie knew better. The days here passed with monotonous sameness, the thick-walled building shrouded in a cathedral-like silence punctuated by the yapping of two Scots terriers owned by a young woman living anonymously upstairs, or by the laughter of an adjutant's visiting children. Not surprisingly, Hitler's staff slipped out when they could to the companionable hostelries down in Berchtesgaden, or to villages further along the valley. Hitler himself slept all morning, while the servants silently cleaned the panelling, polished the red marble staircase or dusted the costly works of art – here a Tintoretto or Tiepolo, there a small Schwindt. Lunch was taken at one communal table presided over by Hitler, with the young woman on his left: the talk revolved around film, theatre or fashion. If Herr Bormann came, Hitler gently ribbed him over his agricultural ambitions or the extravagant and malodorous model dairy recently built by the Party a few hundred yards away.

In short, here Hitler was the country squire. In loose tweedy clothes he set out on long strolls with his invited guests in company. A number of firm paths had been laid out and a small tea pavilion built, with a breathtaking view along the valley towards the forbidden countryside of Salzburg – in the outlawed Hitler's native Austria. In this pavilion he could sit for hours listening to the

* Given to me by Jodl's widow.

small talk of his friends. In later years he quietly dozed off until it was time to walk back to the Berghof for supper and the film. At supper, the ladies dressed more formally. But the meals were of puritan simplicity: earlier, Hitler had eaten meat, but he had suddenly pronounced himself a vegetarian after a suicide tragedy in his town apartment in Munich in 1931 – a fad for which he later offered various excuses: that he had noticed body odours when he ate meat: or that the human jaw was designed for vegetarian meals. This view was shared by his dentist, Professor Johannes Blaschke, who was also a vegetarian. "You'll see, doctor," Hitler told a specialist in 1944, "just how little influence I have on my own household: I'm their Chief, but I'm the only vegetarian, non-smoker and teetotaller. They'd all be far better for it if they lived as healthily as I do." Meantime he regaled his Berghof guests in revolting detail with the various processes he had observed in a slaughterhouse, and all the distracting endeavours of the young woman at his side failed to stop him inflicting this on each new unsuspecting visitor to the Berghof.

After supper, the tapestries in the Great Hall were drawn back to reveal a projection room and cinema screen, and a movie film was shown. Hitler followed this practice nightly until Europe dissolved into war at his command – from which day on he never saw another feature film. His appetite for movies was prodigious, but Bormann efficiently submitted weekly lists to the propaganda ministry and asked for certain regular favourites like *The Hound of the Baskervilles* and *Mutiny on the Bounty* to be permanently available at the Berghof for the Führer's entertainment.

It was here at the Berghof that Hitler proposed to stage his next coup – a conference with the Austrian chancellor, Kurt Schuschnigg, that would spell *finis Austriae*.

Relations with Austria were formally governed by a treaty of July 1936. This purported to restore to the Austrian Nazis a semblance of legality; but the Schuschnigg regime had done little to implement it. Schuschnigg himself was autocratic and wilful, and refused to accept the harsh realities of Central European politics. To his friend the police president of Vienna, he once admitted that Austria's future was "of course" inseparable from Germany's – but he was damned if he was going to put up with Berlin dictating his own foreign policy to him. In many respects he resembled Hitler: a dictator, unsociable and little-travelled; but he possessed only a tithe of Hitler's demonic stature, debating ability and ruthless cunning, so that in any encounter he was bound to come off worse. It was to be a famous meeting, but what happened there has been obscured by specious accounts by the main participants – culminating in those during the post-war trial of Schuschnigg's own foreign minister, Guido Schmidt.

Such a meeting had long been Schuschnigg's dream: he would talk to Hitler "man to man", he said. Hitler was initially only lukewarm, but told his special ambassador in Vienna, Franz von Papen, in the first week in January that the meeting might take place at the end of the month. Throughout January, there were ugly incidents in Austria and rumours in Berlin. On the eleventh, at Hitler's New Year diplomatic reception, François-Poncet happened to express a hope that 1938 would not be seeing any of Hitler's "Saturday surprises" – to which the Nazi foreign minister, Neurath, replied that the internal situation in Austria gave cause for concern. Over dinner with the Austrian envoy, Stefan Tauschitz, on 21 January, Neurath amplified this: "If a boiler is kept heating, and there's no safety-valve, it's bound to explode." This was a reference to the continued internment of Austrian Nazis, against the letter of the July 1936 treaty. (This was the day of Hitler's secret speech to his generals, announcing his plan to conquer new Lebensraum by force.*) Next day Schuschnigg learned that Hauptmann Josef Leopold, leader of one faction of the warring Viennese Nazis, had recently bragged to the private secretary of Sir Oswald Mosley – the British fascist leader – that the Austrian Nazis were going to stage an armed uprising in the spring, aided by the German Reich. On the twenty-second, Vienna learned from Berlin that Göring was secretly boasting that the Reich's difficulties in paying cash for Austrian raw materials would disappear in the spring. That sounded sinister. Three days later, Leopold's headquarters in Vienna was raided by Schuschnigg's police; the police found documents relating to a *coup d'état* in the spring, coupled with an invasion by the German army "to prevent further bloodshed". Hitler sacked Leopold – although we cannot easily say whether his fury was at Leopold's plotting, or at having allowed the plans to be captured so easily.

Perhaps it is important, before we witness the Berghof meeting itself, to recall that these last days of January 1938 were also seeing Hitler's domestic crisis, culminating in the dismissals of Blomberg and Fritsch: over the next two weeks or so, Hitler was playing an intricate two-handed game.

On 26 January, the very day of the confrontation staged by Hitler in his library between General von Fritsch and the blackmailer,† Neurath tele-graphed from Berlin to Vienna the Führer's proposal that the Berghof meeting should take place on about 15 February. It was all part of the same game, and Hitler admitted as much to Keitel, Chief of the OKW. Five days later Alfred Jodl's diary quoted Keitel: "[The]Führer wants to switch the spotlight away from the Wehrmacht, make Europe catch its breath. . . . Schuschnigg had better not take heart, but tremble."

* See page 67.
† See pages 9–10.

Two days later, on 2 February 1938, Hitler walked across the Chancellery garden to the foreign ministry, briefly discussed the forthcoming meeting with Schuschnigg, and then bluntly accepted the aged Baron Konstantin von Neurath's resignation – offered but not accepted a couple of weeks before. Turning a deaf ear on the horrified warnings of Neurath, Hitler appointed Ribbentrop as the new foreign minister.

Joachim von Ribbentrop was excitable, arrogant and short-tempered. Hitler knew it, but saw in him the ideal diplomatic secretary – a loyal henchman who would channel his political directives to the missions abroad with the same unquestioning zeal as General Wilhelm Keitel was to display in OKW affairs. Ribbentrop aroused antagonism everywhere. One voice, that of an army general (Carl Heinrich von Stülpnagel), summarized the main objections to him:

> Indescribably vain and so sure of himself that he never listens to advice. His idea of foreign policy is this: Hitler gives him a drum and tells him to bang it, so he bangs the drum loud and strong. After a while Hitler takes the drum away and hands him a trumpet; and he blows that trumpet until he's told to stop and play a flute instead. Just why he's been banging and trumpeting and fluting, he never knows and never finds out.

Ribbentrop was a year younger than Hitler. He had served as an officer in a good Prussian regiment, and was a good horseman. In post-war years he had built up a thriving export-import business in wines and spirits; with his increasing affluence he had bought a villa in Berlin's fashionable Dahlem suburb, and married into the Henkel champagne family (he was *not*, as was said, "a commercial traveller"). Count von Helldorf, who had served with him in the Twelfth Hussars, introduced him to Hitler; and it was in Ribbentrop's villa that the crucial meetings between Hitler and Chancellor Franz von Papen had taken place, culminating in the emergence of the Nazis in coalition government on 30 January 1933.

Hitler regarded this rich newcomer as somebody with influential connections abroad, somebody who might secure results where the doddering diplomats of Wilhelm Strasse were eminently failing. Ribbentrop had become diplomatic adviser to Rudolf Hess, Hitler's deputy since April 1933, and he had founded the "Ribbentrop Bureau", in unofficial competition with Neurath's ministry. Ribbentrop had been allowed a number of dazzling but relatively easy personal triumphs, like the Naval Agreement of 1935 and the Anti-Comintern Pact of 1936. There is no doubt – because Hitler so informed his adjutants – that he had selected his London ambassador to replace Neurath in the forlorn hope that this would flatter opinion in the British capital.

This, then, was the foreign minister with whom Hitler now stormed into the arena of world politics: now that he had divested himself of his tiresome and over-conservative generals and ministers, and because he had a powerful army, a united people and a clear sense of purpose, Hitler proposed to seize the initiative in Europe. He trusted Ribbentrop – like Keitel – not to intrigue against him. He apparently disclosed to him only his more immediate geographical ambitions (Austria, Czechoslovakia, the former German province of Memel – seized by Lithuania in 1923 – Danzig and the "Polish Corridor", the strip of land linking Poland to the Baltic but separating East Prussia from the rest of Germany). Ribbentrop for his part respected Hitler's confidences: he was a gentleman, with a sense of the *korrekt* that was inflated to almost ludicrous proportions: he refused for instance to accept from Hitler one penny more than he had earned as a businessman. He declined to discuss with post-war American investigators the backstairs intrigues over King Edward VIII, or Count Galeazzo Ciano's ability – since he was now dead – or even the details of his August 1939 secret pact with Stalin, since it was still secret, "as a matter of international courtesy"!

Among those who fell under the axe wielded by Hitler to end the Blomberg-Fritsch crisis was Franz von Papen – since 1934 his special envoy to Vienna.

Papen left Vienna, seething with rage, and arrived at the Berghof late on 6 February 1938 shortly after Hitler himself. Hitler promptly sent him back to Vienna with instructions to invite Schuschnigg to the Berghof on the twelfth, a Saturday. Papen pocketed his pride and did so. Over the next few days, he, Guido Schmidt and Schuschnigg discussed what demands each side had to make of the other. The German proposals were stated by Hitler's agent, Wilhelm Keppler. Schuschnigg agreed in principle to appoint pro-German ministers of finance and security – the latter being the lawyer Dr Arthur Seyss-Inquart, a "respectable" Nazi sympathizer; this would ensure that persecution of the Austrian Nazis would cease. In return, Hitler agreed to close down the Nazis' HQ in Vienna. Under further pressure from Papen, Schuschnigg accepted Hitler's invitation.

Hitler set his stage with the care of a Bayreuth producer. The guard barracks on the approach road were filled with "Austrian Legion" units: there were 120,000 men in the legion, outnumbering Austria's legal army two to one. The SS sentry manning the gate on the final approach growled in unmistakable Carinthian dialect. And as Hitler marched down the steps in brown Party tunic, red swastika armband and black trousers to meet the half-track bringing Schuschnigg's little group up the ice-bound lanes, he was accompanied by Reichenau and Luftwaffe general Hugo Sperrle – "my two most brutal-looking generals," he later chuckled to his adjutants. The Austrian chancellor made a bad impression on the prudish Führer. He remarked to his staff that Schuschnigg had not shaved and his nails were dirty; and when he introduced them to

Schuschnigg, the chancellor bowed slightly, clicked his heels to each and murmured, "Schuschnigg – , Schuschnigg – ," just like a provincial schoolmaster.

Luftwaffe adjutant von Below recalls that the interview was supposed to last only one morning. It dragged on until 11 P.M. and its flavour was well illustrated by Hitler's own May 1942 recollection: "I won't ever forget how Schuschnigg shrivelled up when I told him to get rid of those silly little barricades facing our frontier, as otherwise I was going to send in a couple of engineer battalions to clear them up for him." They spoke at first *à deux*, in the privacy of his long, first-floor study. Hitler heaped rebukes on Schuschnigg for his autocratic regime's anti-German, anti-democratic and brutal attitudes. He had decided to solve the Austrian problem *so oder so*. For a time, he bluffed, he had intended invading Austria on this coming 26 February – a Saturday – but now his advisers had submitted a plan to him; he had accepted it, and now Schuschnigg must sign it too. "This is the first time in my life I have ever changed my mind," he said. At one stage he suggested a plebiscite in Austria – with himself campaigning versus Schuschnigg. Schuschnigg put up a stout fight.

Over lunch, Hitler's generals loudly discoursed on the Luftwaffe and its new bombs. Hitler talked about his Panzer armies of the future. Schuschnigg prodded at his food without appetite. Then Hitler subtly changed his tone, and turned with enthusiasm to his plans to rebuild Hamburg with giant skyscrapers bigger than New York's; and he sketched the giant bridge that he and Todt were going to throw across the River Elbe – the longest bridge in the world. "A tunnel would have been cheaper," he admitted. "But I want Americans arriving in Europe to see for themselves that anything they can do, we Germans can do better." He also announced that later in 1938 a new warship was to be launched with the name of Admiral Tegethoff – the Austrian hero who had sunk the Italian fleet in the Battle of Lissa in 1866. "I'm going to invite both you as Austrian chancellor and Admiral Horthy to the ceremony," Hitler promised Schuschnigg. This generated such enthusiasm that when Hitler withdrew after lunch with Ribbentrop – to draw up the document that Schuschnigg must sign – some of the Austrian visitors loudly proclaimed "Heil Hitler", to everybody's embarrassment.

This mood changed sharply when Schuschnigg saw the proposed agreement. It required him to appoint Seyss-Inquart as minister of security and Dr Hans Fischböck as minister of finance, to prepare economic union between Austria and Germany. A hundred officers were to be exchanged between the Austrian and German armies. All imprisoned Nazis were to be amnestied and reinstated. In return Hitler would publicly reaffirm the treaty of 11 July 1936 and Austria's national sovereignty. Ribbentrop bluntly told Schuschnigg that these terms were not open to negotiation. A new battle between Hitler and Schuschnigg began, and both Keitel and Dr Kajetan Mühlmann testified that it was not a gentle process obtaining Schuschnigg's signature.

Mühlmann – an art-historian and Austrian Nazi sympathizer – had "happened" to be down in Berchtesgaden that day; Papen had called him up to the Berghof to advise Hitler. Hitler asked whether Schuschnigg was likely to adhere to the agreement, indicating: "I myself don't believe he will." Mühlmann disagreed. While they were talking Ribbentrop came in and complained. "Mein Führer, I've reached agreement with him on every point except one: he won't appoint Seyss-Inquart as minister of security." Hitler retorted, "Tell him that if he doesn't agree, I'll invade this very hour!" (This was bluff.) Shortly after, Papen entered: "Mein Führer, there are smiles all round now." But even now Schuschnigg was insisting on six days' grace, as only President Miklas could appoint new ministers. Hitler called him back into his study and resumed his bluster. Once he threatened, "Do you want Austria to become another Spain?" Then he threatened that Schuschnigg should not set much store by Italian military aid: Italy was still weak from her warring in Abyssinia and Spain, and her army was valueless. "In any war 10,000 German soldiers would suffice to thrash the entire Italian army!" Then he asked Schuschnigg to step outside, and as the door opened he called out into the Great Hall: "General Keitel!"

When Keitel hurried in, asking what was wanted, Hitler just motioned him to a chair: "I don't want anything. Just sit there." This dumb charade lasted ten minutes before Schuschnigg was called back in. Papen expressed embarrassment later at this treatment of the visiting chancellor, but Hitler had sized up his opponent well: now Schuschnigg initialled the final draft of the agreement without further objection. He seems to have fallen wholly under Hitler's hypnotic influence – although to his credit he had withstood it for longer than many of the Wehrmacht's most seasoned generals later did. "I have to admit", he told a Viennese intimate two days later, "that there's something of the prophet about Hitler."

For all Hitler's tough talk, the evidence – quite apart from the warship-launching ceremony that he was planning – is that he had no intention of starting a forcible invasion of Austria, provided that Schuschnigg kept his part of the bargain. (Wilhelm Keppler had warned on the seventh that Schuschnigg was governed by "periodic moods".) Hitler told his Luftwaffe adjutant that Austria would come closer to the Reich of her own accord now – perhaps that very autumn of 1938 – unless Schuschnigg committed some *Dummheit* meantime. To deter Schuschnigg from second thoughts, however, he ordered the OKW to fake preparations for an "invasion"; Canaris personally arranged this at Abwehr regional headquarters in Munich. At first these fears seemed groundless. Shortly after Hitler's return to Berlin, he learned on 15 February that President Miklas had ratified the Berghof agreement. Hitler was host to the diplomatic corps that evening: the Austrian envoy Stefan Tauschitz reported to Vienna afterwards that congratulations were showered on him by Göring, Goebbels and Hitler himself; the envoy for his part congratulated Ribbentrop that his first act as foreign minister had been crowned with such success. Hitler announced to the diplomats that the "age of misunderstandings" was over – nobody would ever again be able to sow discord between German and German. The *Sunday Express* suggested that the triumph was all Schuschnigg's, and the *Daily Express* informed its readers that "in the Austro-German poker game" Schuschnigg had played his trumpcard.

It was not long before this tone changed, however. As though on a given signal, the British and French newspapers began printing lurid stories of Hitler's Berghof "blackmail". The upshot was that only six days after Schuschnigg's visit, on 18 February 1938, the German air force received its first ever provisional order from Göring to investigate possible operations against London and southern England, in case war with Britain broke out. Somebody seemed to be inciting Schuschnigg: Ribbentrop's personal Intelligence office, run by Rudolf Likus, learned that once back in Vienna, Schuschnigg had privately declaimed, "The man we had to deal with at Berchtesgaden would have been locked up in a sanatorium long ago if he had stayed here in Austria." More ominously, Likus reported that the chancellor and Guido Schmidt had "recovered their balance" and that they were working to sabotage the Berghof agreement.

Hitler adhered to it – sedulously, one might think. In his next Reichstag speech, on 20 February, he referred warmly to the agreement and praised Schuschnigg's statesmanship; he publicly committed himself to the July 1936 treaty. Next day he summoned the radical Austrian Nazi, Josef Leopold, to Berlin and dismissed him. Hitler informed Leopold's successor that from now on there was to be a different approach towards Austria: the Nazi Party there must learn to keep inside the law. To Ribbentrop and five Austrian Nazis on 26 February 1938 he repeated that he had abandoned for ever all thought of using force against Austria. Time, he said, was in his favour. Provided the Berghof agreement was honoured by both sides, the Austrian problem would solve itself.

By early March, however, there were straws in the Austrian wind indicating that a crisis was again brewing. On the third, Colonel Jodl recorded in his notes: "A hundred [German] officers are to be posted to Austrian units. The Führer intends to speak to them personally. Their job will be to ensure not that the Austrian forces fight better against us – but that they don't fight at all."

Meanwhile, the other fruits of Germany's new military strength were ripening. On 3 March 1938 the long-announced new British,"initiative" materialized. It was brought from London by the ambassador, Sir Nevile Henderson: Henderson spoke German and knew his stuff, and Hitler had taken a liking to him for all his foppish mannerisms and the red carnation that flowered eternally in his buttonhole. Even in May 1942 he still compared Henderson favourably with predecessors, the "permanently tipsy" Sir Horace Rumbold and the "total cretin" Sir Eric Phipps.

In strictest confidence, Henderson reported to Hitler the offer approved by Chamberlain's Cabinet. Chamberlain himself had explained it to the Cabinet's foreign policy committee on 27 January as a deal whereby Nazi Germany "would be brought into the arrangement by becoming one of the African Colonial Powers . . . by being given certain territories to administer."* In return, Germany would be expected to limit her armaments and to recognize the status quo in Europe. Hitler listened to the ambassador's ten-minute speech with a scowl, then launched into a ferocious thirty-minute reply. Henderson quoted him as saying, "Nothing could be done until the press campaign against him in England ceased. Nor was he going to tolerate the interference of third parties in Central Europe." (Probably from FA wiretaps he had learned that Britain was encouraging Schuschnigg to disregard the Berghof agreement.) He refused to consider unilaterally limiting armaments, so long as the Soviet Union's rearmament continued unchecked. "One could place as much confidence in the faith in treaties of a barbarous creature like the Soviet Union as in the comprehension of mathematical formulae by a savage. Any agreement with the Soviet Union is quite worthless."

Henderson patiently outlined the colonies offered, on the globe in Hitler's study. Hitler challenged whether Belgium and Portugal – the governments administering these tracts of Africa – had even been consulted; he asked what was so difficult about simply giving back the East African colonies "robbed" from Germany after the World War. His own gaze, of course, was still fixed on Lebensraum in the east. He did ask Joachim von Ribbentrop to return to London in person to take formal leave as ambassador – an act of calculated blandishment. He instructed Ribbentrop to find out whether Chamberlain seriously desired entente, or was his initiative just a tactic to disrupt the Axis? His more general instructions to Ribbentrop were reflected by Ribbentrop's remarks to Baron Ernst von Weizsäcker on 5 March, when he invited him to become his new state-secretary. Ribbentrop warned Weizsäcker that a "basic acceptance of the Führer's policies" would be necessary, then talked of

* All his colleagues, including Eden, had approved the plan. Chamberlain wrote privately on 30 January, ". . . I have had a 'scintillation' on the subject of German negotiations. It has been accepted promptly and even enthusiastically by all to whom I have broached it, and we have sent for Henderson to come and talk it over with us."

... a "grand programme" that cannot be accomplished without the Sword. It will therefore take three or four more years before we are ready. . . . Where exactly the fighting will be, and wherefore, is open to later discussion. If at all possible, Austria is to be dealt with [*liquidiert*] before 1938 is out.

The meeting with Henderson had been in the Berlin Chancellery. Here in Berlin, Hitler found army opinion still unsettled by General von Fritsch's enforced resignation as C-in-C, his replacement by Brauchitsch, and the creation of the OKW to control all three services. There were sounds of distant thunder as the service staffs marshalled their separate arguments for an all-out assault on the OKW idea.

The General Staff's opinion was submitted in a document dated 7 March 1938, signed by Brauchitsch as C-in-C. General Walther von Brauchitsch was a man of powerful religious convictions, quiet and unassuming; he found sanctuary in the Bible on his bedside table, and kept to himself his hostility to the Nazi Party. He dressed punctiliously, but spoke – like Robert Ley – with a naturally slurred speech that suggested inebriation. In these first months of his office he forfeited much respect in Hitler's eyes by supporting the campaign waged by General Ludwig Beck, the chief of the General Staff, against the OKW. It was Beck who drafted the memorandum of 7 March, together with his deputy chief, Erich von Manstein – a rehash of proposals already put once to Hitler several weeks before, which stated basically that the army should have predominance in any Wehrmacht command.

The memorandum enables us to examine Beck's sagacity. Viewed in the subsequent light of a world war waged largely by the strategic bomber and the submarine, it is a dismal disappointment. In part it gratuitously insulted Hitler, as well as ignoring his own reorganization decreed on 4 February. In bygone times, the document conceded, any monarch could also be a warlord if he chose – Frederick the Great and Napoleon were examples; but now "even a genius" could not manage both political and military leadership. Beck rightly argued that there were two quite distinct functions in a war – the organization of the domestic war economy by a "Reich Secretary for War", and the conduct of strategic operations by a "Reich Chief of General Staff"; but he claimed that since in Germany the senior service was the army and the balance of future wars would lie in the army's hands, clearly the army should provide that strategic leadership, because only the army could defend one territory or conquer another:

The more there comes to the fore a war in the east, which will be a matter of the conquest of territory, while an impregnable wall is erected in the west, the more it becomes obvious that ultimately the success of the army will decide between the victory or defeat of the nation in that war.

A further factor is that, of our eastern enemies, Russia and Poland cannot be mortally injured at sea or in the air; and even if Czechoslovakia's cities and industrial centres are destroyed, she can only be forced at most to surrender certain territories, but not to surrender her sovereignty completely.

To annex a country, to destroy its resistance for all time, it will ultimately always have to be invaded and conquered.

The document predicted that the General Staff could not coexist in wartime with the new OKW operations staff set up under Lieutenant-General Max von Viebahn. "There remains only one conclusion – that the C-in-C of the army [Brauchitsch] must simultaneously act as adviser to the Supreme Commander [Hitler] on all matters of overall military command." Further, the document argued that the navy and Luftwaffe would be confined to primarily defensive roles – to "keeping the sea lanes open" and "defence of the homeland". Of course, Beck could not have foreseen the advent of the atomic bomb; but the possibilities of extended cruiser warfare, of the submarine campaign, of operations like the seaborne invasion of Norway, of the bombardment of Belgrade and the destruction of the Polish, French and Russian air forces were not even contemplated.

All this merely proved to Hitler how reactionary and outmoded his General Staff was. He angrily told his adjutants that the document was calling for the precise opposite of what he had ordered on 4 February. "If the army had had any say in things," he reminded Major Rudolf Schmundt, "the Rhineland would still not be free today; nor would we have reintroduced conscription; nor concluded the naval agreement; nor entered Austria. Even Blomberg acted like a hysterical old woman over each of these issues."

Hitler instructed Keitel to draft a formal reply disposing of the General Staff's arguments.

Providence gave Hitler the means to ride out the storms blowing up amongst his generals.

Towards midday on 9 March 1938 he learned that Schuschnigg was to spring a snap plebiscite on Austria in just five days' time. This was the *Dummheit* Hitler had been waiting for. Obviously the Austrian chancellor was trying to squirm out of the solemn Berghof agreement. Such a plebiscite would not only violate Austria's own 1934 constitution but – as Hitler shortly found out – its one question had been so formulated that any Austrian voting "No" to it could be charged with high treason (since voters had to state their names and addresses on the ballot papers). In fact Schuschnigg's plan caused controversy even in the "Fatherland Front", the only party permitted in Austria: some of his ministers felt the voting age should be 18, with only FF members allowed to vote; others recalled that the constitution defined the voting age as 21; Schuschnigg arbitrarily raised it for the plebiscite to 24 – the Nazis being primarily a Party of youth – and stipulated that votes were to be handed to FF officials, not the usual polling stations. There were no up-to-date electoral registers (Austria, being a dictatorship, had not voted for years). He declined to postpone the vote by four weeks, as this would give the nationalists time to organize a "No" vote. In fact under the plebiscite's *ad hoc* rules, all but the most determined – nay, foolhardy – opposing votes would be counted as "Yes": for example, even if one of the printed "Yes" ballot papers were to be crossed out and marked with a large "No" it would still count as a "Yes". There were no printed "No" ballot papers. No wonder that Weizsäcker, Ribbentrop's state-secretary, caustically termed it "a poor copy" of Hitler's cheap plebiscite tactics.

For two days Hitler was of two minds whether to invade Austria at once, before the day of the plebiscite. His immediate action was to fly his agent Keppler to Vienna to prevent it, or failing that to insist on a supplementary question sounding the Austrian public on its attitude towards union with the Reich. That evening Schuschnigg formally announced the plebiscite. Hitler listened to the broadcast from Innsbruck, then pounded the table with his fist and exclaimed, "It's got to be done – and done now!" A month later he announced, "When Herr Schuschnigg breached the Agreement on 9 March, at that moment I felt that the call of Providence had come."

Not that that call had come at an opportune moment for the Führer. Ribbentrop was in London, Brauchitsch and his senior generals were attending manoeuvres in Thuringia, Reichenau – who commanded Fourth Army Group, with Guderian's panzer force – was in Cairo and Milch was on leave in Switzerland. Towards midnight Hitler mustered his principal henchmen, Göring, Goebbels and Bormann on the Chancellery and announced his resolve to force a solution of the Austrian problem now. Ribbentrop's private secretary, Reinhard Spitzy, was rushed to London with a letter asking him to report immediately what Britain's probable reaction would be. Learning that General Edmund von Glaise-Horstenau, a pro-German Austrian minister, "happened" to be lecturing in Stuttgart, Hitler summoned him by phone to Berlin to discuss ways and means of forcing Schuschnigg's downfall. "Ribbentrop is far away in London," Hitler lamented, "but I've still got Neurath – he's a deliberate and careful fellow. I'll send for him."

His main worry was not Austria's tiny army of barely 60,000 men, but her powerful neighbours and friends. From telegrams decoded by the Forschungsamt Hitler later saw that France had wanted to intervene jointly with Britain and Italy to protect Austria's sovereignty, even if this meant war. The British envoy in Vienna had approved this, but was promptly disowned by

London – Lord Halifax, Eden's successor, refusing to give such a guarantee. The French foreign minister had informed Vienna: "Britain would not be prepared to encourage Herr Schuschnigg to resist." Hitler was to take great pains drafting a letter next day to Mussolini explaining his decision, and begging his approval. In his unpublished diary on 11 March, Alfred Jodl was to note, "Italy's the most ticklish problem: if she doesn't act against us, then the others won't either."

By 10 A.M. on 10 March, when Keitel was summoned to the Chancellery, Hitler had provisionally decided to invade two days later. Neurath, well pleased to have Hitler's ear again, also advised a rapid grab at Austria. Keitel sent back a messenger to the OKW building to fetch any contingency plans for such an invasion. But despite Blomberg's explicit directive of June 1937 there were no plans, except for "Otto" – devised to thwart a Habsburg restoration.* Viebahn sent Jodl to the Chancellery with the draft of Plan Otto. Keitel meanwhile went to fetch General Beck, and asked him what plans the General Staff had made for Austria. Beck gasped, "None at all! No plans have been laid at all!" He repeated this to Hitler when they got back to the Chancellery. The most he could mobilize would be two corps, with some panzer and infantry reserve divisions. Hitler told him to be ready to invade on Saturday morning, 12 March.

Beck primly declaimed: "I cannot take any responsibility for an invasion of Austria." To which Hitler retorted, "*You* don't have to. If you stall over this, I'll have the invasion carried out by my SS. They will march in with bands playing. Is that what the army wants?" Beck bitterly reflected, in a letter to Hossbach in October, that this was his first and last military conference with Hitler, and it had lasted just five minutes.

Even so, his staff worked with commendable speed. By 6:30 P.M. it had issued mobilization orders to the Eighth Army in Bavaria. So, where there was a will there was evidently a way. The Luftwaffe raised none of these obstacles. Göring – a field-marshal now – immediately made 300 transport aircraft available for propaganda flights and leaflet operations. Diplomatic officials also moved fast, as Weizsäcker's diary shows that day:

> 6:30 P.M., hear from Neurath that we're to invade on 12 March. We discuss all the diplomatic steps. Above all I insist that we rig internal events in Austria in such a way that we are requested *from there* to come in, to get off on the right foot historically. It seems a new idea to Neurath, but he'll implant it in the Reich Chancellery.

At about 8 P.M. Odilo Globocnig, the Trieste-born Austrian Nazi – and one of the gangsters primarily responsible for the later Jewish Extermination

* See page 62.

horrors – arrived at the Chancellery with a letter that Seyss-Inquart had written the day before to one of Schuschnigg's ministers, Guido Zernatto: Seyss-Inquart warned that the plebiscite was unconstitutional and unfair. Hitler read the letter out. Neurath suggested that Seyss-Inquart should telegraph an "appeal" for German intervention to Hitler – in line with Weizsäcker's idea. Hitler agreed, and himself wove this strand around Seyss-Inquart's neck by drafting a suitable text. The telegram (which Seyss-Inquart never even saw) appealed to Hitler to send in troops to restore order because of unrest, murder and bloodshed in Vienna.* Göring was unhappy about the idea, but Hitler could never forget 1934, when Mussolini had put five army divisions on the Brenner after the Dollfuss murder: Hitler wanted German troops, not Italian or Czech, to fill the vacuum in Austria, even if they were not otherwise needed.

Over dinner in his villa, Göring handed the draft telegram to Glaise-Horstenau to take back to Vienna. Hitler had already given the Austrian general two other documents – a speech for Seyss-Inquart to broadcast next evening, 11 March; and a veiled ultimatum with a deadline to be handed to Schuschnigg himself. At 2 A.M. he issued the directive for the Wehrmacht operation, "to restore constitutional conditions" in Austria. "I myself will take charge of the whole operations. . . ."

Evidently Hitler did not sleep much that night. When Ribbentrop's private secretary, Reinhard Spitzy, flew back from London, arriving at 4 A.M (Hitler had himself telephoned him, using a code-name, the evening before) the Chancellery was still swarming. Hitler offered him breakfast and read Ribbentrop's verdict on Britain's likely response – "I am basically convinced", the minister had written, "that for the present Britain won't start anything against us herself, but will act to reassure the other powers." Later, Schmundt told Hitler that the General Staff was inquiring what to do if Italian or Czech troops were encountered on Austrian territory; Hitler ruled that Czechs – but not Italians – were to be treated as hostile.

The telephone lines between Berlin and Vienna buzzed with all the plotting. Hitler evidently forgot that these lines ran across Czech territory. A failure at the Chancellery telephone exchange even obliged him to conduct his conversations from a phone booth in the conservatory. The Forschungsamt's own wiretaps on the conversations were found later in Göring's files, so we know what was said.

Hitler's special agent, Wilhelm Keppler, was keeping a weather eye on Seyss-Inquart in Vienna now, to ensure that this vacillating and overlegalistic

---

* His widow, Frau Gertrud Seyss-Inquart, granted me access to his papers, and among them I found a long account of this odd affair. Most likely is that Keppler sent the telegram from Vienna. Seyss approved it *post facto*, though with misgivings. "My responsibility lies in having permitted the Reich to use my name after the invasion began. I believe I did not learn of it [the telegram] until early on 12 March." He was hanged at Nuremberg in 1946.

minister did just as the Führer told him. Keppler had also conveyed to Vienna a list of the Nazis who were to be foisted on to the new Austrian Cabinet; they included Göring's brother-in-law, Dr Franz Hueber (referred to in the wiretaps as "Ullrich"), who was to control justice and foreign affairs, with Dr Fischböck for economics and Ernst Kaltenbrunner for internal security.

That morning, 11 March, Goebbels's chief aide Alfred-Ingemar Berndt confidentially briefed Berlin press representatives: "Rather more emphasis is to be put on the events in Austria today – the tabloid newspapers are to make headlines of them, the political journals are to run about two columns. You are to avoid too much uniformity." Brauchitsch conferred at the Chancellery for most of the day. Hitler, he found, had also ordered SS troops to participate in the invasion, with regular army officers attached as advisers to each of the three SS regiments concerned. When General Heinz Guderian asked if he could deck out his tanks with flags and flowers to emphasize the "peaceful" nature of their operation, Hitler agreed wholeheartedly.

For several hours beyond the deadline set by Hitler in his ultimatum, Schuschnigg prevaricated – hopeful that the Nazis were only bluffing. From the phone booth Göring's voice could be heard shouting orders to his agents in Vienna. Göring's task was to ensure that Schuschnigg resigned before nightfall. Schuschnigg did at last postpone the plebiscite, but – after discussing this with Hitler – Göring phoned Seyss-Inquart that this was now not enough. The Austrian chancellor had violated the Berghof agreement and would have to resign. The Führer wanted clear information by 5:30 P.M. as to whether or not President Miklas had invited Seyss-Inquart to form the new Cabinet. Seyss-Inquart expressed the pious hope that Austria would remain independent even if National Socialist in character. Göring gave him a non-committal reply.

Five-thirty came and went: Göring learned that Schuschnigg had at last resigned – but now Miklas was planning to appoint somebody else chancellor. "Our people are with him [the president] now," reported Seyss-Inquart. "They're spelling out the situation to him." Göring ordered him and the military attaché, General Wolfgang Muff, to visit the president and tell him, "If our demands are not accepted as set out, our troops will invade tonight, and Austria's existence will be over! . . . Tell him we are not joking. . . . If Miklas hasn't grasped that in four hours, then tell him he's got four minutes to grasp it now." To this Seyss-Inquart weakly replied, "Oh, well."

Since Schuschnigg was believed to have resigned, in fact the Wehrmacht invasion order was cancelled: only police units would move into Austria.

But at 8 P.M. Seyss-Inquart again came on the phone from Vienna: nobody had resigned, and the Schuschnigg government had merely "withdrawn", leaving events in limbo. Moreover, Miklas was still refusing to appoint him chancellor. For half an hour there was agitated discussion of this irregular position, with Göring loudly in favour now of military intervention, and Hitler a passive, pensive listener. Then, as they slouched back from the phone booth to the conference room, Hitler slapped his thigh, looked up and announced: "*Jetzt geht's los – voran!*" ("Okay, we have lift-off").

Whereupon Göring called out to Bodenschatz to set the Luftwaffe in motion. At about 8:30 P.M. Hitler signed the executive order. The invasion would commence next morning.

Hitler did not expect serious opposition. Soon afterwards (at 8:48 P.M.) Keppler telephoned from Vienna that Miklas had dissolved the government and ordered the Austrian army not to resist. By 10 P.M. the all-important telegram – signed "Seyss-Inquart" – had also arrived, appealing on behalf of the provisional Austrian government for German troops to restore order.

By 10:30 P.M. Hitler also knew that Mussolini would look benignly on a German occupation of Austria (the Duce had sharply reproved Schuschnigg over the phoney plebiscite). Hitler hysterically besought his special emissary in Rome over the phone: "Tell Mussolini I will never forget him for this! . . . Never, never, never! Come what may!" And, "Once this Austrian affair is over and done with, I'll be willing to go through thick and thin with him."

As he replaced the telephone, Hitler confessed to Göring that he had never lost faith in Mussolini's greatness – now this was the happiest day of his life. For the first time in over a decade he could return to his native Austria and do what Schuschnigg and his predecessors had forbidden – visit the grave of his parents at Leonding.

He knew Ribbentrop would be furious at missing the morrow's glory. But Hitler felt the minister would serve Germany best as a "lightning conductor" in London over this weekend, and he told his adjutant Wilhelm Brückner to ensure that Ribbentrop stayed on for at least two or three days more. He himself would be in Vienna, if all went well, when he next saw Ribbentrop. Neurath blanched when he heard this, and begged Hitler not to risk Vienna yet – Braunau, his birthplace, perhaps; but not Vienna. Hitler insisted, and ordered absolute secrecy.

For the first time in two days he retired to snatch what sleep he could. But neither he nor Keitel was allowed much slumber, as apprehensive generals and diplomats telephoned frantic appeals to call off the operation before blood flowed. Brauchitsch was observed in dark despair, still fearing armed Italian or Czech intervention. He and Beck repeatedly phoned Keitel and Weizsäcker that night, begging them to intervene. Keitel's own chief of operations, General Max von Viebahn (a close but oversensitive friend of Ludwig Beck), also bombarded Keitel with phone calls, and at 2 A.M. willingly connected General Muff to Hitler's bedside phone. Hitler blasted Keitel, and Keitel forbade

Viebahn to put the importunate attaché or anybody else through to the Chancellery again. Viebahn suffered a nervous breakdown next morning and barricaded himself into an office at the war ministry, where he hurled ink-bottles at the door like some military Martin Luther. (Jodl succeeded him.) Hitler's verdict on the army's senior officers was a scathing one.

Once again, it was Saturday. At 6 A.M. that day, 12 March, Hitler departed from Berlin by plane, leaving Göring in command. At the Munich operations post of General Fedor von Bock, commanding Eighth Army, he was briefed on the operation so far: wildly cheering crowds had greeted the German "invaders", and the Austrian troops, far from resisting, were falling in behind. Veterans of the World War were lining the highways, saluting and proudly displaying the long-forgotten medals on their breasts. Czechoslovakia – to whom Hitler had given explicit assurances – did not bestir herself. Indeed, as Hitler sardonically commented to the profusely weeping general seated beside him – Franz Halder – Czechoslovakia seemed very anxious to oblige him all of a sudden! Her turn would come.

Hitler crossed the frontier near Braunau at about 4 P.M. and drove on toward Linz, where he had summoned Dr Seyss-Inquart to await him. He stood erect in the front of his open dark-blue Mercedes, saluting or waving as his driver, Erich Kempka, changed down through the gears to avoid running down the hysterical crowds pressing into their path. It was dusk by the time they reached the city centre, packed with a million clamouring Austrians. (As Sir Alexander Cadogan of the Foreign Office later admonished Henderson, "I can't help thinking that we were very badly informed about feeling in that country. . . . We only forbade the Anschluss to spite Germany.") From the city hall's balcony Hitler spoke to the crowds: "If Providence once sent me out from this fine city, and called upon me to lead the Reich, then surely it must have had some mission in mind for me. And that can only have been one mission – to return my beloved native country to the German Reich!"

He dined with Seyss-Inquart and Keppler that evening, and rested in Linz next day, 13 March. In the afternoon he drove to Leonding, where his parents lay.

By the time he returned, an idea – which had occurred to him during the night – had taken definite shape. Originally, he had planned an autonomous Austria under his own elected presidency; but could he not now afford to proclaim Austria's outright union with the Reich, i.e. the Anschluss? The public obviously supported him overwhelmingly. He sent a messenger by air to Göring, asking his opinion. And he telephoned Keppler in Vienna, to ask Seyss-Inquart to put the idea to his Cabinet at once.

Göring had heard of the jubilation at Linz, and in fact sent Milch to make the same suggestion. Milch landed there at 5:09 P.M. Hitler told him he had already decided. When Seyss-Inquart and Keppler arrived there that evening they confirmed that the Cabinet agreed to the Anschluss with the Reich.

Thus was Hitler's decision taken – not as the upshot of a long-contrived conspiracy, but as an improvisation of which even Göring was to learn at Karinhall, his country mansion, from a chance remark dropped by the Austrian envoy, Tauschitz.

"There is but one moment when the Goddess of Fortune passes by," Hitler observed to his adjutants. "And if you don't grasp her by the hem, you won't get a second chance."

We need not follow Hitler's triumphal progress next day onward to Vienna, albeit the crowds in the capital were less rapturous than had greeted him at Linz. Cardinal Theodor Innitzer, Archbishop of Vienna, had telephoned him for permission to ring all the church bells in Austria to welcome him, and he asked for swastika banners to decorate the steeples as Hitler drove into the capital: such was the paradox and tragedy of Austria. Behind the Führer came the herds of outlawed Austrian Nazis, embittered by their years of exile and eager for revenge. After the glitter and panoply and spectacle, it was their rampages in the back streets and the prison camps that again marred History's view of Hitler.

At 2 P.M. on 15 March he took the salute at a great military parade at the Maria-Theresia monument. Wehrmacht troops marched past together with Austrian regiments, garlanded alike with flowers and flags. A thousand bombers and fighters of the two air forces – led by one German and one Austrian general – thundered low over the capital's rooftops. It brought lumps to many a throat to see Austrian dragoons parade again with German soldiers, to the strains of the Prince Eugen March. Baron von Weizsäcker, who had arrived with Ribbentrop, wrote that day: "Which of us does not recall that oft-repeated question of earlier years: What did our World War sacrifices avail us?"

Here was the answer, and all the Viennese diplomatic corps appeared on Hitler's podium to witness the demonstration – with the haughty exception of the British and French envoys. This was no Goebbels spectacular, the whole city was wild with frenetic acclaim.* They were seeing the rebirth of German greatness, of a nation defeated despite bloody self-sacrifice, dismembered in armistice, humiliated, crippled by international debt and yet once again arising

---

* The private files of Mr Justice Robert H. Jackson – the US chief prosecutor at the Nuremberg Trials – reveal that the newsreels shown there as evidence were doctored in November 1945 by his staff, to remove the scenes of popular acclaim for Hitler's troops as they entered the Rhineland, Austria and the Sudeten territories, "In all of which flag-waving, smiling faces and the presentation of flowers help to nullify our notion that by these acts these people were planning or waging a war against their neighbours."

in the heart of Europe – a nation united by one of their humblest children, a Leader promising them an era of greatness and prosperity.

As darkness fell upon Vienna, now a mere provincial capital, Hitler fastened himself into the seat of his Junkers plane – sitting left of the gangway so that he could gaze upon Austria as they flew back to Germany. They flew towards the sunset, the craggy Alpine skyline tinged with ever-changing hues of scarlet and gold. Keitel was looking out over Bohemia and Moravia, to the right. With tears in his eyes, Hitler called the OKW general's attention to Austria. "All that is now German again!"

After a while, he leaned across the gangway again. Keitel's adjutant, sitting behind them, saw Hitler show a crumpled news cutting he had been clutching ever since leaving Vienna. He had torn it out of the morning's newspaper. It was a sketch map of the Reich's new frontiers. The shaded area of Czechoslovakia was encircled now on three sides. Hitler superimposed his left hand on the map, so that his forefinger and thumb emcompassed Czechoslovakia's frontiers. He winked broadly at Keitel, and slowly pinched finger and thumb together.

"Green"

This was the beginning of Hitler's new-style diplomacy.

His victories in Central Europe were won without the sword – they were won by power-politics and opportunism, by bluff, by coercion, by psychological operations and by nerve-war.

On each occasion he carefully gauged his potential enemies. He satisfied himself that the western powers would not fight provided he made each claim sound reasonable enough. The west was weak and unready, and he was not. France in particular was corrupted by creeping revolutionary influences from the left. When General Walther von Brauchitsch had proposed to him, on 9 March 1938, the strengthening of Germany's defences along the Moselle and Rhine rivers by early 1939, and the erection of fortifications on the Belgian, Dutch and Luxembourg frontiers by the spring of 1940, the Führer had seen no need for greater urgency. He was to explain, in a secret speech to Nazi editors on 10 November, "The general world situation seemed more favourable than ever before for us to stake our claims."

His next victim would be Czechoslovakia. Jodl's diary shows that Poland let Hitler know through Intelligence channels that in that event she would join the Nazi cause. Through the same channels, Czechoslovakia indicated her willingness to seek a solution to the problem of the Germans living in the Sudeten territories, where 3,200,000 Germans had been trapped on the Czech side of the frontiers redrawn in 1919. Eighty per cent of them were hostile to the Prague government, according to the German diplomatic experts. The Czechs discriminated against them in employment – in the civil service for instance – and they were treated harshly by Czech law courts. But Hitler had no desire for any solution the Czechs might propose. He wanted to occupy the Sudeten territories, because here were the Czech frontier fortifications of which General von Fritsch had warned him in 1937.

On 19 March 1938, Hitler conferred with Nazi Party leaders. That day

Goebbels issued a secret circular to Nazi editors to use the word *Grossdeutsch* – Greater German – only sparingly as yet. "We must avoid the impression that Germany's demands are satisfied by the union of Germany and Austria. That is not the case. Obviously other territories belong to the actual Grossdeutsches Reich and claim will be laid to them in due course." (An almost identical press directive was issued one year later.*)

At the conference, Hitler mapped out plans for a vote to be held throughout Germany and Austria on 10 April, to confirm the Anschluss. The question on the ballot paper was: "Do you accept Adolf Hitler as our Führer, and do you thus accept the reunification of Austria with the German Reich as effected on 13 March 1938?" Unlike Schuschnigg's phoney plebiscite, it was a genuinely secret ballot. The result staggered even Hitler: of 49,493,028 entitled to vote, 49,279,104 had cast votes, and of these 99·08 per cent had voted "Yes" – altogether 48,751,587 adults had stated their support of Hitler's action. This was a unanimity of almost embarrassing dimensions.

His election campaign had taken him the length and breadth of both countries. On the seventh he had turned the first spade's depth of a new autobahn system in Austria. One of his doctors, Hanskarl von Hasselbach, later wrote: "The people lined both sides of the roads for mile after mile, wild with indescribable rejoicing. Many of the public wept openly at the sight of Hitler." By that time German laws had already been enforced in Austria, and these had brought Nazi methods in their wake. Thousands of Communists and anti-Nazis had been rounded up and interned in concentration camps.

Hitler instructed Ribbentrop that the former chancellor, Kurt Schuschnigg, was to be well-treated in spite of everything, and housed in a quiet villa somewhere. But in later years – like so many other Hitler directives – this came to be overlooked, and Schuschnigg went to a concentration camp too.

Hitler had initially instructed the OKW that the next step, Czechoslovakia, must wait until Austria had been "properly digested" The Austrian armed forces had to be kitted with Wehrmacht uniforms and equipped with German *matériel*. But already it was time to start subversive activities in the Sudeten territories.

On the afternoon of 28 March he discussed tactics with Konrad Henlein, the leader of the Sudeten German Party. Henlein had been discovered by Admiral Wilhelm Canaris in 1935 and schooled by the Abwehr in subversive operations. Skilled in the verbal patter of democracy and diplomacy, but otherwise a suspected homosexual of simple intellect, Henlein had built up a powerful political organization amongst the 3,200,000 Sudeten Germans. He had been

* See page 192.

given some support by SS Gruppenführer Werner Lorenz of the Volksdeutsche Mittelstelle – the Central Office of Ethnic Germans – but Himmler and Heydrich had cold-shouldered him and barred his access to Hitler until now.

Hitler conferred with him in top secret, together with Ribbentrop and Lorenz. He assured Henlein of support, indicated that he would deal with the Czech problem "in the not too distant future", and gave him two related missions: the first was to formulate a series of demands on the Czechs of such an extent that, though ostensibly quite reasonable, there was no danger that Dr Eduard Beneš would actually entertain them. Secondly, Henlein was to use the influence he evidently had in London to prevail on the British not to interfere.

On the same day, 28 March, Keitel signed an important OKW instruction to the army and air force to modernize the main bridges across the Danube and main roads in Austria leading towards Czechoslovakia, to assist the strategic movement of troops against that country. On 1 April the General Staff telephoned General Wilhelm von Leeb to report in five days' time to Beck about his employment in time of war: Beck told Leeb he was to command Seventh Army, which would operate from Austria against Czechoslovakia. Leeb's pocket diary shows him later in April touring the Austro-Czech frontier from one end to the other.

At this stage Hitler met little army opposition. Beck's hostility to the Czechs was well known (Manstein described it in a letter of 21 July as a "fierce yearning" by Beck for the destruction of Czechoslovakia). In December 1937, Beck had referred to her, in conversation with Jenö Rátz, the Hungarian Chief of General Staff, as an appendix on German soil: "As long as she exists, Germany can't fight any war." Beck was, it must be said, a gifted but essentially old-fashioned theoretician. His mind was closed to all save the possibilities understood by his own profession. His stated view was that Czechoslovakia was impregnable to military assault – he seemed unaware that modern states were vulnerable to attack by other means, that the army was only one weapon in Hitler's arsenal, that he also had a Luftwaffe, an OKW to control sabotage and subversion operations behind enemy lines, and a noisy propaganda machine.

Unlike the General Staff, Hitler and the OKW saw their future campaigns as a whole – not just in terms of guns and gunpowder. The Luftwaffe did not challenge him outright, although its lower echelons did warn Göring uncomfortably of the risk should Britain declare war. Unlike his generals too, Hitler knew many of the cards his opponents held: useless though Canaris's Abwehr was for Intelligence purposes, there were other agencies that provided Hitler with invaluable data. The code-breakers' intercepts of François-Poncet's secret cables have been referred to; the telegrams between Paris and French missions abroad were also being regularly deciphered, as were the despatches from the Italian and Hungarian embassies in Berlin – which revealed to the Forschungsamt, for instance, that Hungarian foreign minister Kolomán von Kánya was regularly passing tips on Nazi plans to the British.

Many a Hitler decision – that infuriated his generals by its seeming lack of logic at the time – can probably be explained by the work of Göring's Forschungsamt, Ribbentrop's ministry and the naval staff's cryptanalysis branch. His confidence that Britain did not mean war in 1939, his March 1940 knowledge of Britain's plan to invade neutral Norway, and his July 1940 decision to prepare an invasion of Russia were just three later examples.

Hitler's architectural planning betrays something of his future intentions, too. A studied recklessness with public funds was sweeping German architecture out of the pre-1933 doldrums. After years of uncertain, halfhearted designs a squat, pretentious style was beginning to characterize the new public buildings – frequently dictated by Hitler himself, as he was prone to issue thumbnail sketches of the grand boulevards and buildings as he wanted to see them. By February 1938 he had decided that Munich would get a colossal new central station, with a dome 300 feet high – the biggest steel-framed structure in the world at that time.

The 1936 Olympic stadium in Berlin, by Werner March, and the war office and Luftwaffe buildings were still the products of Germany's older school of architects. Hitler disliked them, and appointed the youthful Albert Speer as chief architect to Berlin, and the self-taught Hermann Giesler in Munich.

Chance remarks betrayed his inner ambitions. When Speer – commissioned to build a gigantic new Reich Chancellery in Berlin – reported that he could do it in twelve months, Hitler commented that it would be useful for receiving and impressing the "little nations". One evening in October 1941 – with his armies poised to capture Moscow – Hitler explained in private:

> When one enters the Reich Chancellery one must have the feeling that one is visiting the Master of the World. One will arrive there along wide avenues containing the Triumphal Arch, the Pantheon of the Army, the Square of the People – things to take your breath away! It's only thus that we shall succeed in eclipsing our only rival in the world, Rome. . . . For material we shall use granite. Granite will ensure that our monuments last for ever. In ten thousand years they'll still be standing. One day, Berlin will be the capital of the world.

He enlarged on this to Speer, explaining his project for a vast stadium at Nuremberg capable of seating over 350,000 spectators: "In future all the Olympic Games will be held there."

Hitler first saw Rome later that year. Entries in Weizsäcker's diary indicate that Hitler regarded Italy and Britain as holding the key to his plan to conquer Czechoslovakia and the east.

On 29 March, Ribbentrop mentioned to Weizsacker that neither he nor Hitler wanted to slam the door on Britain altogether, despite her traditional opposition to whichever European power was strongest. But Germany's ties with Italy were now a fact, and Hitler wanted to sign a treaty with Mussolini during the forthcoming state visit in May. Hitler adopted the same line on Italy when he saw off Hans-Georg von Mackensen as the new ambassador to Rome on 2 April: he had decided to write off the disputed South Tyrol region in Italy's favour – Germany's frontiers with Italy, Yugoslavia and Hungary "are permanent". The drive to the Mediterranean would go no further. "Our aspirations", said Hitler, "are to the north. After the Sudeten Germans our target will be in the Baltic. We must turn our interest to the Polish Corridor and, perhaps, the other Baltic states. Not that we want any non-Germans in our domain – but if rule any we must, then the Baltic countries."

Weizsäcker also recorded that Hitler had told Neurath on 20 April, his birthday, that foreign triumphs were now coming thick and fast – but one must not attempt too much too soon. The main thing was to avoid impulsive acts. He would bide his time, prepare properly, then strike like lightning.

The moment for settling the Czech affair was up to Mussolini, because Hitler dared not risk it until he was sure of his support. This in turn depended on Mussolini's ambitions: if the Duce regarded his life's work as done, Hitler would be obliged to shelve his own ambitions. But if, in Rome, Mussolini told him in confidence that he was planning to extend his African empire, then Hitler could make Italian support over Czechoslovakia the price for German support in Africa. And then, as he once ruminated to Schmundt during April, "I'll return from Rome with Czechoslovakia in the bag."

On 21 April he instructed Keitel to draft a suitable OKW directive. The tactical ideal would be a surprise invasion of Czechoslovakia, but world opinion would rule that out unless, for instance, some anti-German outrage occurred there like the murder of their envoy in Prague. A surprise invasion from "out of the blue" was, Hitler expatiated, a procedure proper only for the elimination of "our last continental enemy". (Was he already thinking of the invasion of Russia? The records do not help us.)

The rapid collapse of Czech resistance would be vital in dissuading the west from intervening. So the German army and air force must strike simultaneously, leaving her isolated and demoralized, while German armour poured ruthlessly through Pilsen towards Prague. In four days this main battle must be over. Major Schmundt laboriously typed the secret record of Hitler's remarks himself.

Next day, 22 April, Hitler sent on a pretext for the Hungarian envoy in Berlin, Döme Sztójay, and confided to him that in the coming carve-up of Czechoslovakia the Reich had no interest in Slovakia, and it would be up to Hungary to recover the territory she had lost there after the World War, including "Hungary's old coronation city", Bratislava (Pressburg). Sztójay reported this splendid news to Kánya in a handwritten letter.

Two days later, at a Karlsbad rally, Henlein announced an eight-point programme calling on Prague to grant his Sudeten Germans autonomy and the right to adopt German nationality.

Thus Hitler's planning entered its first active ·phase.

The big military parade marking Hitler's forty-ninth birthday had reminded him that his years were drawing on. An adjutant heard him remark for the first time that his vitality and sharpness of decision were now at their peak, but would soon begin to decline. Moreover an assassin's bullet might always cut him down – in Italy, perhaps.

On 23 April, therefore, he signed a secret decree confirming Göring as his deputy in Berlin, while Hess continued to manage the Party in his absence. On 2 May 1938, Hitler wrote out a private testament, and handed it in a sealed envelope to Dr Lammers, head of the Reich Chancellery – a rare documentary glimpse of Hitler as a human being, putting his affairs in order, arranging his own funeral and disposing of his personal effects to his family and private staff.

The entire Reich government assembled at the Anhalt station in Berlin to bid him farewell for Rome that day. The last time he had seen Italy, in 1934, the unimpressed Italians had consigned him to a hot palazzo in Venice with unopenable windows and myriads of mosquitos. In his bedchamber he had searched in vain for a light-switch, and finally clambered on to a chair to unscrew each scalding light-bulb in the chandelier. But this time, in May 1938, Mussolini had laid on a lavish reception that outshone even the welcome Hitler had prepared for him eight months before.

For a week in Italy, Hitler could cynically survey the Roman scene and weigh the powers of the Duce against the prerogatives of the King. Nor that his own court was modest in size: trainloads of interpreters, masters of ceremony, servants, doctors, diplomats and adjutants had followed him, the luggage cars were mobile wardrobes packed with gala uniforms, swords, daggers and bejewelled medals. As his special train hauled into Rome's suburbs next afternoon, 3 May, he marshalled his private staff and warned them sternly not to burst out laughing at the sight of a diminutive figure kneeling on the platform, weighed down with gold braid: for that was the King of Italy, and he was not kneeling – that was his full height.

Yet there was no escaping the tiny King Victor Emanuel III, for technically he was Hitler's host. Some days Hitler had difficulty in meeting his fascist confederate at all. The royal camarilla could not have angered him more had they actually conspired to humiliate this son of a Braunau customs official, this plebeian dictator from the north. In Naples he found himself inspecting a guard of honour as the only civilian, with top hat in hand and wearing evening dress. In Rome the gates of the King's villa were accidentally locked in his face. Not that Hitler disliked the King personally. When he visited the villa, the monarch had to operate the tiny electric passenger lift himself. "He's quite a decent fellow," Hitler chuckled to his private staff."The way he stood next to me, pressing the buttons, I quite liked him. But I can't stand the moth-eaten types around him."

The Italians were never noted for their phlegm. Every railroad station was beflagged, the railway embankments swarmed with cheering villagers, the very oxen had swastikas painted on them. In Rome a million citizens lined the route from the station – among them the young lady from the Berghof, her fare paid privately by Hitler. She was hoisted on to the shoulders of an anonymous Italian so that she could glimpse the glittering cavalcade pass by. For Hitler's benefit, the ancient ruins were lit by searchlights and the Colosseum and Capitol were shrouded in artificial white and coloured smoke-clouds and illuminated by Bengal fireworks, so that they seemed to burn again before this modern Nero's eyes. The royal coach swayed through the breach newly carved in the city wall to the Quirinale Palace, placed at his disposal. Mussolini followed King and Führer more humbly in a limousine.

Here at the palace, Hitler encountered suffocating palace etiquette for the first time. The noble Italian chief of protocol bowed before him and then led his guests up the long, shallow flight of stairs, striking every red-plush carpeted tread solemnly with a gold-encrusted staff. He was accustomed to this measured tread, but not Hitler: the nervous foreign visitor fell out of step, found himself gaining on the uniformed nobleman ahead, stopped abruptly, causing confusion and clatter on the steps behind, then started again, walking more quickly until he was soon alongside the Italian again. The latter affected not to notice him, but perceptibly quickened his own pace, his lacquered slippers and silken stockings flashing, until the whole throng was trotting up the last few stairs in an undignified Charlie Chaplin gallop.

There were other flaws. Ribbentrop had ruled that the ladies in the German party were not to bob a curtsey to the royal family, but "show slight obeisance". (All obeyed with one solitary exception – Frau Marga Himmler. Hitler was furious.) Earlier, Ribbentrop had prevented him making another gaffe: Hitler had proposed giving Italy a planetarium. Ribbentrop pointed out that Italy already had two, both somehow wangled out of Germany as post-war reparations. "It would seem to me therefore", Ribbentrop observed in a note, "That the gift of a planetarium to Mussolini might be somewhat out of place." Hitler gave him a Zeiss telescope and equipment for an observatory instead. As a further gift, Hitler publicly renounced Germany's claim to the South Tyrol in his banquet speech in Rome.

The royal insults to Mussolini seemed however to Hitler to intensify as the days passed. At a *dopolavoro* display only three gilded chairs were provided for the royal couple, Hitler, and Mussolini; inevitably the two dictators had to stand, leaving the third chair empty, while a hundred thousand Italians looked on. At a concert at the Villa Borghese, the nobility occupied the front rows while the soldiers Rodolfo Graziani, Italo Balbo and Pietro Badoglio were crowded back into insignificance. This was repeated at the military parade at Naples – Hitler found himself backed by a perfumed wall of lords- and ladies-in-waiting, screening the generals behind them. He boorishly remarked out loud that these were the generals who had brought the King his Abyssinian empire; at which the row behind him melted away until the generals were in front.

Later, Wiedemann subsequently testified, Hitler petulantly announced to Mussolini: "I'm going home. I didn't come to see the King, but you, my friend!"

But he stayed until 10 May. He returned to Berlin with mixed impressions. He often spoke afterwards of the fine architecture and galleries of Florence. But his worst fears of Italy's military worth were confirmed. In German eyes the Duce's most modern weaponry, proudly paraded in Rome, was already obsolete. The naval display he saw at Naples – when eighty Italian submarines surfaced simultaneously in formation and fired their guns – was pure stop-watch theatre, of no military worth whatever. He confessed, too, that he was aghast at Mussolini's ignorance of military technology – he would be at the mercy of his generals, and they had sworn their allegiance to the King.

The political benefits were less than he had hoped. The Italians had ducked out of signing the draft alliance that Ribbentrop had taken with him, and in Weizsäcker's words, "dealt us a slap in the face with an improvised draft treaty of their own, more akin to an armistice with an enemy than a bond of loyalty signed between friends." "The journey", Weizsäcker added in his diary, "turned out to be a lesson for us, and a sobering one at that." Mussolini had secretly affirmed that in any conflict between Germany and Czechoslovakia he would stand back, "his sword in its scabbard". That was somewhat ambiguous: "Is that supposed to encourage us or warn us?" mused Weizsäcker. "The Führer takes it as an encouragement."*

---

* Keitel's adjutant recorded Hitler's words at a secret speech to generals on 15 August 1938: "What will Italy's position be? I have received reassurances (visit to Italy). Nobody's going to attack us!"

Unhappily, no full record exists of Hitler's pregnant remarks to Benito Mussolini, uttered aboard the battleship *Conte Cavour*. He agreed that Italy should become the dominant power in the Mediterranean, while – for economic reasons – "Germany will step out along the ancient Teutonic path, towards the east." (These words he recalled saying, in 1939.)

Hitler's visit to Rome had discredited the monarchy in his eyes for all time. The royals were all that he was not. One anecdote circulated long afterwards among his staff. One of his ministers inquired of Prince Massimo whether he really was descended from the ancient Roman general, Fabius Maximus. He loftily replied, "I probably am. The story has been knocking around my family these last two thousand years."

To his intimates, Hitler had in earlier years occasionally hinted that he would one day retire and pass supreme command over the new and prosperous world empire he had created to a contender of royal blood. He would then live his last years as a pensioner in Munich, Regensburg or Linz, dictating the third volume of his memoirs to Fräulein Johanna Wolf, the more elderly of his secretaries. There were moments when he pulled out his thumbnail sketches of his dream house, shaded in a few more lines, and returned them to his safe. He had in fact discussed with the late President Hindenburg his plan to restore a Hohen-zollern to the throne – not so much the Crown Prince, Friedrich Wilhelm, whose wife had insulted him once before he came to power – as one of the Prince's sons instead. Hindenburg had welcomed the idea.

What Hitler saw in Rome put all thought of that out of his head for ever. Indeed, the visit had a remarkable sequel: on his return to Berlin, he had Göring contact the former Social Democrat leaders like Carl Severing, Gustav Noske, Otto Braun and Paul Löbe and *increase* their pensions – in recognition of their having dispensed with the monarchy.

Nonetheless, he sent routine birthday greetings on 6 May to Crown Prince Friedrich Wilhelm. The Prince replied with congratulations for Hitler's con-tribution to peace in Europe. Hitler dourly remarked to Wiedemann – as the adjutant recorded a few months later – "I'm not here to ensure peace in Europe; I'm here to make Germany great again. If that can be done peacefully, well and good. If not, we'll have to do it differently."

He had evidently decided not to wait over Czechoslovakia. Weizsäcker recorded on 13 May, "He's thinking of dealing with the Sudeten German problem before the year is out, as the present balance of power [*Konstellation*] might otherwise shift against us." A cunning propaganda campaign was worked out, beginning with deliberate silence on the dispute. Goebbels' chief aide, Alfred-Ingemar Berndt, briefed the tightly-reined Nazi editors on the thirteenth: "You are again reminded that you are not allowed to report minor incidents in Czechoslovakia." (He repeated the warning on the eighteenth and the twentieth.) There was a *psychological* battle to be won.

Meanwhile, Hitler applied his mind to the supposedly impregnable Czech frontier defences. The OKW advised him that the fortifications were formidable – there were big gun-sites, proof against all known calibres of artillery, at hundred-yard intervals, and machine-gun bunkers in between. The heavy machine-gun nests would withstand 21-centimetre shellfire, and the lighter ones up to half that calibre. Hitler decided that the attack would have to come from *within* the fortifications simultaneously with the main invasion from without (for which the German army must begin training special shock-troops). This breaching of the fortifications would be followed by a rapid armoured penetration into Czechoslovakia, while the Luftwaffe bombers struck simultaneously at Prague.

The strategic line-up against him was now much clearer. Italy would not interfere. Hungary had claims of her own on the predominantly Magyar regions of the Carpatho-Ukraine in Slovakia. There were also Polish minorities involved – the Poles were no friends of the Czechs. Russia was still a negligible political factor. France was morally weaker than in 1914 and like Britain incompletely armed, and while willing to hurt was afraid to strike.

Britain was Hitler's biggest worry now. His agents in Vienna had captured papers revealing the extent to which the British envoy there had egged Schuschnigg on against Berlin. Britain's links with France and the United States were growing stronger: from diplomatic and Forschungsamt sources Hitler was aware of the Anglo-French staff talks in London – a code telegram of the US ambassador in London, Joseph Kennedy, reached Hitler early in May indicating that while Britain was prepared to force the Czechs to accept some of Hitler's terms, he would not be given a free hand in Central Europe. A British military mission was known to be in the United States and Canada placing contracts for war equipment.

War with Britain – against his will – was thus becoming more likely. All his service commanders realized this. After a joint conference with the navy on 4 May, the Luftwaffe's deputy chief of operations, Colonel Hans Jeschonnek, wrote: "The general political situation has radically changed recently, with Britain emerging increasingly as Germany's principal enemy." The United States would probably act "at first" only as an arms supplier for the west, he predicted. The Führer had already stated quite plainly to Raeder in January that they needed a bigger battle fleet, and Raeder in turn had put the heat on to the shipyard managers, telling the directors of the Germania Yards on 2 March 1938, for instance, "The Führer's impression is that the naval construction programme is not progressing fast enough. He compares the naval construction effort with the Luftwaffe's dynamic advance and with the energy with which

Field-Marshal Göring intervenes and spurs all his factories on." But the yards lacked skilled labour, welders, and materials, and Raeder caustically pointed to the reckless increase in public construction projects competing with the re-armament programme – the Volkswagen works, the Munich subway, the reconstruction of Berlin, Nuremberg, Hamburg and much else. Hitler turned a deaf ear on his protests.

On 17 May 1938, the Führer flew with Schmundt to Munich, where Martin Bormann was waiting for him with a column of automobiles. At a stately speed the convoy of heavy dark-blue Mercedes swept south toward Berchtesgaden, with Hitler's open supercharged Mercedes in front and his escort and luggage bringing up the rear. From time to time Hitler glanced at the speedometer to check they were not exceeding his personal speed-limit of fifty miles per hour.

After two hours the whine of the engine pitched higher as they wound up the narrow lane scaling the Obersalzberg to the Berghof. His housekeeper and domestic staff were marshalled on the terrace to greet the returning dictator – the sentries had telephoned warning to them from the valley below. Orderlies stepped forward and opened his door, and he vanished into the Berghof. He could hear the Scottish terriers yapping in the distance, he scented the familiar odours of wood and wax polish, and thrilled to the Great Hall's spectacle of the world, as it could seem, spread out at his feet below.

Picking his way along the narrow paths laid out on the Obersalzberg mountainside, Hitler began to think aloud to Rudolf Schmundt and his other trusted adjutants. He still felt uneasy about his army generals. Fritsch was gone but there was still Ludwig Beck, the Chief of General Staff, and Beck was an officer wallowing in the easy and outmoded notions of the Hundred-Thousand Man army – "more at home in his swivel chair than a slit trench", Hitler sniggered. And there was Gerd von Rundstedt, the army's senior-ranking general, whom Beck had proposed as C-in-C: Rundstedt had deeply offended Hitler recently by advising him coarsely to have nothing to do with that "negroid asshole" Mussolini. Small wonder that General von Viebahn, rifling through Keitel's desk when the OKW chief was away parading with Hitler through Vienna, chanced upon a note by Keitel to the effect that Beck and Rundstedt were both due for retirement in the autumn! In Austria, however, Hitler had renewed his acquaintance with Franz Halder, Beck's deputy, of whom he had already formed a fine impression during the big September manoeuvres. He decided to replace Beck by Halder soon. Meanwhile Hitler turned for military advice to the OKW and not the General Staff, "an establishment for learning to lie", as he described it to his adjutants.

In Berlin, Hitler had already asked the OKW to draw up an interim directive for "Green", the attack on Czechoslovakia. It reached the Berghof on 21 May. It opened with Hitler's basic definition, "It is not my intention to destroy Czechoslovakia in the immediate future by military action unless provoked . . . or unless political events in Europe create a particularly favourable and perhaps unrepeatable climate for doing so."

If Hitler had still planned to shelve the Czech problem, his mind was changed by the news that reached him that same day, 21 May 1938. Two Czech policemen armed with rifles had shot dead two Sudeten German farmers, Böhm and Hoffmann, near Eger; and the Czech government was mobilizing nearly 200,000 troops on the – as yet wholly false – pretext that Germany was already concentrating troops against her in Silesia, Saxony and northern Austria. That evening, Hitler ordered Keitel and foreign minister Ribbentrop to meet him in Munich. Both flew down from Berlin next morning. In a secret speech six months later Hitler was to relate: "After 21 May it was quite plain that this problem would have to be tackled – *so oder so*! Any further postponement would only make it tougher, and its solution even bloodier."

Ribbentrop arrived in Munich gloomy. Brauchitsch had warned him before he left Berlin that the German army was not ready for an attack on Czechoslovakia. Hitler seems not to have fully accepted this, because after Keitel flew back to Berlin, Schmundt forwarded to him lists of questions asked by the Führer. Could enough troops be mobilized without putting the western powers on guard? How strong were the German divisions concerned? What was the composition of the 2nd Panzer Division, and how strong would a German armoured force have to be to carry out the invasion by itself? Could the western frontier be strengthened by temporarily arming the construction gangs?

The OKW's replies, cabled to the Berghof, put a damper on any idea of immediate action except in an emergency: Brauchitsch was said to have "other plans" for employing their armour and – as Ribbentrop had faithfully conveyed to Hitler – the army's firepower was quite inadequate. The new heavy infantry howitzers (15-centimetre trench mortars) could not enter service before autumn, because no live ammunition would be available before then. To attack the enemy fortifications now, Hitler would have only twenty-three 21-centimetre howitzers and of these, eight were in East Prussia.

All week Hitler grappled with the decision – to attack now or later? German blood had been spilt by the Czechs, and his pride was mortified by the anti-German outburst in the foreign press. Hitler learned from the Likus reports that the British and French embassies were stoking up the controversy in Berlin. Lord Halifax was tactless enough to write to him urging him not to make the situation worse – as though it was *he* who had mobilized. For months afterwards the behaviour of the Fleet Street editors rankled him. "Twice I told the British ambassador that not one German soldier had been moved, and yet still the newspapers started their vile campaign against Germany."

The Czechs and the British even maintained that only Beneš's mobilization order had forced Hitler to climb down – and this stark untruth was the bitterest pill for him to swallow. By Wednesday 25 May his mind was made up. The intellectual process involved by this was evident to his private staff. They could hear him pacing up and down inside his locked room hour after hour at night; but by morning the mental storm of uncertainty had subsided, his face was clear and relaxed, the decision was within him. On Thursday he returned to Berlin; on Friday he received Admiral Raeder to discuss long-term naval problems (to which we must shortly return); and on Saturday 28 May he called a wider conference of ministers and generals, including both Beck and Halder (Beck had merely smiled, and told Hitler's army adjutant Gerhard Engel, "Give the Führer my regards but say I don't know if I can come, as I'm busy on a memorandum I'm going to send him shortly.")

Beck appeared nonetheless on the appointed afternoon, as did Göring – who apprehensively whispered to Wiedemann, "Does the Führer really imagine the French won't do anything if we weigh into the Czechs? Doesn't he read the Forschungsamt intercepts?" – Brauchitsch and Neurath.* Ribbentrop was not in evidence but his liaison officer, Walther Hewel, came with Baron von Weizsäcker. Hitler spoke that afternoon for three hours, using his own hand-written notes. He stressed that he alone was responsible – "Far-reaching decisions can only be taken alone," Beck's record of his speech observed – and announced his decision as follows, according to Wiedemann's recollection: "It is my unshakeable resolve that Czechoslovakia shall vanish from the map of Europe." He explained to them why he had not reacted immediately to the provocation of Prague's mobilization: firstly, the German army was not yet ready to penetrate the fortifications; and secondly, Germany's cover in the west was at present inadequate to deter France. Therefore he would stay his hand for the next few months. "No amount of provocation will force me to change this attitude," he assured them. The coming months would meanwhile give time to prepare the German public psychologically for war.

He warned them not to imagine that this time Germany would just teeter on the brink. With British rearmament still three years from completion, and the French forces similarly unprepared, this moment of fortune must be grasped now. "In two or three years their temporary weakness will have passed."

According to Wiedemann, Hitler even added: "Once this Czech business is over and done with, I'll give you four years to prepare for a settling of scores with the western powers."

* Neurath was acting President of the otherwise inactive "Secret Cabinet Council" established in the wake of the February crisis.

Neither Beck nor Brauchitsch voiced any comment.

Hitler had not indicated to them precisely when "Green" would begin. He appears to have hinted that it would not be before the end of September 1938 – and perhaps not even until March 1939, because Neurath told Wiedemann as they left the Chancellery, "So, we have at least another year and a lot of things can happen before then."

At the Berghof, Hitler had already decided to accelerate the construction of a mighty West Wall – two parallel defence-zones, the forward one to be built and manned by the army, the rear by the Luftwaffe. On 27 May he had issued the new figures to the army: it was to speed up work on the existing 1,360 concrete pillboxes and to build in addition 1,800 pillboxes and 10,000 bunkers in the west by 1 October 1938 – a daunting task indeed. He also ordered that Reich Labour Service (RAD) workers were to be trained in the use of rifles, machine-guns and hand-grenades so that they could man the West Wall in an emergency while the regular army was fighting in Czechoslovakia.

The services reacted characteristically to Hitler's decisions. That same evening, 28 May, Göring arranged to confer next day with senior Luftwaffe generals; operational planning for "Green" began at once, and on 1 June the air ministry issued complete orders for the erection of Air Defence Zone West. The army's General Staff was more conservative and complied only reluctantly with Hitler's directives. Beck felt obliged to agree with Brauchitsch that Hitler's measures must be humoured "for the time being". (Hitler obviously recognized the reluctance of these old army workhorses to bite the snaffle because he commented cynically to Göring, "These old generals will just about manage Czechoslovakia – after that we'll have four or five years' grace anyway." This hurtful comment was swiftly transmitted to Beck by Wiedemann.) On 30 May and again on 1 June, Todt's diary shows that he lunched with Hitler. Hitler asked him to build the West Wall. Todt agreed; the ill-defined line between his and the army's responsibility resulted in much friction.

The German navy was a special case. While still at the Berghof, Hitler's naval adjutant – the cigar-smoking ex-destroyer-captain Karl-Jesco von Puttkamer – had cabled Admiral Raeder to stand by for a meeting with the Führer in Berlin on 27 May 1938. Puttkamer tipped him off that Hitler was going to ask for a further acceleration of the battleship and submarine construction programme, since "the Führer must now assume that France and Britain will rank amongst our enemies".

In Berlin on the twenty-seventh Hitler informed Raeder that he wanted the new battleships *Bismarck* and *Tirpitz* completed by early 1940. He also demanded an increase in the armament of the battlecruisers *Scharnhorst* and *Gneisenau*, the expansion of naval shipyard capacity, the completion of the total percentage of submarines permitted under the 1935 Anglo-German agreement as soon as he gave the word, and rapid development of an artillery U-boat. The 500-ton (type VII) submarine was to go into mass-production.

The admiralty again asked for the closing-down of non-military construction projects like the Munich subway (which Hitler had initiated as recently as 22 May) and the Volkswagen factory (of which he had laid the foundation-stone four days later) to release skilled labour. Hitler refused. As for the dates Hitler had set, the admiralty hoped that *Bismarck* might be completed before December 1940, and *Tirpitz* might enter service one month later.

Hitler obviously gave Raeder the impression that the naval part of the war – i.e. the war with the west – would not begin before 1944 or 1945. Such was the contingency plan subsequently analysed by Raeder's chief of naval operations, in investigating the strategic problems raised by a war with Britain. It was on this basis that the naval staff was to formulate, some months later, its new ship construction programme, the Z-Plan. Raeder had also evidently stipulated to Hitler, at their meeting on 27 May, that in any war in the west the Nazis' first strategic aim must be to extend their coastal base by the occupation of neutral Belgium and Holland: because Hitler mentioned this in his secret conference with the ministers and generals next day.

His policies now turned therefore on destroying Czechoslovakia within four days – so rapidly that her allies could not intervene. It would take France at least four days to mobilize. To Schmundt he outlined the campaign as he envisaged it: on Day One – 1 October, say – his Fifth Columnists could sabotage the Czech "nerve centres" while the fortifications were seized by Trojan-horse methods or bombed by the Luftwaffe. On Day Two camouflaged units, no doubt in Czech uniforms, would secure key bridges and targets between the enemy fortifications and the German frontier. Across these bridges on Day Three the army's lorried units would move in to relieve the troops that had dug in among the fortifications; and on Day Four the divisions waiting on the frontier would follow, while a motorized formation and the 2nd Panzer Division lunged into the heart of Czechoslovakia.

The final OKW directive that Hitler signed on 30 May suggested no date for the attack. But Keitel ordered the Wehrmacht to be ready by 1 October. And now the document began, "It is my unshakeable resolve to smash Czecho-slovakia by means of a military operation." Hitler reserved to himself the choice of the right moment. Tactically and politically, the ideal campaign was one that opened with a lightning attack "in consequence of some incident whereby Germany is provoked beyond the bounds of endurance". As he had declared in his secret speech of 28 May, the propitious moment, if it came, would have to be seized: but chance was something that the orthodox politician, at least, could not control.

The Other Side of Hitler

While the German screw was slowly turned on Czechoslovakia during the summer of '38, Hitler stayed at the Berghof and succumbed to the lazy routine of a country gentleman. He was surrounded by his personal friends and their womenfolk.

Only rarely were generals or ministers seen here. He rose at ten, read the papers, lunched with Martin Bormann or one of the doctors, strolled, watched a movie, and retired between ten and midnight. Once he stayed up until 3:15 A.M. to hear the result of the boxing match in the USA between Max Schmeling and the negro Joe Louis; but his champion was defeated and for days afterwards his adjutants grinned as they handed him the dutifully-translated telegrams sent by US citizens to the Führer: "Herrn Adolph Hitler, Berlin, Germany," cabled one correspondent from Colorado, "How do you feel after tonight's defeat of Nazi number one pugilist, defeated by Afro-American. Nazi stock going down here." Another came from Los Angeles: "You congratulated Schmeling too soon. American negroes are perfect in praying, economizing and fighting. You try it sometimes." And another, "Our sympathies on the disgraceful showing Herr Max made tonight. Just about as long as you would last if we tied in to Germany."

When in Munich, Hitler invariably lunched at the Osteria, his favourite wine restaurant three doors from the Party's old offices at Schelling Strasse in Munich. It had a small Italian garden, one tree and a fountain. He always sat at the same table: it is still there, unmarked, and his intimates still recognize it and choose to sit there. His secretary Christa Schroeder shared his vegetarianism, and so did Bormann – to stay close to his Führer. Once, that electric summer, she tried to cheer him up with a local variation of the old "two alternatives" gag: it began, "They say there are two alternatives, either there will be war or no war," and rambled on through the increasingly nauseous stages until this was reached: ". . . And if you're just injured, that's good, mein Führer, but if you get killed – then there are again two alternatives. Either they give you a private grave, or you're thrown into a mass grave. If you get a grave to yourself, that's good, mein Führer, but . . ." Here Bormann stopped her, as Hitler was hooting with laughter. "If you can put the Führer in a mood like this just twice a year, Fräulein Schroeder," commended Bormann, "then you've earned your salary."

Hitler's adjutants and military advisers went on routine summer furloughs. Jodl and Schmundt took five weeks until the end of July, Keitel then went until mid-August. Late in June 1938 a new naval adjutant arrived, a dour Frisian navy commander, Alwin-Broder Albrecht; Puttkamer returned to the destroyers. The elegant Luftwaffe adjutant Nicolaus von Below was still there, as was the new army adjutant, the brash and jocular Gerhard Engel. Himmler had also provided Hitler with a young, good-looking SS lieutenant (*Obersturmführer*) as an ADC, Max Wünsche; and Wünsche's diary of the Führer's activities that summer gives a vivid impression of the dictator's life and ordinances – the regular visits by Schmundt or Bodenschatz, the rarer audiences granted to Brauchitsch, and the almost complete absence from the Berghof of gauleiters and other Nazi Party dignitaries.

Once, the new SA chief of staff, Viktor Lutze, gatecrashed the Berghof. Hitler afterwards ordered his sentries to refuse access to anybody else, regardless of rank, who tried to see him without appointment. The Berghof was his private residence, and several times during the coming crises Bormann or Lammers issued circular notices to that effect. Here the Führer could hob-nob in peace with his court photographer, Heinrich Hoffmann, his press chief, Otto Dietrich, or the various ladies who currently found his favour. The Wünsche diary records young Albert Speer as a frequent visitor, or telephoning ingratiatingly to report the birth of a daughter. Less frequently came Himmler or Ribbentrop. But the diary shows too that even dictators could have secrets – once he commanded Bormann to purchase a private car specially, as he desired to undertake a motor journey somewhere "incognito".

As absolute dictator, Hitler put himself above the law. He had often used his position earlier to surprising effect. In an early Cabinet meeting (on 8 June 1933) he came out against the death penalty for economic sabotage: "I'm against using the death sentence because it's irreparable. The death sentence must be reserved for only the gravest crimes, particularly those of a political nature." Julius Schaub has testified to Hitler's annoyance at learning from Raeder during the 1934 visit to Kiel that a crew just back from the Far East had not been allowed on shore until Customs inspected their warship; Hitler pointedly asked what sailors could possibly purchase on their meagre pay, and directed an immediate signal to the finance ministry to abolish the rule forthwith. Cheers rang round the navy.

His contempt for lawyers was notorious and not unjustified. In 1935, he had just written out his own testament – at a time of acute depression over the polyp in his throat – when he learned that the Supreme Court had nullified an old lady's testament because she had written it on headed notepaper, instead of writing out her address in longhand! Hitler sent for Franz Gürtner and drafted a special law reversing the absurd ruling; but when he came to rewrite his testament in May 1938, he wrote it out in full in longhand nonetheless. (This did not prevent post-war lawyers from voiding it all the same, on government instructions.) In some cases Hitler's hatred even extended to police officials, and judges too. After reading the court file on Töpken, who had murdered a Frau von Ledebur in August 1942, he had directed as follows (as Lammers hastily informed Gürtner):

> In many cases it will undoubtedly be necessary to determine whether there were sexual relations between two people or not. But if this much is known, it is wholly superfluous to probe for closer particulars as to how and where such sexual intercourse took place. The cross-examination of women in particular should cease!
>
> Every time that cross-examining police officials or judges keep probing for details as to the how and where of the sexual intercourse, the Führer has gained the very clear impression that this is done for the same reasons that the same intimate questions are asked in the Confessional box.
>
> The Führer wants clear instructions issued for the abolition of unnecessary interrogations.

By 1942, Hitler's orders were graven in the blood of millions across the continent. But Wünsche's diary shows some of the matters exercising Hitler's mind in the summer of '38. On 17 June 1938, "Führer orders the pedestal of the Strauss bust to be changed." On 7 July, "The Führer commands that the sockets of flagpoles required more than once are to be made permanent." Five days later, "On the drive to the Berghof a letter was passed to the Führer. In this, a man complains that he has still received no reply to a letter sent two years ago (Bouhler's chancellery). The Führer is very annoyed and orders that every matter addressed to him is to be seen to as a matter of urgency." On the fourteenth, Hitler is "deliberating whether it might not be possible to manufacture all cigarettes without nicotine content"; a few days later he "commands that no more smoking is to be permitted at the Berghof".

This solicitousness extended to road safety: "4:45 P.M., the Führer confiscates the driving licence of SS General [Fritz] Weitzel's chauffeur for six months and details the Reichsführer [Himmler] to proceed strictly against traffic offenders. The Führer himself will order the imprisonment of any Party official, including even gauleiters, if they cause any more traffic accidents." The Wünsche diary also recorded small unpublicized acts of humanity: "The

Führer will act as godfather to the triplets of Frau Feil of Kirchanschörung. A pram is on order in Munich, and 300 marks have been sent to the mother. Doctors' bills will be taken care of." On 21 July, Wünsche recorded, "Lunch at the Osteria. The Führer commands that the woman who passed the letter to him during the journey from the Obersalzberg is to be given help. SS Colonel [Hans] Rattenhuber is given 300 marks for this purpose."

This was the "popular dictator" – friend of the arts, benefactor of the improverished, defender of the innocent, persecutor of the delinquent. His compunctions of 1933 about the death penalty, however, were gone. "The Führer signs the new law providing the death sentence for highway robbery"; and precisely one week later, "The Führer countersigns the death sentence passed on the highway robber Götze." More ominously the diary also observes him interfering in judicial processes: "The Führer commands that Salzberger, the woman-killer, is to be sentenced as rapidly as possible. Justice Minister [Franz] Gürtner is informed of this." But these methods ostensibly produced results: the gangsterism withered as rapidly as it had sprung up – to be replaced, of course, with a gangsterism of an altogether more sinister kind.

All of Hitler's staff wishing to marry – from field-marshal down to his humblest adjutant – had to secure his permission first. The Blomberg incident was a notorious example; the Alwin-Broder Albrecht case had yet to come.* Sometimes, while he did not refuse consent, he did what he could to break the match. He took a personal interest in the prospective wives of army officers, requiring to see their photographs and frequently guffawing over the oddities of the match proposed. SS officers had in addition to obtain clearance from the RuSHA (*Rasse-und Siedlungshauptamt*) – the racial purity agency. When in August 1936 Hitler's capable chauffeur Kempka proposed to marry one Rosel Bubestinger, Schaub at first wrote asking for express clearance – until her ancestry was found to be askew; then Schaub telephoned the RuSHA *not* to hurry the clearance, "but on the contrary to protract it to stop them marrying. This is the explicit instruction of a Senior Person."

In every respect Hitler's own relationship to women was normal, but he refused to marry. When Puttkamer announced his engagement on 24 March 1938, Hitler lamented: "You're lucky – you can marry. I never can!" True, he had proclaimed it as the duty of every German family to produce four children: but he feared producing a Cromwell-type dynasty, and there were cynical reasons to remain single. He had the female vote to consider. He was wedded to Germany, he liked to say. To Henriette Hoffmann, the photographer's daugh-

---

* It led to a complete rupture in Raeder's relations with Hitler for three months, from June to August 1939. See page 212.

ter, he once jested: "You see, at first I was too shy and unimportant, and women were wondrous creatures far out of reach. After that I was a starving soldier, and who was going to show an interest in me then; and now I'm head of state – can you imagine me keeping a lover's tryst?" In the Twenties he had picked up women casually – Emil Maurice, Hitler's driver, told Hitler's secretaries once that he drove him to Berlin and "organized" girls for him for an evening's amusement, for which Hitler afterwards confessed he gave them twenty marks apiece.

There were indeed relationships – the names of Emmi Maree, Jenny Haug, Ada Klein and Mitzi Reiter figured briefly in his earlier life. But the first woman to have a more permanently disturbing effect on him was his stepniece Geli Raubal, the daughter of his half-sister Angela. Geli's tragic death in a locked room of Hitler's Munich flat marked the turning-point in his career – a moment when he braced himself for the future, casting off all fleshly pleasures in the most literal sense, and dedicated himself to Germany's future. She had first come into his life in 1926, as an eighteen-year-old brunette on an outing from her high-school; Hitler had commanded Schaub to show her over Munich. The next year she had moved there indefinitely, renting a furnished room next to the house in Thiersch-Strasse where Hitler, her uncle, then lived. When he moved to Prinz Regenten Platz he rented a room for her in the next-door apartment of his housekeeper, Frau Anni Winter. She furnished her room with bright, modern furniture in marked contrast to the heavy brown pieces that filled Hitler's flat.

Hitler paid for Geli's opera lessons, and she accompanied him on evening outings or to the Obersalzberg. Henny Hoffmann has described in a manuscript the atmosphere on those private excursions of the late Twenties. "I can still see her smiling seductively and embracing Hitler and saying, 'Uncle Alf, let's all drive to Lake Chiemsee for a picnic.' And usually he gave in." Then Maurice would drive, while Hitler sat in front and the girls in the back with Wilhelm Brückner, and the Mercedes would roar down the highway to the lake's shores; the chequered tablecloth was laid out, Frau W's sandwiches were unpacked and Hitler and his friends vanished into the leafy shade to read their newspapers, while the young girls chastely removed their garments and splashed about nude in the warm lake water. (Hitler never swam; he argued that Friedrich Ebert's photograph in bathing trunks had contributed little to his popularity.) Hitler swore that "when he came to power" he would build a fine watering-place on this spot, and so he did: but it has been restricted to US occupation forces personnel ever since 1945, like the Platterhof Hotel that Bormann built.

There is no doubt that Hitler grew attached to Geli. Once he went down on bended knee to her. He did not know how to take photos but he sketched her often.* One of his doctors, Karl Brandt, was to write, before his execution by the Americans, of the moral comfort and support this young girl gave Hitler in his years of struggle. "I remember the emotion with which Hitler spoke of her in earlier years – it was akin to the worship of a Madonna." Geli had the cheerful resolution that Hitler valued in a woman – he compared her face to the sphinxes of the Upper Belvedere in Vienna. (He had long taught himself not to betray emotions. "Mark this," he had told little Henny Hoffmann at her mother's funeral, "Let no person look into your heart!" He took the child's hand in his during the chilling ceremony and commanded her not to cry.)

Geli was probably deeply troubled by all this. She certainly never had intimate relations with him, but he jealously guarded over her. From what she told her real lover – Emil Maurice – Hitler held her in a gilded cage, consumed by desire for her and the recognition that he must not touch her. He dismissed Maurice in 1928 when he found out about the affair, and Maurice successfully sued for reinstatement before the Munich industrial tribunal. Yet Geli too was jealous of other girls. In 1930, she cajoled her uncle to take her to the Oktoberfest in Munich, and while Hitler tucked into roast chicken and beer she saw Heinrich Hoffmann arrive with a comely fair-haired girl in tow, whom he laughingly introduced to all and sundry as "*my* niece". Geli suspected this was a jibe at her, and objected to being put into the same category as "that monkey girl" – a hostile reference to the black long-haired coat worn by the girl.

Geli next saw the girl in a photograph beaming at her from Hoffmann's studio window in Amalien Strasse, where the Schaubs went in May 1931 to have their wedding photos taken. This was Eva Braun, aged twenty-one, one of Hoffmann's more decorative assistants. Hitler often saw her now, as he frequently visited Hoffmann's offices. But his affections belonged to Geli. In later months Eva took to slipping *billets-doux* into Hitler's unsuspecting pockets. On one occasion Geli found the message first.

In September 1931 this affair ended. Hitler had left Munich for a speaking engagement in Hamburg, when his car was overtaken by a message that Rudolf Hess had telephoned urgently from Munich. Hitler phoned him back from Nuremberg. Hess told him that Geli's body had just been found in her room – locked from the inside – shot through the heart with Hitler's own 6.35-millimetre Walther pistol.

Hitler had recognized that something was wrong when she helped him pack the day before. He had gone back upstairs to say goodbye, stroked her cheek and whispered something to her; but she had reacted coldly and irritably, and Frau Schaub told him later that day that Geli had been distracted and almost in tears. More than that we can never know for certain – Hitler jotted down three

* Once Hitler deftly sketched a self-portrait on a card, then two likenesses of Geli Raubal on the other side. The originals of these are printed in this book (see facing pages 71 and 102).

possible motives for her suicide on a scrap of paper, but dismissed each in turn as absurd. She was buried in Vienna a few days later. The Austrian authorities allowed Hitler in briefly to pay his last respects.

The emotional damage suffered by Hitler over this was never repaired. Hans Frank, his lawyer and close friend, never saw him again in such a state until Rudolf Hess's startling defection ten years later. On Hitler's orders Geli's room was locked and left as it was, with her carnival costume, her books, white furniture and property scattered about it as on the day she died. In his May 1938 testament he ordained, "The contents of the room in my Munich home where my niece Geli Raubal used to live are to be handed to my sister Angela" – Geli's mother. From that moment on Hitler became an ostentatious vegetarian of ever crankier eating habits; and – even odder – the politician who had taken pleasure in strumming quietly on the piano given by the Bechstein family, never played another note again.

A few days later Hitler found another note from Eva Braun in his pocket, expressing her sympathy.

Eventually she filled part of the void left by Geli's suicide, but she had little of Geli's character. "The greater the man, the more insignificant should be his woman," Hitler defined in 1934 – and the simple Eva fitted the bill exactly. A former convent schoolgirl, she had the simple round features of a Deanna Durbin, but she gained in assured charm as she grew older. Over the years she became the Lady of the Berghof, and commanded the respect of the married women privileged to meet her there; inevitably she excited hostility from the spinsters, however – the dislike she engendered in test-pilot Hanna Reitsch endured to 1945, when Hanna secretly tore up the last letter that Eva had trusted her to convey from the Berlin bunker to her family. Another spinster who impressed Hitler was the moviemaker Leni Riefenstahl, whom he first met during the election campaign of May 1932: her films became classics of their genre, and she liked the envy that they caused. Leni and Hanna did little to smother the rumours that they had been the Führer's mistresses, which they almost certainly never were.

By this time Hitler was interested only in Eva. He took at first to inviting her to tea in his Munich apartment. She fell in love with him years before he with her, it is true, and she resorted to great cunning in winning him. She faked her own May 1935 diary threatening suicide, and left it lying around for him to find. She was infuriated by Hitler's long absence at the Berghof, especially as she learned that one of German society's most notable beauties, Baroness Sigrid Laffert, was a regular house-guest there: probably at Hoftmann's suggestion, Eva swallowed a dose – not an *over*dose – of sleeping tablets and was "rushed to hospital". In fact she went in for a long-planned routine operation. Hitler hurried back to Munich, aghast at the mere threat of a second suicide scandal around his name. The "diary" was shown to him. Upon her discharge, the artful Eva was powdered a sickly hue and displayed to him, while her women friends cackled upstairs. At dinner, Hitler remarked warmly on her devotion to him. By 1936 her association had taken on a more permanent character: she attended the Nuremberg Rally and lived with his entourage in the Kaiserhof Hotel. It was here that Frau Angela Raubal, Geli's sorrowing mother, met her face to face: the indignant mother marshalled half the ladies in the hotel, including Henny Hoffmann, in her support, while the rest sided with Eva. It was open war, until Hitler packed Angela off from Nuremberg and vengefully told his half-sister to vacate the Berghof forthwith, where she had kept house for him. Eva Braun moved in to a permanent apartment at the Berghof – with a bedroom, drawing-room and bathroom, to which Hitler soon added Hoffmann's unused darkroom, because she was a keen photographer herself.

The Berghof now became *her* gilded cage, but she liked it. When official guests came she withdrew tactfully up the red marble staircase to her apartment, or even to the attic, and immersed herself in old movie magazines. She knew that Hitler would never present her in public as his wife. He remonstrated to Schaub, "I've told her a dozen times I won't marry her, as I can't tie any woman to my life." Schaub suspected that Hitler's feelings for Eva just did not go deep enough, but in retrospect this seems unlikely: over the years both exchanged hundreds of handwritten letters (they filled a trunk, which was looted in August 1945 by the CIC and vanished with the unit's commander when he returned to New Mexico).

One thing is certain: Hitler did remain faithful to Eva, and his sex life was at first quite normal. But over the last ten years of his life his natural libido *was* somewhat diminished – Hitler's medical records display only half the usual secretion of testis hormone in his blood, comparable to that of a busy executive or a man serving a long prison sentence. An October 1944 medical examination revealed no organic abnormalities in the Führer. Before Eva, there had been other women; but, as Hitler confided to an ADC – Otto Günsche – he had always avoided promiscuous women, fearing venereal disease just as in later years he kept people with common colds at a distance.

What else can be said about Eva Braun and Adolf Hitler? His staff were aware of her, but kept the secret well. Puttkamer, closest of his military adjutants since 1935, did not set eyes on her for four years. Emmy Göring was never introduced to her. The staff referred to her as "E.B.", addressed her as "madam", and kissed her hand. Hitler would call her "Patscherl"; she referred to him – as did all his staff – as "Chief". She avoided using his name in public; or quietly called him "Adolf". There was clearly an empathy in life between them, of an intensity not really documented except by their chosen manner of departure from it – the suicide pact in 1945. She remained his anonymous shadow to the end.

There had been a very different category of women in Hitler's life in the Twenties – grand political ladies with social salons.

One was Frau Elsa Bruckmann, wife of a wealthy Munich publisher. She was witty, rich and a Romanian princess as well. She had supported the Party since 1922, and took to telephoning "Wolf" – as Hitler's intimates called him – to come and meet selected industrialists or intellectuals. It was at her salon that Hitler had met Professor Karl Haushofer, the geo-politician, and the architect Ludwig Troost. In 1926 she had saved the Nazi Party from insolvency.

In later years Frau Lotte Bechstein had displaced her. She had met Hitler as early as 1921 or even 1920. An ample woman of ostentatious riches and jewellery, Frau Bechstein was the wife of the wealthy and anti-Semitic piano-manufacturer Edwin Bechstein. She brought gifts to Hitler in Landsberg prison, and although twenty-five years his senior she had fostered him as her *enfant gâté* and kept Frau Bruckmann at a distance She taught him the social graces and introduced him to Berlin high society. Hammerstein and the other Reichswehr generals were frequently invited to her gatherings – until she in turn was supplanted by Viktoria von Dirksen, the stepmother of ambassador Herbert von Dirksen, and aunt of Sigrid Laffert.

In the Berlin drawing-room of this bewigged female battle-axe the diplomats and deposed royalty regularly met. André François-Poncet, the French ambassador, once slyly remarked on seeing her sail in: "That is how I imagine that Joan of Arc would have looked if she had survived to a great age; but, thank God, the British burnt her first!" Hitler needed only to swear Frau von Dirksen to absolute secrecy on any given topic, to ensure that it spread like lightning to every foreign embassy in Berlin. (Later he employed the witless Count Ciano as an even swifter channel of misinformation to the enemy.)

The only other woman whose company he valued was Gerti, the young widow of Professor Ludwig Troost. He took her under his wing, made her a professor and consulted her on colour-schemes for the fine new buildings rising in Germany. Her influence must have been considerable, because she had only to take exception, for instance, to a 1943 article about Ludwig's work in the *Frankfurter Zeitung* for Hitler to order it summarily closed down, despite horrified protests from both Goebbels and Amann, who were aware of its foreign prestige value (it was the only quality daily left in Nazi Germany).

Ludwig Troost had died before his House of Art in Munich was completed. Hitler had first met him at Frau Bruckmann's in 1928, and that same day told the architect: "When I come to power, you will be my architect. I have great plans in mind and I believe you are the only one who can carry them out for me." But Troost did not live that long. As Hitler gave the House of Art's foundation-stone the obligatory three taps the shaft of the silver-headed hammer broke, a high-degree omen of ill-fortune for the architect: as the local architect, Schiedermayer, whispered to Hitler:*"Dös bedeudt a Unglück"*.

As usual, Hitler himself had sketched the rough outlines for the House of Art on the back of an Osteria menu one day in 1931 – a gallery of stern Grecian lines which even today is mocked by some as Munich's "Athens Station". It opened in 1936, and by 1938 was recognized by the Party as a stable, Nazi-conservative breakwater in the running tide of decadent and Jewish art. He himself treasured in his flat a picture book of the Palace of Knossos, in Crete, and this influenced his archtectural tastes. He sketched hundreds of monuments, memorials, arches, bridges and temple-like structures, in pen-and-ink, with a remarkably good eye for proportion and perspective, though showing a propensity for over-rich designs like those of Gottfried Semper, who had erected many of Vienna's nineteenth-century buildings. It was Troost who influenced Hitler more towards neo-classical designs – the soaring shafts of granite and marble, and the squat, oblong buildings that were to characterize the twelve years of Nazi rule.

Troost's place as Hitler's chief architect was now filled by the young Albert Speer, who had providently built himself a studio villa higher up the Obersalzberg. They often consulted on Hitler's grandiose reconstruction plans for Germany, announced in his speech of 30 January 1937. Speer wrote in a memorandum on 31 August 1938 on the Obersalzberg,

> Only few people know the scale of the Führer's plans for the reshaping of Berlin, Nuremberg, Munich and Hamburg. These four cities are to receive over the next ten years buildings which are quite capable of swallowing a major part of the building trade's present capacity, whereas our present stone-quarrying capacity is already far short of these buildings' requirements.

After complaining that Cologne, Breslau, Hanover, Königsberg, Münster, Dresden, Magdeburg and Stettin had also jumped on the bandwagon, Speer pointed out that there were not enough architects familiar with Hitler's style to go round:

> By imparting basic design ideas and by frequent personal intervention and by innumerable personal improvements the Führer has created a new artistic school that has without doubt the elements of a viable and general architectural line. But at present only a few architects are spreading the Führer's design ideas – architects who know what matters to him through their close contacts with the Führer. . . .

There is no doubt that – besides war – architecture was Hitler's other great love. He made no secret of these plans. He showed the sketches enthusiastically to visiting statesmen like Milan Stoyadinovich, the Yugoslav prime minister, and Schuschnigg. From 1937 on, the Elbe bridge particularly interested him. On 29 March 1938, Todt recorded in his diary, "Discussion with Führer on the Hamburg suspension bridge." At one time Hitler even investigated the possibility of building a new Berlin somewhere in Mecklenburg, on Lake Müritz – like some Nazi Washington or Brasilia – as the present Berlin was built on sand, with all the architectural problems that that implied.

Speer's new Reich Chancellery building was already taking shape in Wilhelm Strasse. Hitler also planned a huge Congress Hall, a building so vast that a giant image of the speaker would have to be thrown by television techniques on to a screen above his podium. Throughout 1938 – in fact, until the last days of his life – this would-be architect sketched the buildings and façades as he envisaged them, while his faithful Speer did the "general staff" work, made scale models from the sketches, for Hitler to eye from every angle. Finally the buildings themselves took shape, built not of the concrete and steel of the mid-twentieth century but of the materials of classical Mediterranean culture – granite and marble.

Hitler wanted the monuments of the Nazi rebirth to last millenia. On 17 December 1938, when Todt put to him Professor Wilhelm Thorak's plans for a gigantic monument to Labour, this became very clear. Todt recorded, "The Führer expressed reservations about using Untersberg stone. The Führer wants this monument in particular to last for centuries. . . . The Führer recommended us to consider whether a reddish granite or something similar of absolute permanence should not be used, so that this gigantic monument will still be standing in a thousand years in all its nobility despite atmospheric erosion."

Driving up and down Germany, Hitler saw his dreams come true. He revelled in these motor journeys. He liked to see the faces and hands of the German construction workers and accept their cheers. Once – shortly after Hitler reintroduced conscription – Wiedemann murmured to him, "You still have the people with you, the question is: how much longer?" Hitler indignantly replied, "They're behind me more than ever – not 'still'. Come on a drive with me – Munich, Stuttgart, Wiesbaden – then you'll see just how enthusiastic the people are!" When Wiedemann later warned that there was public criticism of Goebbels, Hess and Göring he retorted: "My dear Wiedemann, take a look at the newsreels and you'll see how much my men are adored." Once Wiedemann proposed Hitler should, once a week, meet two citizens picked at random to hear the real public opinion. Hitler refused. "I'm going to motor around the country again this summer and talk at public meetings – that's the best way to meet the people."

He could not take criticism. In early 1939, after his dismissal as adjutant, Wiedemann wrote for his personal papers a short sketch of the small talk at Hitler's table:

It was virtually monopolized by the Führer. The others just listened and nodded approval. All argument, however reasoned, was virtually impossible. Goebbels was the only one to make wisecracks or pull people's legs – not very nicely but always elegantly. The Führer used to tell anecdotes of the World War – though less often in *my* presence – and of his own childhood and youth experiences, and he revealed a lot of whatever he happened to be mulling over at the time. So those lunching with him before a big speech had a pretty fair idea of what he was going to say. In earlier years I was astounded and often shocked at his unbridled remarks about the Jews, the Church, the bourgeoisie, the civil service, monarchists, et cetera. Later on it left me stone cold, as it was always the same thing.

Whetting the Blade

Less regular visitors that summer of '38 were the military. Occasionally they gathered in the Berghof's Great Hall – army and air force generals, or experts on fortifications, standing uncomfortably on the terracotta-red carpet or staring uneasily at the oak-panelled ceiling until the Führer came downstairs to hear them out.

He could not fathom his generals. To Hitler, a new nation's first war was as essential as cutting teeth to a growing child. Six years from now, on 22 June 1944, he put this blunt philosophy to a secret audience of newly-promoted generals:

> Whatever is born into this world must suffer pain on its arrival. The first sign of life that a child gives as it leaves its mother's womb is not a cry of joy but a cry of pain. The mother too feels only pain. And every nation emerging in this world is also accompanied by trials and suffering; that's the way things are.
>
> If the birth certificate of some new state is just a paper treaty, then it's not worth anything. The birth certificate of nations must always be written out in blood. That may sound harsh, and it may be hard, but it's in the nature of things. It will then survive the longer for it.

He had ordered most of the senior army and air force generals to witness a Luftwaffe equipment display at Barth airfield, in Pomerania, on 13 June 1938. (It was on this occasion that the Fritsch acquittal findings were read out to them.)* Brauchitsch addressed them in an otherwise empty hall, and revealed that Hitler had decided to deal with the Czech problem by force. He confessed to them that he had failed to get Hitler to reinstate Fritsch fully, but, he said, in view of "Green" he was not going to press the consequences.

The Luftwaffe worked hard all summer planning bombing-attacks on Czech

* See pages 18–20 above.

cities and airborne operations. But all this was anathema to the effete and elderly Reichswehr generals – especially Ludwig Beck, the Chief of General Staff. While Brauchitsch correctly saw it as no part of his duty to question a basically political decision, Beck fired off wordy memoranda all summer, using increasingly spurious arguments against "Green". Germany, he warned, might well defeat Czechoslovakia – but not the world. Even if Hungary did attack simultaneously, he added, the campaign would still last at least three weeks; but the new West Wall could not hold out more than two weeks against the French. Beck described Hitler's emergency plan to arm Labour Service battalions to man the West Wall as "a military impossibility".

Beck's memoranda were less criticisms of Hitler's ambitions than attacks on the competence of the new OKW joint Wehrmacht command. Indeed, Beck thoroughly approved of the idea of destroying Czechoslovakia. But, procrastinator that he was, he preferred it all to come "in the future" – not now, when he was Chief of General Staff. The least that Germany must do, he insisted, was consolidate her alliances, and particularly start staff talks with Hungary, before launching this new adventure.

Both Hitler and Brauchitsch ignored him. So Beck's memoranda grew both shriller and gloomier, until by mid-July 1938 he was threatening Brauchitsch that he would call on the leading army generals to resign with him if the Führer would not abandon his intentions. Brauchitsch showed the document to Hitler. Beck's thinking was riddled with fallacies – i.e. that German arms production could never be increased (which Todt and Speer were to disprove quite dramatically in the Forties); or that all Germany's allies were weak and unreliable, while her enemies were resolute and powerful. To appreciative audiences like Todt, Schmundt and Engel, Hitler tore Beck's arguments to shreds: thus, Beck had included France's *garde mobile*, police and *gendarmerie* as well as her regular army, but he had not added to the German army strength the equivalent SA, SS or police battalions. "Beck should not think me stupid," he complained.

In the coming autumn crisis, Hitler's nerve was to remain intact – but not his generals'. His gamble duly came off, and when it was all over he recounted in secret to handpicked Nazi editors what it was like:

> You can take it from me, gentlemen, it was not always easy either to take such decisions or to stand by them, because obviously the whole nation does not throw its weight behind them, far less the intellectuals: there are, of course, lots of gifted characters – at least they regard themselves as gifted – and they conjured up more obstacles than enthusiasm about such decisions. That's why it was all the more important that I stood by the decisions I took back in May and carried them out with iron determination in face of every opposition.

In the first century AD the Roman legions built *limes*, or "threshold" fortifications, to safeguard the frontiers of their territories in Germany and
England. Hitler too called his 1938 western defences his Limes Plan. Under the
overall command of sixty-year-old General Adam, thirty-six infantry battalions and thirty engineer battalions were building the new West Wall, aided
by Todt's autobahn experts and young Labour Service conscripts. There was
one labourer to every yard along the entire West Wall sector from Aachen on
the Belgian frontier down to the Istein Block near Basle.

Hitler had a low opinion of the army's engineers. He found the army's
Inspector of Engineers and Fortifications, General Otto Förster, quite ignorant
of bunker specifications and modern weapons technology. Mistrustfully, he
sent Göring and Luftwaffe experts to inspect the army's progress with the West
Wall early in June. Of course, fortification efforts here had not begun until after
the remilitarization of the German Rhineland in March 1936, and there had
been little money or steel available in the two years since then. In consequence,
by early 1938 only 640 blockhouses had been completed here and – until
Hitler's recent demand for twelve thousand more – the army had only been
planning to add another 1,360 during 1938. Göring, no flatterer of army
generals, called at the Berghof on 14 June and together with Todt delivered a
devastating report on the Limes Plan progress made by the army so far.
Virtually nothing had been done, he claimed: for instance, the entire Istein
Block boasted only two puny machine-guns.

The comparisons were not fair to Adam, because he had first had to solve all
the problems of accommodating, feeding and supplying the huge construction
force. And while Todt's mass-production of the earlier pillbox designs would
not begin until early August, the army was struggling with much more complex
sites. Hitler was however very angry, and sent for Brauchitsch. Brauchitsch in
turn required Adam to visit the Berghof on 30 June. Adam did not mince his
language; he described Hitler's order to erect 12,000 bunkers by 1 October as
impossible. "It's written in the stars", he put it, "how much we'll have done by
autumn." He put the blame squarely on Todt and on the young Labour Service
conscripts – whose physique was just inadequate for such arduous work. Hitler
retorted that Fritz Todt was the man for the job. "The word 'impossible' is
unknown to him!" Todt himself was puzzled by all this army rancour, and wrote
that day to the adjutant of Rudolf Hess, Alfred Leitgen: "Working with the
Wehrmacht is very interesting. You put up with a lot of things that frankly you
don't expect after five years of National Socialism."

The outcome of Adam's visit to the Berghof was a remarkable document,
dictated by Hitler over the next two days to his secretary, Christa Schroeder – a
wordy essay on fortifications design and infantry psychology, deriving from
Hitler's own unforgettable experiences of the trench-warfare of the First World

War. It turned on his insistence that the West Wall, unlike the enemy Maginot Line facing it, must conserve the fighting power of its defenders, not just their bare skins. He ridiculed the monstrous *Infanteriewerk* designed by the army engineers: it cost millions of marks, housed 140 soldiers, but sprouted only a couple of small machine-guns, with perhaps a third to cover its own entrance. Hitler's ideal was a small, well-designed, gas-tight pillbox that could be easily mass-produced and scattered in depth along the line, to shelter his infantry from the enemy's softening-up bombardment: thousands of these would present the enemy with more targets than their artillery could ever eliminate. Once the bombardment was over, these pillboxes would disgorge their troops, their weapons unscathed, into the open to engage the subsequent French infantry attack – they would rush out machine-guns, grenade-launchers and rifles and mow the enemy down. The slogan would be, "Out into the open!" "To be killed then is honourable," Hitler explained, "but to get smoked out of a blockhouse is not only cowardly but stupid."

Walter Warlimont – who saw this document – and a later Chief of General Staff, Kurt Zeitzler, both had high praise for Hitler's insight into the soldier's needs. He knew what the Becks did not – that the infantryman was a human being with mortal fears and the need for sleep, food, fresh water and shelter. The memories of the World War still haunted him: how many of his comrades had died needlessly, while going to the latrines, just because of the shortsightedness of the Otto Försters who had forgotten to provide them in the bunkers? "Particularly the younger soldiers in combat for the first time will need to relieve themselves more frequently," Hitler dictated. Elsewhere his document observed, "Only somebody who has fought a defensive battle for weeks or months on end will know the true value of a flask of drinking water, and how happy the troops are when they can just brew up some tea or coffee." He also wrote: "For acoustic reasons if nothing else, these pillboxes must be clad with wood if possible (or failing that, sheet metal) inside. Only this will prevent the rain of particles that occurs in a heavy bombardment, and the consequent psychological effects. If sheet metal is used, then visible wooden pegs are to be inserted into it to enable hooks, nails and the like to be affixed to it."

As Otto Förster later complained, "The Führer was interested in the very big issues, and also in the tiniest details. Anything in between did not interest him. What he overlooked was that most decisions fell into this intermediate category." It is significant that Hitler rode roughshod over even his most beloved projects to provide the West Wall with what it needed. On 4 July he dictated to Fritz Todt that building projects that could not be ready that year must take second place to this Wall, "which is a project that will make any further work in peacetime possible," as Todt admonished State-Secretary Werner Willikens next day.

All that summer Hitler's adjutants saw him sketching new bunker designs. He laid down how thick the concrete should be, the amount of steel reinforcing, the position of each girder. The sketches became blueprints, the blueprints became wooden forms and webs of reinforcing, the millions of tons of concrete were added, and at the rate of seventy sites a day the West Wall took shape. The Limes Plan was employing 148,000 workers by late August; the army engineers provided 50,000 more. A hundred trains a day transported the construction materials to the west; and 8,800 lorries shuttled between railhead and construction site. He decided the position of each blockhouse, and where the heaviest weapons were to be emplaced. Six batteries of former naval 170-millimetre guns were to be sited so that they could bombard the French towns of Strasbourg, Colmar and Mulhouse in retaliation for any French attack on German towns. On 12 August, Todt was again summoned to the Berghof and ordered by Hitler to build an intermediate position, consisting of hundreds of the heavy strongpoints he had himself sketched. Todt decided to shut down work on several autobahn sections to find the five or ten thousand workers, gangers and foremen necessary – of course, only those who had no call-up papers would be of use. Hitler had ordered Todt to find them by 15 October (which might be taken to imply that he was planning nothing definite before then).

How much of all this effort was serious, and how much pure bluff, we shall never know. He often made warlike remarks to his intimates that seemed destined more for consumption in Prague. Retaining Ribbentrop's secretary Spitzy after one conference on 2 July 1938 in Munich, Hitler took a map of Czechoslovakia and ran his thumbnail down the line dividing Slovakia from Bohemia and Moravia: "That will be Germany's new frontier," he said.

The Hitler that the foreigners saw was often a clever act. Spitzy himself once witnessed this scene, after an excellent luncheon with Hitler and his private staff: a manservant announced the arrival of a British emissary on a matter of great urgency. Hitler started up in agitation. "*Gott im Himmel!* Don't let him in yet – I'm still in a good humour." Before his staff's eyes, he then worked himself up, solo, into an artificial rage – his face darkened, he breathed heavily and his eyes glared. Then he went next door and acted out for the unfortunate Englishman a scene so loud that every word was audible from the lunch table. Ten minutes later he returned with sweat beading his brow. He carefully closed the door behind him and said with a chuckle, "Gentlemen, I need tea. He thinks I'm *furious!*"

Hitler was one of the masters of psychological warfare, and he used every trick at his disposal. He mapped out with Goebbels a crescendo of press intimidation in the Nazi-controlled newspapers. "Thank God they all read

German and take our newspapers," he remarked about his opponents with a snigger, in November. (In August, he explained his method to his generals: "Put the wind up them – show them your teeth!") Each day he scanned the Forschungsamt's latest wiretaps on the phone conversations between Prague and Czech diplomats abroad, to keep track of his own success. He deliberately spread misinformation about the actual date of any planned invasion. On 22 May he had received Henlein in secret; two days later Henlein confided to the Hungarian military attaché in Prague, Eszterházy, "The Führer has assured me that the present gap in the West Wall will be sealed in eight or ten weeks, and then he'll tackle the Czech problem." On 15 July he briefed Wiedemann, whom he knew from the wiretaps to be a chatterbox, to tell Lord Halifax on his coming trip to London that the deadline was March 1939. On 9 August he stressed to Fritz Todt that work on the West Wall would continue to 1 October at least, "probably even until 15 October – in short, until the first shots ring out." Two days later he ordered Halder to have the six 170-millimetre gun batteries ready to open fire by the last day in September.

As Hitler explained somewhat superfluously to Wiedemann before his departure, he was a revolutionary and as such unapproachable by the techniques of old-style diplomacy. In a two-hour conference with Ribbentrop on 12 July, Hitler instructed him to "talk tough" on Czechoslovakia. If the western powers intervened, then they too would be defeated. Göring's Luftwaffe, Ribbentrop must say, was invincible (it had certainly devised blind-bombing techniques on radio beams for "Green"). He himself, he told Ribbentrop on a later occasion, would be in one of the first tanks invading Czechoslovakia!

Wiedemann's visit was a sequel to one by Albert Forster, the Danzig gauleiter, to London. On 14 July he had met Mr Winston Churchill, and told him that he saw no real cause for dispute between Britain and Germany: "If Britain and Germany could only come to terms," Churchill sceptically noted him as saying, "they could share the world between them." Forster invited Churchill to meet Hitler; Churchill admitted, "I gave a noncommittal reply." With Halifax, Wiedemann had more luck. Hitler had briefed him to indicate that "by threats, pressure or violence people would get nowhere with him". He was to say that an entente with Britain was possible, but not until Central Europe had been tidied up; and that Hitler was going to solve the Sudeten problem *so oder so*. "If they ask you about our western fortifications," Hitler said, "tell them we saw on 21 May just what to expect of France and Britain. And that's why we're building these fortifications."

Three days later, on 18 July 1938, Wiedemann flew back to Berchtesgaden. The most revealing words were those spoken by Lord Halifax as he accompanied Wiedemann to the door of his Cadogan Square flat. Halifax confided to Hitler's adjutant that his one ambition in life before he died was to see the

Führer, "at the side of the King of England, driving to Buckingham Palace to the cheering of the crowds".

Hitler's army generals viewed the immediate future, it must be said, less festively.

Early in August he learned from General von Reichenau that there had been a mutinous gathering on 4 August of the most senior generals, passively presided over by Brauchitsch himself. Beck had read out his latest anti-war memorandum, and called for concerted opposition by the army. (As Hitler quipped to his staff, Beck was only ever able to make up his mind when his decision was *against* doing something!) But Reichenau had urged the generals not to interfere with the Führer's political decisions.

Hitler's response to this meeting aroused some controversy. He called to the Berghof's Great Hall not these same generals but their chiefs of staff. The Luftwaffe equivalent ranks were also invited. After they had been well feasted, Hitler spoke to them for three hours about his plans. But when he spoke at one point of the West Wall as though it already existed and was capable of holding off the French, some of the generals loudly murmured dissent. One of them, Major-General Gustav von Wietersheim, quoted his superior, General Adam – perhaps erroneously – as predicting that the Wall could be defended for three weeks at most. To Hitler this seemed proof of the infection that Beck was spreading. His irritation became more visible as Wietersheim droned on; he began to leaf through his notes and suddenly interrupted him with a torrent of facts and figures on the quantities of concrete, iron and steel, and labour invested in the fortifications. Wietersheim stammered, "I wasn't aware of that." Hitler declaimed, "I'm telling you, General, the position there will be held not for three weeks but for three years!"

On the day after the meeting, General von Leeb (Seventh Army) learned of it from his chief of staff, Manstein. "He's just come from the Führer," Leeb put in his diary of 11 August. "Thinks the chips are already down." Hitler for his part expressed to his adjutants bitter disappointment at these products of Beck's vaunted General Staff: "What manner of generals are these – that one has to whip to war instead of holding them back?" he asked in exasperation.

An immediate antidote to the poison spread by Beck's philosophies had to be found. Hitler believed a noisy demonstration of cordite and shell against concrete would do the trick. He invited this time all the army's senior generals to attend, at the Jüterbog artillery school on 15 August. He even considered inviting the hapless General von Fritsch but decided against: "It might be too distasteful for him," he explained to von Below.

He had in fact planned several such artillery demonstrations for this summer. On 10 November he was to explain to his appreciative Nazi editors: "I was frequently asked, 'Do you think that proper? I mean, for months now all round Czechoslovakia there's been this continual gunfire, day and night at every artillery range – they're loosing off live ammunition without pause. You're attracting everybody's attention!' But I was convinced that these months of activity would slowly but surely get on the nerves of the gentlemen in Prague." It is in this context – of deliberate, systematic psychological warfare – that the confidential instructions handed out to Nazi editors in Berlin on 15 August are to be understood: "The Führer and Reich Chancellor", these stated, "will be taking part in troop manoeuvres over the next few days. Every day news items and photographs will be distributed. The High Command asks for them to be published clearly, but not too prominently, as fast as possible."

At Jüterbog construction workers had erected exact replicas of the Czech frontier fortifications, using air photos and blueprints obtained by secret agents. Now Colonel Walter Model, head of the General Staff's experimental branch and a keen Nazi, staged an infantry assault on them. Hitler was delighted, but not his generals: according to one, Curt Liebmann, it was "pure theatre, with much *donner und blitzen* and shouts of Hurrah!" Model pronounced that there was no problem. Hitler congratulated him. General Beck, as Model's superior, was furious but could say nothing. Now Hitler ordered the 150-millimetre howitzers to open fire on the "Czech bunkers", followed by other guns – including the high-velocity 88-millimetre anti-aircraft guns, of which he had ordered one hundred placed at the army's disposal for the assault. After the deafening barrage stilled, he clambered through the smoking and battered concrete hulks while Keitel's adjutant – the Luftwaffe captain Wolf Eberhard – struck matches to illuminate the gloom. The actual damage was disappointing: only direct hits on the embrasures had any real effect. But Hitler emerged grinning, knocked the dust off his brown Party tunic and loudly professed himself astonished at the devastation.

In the mess he spoke ninety minutes to the generals, revealing – but only in tantalizing retrospect – his timetable. Erhard Milch began noting thus: "15 August 1938, Führer speech to generals, 2:45–4:15 P.M. A glimpse into his thinking, his mind is made up!!" – but then, fascinated by the speech, Milch put his pencil away. But Eberhard wrote a complete record for Keitel's benefit. This shows that Hitler rehearsed, as he had in part on 5 November and 28 May, the problem of Lebensraum and the devastating food crisis that would grip Germany in fifteen years. ("It is my one great fear that something may befall me personally, before I can put the necessary decisions into effect," Hitler explained.) He had already taken the first seven steps: he had founded the Party to "clean up" Germany; established political unity in 1933; walked Germany out of the League of Nations and thus restored her freedom of action; rearmed; reintroduced conscription; remilitarized the German Rhineland; and reunited Austria with the Reich. The eighth step now lay ahead: "However the situation may develop, Czechoslovakia has got to be eliminated before anything else." Some might argue, he agreed, that Germany's rearmament was as yet incomplete: but there was no such thing as completeness in armament. How often had he himself been faced by two alternatives – to wait, or to exploit a politically favourable moment despite his own military weakness. "In political life you must believe in the Goddess of Fortune," he declaimed. "She passes by only once, and that's when to grasp her! She will never come by that way again."

In his assessment of the enemy powers, Hitler differed sharply from the "effete voices" – as he called them – of the General Staff. Britain's rearmament was barely one year old: "They'll recoil as long as we show no signs of weakness." The quality of France's artillery and aircraft was highly dubious, and if she withdrew troops from Africa to employ against Germany, then Mussolini would be able to fulfil Italian ambitions in Tunisia. Of Russia, Hitler had no fears whatever. As for Czechoslovakia herself, nerve-war methods like this Jüterbog display would do as much as anything: "If somebody is forced to watch for three long months while his neighbour whets the blade. . . ." (Hitler left the sentence unfinished.) In his view, after a brief spell of fanatical ("Hussite")* resistance, Czechoslovakia would be finished. Hitler concluded his speech, "I am firmly convinced that Germany will win and that our National Socialist upbringing will see us through." And he added, "I believe that by the time this year is out we shall all be looking back on a great victory." In Berlin next day, 16 August, Leeb privately entered in his diary: "Chips down. Führer convinced Britain and France won't intervene. Beck opposite opinion, gloomy mood."

Beck was horrified by all this. On 17 August, Hitler again spoke to his generals, this time at Döberitz. After Model's infantry assault display at Jüterbog, Beck had exclaimed to Adam, "After a graphic display like that, the man [Hitler] will only go more berserk." They discussed resignation – but Beck said he was going to wait until Hitler "threw him out". When he heard of Hitler's speeches, however, Beck correctly interpreted them as a personal attack and submitted his resignation to Brauchitsch on the eighteenth. Even now Hitler scored a last triumph over the wretched general: Hitler asked him to stay on, to all appearances, for the time being "for reasons of foreign policy". And Beck, who had so recently urged a mass demonstration by all army generals against Hitler, meekly agreed – thus striking the last weapon from his own hand. He probably hoped for an Army Group, and Brauchitsch did nothing to dispel the delusion. Nothing was further from Hitler's mind.

By the end of August 1938, General Franz Halder, fifty-four, a Bavarian of

* The reference is to Jan Hus, the Czech patriot and revolutionary.

slight physique and a mild, pedantic temperament, had taken over the General Staff. Beck was out – right out – and did not encroach on the Führer's consciousness again until 20 July 1944.

Throughout August 1938, the "whetting the blade" continued. When the chief of the French air force, General Joseph Vuillemin, was shown round the Luftwaffe's installations, Göring and Milch arranged a spectacular and deceitful display from one end of Germany to the other. Advanced non-operational fighter prototypes were described to the goggling French delegation as being already in mass-production. All available Messerschmitt 109s and 110s were leapfrogged from one airfield to the next for the visitors' inspection. They secretly advised Paris that the French air force would not last many days against the Luftwaffe – and no doubt Hitler learned of this too from the FA intercepts.

But when he tried to bribe the Hungarians into promising outright support of his invasion of Czechoslovakia, he was disappointed. Hungary had been severely dismembered and disarmed after the World War, losing slabs of territory to all her neighbours – Romania, Yugoslavia and Czechoslovakia. But a flamboyant week-long state visit by the Hungarians, coupled with window-rattling military parades and the launching of a battlecruiser named *Prinz Eugen* in their honour,* failed to extract more than conditional undertakings from their Regent, Admiral Nikolaus von Horthy. In their last meeting, on 22 August 1936, Hitler had apparently given Horthy the clear impression that there would be no war before 1942 (in fact the Führer had then issued his secret orders for the Wehrmacht to be ready for war in four years).† Next year, Beck had indicated that the target year was 1940, and – as the Hungarian defence minister Jenö Rátz confided to Keitel on 22 August 1938 – Hungary had laid plans accordingly.

Hitler had used all his gangster methods to impress the visitors. Knowing that Madame Horthy was a devout Catholic, he had placed a prayer stool and crucifix in her rooms, and a large bouquet of lily of the valley, her favourite flower. Then he took Horthy and his staff aboard the state yacht *Grille*, so that the old admiral could feel the throb of engines and the pull of the waves beneath his feet again. That day, 22 August, passed without incident until evening when the Forschungsamt, routinely monitoring the Hungarians' telephone conversations between Kiel and Budapest, reported that at a meeting of foreign ministers of the Little Entente in faraway Bled the Hungarian delegation had apparently formally renounced all use of force against Czechoslovakia; the wiretaps showed that Horthy, Kánya and his prime minister, Bela

---

* Italy had objected to the original choice of name, *Admiral Tegethoff*, offered by Hitler to Schuschnigg (page 75).
† See pages 50–1.

von Imrédy, had retrospectively sanctioned this. This cast a cloud over the entire state visit.

The secret meetings which began next day, during a sea trip to Heligoland, were stormy. In the morning Hitler conferred privately with Horthy, while Ribbentrop and Weizsäcker took on Imrédy and Kánya. Ribbentrop accused Kánya of stabbing Germany in the back with the Bled Agreement, and refused to accept Kánya's explanations. Kánya said, "Then I'll explain it all again as slowly as I can." And when he finished he added condescendingly, "Perhaps now even Herr Ribbentrop has understood?" Hitler fared no better with Horthy or Imrédy. The Regent declared his willingness on principle to participate in "Green", but 1938 was far too early. Horthy picturesquely reminded Hitler that Hungary had "150 Yugoslav camps" along her other borders. When he then began to enlarge on the risk that "Green" would unleash a world war, resulting in Germany's defeat by the British navy, Hitler impatiently broke in: "Rubbish! Hold your tongue!" Horthy complied – deeming it unseemly, he later wrote, to indulge in a shouting match. To Hitler it was inconceivable that Hungary was so reluctant to fight to regain her part of Slovakia. As he sourly pointed out to Imrédy that afternoon, "This is going to be a cold buffet. There'll be no service – everybody will have to help himself." (Hewel retailed the remark to Spitzy afterwards; Jodl also noted it down.)

They returned by separate trains to Berlin on 24 August. On the train, Admiral Raeder asked for a private talk with Hitler on the likelihood of "naval warfare with Britain". In the presence of Hitler's naval adjutant Albrecht, Raeder set out calmly the formidable strategic problems that Germany would face in a sea war. Hitler listened politely, and ended their interview after an hour with the words: "Herr Admiral, what you and I have been discussing is pure theory. Britain will not fight."

The German pressure on their visitors was intense. Brauchitsch had put it direct to the Hungarian military attaché, Kálman Hárdy, that Hungary should participate in "Green"; Hárdy had referred him to his superiors. Kánya asked to see Ribbentrop in Berlin on 25 August, and disclosed to him that Hungary's military prospects were not quite as bad as he had thought: "We shall have made sufficient rearmament progress by 1 October to be able to participate after all." Keitel visited Rátz in his hotel the same day and again emphasized Hitler's firm resolve to occupy Czechoslovakia; he added that only the date was uncertain, but that any fresh atrocity by the Czechs would trigger it. When Rátz asked the Führer next day – according to the Hungarian record – what would be considered as Czech provocation, Hitler replied: "The murder of German citizens." (This reply was significant, as will be seen.)

With a concealed SS bodyguard of two thousand security agents, Hitler set out late on 26 August 1938 from Berlin for a much publicized inspection of the West Wall. By 8:00 A.M. his special train was at Aachen near the Belgian frontier – here the West Wall ended, for Hitler wanted the Belgians to realize that their country would become a battlefield if they joined France's cause.

At Aachen he was met by General Adam, whom General von Brauchitsch had ordered to accompany the Führer. Adam indicated that what he had to say was secret, and asked for Himmler, the labour-service chief Konstantin Hierl and Fritz Todt to leave the dining-car temporarily. Brauchitsch, Keitel and Jodl remained. General Adam stoutly began, "As general commanding the western front I obviously have a far better insight into the situation here than anybody else, and my worries are consequently bigger." Hitler interrupted menacingly, "Get to the point!" Adam faltered, then embarked on a long-winded warning that they would not have completed more than one-third of the West Wall at most by the time the winter frosts set in; and that he, as the military commander responsible, must always take the most dangerous possible situation into account, namely that the western powers would march. "I believe", he added, "that if we start fighting in the east that possibility will become a certainty!"

Adam got no further. Hitler interrupted again, this time finally, thanked him curtly and ended the conference. In a convoy of three-axled cross-country vehicles, he toured the construction sites with Adam's sector commanders. The whole west country was alive with activity – he was reminded of the approaches to the beehives Bormann had erected in the woods near the Berghof: the narrow country lanes were choked with thousands of heavy trucks carrying sand, gravel, steel, cement and tarpaulin-sheeted objects that were obviously guns and ammunition, westwards to the Wall.

He returned to the train for further conferences and to sleep. The General Staff's records show that these secret conferences were more monologue than dialogue in character. He tried to convince the generals that France would not risk serious intervention while menaced by Italy in North Africa and along her Alpine frontier. Here on the western front, he claimed, Germany would have 2,000 tanks and, above all, the outstanding anti-tank mine as a weapon. General Adam remained pessimistic, pointing out that in important sectors of the Wall each division would have to hold a thirteen-mile front, and elsewhere considerably more. During the initial phase while Czechoslovakia's frontiers were being breached, Adam would have no reserves for the west. And what if Belgium and Holland attacked simultaneously with the French? Hitler stubbornly rejoined, "I will not call off the attack on Czechoslovakia."

Adam saw technical and timetable problems in Todt's monopolizing all rail transport for the Limes Plan. Hitler did not. On 28 August he congratulated everybody loudly on the progress made with the Wall. "I am convinced that

German troops can never be shot out of these positions," he declared. On the 29th – the last day of the tour – he proclaimed to the generals: "Only a scoundrel could not hold this front!" General Adam stood there "with his tail between his legs", according to Keitel's adjutant Eberhard. Hitler rebuked the unfortunate general, "I only regret that I am Führer and Chancellor, and not C-in-C Western Front!" It was obvious to Keitel that Adam's days were numbered.

Munich

Well might the generals ask themselves what their Führer really wanted. When Franz Halder now first reported to him as the new Chief of Staff on board the *Grille* on 22 August 1938, Hitler teased him: "You will never learn my real intentions. Not even my closest colleagues, who are convinced they know them, will ever find them out."

One thing was certain. That summer Hitler really wanted a war – whether to write out the "birth certificate" of his new Reich in blood, or to "forge the Austrians into a worthwhile component of the German Wehrmacht", as he had explained to the generals on 15 August, or to have a war just for its own sake. "Clausewitz was right," he exulted to Schmundt, Wiedemann and the other adjutants leaving another military display in East Prussia some days later: "War *is* the father of all things." This was Hitler's favourite misattributed quotation.* He repeated it in his secret speeches to new officers on 30 May 1942, in the first line of his speech to the generals on 27 January 1944, again on 22 June 1944 and in his midday war conference of 9 January 1945 – when even his most ardent followers had long grown tired of Hitler's war.

Confronted by fumbling democracies who desired only peace at apparently any price – indeed, by men who wanted to see him cheered all the way to Buckingham Palace or, as his Paris embassy had recently cabled, fêted as a great statesman if only he would not make war – Hitler's position as a dictator actually thirsting for hostilities was a powerful one. He told his generals that he wanted Germany's older troops, the thirty to thirty-five year olds, to see some combat action in this Czech war; the younger soldiers could taste blood in the next. Admittedly, there were by early September 1938 minor contra-indications: Hungary was "hesitant", Italy was "dubious" – but Germany's 1938 harvest was an excellent one. It was as though Providence herself was smiling on Hitler's venture.

Opinion at top level was – and remained – divided as to whether Hitler was bluffing or not. We still do not know for sure. Weizsäcker wrote privately on 1 September, "None of this would prevent me from laying a (small) wager even

* The words were actually uttered by Heracles (534–475 BC): "War is the father of all things, of all things it is king."

now that we will preserve the peace in 1938." But three days later Ribbentrop again informed him that Hitler and he were assuming that "Green" would begin "within six weeks". For technical reasons, "Green" could not begin before 1 October anyway; but equally, for the best flying weather, it ought not to be delayed after the fourteenth. Hitler loudly hinted that he might postpone it until the spring, but his staff believed that that was not his intention: for by then the Czechs might well round up Konrad Henlein – and the leader of the Sudeten German Party was Hitler's "secret weapon" for breaching the Czech fortifications. Besides, Henlein's followers were to furnish the pretext needed to justify and unleash the German invasion.

Hitler had secretly counselled, several times during July and August 1938, with Henlein and his chief lieutenants. Henlein was by no means enthusiastic about "Green". At Bayreuth on 23 July he vainly tried to dissuade Hitler from using force; Hitler replied that his young Wehrmacht needed a taste of fire. At the Breslau gymnastics festival a week later they again met: Hitler invited him up to his hotel room – but once the door closed, he told Henlein he had nothing to add to the instructions he had long given him. Evidently this was a crude continuation by Hitler of the war of nerves: an act for the benefit of the journalists ringing the hotel. In mid-August, Henlein's coarse deputy, Karl-Hermann Frank, came to the Chancellery and tried to convince Hitler that maps of Bohemia and Moravia showed that the distribution of Czech and German population groups was such that "self-determination" alone would eventually bring Czechoslovakia into Hitler's grasp. He found he was talking to deaf ears. Hitler was out for blood – Frank quoted Hitler shortly after as saying that he wanted Benes captured alive, so he could hang him personally!

By this time Hitler – as will be seen – had begun examining with his OKW staff ways of controlling the climax that would unleash "Green". On 26 August he ordered Frank to prepare to manufacture incidents in the Sudeten territories.

The snag was the British negotiating team now lodged in Prague under a venerable Liberal peer, Lord Runciman. Underlying all Hitler's instructions to Henlein since late March had been one theme: to do anything to avoid reaching a compromise solution with the Czechs. But outwardly Hitler had to appear to be heeding the British proposals. The British were minded to force Beneš to swallow all Henlein's eight Karlsbad proposals – but Hitler, of course, wanted more than that. By now he wanted all Czechoslovakia, not just control of the Sudeten regions. This explains Hitler's irritation when Henlein's Berlin agent, Fritz Bürger, brought the Runciman proposals to Munich on 29 August. "What business do the British have, poking their noses in?" exclaimed Hitler. "They ought to be looking after their Jews in Palestine!" He told Bürger the British were just playing for time to rearm. If Britain interfered when "Green" began, then the Luftwaffe would deal with her.

An apprehensive Konrad Henlein appeared himself at the Berghof on 1 September. Hitler showed him over Martin Bormann's model dairy – built at great expense to supply the SS barracks. ("God knows the price of a pint of your milk," Hitler used to bully him.) He wisecracked to Henlein: "Here are the representatives of the National Socialist Cow Club!" He was evidently in high spirits – but not Henlein. Hitler repeated that he still planned the military solution: Czechoslovakia was to be eliminated "this September". He told Henlein not to let the British bamboozle him – he was to keep on negotiating with Prague, and start manufacturing "incidents" from 4 September. When Hitler saw him off from the Berghof at 3:30 P.M. on the second, he is alleged to have laughed: "Long live the war – even if it lasts eight years."

Perhaps it was all bluff, intended for the eyes and ears of Beneš and his advisers. (There are clues that Hitler was using Henlein as a powerful psychological weapon – for instance, a secret directive to the Nazi press a few days later: "There's to be a reception at Nuremberg attended by Konrad Henlein and others. Henlein is not being mentioned in the official report on this, but there is no objection to the publication of photographs that may show him attending this reception.") Henlein, however, took Hitler at his word about a coming war, and returned to his followers in despair: he realized that the wretched Sudeten Germans with their legitimate grievances were becoming pawns in a much larger struggle.

Henlein was not alone in his anxiety. The Nazi-conservative finance minister, Count Schwerin von Krosigk, tried in vain to see Hitler, then sent in a memorandum formulated in quite clever terms, urging Hitler to delay "Green" until later. Time, but not money, was on Germany's side, he advised: the Reich was facing a serious financial crisis because of the inflationary rumours of a war starting on 1 October. He believed that the British were not bluffing, and that the German public lacked the inner resolution to fight a new war. "It will not be able to bear for long the hardships of war, large and small – the ration cards, the air raids, the loss of husbands and sons." So wrote Krosigk on 1 September in his memorandum to Hitler.

In his speech to Nazi editors two months later Hitler parcelled it into the same category as those from Ludwig Beck, and attributed it to "the hysteria of our top ten thousand".

He turned an equally deaf ear on his diplomats. The moderate Konstantin von Neurath tried to see him on 1 September, and was refused. When his ambassador in London, Herbert von Dirksen, tried to bring him a private message written by Neville Chamberlain on 8 August, Hitler refused to receive him too. When his ambassador in Paris, Count Johannes von Welczek, quoted to Berlin the French foreign minister's clear warning that France would stand by Czechoslovakia, Hitler pushed the telegram aside and said it did not interest him. Hans Dieckhoff, his ambassador in Washington, was given equally cavalier treatment.

All three ambassadors demanded peremptorily to see Hitler. But it was not until the annual Party rally at Nuremberg that he condescended – turning to Wiedemann and instructing: "Well, show the *Arschlöcher* [assholes] in!" Chamberlain's now five-week-old message did not interest him; so this, Dirksen's only meeting with Hitler, was over in five minutes. On Ribbentrop's advice Hitler instructed all three ambassadors not to return to their posts for the time being. He had literally no time for the foreign ministry – or its methods. The diplomats were in uproar – like a chicken-run into which a fox has wriggled. Weizsäcker indignantly wrote for the record, "After hearing out Messrs. Dieckhoff, von Dirksen, Count Welczek, [Hans Adolf] von Moltke [ambassador in Warsaw] and [Hans Georg] von Mackensen [Rome] on 7 September, I reported as follows to Herr von Ribbentrop on the eighth: 'The opinion of all these gentlemen is, with certain shades of difference, in flat contradiction to that of Herr von Ribbentrop inasmuch as they do not believe that the western democracies will abstain in the event of a German-Czech conflict.' I added that my own opinion is well enough known to Herr von Ribbentrop as it is."

Hitler's own routine was hardly that of a dictator preparing for war. On 30 August 1938 he was to be seen spending the day visiting architects and art galleries in Munich: he inspected the models of Speer's new Chancellery building and purchased paintings for the "Führer Building" (*Führerbau*), the Party HQ. Lunch was at the Osteria with Bormann and Unity Mitford. The evening was passed idly at the Berghof, watching two unsatisfying Hollywood movies – both of which Hitler peremptorily halted in mid-reel.

After midnight, Major Schmundt brought to him planning papers relating to the phoney "incident" that was to be staged to justify "Green". The OKW had drafted a three-page memo on this, on 24 August (which explains Hitler's remarks soon after to Bürger and Rátz); this was what Schmundt now submitted to him. The OKW argued for the main "incident" to be staged when the weather was favourable for the Luftwaffe; and it must be early enough in the day for authentic word to reach OKW headquarters in Berlin by noon of the day before the Nazi invasion. The interval was unavoidably brief. It would put the Germans in enemy territory at the mercy of the Czechs and prevent the issue of any warning to diplomatic missions in Prague before the first air raid on the city. But it would satisfy for Hitler his vital condition for success: surprise.

Naturally, this devious infra-planning by the OKW – whose Abwehr agents would, Jodl believed, have been responsible for staging the actual "incident" – provided the prosecutors at the Nuremberg Trials with considerable mileage. Jodl, writing privately on 3 December 1945, dismissed the accusations thus: "The real provocation of Germany was provided by the Versailles Treaty inasmuch as it handed over 3½ million Germans against their will to 6 or 7 million Czechs."

Within the General Staff a fundamental dispute arose with Hitler over the employment of the army's limited tank strength. Halder had outlined the General Staff plan to Hitler and Keitel aboard the *Grille* at Kiel, using a map of Czechoslovakia. The country would be bisected at its narrow waist by Rundstedt's Second Army, striking south from Silesia, and by the armies of Wilhelm von Leeb and Wilhelm List striking northwards from Bavaria and Austria. To Hitler this seemed wrong: this was precisely what the enemy would expect. He asked Halder to leave the map, and after returning to Berlin he instructed Keitel to advise Brauchitsch that the tanks were to be employed quite differently, concentrated into one force which would drive north-eastward from Nuremberg, through the Czech fortifications and Pilsen and straight on to Prague. The political objective was to capture Prague, the Czech capital, in the very first few days. An added advantage was that the tank force would then come under Tenth Army, commanded by the politically reliable General von Reichenau.

The General Staff disagreed with Hitler's plan. They believed the tanks were needed by the other armies to make up for their weakness in heavy artillery during the infantry assault. Hitler summoned Brauchitsch to the Berghof on 3 September, and dinned in to him why he insisted on his own plan. Originally, he said, the Czechs had not prepared their defences in anticipation of attack from Austria; so their fortifications facing Rundstedt in Silesia were far stronger. "The Second Army might run slap into a second Verdun. If we attack there we will bleed to death attempting the impossible." Equally, List's assault from the south would get bogged down by Austria's ancient railroad system. What the Czechs would not expect would be the attack Hitler planned to deliver with Reichenau and a massed force of tanks. "An army plunged into the heart of Bohemia will settle the issue." Besides, the Czech terrain facing Tenth Army was swarming with Henlein's supporters: he could kit them out in "suitable uniforms" – as Hitler delicately put it – and commit them to battle in the very heart of the Czech bunker systems.

Brauchitsch was unconvinced. The General Staff simply ignored Hitler's plan. Hitler found out, and sent Keitel to make sure. Halder told Keitel that the General Staff's orders had already gone out, and it was too late to alter them. Keitel flew to Berlin early on 8 September and urged Brauchitsch to comply.

But when the OKW chief returned to Hitler in Nuremberg – where the Party rally was approaching its spectacular climax – next morning, all he could report was that both Brauchitsch and Halder flatly refused to alter their plans. The two reluctant generals were summarily ordered down from Berlin and presented themselves that night at Hitler's Nuremberg hotel, the Deutscher Hof. It was particularly galling for Hitler: four days long, hundreds of thousands of his followers had displayed their unquestioning acceptance of his leadership here at Nuremberg. Yet here were his army generals – of all people – treating their own Supreme Commander as though his views were of no consequence.

The row lasted five hours. Halder stated the General Staff case on "Green": while Reichenau's army would have to penetrate line after line of Czech fortifications, the pincer-operation presently planned would take these fortifications from the rear. Rundstedt, he insisted, was confronted only by weak and incomplete fortifications. Hitler replied that they should plan with regard to the enemy's most probable line of action, a sound strategic principle. "No doubt," he conceded, "your planned pincer-operation is the ideal solution. But its outcome is too uncertain for us to rely on it, particularly since for political reasons we must obtain a rapid victory. Politically the first eight days are all-important. We must have made substantial ground by then." He reminded them that history alone showed how hard it was to call off an operation that had only half-succeeded – that was the familiar road to horrors like Verdun. The tanks would be frittered away piecemeal, and when they were needed for the subsequent operations in depth they would not be there.

All this now seems self-evident, but at the time, in September 1938, it was by no means so obvious that Hitler was right. The two generals still refused to give way. In the small hours of the morning Hitler finally ceased reasoning with them and *ordered* them to redeploy the tanks as he had said – they had until the end of the month to do it (he explicitly defined X-Day minus Eleven as 20 September, subject to fair weather). Halder shrugged; but Brauchitsch did a complete about-turn and startled everybody with an effusive declaration of loyalty. After they had gone, Hitler ventilated to Keitel his anger about these cowardly and hesitant army generals: "It's a pity I can't give my gauleiters each an army – they've got guts and they've got faith in me."

Not that Keitel's OKW entirely escaped Hitler's censure in these nerve-racking days. Italy had inquired about the "likely date" of "Green" – a secret that Hitler refused to impart to such a gabby ally – and Canaris was sent to Rome for consequent discussions with the Italian Chief of General Staff, Alberto Pariani; the OKW Intelligence chief returned with word that Mussolini was extremely reluctant to help Hitler over Czechoslovakia, a summary which grossly distorted Italy's true posture. Secondly, Keitel's economics section chief, Georg Thomas, had drafted a very pessimistic report on the size and invulnerability of Britain's arms industry. Göring channelled both Canaris's and Thomas's reports to Hitler to discredit the OKW.

To shame these defeatist generals, Hitler alluded to them in withering terms at the Nuremberg rally, while they listened stonily from the front rows. He announced the award of the hundred-thousand Reichsmark National Prize to Fritz Todt for building the West Wall – a gratuitous slight to the army engineers which they took out on Todt over the next months. Worse, Hitler contrasted the "plucky rifleman" who risked his life in the trenches, with the asinine generals whose courage appeared to wax only as their distance from the shooting increased. The generals did not applaud, and when the Minister of Posts hissed at General Adam, "Clap!" the general rounded on him and loudly demanded, "Is this a vaudeville act, then?"

The auguries were unmistakably set for war. Only about forty thousand Labour Service conscripts could be spared for the rally – the rest were working on the Wall. For five hours on the eleventh Hitler stood in his car at Adolf-Hitler Platz in Nuremberg, hatless under the broiling September sun, taking the salute as 120,000 SA and SS men marched past, breaking into the spectacular high-kicking "parade step" as they came within sight of their Führer. His big speech of the twelfth had been awaited with apprehension by diplomats and generals alike, for its tone towards Czechoslovakia. The diplomats had noticed his signs of nervous strain for days before: his hands clenched and unclenched, he joked weakly with them at their formal reception, and even allowed the French ambassador to press a lily into his hands – the symbol of France. "It is a sign of peace as well," explained François-Poncet eloquently, "and should be worn by those who desire to work for peace." Hitler divested himself of the lily as soon as he decently could.

Next day the German newspaper headlines read: SELF-DETERMINATION FOR THE SUDETENLAND. – THE FÜHRER DEMANDS AN END TO SLAVERY. But the political content of the speech had been ambiguous. The British ambassador found it sane, a good debating speech; the Führer had burned no boats and stopped several yards short of the actual brink. He was raising no fresh demands, not even for a plebiscite in the Sudetenland, nor had he hinted at a date. But the speech contained enough inflammatory material to produce a slow-burn reaction in the Sudetenland – not a spontaneous uprising by the Germans, but excitable demonstrations which the Czechs moved savagely to suppress.

On 13 September, Prague proclaimed martial law around the city of Eger. Things were going just as Hitler planned. Karl-Hermann Frank gave Prague an ultimatum to repeal martial law, however, a gesture which did cause Hitler some consternation. The Czechs heard him telephone Henlein and ask what he proposed if the ultimatum expired unanswered? Henlein responded, "Then I shall immediately dissolve my negotiating team [in Prague] and break off the talks with the Czech government." Hitler was relieved: "That's good, Henlein! Very good! Excellent! An excellent idea!" That would make Beneš himself appear to bear the blame. The Nazi press proclaimed next day, the fourteenth: CZECH MURDER TERROR NEARS ANARCHY. GERMANS SLAIN BY CZECH GUNS. Jodl's diary records that a flood of Sudeten Germans had begun crossing into Germany. Goebbels's chief aide, Berndt – he later became Rommel's lieutenant in Africa – harshly fanned the propaganda flames, directing editors at a conference next day to keep hammering ruthlessly away about the atrocities in the Sudetenland: "We can chalk up all our triumphs so far to our ruthlessness," he announced, "and we may be able to chalk up a lot more."

From the Sudeten town of Asch on the evening of the fourteenth Karl Frank telephoned Hitler to appeal for German troops and tanks to intervene right now. Hitler responded: "Frank – bide your time. The time isn't ripe yet." Indeed, it was not. A most unexpected event had occurred. Late the previous night, 13 September, the British ambassador had handed to Baron von Weizsäcker a letter in which Neville Chamberlain, aged seventy, offered to fly at once to Hitler to find a peaceful solution. Hitler was spending the fourteenth with Ribbentrop, visiting Bormann's house at Pullach outside Munich, and this evidently caused some delay; but at 2:30 P.M. his acceptance of Chamberlain's proposal reached Berlin. He could hardly have refused the offer, and he was nettled to have lost the initiative like this, however briefly. He half-expected the old gentleman to issue to him a stern warning that Britain was going to fight – even though all the secret intelligence indicated the contrary.

The "brown pages" – top secret wiretaps by Göring's Forschungsamt – were pouring into the Berghof by courier. Only that morning, Jan Masaryk, the volatile Czech envoy in London, had talked by telephone to his foreign ministry in Prague about the likelihood that Hitler *would* attack. ". . . But if he marches, then everybody else will march, won't they?" Prague had asked him; Masaryk was not so hopeful: "I think after a while they will. But people here won't look me in the eye. They're just an uncouth rabble!" The voice in Prague exclaimed, "No! Impossible!" "They're just stupid people who've got fifteen cruisers," explained Masaryk, "and they're frightened of losing them." He said that he himself was in telephone contact with President Roosevelt and other Americans, and they were doing all they could: but, as for France, "There are quite a few ragamuffins there too."

The tone of these remarks told Hitler volumes about morale in London and Prague. Hitler's illicit knowledge of these – previously unpublished – conversations explains much of his sureness over the next two weeks. The wiretaps showed, significantly, that Chamberlain was keeping Masaryk in the dark and probably even delaying his incoming telegrams from Prague for days on end – knowing that the envoy was feeding secret documents and slush funds to anti-Chamberlain elements in Britain including Winston Churchill. Thus, ironically, Masaryk was obliged to rely even more heavily on the telephone lines to Prague, and these in effect ran across Hitler's desk at the Berghof. The daily FA wiretaps showed the Czech envoy mouthing the most obscene insults about the western statesmen, appealing to Prague for still more cash – urgently – and plotting with Churchill, the Labour Party leader Clement Attlee and his Paris colleague the early overthrow of the Chamberlain and Daladier regimes. It was all evidence of the most useful sort, and Hitler knew how to exploit it.

Now, at 9:50 P.M. on 14 September 1938, Masaryk put through an urgent call to Dr Beneš himself. "Have you heard about Chamberlain?" "No." "He's flying to Berchtesgaden at 8:30 A.M. tomorrow!" The wiretap analysis continued, ". . . After a lengthy pause Beneš exclaimed, obviously horrified, 'It's not possible!'" Masaryk replied that Chamberlain would be accompanied by William Strang – a trusty friend of Czechoslovakia – but also by "that swine" Sir Horace Wilson.

At 12:30 next day Hitler, at the Berghof, got word that Chamberlain's plane had landed at Munich. He nervously conferred with Keitel, who had flown down from Berlin with the OKW's timetable for "Green" – Hitler wanted to be prepared for every eventuality. A thirty-man SS guard of honour formed up on the terraces outside the Berghof towards 5 P.M. Hess sent cars down into the valley to meet Chamberlain's train, and at six the English party arrived. Chamberlain was in the familiar dark suit and stiff wing-collar, with a light-coloured necktie and a watchchain across his waistcoat.

Upstairs in his study Hitler began his usual tirade about the mounting Czech terror campaign. He claimed that 300 Sudeten Germans had been killed already, and threatened that if Britain continued to talk of war he would revoke the naval agreement. But Chamberlain had not come to talk of war – far from it. "If Herr Hitler really wants nothing more than the Sudeten German regions," he said in effect, "then he can have them!" Hitler, taken aback, assured him he had no interest whatever in non-Germans. He told his adjutants afterwards that he had taken quite a liking to the old gentleman. Chamberlain, wearied by his first-ever aeroplane ride, returned to London.

In fact Chamberlain had thrown something of a spanner in the works of "Green". Hitler might not get his little war after all. But the Führer was buoyant as he discussed the conversation that evening with Ribbentrop and Weizsäcker, midst scenes of great glee. Weizsäcker – evidently soon after – wrote this personal record:

> By making no bones about his brutal intention of settling the Czech problem now – even at the risk of a general European war – and by indicating that he would then be content in Europe he [Hitler] had prodded Ch[amberlain] into undertaking to work towards the ceding of the Sudeten regions to Germany.

He, the Führer, had not been able to refuse a plebiscite. If the Czechs reject this the way will be clear for a German invasion; if the Czechs yield, then Czechoslovakia's own turn will not come until later, for instance next spring. There are in fact distinct advantages in disposing of the first – Sudeten German – stage amicably.

In this confidential discussion the Führer did not conceal that he has taken a future war into account, and is fostering much further-reaching plans. For this he volunteered not only nationalist motives, but what might be termed educational ones as well, or ones of latent dynamism.* He radiated self-confidence and fearlessness in war and foreign policy, and spoke quite unambiguously of his own personal responsibility for steering Germany through the inevitable passage of arms with her enemies in his own lifetime.

The Führer then related a number of details of his talk with Chamberlain itself – the little tricks of bluff and bluster with which he had fenced and duelled his conversation partner back into his corner.

In fact Chamberlain and the French proposed to give Hitler all areas with over 50 per cent German population, while Lord Runciman's main proposal was rather less – those areas with over 75 per cent Germans. Not surprisingly, Chamberlain kept this from the Czechs on his return to London. Jan Masaryk was heard frantically telephoning Dr Beneš that "Uncle" had not yet told anybody anything about his Berghof talk with Hitler. The Czech envoy added delicately, "May I ask for money to be sent if I am to do anything? . . . I need just enough, you understand?" Beneš did: "I will put it in hand at once."

Weizsäcker's record leaves no doubt that Hitler had no intention of letting Chamberlain fob him off with just the Sudeten regions: they would do nothing for his grandiose Lebensraum strategy. But he had to tread very cautiously for a while. The "incidents" now multiplying in the border areas must not appear Reich-inspired in any way. When Canaris telephoned the Berghof to ask whether his guerrilla and sabotage units there should start their dirty work, Keitel instructed: "No, not for the time being." Hitler had developed a surer method – a Free Corps, ostensibly raised spontaneously by the aggrieved Sudeten Germans inside the Czech frontier. In fact about ten thousand of Henlein's supporters had fled into Germany over the last week: Hitler ordered the Wehrmacht to equip them with suitable weapons – namely with Austrian-made Männlicher rifles – and with winter coats and headgear and to return the men to Czechoslovakia under cover of darkness. These irregulars would be aided by regular German army and SA officers as advisers, and provided with motor transport by the Party. Hitler disclosed this plan to Karl-Hermann Frank on 16 September in a two-hour conference. The Henlein Free Corps would

* A distinct echo of Heracles again (see page 129). A year later Weizsäcker recalled, "From the Reich Chancellery emanated the slogan that Germany's youth needed a war to steel itself. The war against Czechoslovakia took on the character of *l'art pour l'art* [art for art's sake]."

carry out irregular missions and commando-type sorties into the Czech frontier positions each night. Their aim would be – as Schmundt explicitly telegraphed to the OKW next day – "to protect the Sudeten Germans and keep up the level of disturbances and clashes". Lieutenant-Colonel Friedrich Köchling was provided as OKW liaison officer to the Free Corps. Late on 17 September, Hitler briefed him that this force – a ragged army eventually numbering fifteen thousand men – was to start machine-gunning Czech border posts, attacking patrols and executing general "terrorist" operations. These were desperate methods, but Hitler still aimed at capturing all of Czechoslovakia. As the *Völkischer Beobachter* headlined: THE TIME FOR COMPROMISE IS OVER.

In the summer of 1937, Martin Bormann had observed how his Chief liked strolling down to the tea pavilion, and he decided to perform a feat that would outclass even the Planting of the Lime Tree – he would construct for the Führer a new tea-house to rival any other in the world, as would befit him. In August 1937, Bormann had selected the craggy peak of the 5,500-foot Kehlstein, not far from the Berghof, and personally hammered in the marking pegs together with Fritz Todt. Engineers built a well-paved road most of the way up, and now, by 16 September 1938, the "Eagle's Nest" was finished. At 4 P.M. Hitler, Todt and Bormann drove up to the new eyrie – Bormann proud, but Hitler sceptical. He had known nothing of Bormann's surprise plan until it was too late to revoke; according to Julius Schaub, Hitler blamed it on Bormann's *folie de grandeur*, smiled indulgently and let himself be persuaded that it would serve to impress foreign visitors.

The new road ended some way below the Kehlstein's peak. A parking area had been blasted out of the rockface, into which were set massive bronze doors guarded by sentries and topped with a granite slab reading, "Built 1938". The doors swung open and the car drove on into the mountain along a 170-yard tunnel wide enough for two cars to pass. At the tunnel's end was a circular vault not unlike a church choir: facing them were bronze sliding doors. Bormann invited Hitler into the windowless room beyond the doors – an elevator with walls of polished brass and mirrors and upholstered chairs. They were lifted noiselessly to the very crest of the Kehlstein. As Hitler stepped out, he found himself looking over a view even more majestic than from the Berghof. There was a large, wood-panelled dining-room with a fireplace hewn from reddish-brown Italian marble inscribed with a carved swastika. The whole building was warmed electrically through the stone-paved floor. There was a powerful stand-by generator with a submarine-engine in case the electricity supply failed.

Hitler spent an hour up here. He was in fact silently alarmed by the thumping of his heart at this altitude, and he was short of breath (this he told his doctors). He visited this eyrie twice more over the next few days, bringing Himmler and

Goebbels, Ribbentrop and the British journalist Ward Price. But he was a man of set habits, he did not warm to this artificiality – though he did not want to hurt Bormann by saying so – and he seldom saw it afterwards.

There were now two weeks to go before "Green". Certain sections of the OKW's timetable were already in force. At a dozen training grounds on the periphery of Czechoslovakia carefully-phased manoeuvres were beginning, drifting now towards the border and now away, apparently at random, maintaining the strain on Czech nerves – but with one overriding directive: on X-day eve the manoeuvres must apparently be moving away from the border, until the actual hour for "Green" struck.

Chamberlain had promised to return with his Cabinet's agreement. Meanwhile, Hitler was well informed on developments in London. From the FA wiretaps he knew that Lord Runciman's report of 16 September had recommended pressuring Dr Beneš to cede the Sudeten territories and neutralize what remained of his country.* He also knew that French premier Edouard Daladier and foreign minister Georges Bonnet had arrived in London on the eighteenth to confer on the actual terms to be dictated to Beneš, and that Czech envoy Masaryk was still being left in the dark. At 1:20 P.M. on the nineteenth Masaryk was heard plaintively telephoning Beneš, "The uncles here are in session and haven't breathed a word to anybody yet. Only the person you spoke to yesterday made any great impression here with his views. Chamberlain's secretary told me that today." Beneš referred to the rumours he had heard – to plans involving Hungary and the Carpatho-Ukraine, in his view all quite out of the question. Masaryk confirmed, "They are talking about ceding territories and suchlike, you know." After more discussion Masaryk added vehemently, "I haven't the slightest intention of going over there [to Downing Street]. They haven't sent for me, so what I say is, shit them, Mister President!" During the afternoon the Anglo-French plan was finally communicated to Beneš – but not to Masaryk. It virtually instructed Beneš to surrender: he was to cede to Hitler all areas with more than 50 per cent German population. Beneš told Masaryk the gist of it on the phone at 7 P.M., and asked hopefully what people like Churchill thought. Masaryk responded, "When I asked them, they said they couldn't give us advice, but they hoped we won't take it lying down." He added, "75 per cent would be one thing, but 50 per cent – that's impossible." Beneš sighed, "Frightful!" Masaryk expressed profound contempt for the British statesmen: "They haven't looked at maps or anything!"

* On 16 September 1938 Masaryk phoned Beneš: "That Lord who wrote that crackpot book has shown me a letter he received from the fat field-marshal [Göring]. In his letter Göring says, 'If Czechoslovakia cedes the territories and revokes her treaty with Russia, she'll be left alone.'" Lord Londonderry, author of *Ourselves and Germany*, was probably meant.

For the next two days Prague offically remained silent. Beneš was heard explaining to Masaryk that he was searching for some formula, neither Yes nor No, to enable him to keep honourably negotiating. Masaryk referred contemptuously to Chamberlain's approaching return to Germany: "The old man's packing his bags again, he's in quite a dither." Again he asked for slush funds to be urgently rushed to him in London: "The balloon will soon go up and I'll find myself without a penny."

By early 19 September, Henlein's Free Corps terror squads had begun operations. (The day before, the *Völkischer Beobachter*'s cynical headline read, PRAGUE SYSTEMATICALLY SENDING IN MURDER GANGS.) During the twentieth, reports of shooting outbreaks multiplied. The Czech army was moved closer to the border. Hitler's own generals persuaded him to limit the Free Corps operations therefore to twelve-man commandos or smaller. CZECHS BEGIN MASS FLIGHT INTO INTERIOR, proclaimed the *Münchner Neueste Nachrichten*. The crisis was climaxing well, in Hitler's view.

That day he resumed his wooing of the Hungarians. Horthy – by now again in Germany as Göring's guest on a shoot – had written privately to Hitler in some alarm over the newspaper reports that Beneš was about to cede the German-speaking regions to the Reich, "leaving everything else as it was". Horthy reminded Hitler that there were Hungarian-speaking regions in Czechoslovakia too, and that these also had a right to determine their own future by plebiscite. (The letter is amongst Horthy's papers in Budapest.) Hitler discussed this with Imrédy and Kánya at the Berghof on 20 September. He assured them that Britain and France were not going to declare war; and he added that he hoped that Dr Beneš was not going to agree to the Anglo-French terms dictated to him, as he intended to destroy Czechoslovakia – the only really satisfactory solution.

At 4 P.M. the same day, Hitler and Ribbentrop received Josef Lipski, Poland's ambassador to Berlin. Hitler had wooed Poland since mid-July; Goebbels' aide Berndt had briefed Nazi editors not to report anti-German incidents in Poland, and to suppress "for the time being" all items that might offend her. On 6 September, Hans Fritzsche had repeated the confidential Goebbels directive: "There are to be no reports published on incidents in Poland . . . however much we may regret it." And three days later there had followed this telling explanation: "It is a basic principle of Third Reich foreign policy only to tackle one thing at a time." Now Hitler had the reward for his forbearance: the Polish ambassador coyly confirmed the Warsaw government's predatory interest in Tešin – a primarily Polish-speaking area in northern Czechoslovakia – and assured Hitler that the Poles "would not shrink at all from using force". It was all very satisfactory. Hitler and Ribbentrop drove complacently to Pullach and spent the evening at Bormann's home. By midnight, he knew that Chamberlain would be coming to Bad Godesberg to meet with him on the twenty-second.

That day, 21 September 1938, Winston Churchill had hurried over to Paris to try to influence the French regime. Oddly, in one respect his immediate ambition coincided with the Führer's: both wanted the Czechs to stand and fight. Churchill's other purpose in going to France was – since he knew that the British secret service also wiretapped the international lines – to communicate with Prague without the knowledge of the Chamberlain government: but as the Nazi wiretaps also covered the lines from Paris to Prague, we can piece together the progress of his visit, as indeed could Hitler.

Churchill was still as ignorant of the details of the Anglo-French plan dictated to Beneš as were his intimate friend Jan Masaryk in London and the Czech envoy in Paris. Hitler must have chuckled as he realized this from the wiretaps. At 2 A.M. on 21 September, the British and French envoys in Prague jointly called on Beneš to accept the plan, "before producing a situation for which France and Britain could take no responsibility". Six hours later, Göring's wiretappers found a cryptic conversation going on between unidentified voices in Prague and Paris, where Churchill still was. The Prague end announced that they had been forced to accept the plan in view of the 2 A.M. *démarche* and since both Britain and France had threatened to leave Czechoslovakia in the lurch completely otherwise. There was only one hope, "Prague" continued: "The Paris person" must at once contact Léon Blum, leader of France's biggest party, and try to replace Daladier as premier with Edouard Herriot; and that person must also get Attlee to do the same in Britain – there was no time to be lost. From a further conversation, this time between Beneš and his Paris envoy at 10:30 A.M., it emerged that Churchill was in touch with the envoy – no doubt he was the "person" referred to – and had also reassured Masaryk in London: "The [Chamberlain] government is here today, but gone tomorrow."

On Churchill's return to London – as was clear from the FA wiretaps of 22 September – he, Anthony Eden and the Archbishop of Canterbury besought Masaryk to obtain for them a copy of the plan dictated to Beneš on the nineteenth; it had been given neither to them nor to Masaryk. Beneš was perplexed at this, since he had cabled it to Masaryk already: obviously Masaryk's post was being selectively delayed by the London GPO. No matter – the wiretaps indicated that Churchill was promising him that Chamberlain would be overthrown by that afternoon, that in Paris three ministers had tabled written protests to Daladier, and that "that oaf" Bonnet was on his way out too.* Masaryk's British friends urged Prague to delay any formal decision on

---

* Sir Eric Phipps, British ambassador in Paris, termed the war group there "small, but noisy and corrupt", in his telegram to London on 24 September.

the plan until the twenty-sixth at least. Masaryk's voice was heard adjuring Beneš:

Mr President, one thing is most important: peace and order must be preserved during the Godesberg talks. Everything depends on it. Public support here is growing like wildfire. But we must not let the [Czech] public hold big demonstrations, as otherwise the Germans will say during the Chamberlain visit, "You see, they've disrupted our talks themselves." And that would be Hitler's big chance. That is what Churchill, Eden and the archbishop want you to know.

Now Hitler knew too; and forewarned – for the Führer – was forearmed. On first hearing that Prague was minded to accept, Hitler had instructed his OKW to consider the administrative problem of an unopposed occupation of the German-speaking areas; Keitel brought with him to Godesberg – where Hitler was to meet Chamberlain – the next week's military timetable and a draft list of twenty-five demands that ought to be put to the Czechs (tantamount to the complete surrender of the Czech defences). But now the FA wiretaps decided Hitler differently. It seemed that while feigning acceptance, Beneš was going to play for time in the hope that Chamberlain and Daladier would be overthrown.

Chamberlain arrived at Cologne Airport on 22 September; a band played the British national anthem. He had brought ("that swine") Sir Horace Wilson with him, as before. At the Rhine Hotel Dreesen in Godesberg – scene of Hitler's historic decisions in June 1934 – Chamberlain was honoured by a company of Hitler's own SS Leibstandarte. But these were the only pleasantnesses. After Chamberlain reminded Hitler of their Berghof agreement, and stated the trouble he had had securing his Cabinet's and France's acceptance, Hitler solemnly pronounced: *"Es tut mir furchtbar leid, aber das geht nicht mehr* – I'm exceedingly sorry but that won't do any longer." He mentioned that Hungary and Poland were also concerned about their minorities in Czechoslovakia. And he must now insist on the Wehrmacht being permitted to occupy the German areas immediately; because if there was any delay the Czechs would cheat, leading to further "terrorization" of the Germans there. Chamberlain felt ill: he considered that Hitler had broken his word. After three hours of this, Hitler would still only answer with verbose arguments; so Chamberlain's placid tones tailed off, he reclined on a sofa and announced he had done what he could – his conscience was clear. As neither side would yield, the talks were broken off – perhaps for ever.

As Chamberlain's party returned by ferry to their splendid Hotel Petersberg, Hitler was sure they would come round: in May 1942 he referred to the two-faced British behaviour here – from the FA wiretaps he already knew of their private willingness to make the concessions he needed, but publicly they still dug their heels in. His annoyance was increased by what he regarded as the studied insolence of the British delegation and their sloppy attire, while he and his officials all wore formal dress or uniform. He later rebuked Henderson, "If any more people in tired suits call on me, I'll send my ambassador in London to see your King in a pullover: tell that to your government." (Hitler told Guderian this on 5 November.)

Sure enough, the British made the next move. From the Petersberg next day, 23 September, Chamberlain sent a note to him explaining that British opinion would not tolerate the new German demands. Hitler replied, also by letter, that he mistrusted the Czechs: they were playing for time. Chamberlain replied tersely asking the Führer to set down his proposals in a memorandum ("Hitherto," Sir Horace Wilson explained on the telephone to London, "it has all been words."). The document was handed to Chamberlain on his return to Hitler's hotel that evening at ten. Chamberlain was frosty. Almost at once, at 10:30 P.M., a messenger brought a note to Hitler: "Beneš has just announced general mobilization over Czech radio."

That galvanized the meeting. Again Hitler seemed to have lost the initiative. He stood up and declared that that was that – here was proof of Czechoslovakia's duplicity. Chamberlain also stood up and prepared to leave. This was not what Hitler wanted and he was saved by Ribbentrop, who suggested that as the British had asked for the memorandum they should at least read it. The awkward hiatus was overcome, and they sat down. The document embodied the OKW's demands and some of Henlein's too, and set a sharp deadline – the Czechs were to begin evacuating the German areas at 8 A.M. on the twenty-sixth and complete it by the twenty-eighth. Chamberlain rightly objected that this was just a *Diktat*. Hitler smugly replied, "It isn't. Look – it's headed Memorandum." Under pressure, he did however agree to relax the deadline to 1 October (his secret X-day for "Green"). "You know," he flattered Chamberlain, "you're the only man I've ever made a concession to." (He had used exactly the same words to Schuschnigg at the Berghof in February.) Chamberlain said he would transmit this memorandum to Prague without comment. At 1:15 A.M. the Führer bade him farewell in the hotel foyer. This was his last territorial claim in Europe, he assured him; Chamberlain replied, "Auf Wiedersehen."

Hitler sat in the hotel garden for some time, watching the Rhine swirl past. After a time he turned and thanked Ribbentrop for having intervened earlier: "You saved the day for us."

The origins of Beneš's sudden mobilization were a mystery, but the mists had cleared by the time Hitler's plane landed in Berlin late next afternoon, 24 September. FA wiretaps established that during Chamberlain's absence from London, the Foreign Office had instructed its representative in Prague to advise the Czech president, in unison with the French envoy, that Britain and France could no longer recommend him *not* to mobilize, but that it was hoped this could be done without disturbing "the old gentleman" at Godesberg – meaning Chamberlain. The British envoy had thereupon seen Beneš at 5:30. Evidently there was a war group operating in London, too.

Chamberlain was reporting to his Cabinet. Masaryk was heard sneering on the phone to Beneš, "The Germans made such mincemeat of him that this morning he could barely manage a stutter."* When Masaryk mentioned the rumour that Hitler was demanding that the Czechs should allow the Wehrmacht in at once, Beneš exploded: "Out of the question!" Masaryk agreed. "I'm saying here that we leant over as far as we could, and we're still willing to do everything for peace. But we can't evacuate our defensive positions at all." "That's quite out of the question," confirmed Beneš, "we can't give up our positions." Masaryk then said, "The people here" – and it is clear whom he meant – "are only afraid that we might yield to pressure again." Beneš reassured him, "Everything's absolutely calm at this end. Our mobilization is going ahead perfectly. Everybody's reporting for duty – even the Germans!"

That Beneš was standing firm was quite pleasing to Hitler too: what was not was the way the western powers were moving. France had now emulated Czechoslovakia and begun partial mobilization – Hitler had not bargained for that until X-day itself. Moreover, elements of the British fleet had put to sea, and the Admiralty was refusing to comment on their destination. On 25 September, France, Britain and Czechoslovakia all rejected Hitler's Godesberg "memorandum". As Beneš told Masaryk to make clear, in announcing this in London, the map forwarded by Chamberlain with the memorandum was not only precisely what Hitler had always demanded: "It is far more – it would mean nothing more nor less than the immediate surrender of our whole nation into Hitler's hands." Beneš added, "Show them all, on the map, how our nation is to be destroyed!" But Masaryk replied, "So far they haven't given me the map. It's a shabby trick. And when I spoke to Halifax even he still hadn't got it. He only knows what 'he' [meaning Chamberlain] tells him." Later that evening Masaryk phoned Beneš that he had, as instructed, rejected the memorandum. "Then they sent for me and I had an hour's talk with them. Their ignorance is so huge that you just won't believe it!"

Turning these FA wiretaps over in his hands, with their revelations about the

---

* At 3:30 P.M. Chamberlain told his Inner Cabinet he thought he had "established some degree of personal influence over Herr Hitler"; he felt Hitler would not go back on his word. At 5 P.M. he told the full Cabinet that Hitler was "extremely anxious to secure the friendship of Great Britain . . . it would be a great tragedy if we lost an opportunity of reaching an understanding with Germany." He believed Hitler now trusted him.

anti-Chamberlain machinations of the Czechs and their barely translatable obscenities about diplomats like Horace Wilson, Hitler saw a distinct possibility of driving a wedge into the enemy camp. He instructed Göring to disclose these brown-paper intercepts to Henderson, although they were of such sensitivity that their disclosure was a hanging offence in Germany; and when Sir Horace Wilson arrived in Berlin to see him on 26 September, Hitler mentioned them to him too.

Meanwhile he had already summoned Keitel at 12:15 P.M. and told him that "Green" would start on the thirtieth or any day thereafter. When Wilson put to him Chamberlain's latest proposal for direct German–Czech negotiations, Hitler already knew of it thanks to Masaryk's loquacity on the phone; he dismissed the idea impatiently, it was valueless so long as Prague would not accept the Godesberg terms. He stated that he would give Beneš until Wednesday the twenty-eighth to accept, or he too would mobilize. "Midnight Wednesday?" the British ambassador somewhat ambiguously asked. "No, by 2 P.M.," said Hitler. Thus the formal ultimatum was spoken.

But the pressure on Hitler was steadily increasing. That afternoon the British Foreign Office publicly warned that if a German attack was made on Czechoslovakia, "the immediate result must be that France will be bound to come to her assistance, and Great Britain and Russia will certainly stand by France." Lord Rothermere privately cabled Hitler to think twice before making his scheduled speech at the Berlin Sportpalast that evening. The speech was rowdy and provocative: the Führer repeated that the Sudeten German areas were his last territorial demand in Europe, and he hinted at a guarantee for the rest of Czechoslovakia. He declared that his troops would march into those areas in five days' time, on 1 October. "Our mind is made up. It is up to Herr Beneš now!"

Next morning, Sir Horace Wilson was again ushered in, and repeated the solemn British warning. Perhaps there was something about his formality that unsettled Hitler, but not enough. Shortly after Wilson left, Hitler sent Schmundt to Keitel with written instructions that the initial shock-troops were to move up to a line from which they could attack on or after the thirtieth. He would issue the secret invasion order at noon on X minus One. Later that afternoon the German army mobilized five divisions along the West Wall. He ordered the Free Corps to step up its terrorist activities. And "to put backbone into the Berliners", he had arranged for an armoured division to parade through the city that evening.

Did he still want war? Weizsäcker, who appeared after midnight with a – somewhat outdated – proposal from Henderson, found the Führer sitting alone with Ribbentrop. Hitler curtly announced that he would now wipe out Czechoslovakia. Weizsäcker pointed out some days later, "This was said only in the presence of Ribbentrop and myself, and was not designed for effect on some third party. So it would be incorrect to assume that the Führer was just putting up a huge and monstrous bluff. It was his resentment over 22 May – when the British jeered at him for 'climbing down' – that was propelling him along the path to war." But it is equally possible that Hitler knew from the FA wiretaps that Weizsäcker was conniving with the British diplomats, and the words were intended for their benefit. We still cannot be sure.

In the coming hostilities, Hitler wanted the SS to play an important part. In Berlin he had several talks with Himmler, arranging for two Death's Head battalions to be equipped with anti-tank and field guns to protect an "autonomous Sudeten German government" being set up at Asch, now wholly occupied by Henlein's troops. Heavy fighting had also broken out in the Jauernig enclave south of Breslau, and Henlein, aided by Canaris's underground movement, had seized power there. SS units were massing in Silesia, and Reinhard Heydrich's task-forces were preparing to round up any Communists imprudent enough to remain in the Sudeten areas when the Czechs withdrew.

Control over Henlein's Free Corps would pass to Himmler on the day "Green" began. In these last days of crisis, Hitler not surprisingly found Himmler's company more congenial than that of the army generals who were still questioning his judgement and challenging his strategy. Hitler leant heavily on generals close to the Party like Reichenau for advice – a situation to which Brauchitsch characteristically resigned himself.

Hitler's ultimatum to the Czechs would expire at 2 P.M. on 28 September. By late on the twenty-seventh, Hitler's own C-in-Cs were beginning to have their doubts. Their military attaché in Paris estimated that France could assemble her first sixty-five divisions on the West Wall by the sixth day of mobilization. In an internal conference, Göring grimly conceded that war seemed inevitable and might well last seven years. A month earlier, on 23 August, he had ordered his Second Air Group (*Luftflotte 2*) to prepare to accommodate three or four bomber wings if war should break out with Britain too.

On 22 September, the Group commander, General Hellmuth Felmy, replied that while in theory his organization could accommodate twelve bomber squadrons from 1 October their aircraft were quite unsuited for war with Britain -- they could carry only half a ton of bombs to a range of about 430 miles; they could not reach the British Fleet's bases; and if Belgian and Dutch air space were not to be violated, they could not even reach important targets in southern England. Felmy wrote, "With the means available, we cannot expect to achieve anything more than a disruptive effect. Whether this will lead to an erosion of the British will to fight is something that depends on imponderable and certainly unpredictable factors. . . . A war of annihilation against Britain appears out of the question with the means at hand."

Göring scrawled an angry comment in the margin and sent the document back to Felmy: "I didn't really ask for a study deprecating our current prospects of success and defining our weaknesses – I'm all too aware of them myself. . . ." This was no time for him to learn that his Luftwaffe had been supplied with the wrong aircraft. Early on the twenty-eighth, the naval attaché telephoned the OKW from London that a reliable source had just informed him that King George VI, on whose "vacillation" Hitler had set such store, had signed the Cabinet's order for mobilization. Only the date needed to be inserted.

Hitler had already ordered his C-in-Cs to come to the Chancellery building at noon to settle their differences over the actual hour for "Green" to begin. At 10 A.M., however, Brauchitsch saw Keitel and begged him to prevail on the Führer not to invade more than just the Sudeten areas. He told Canaris that Germany was in no position to fight on two fronts. Canaris told this to Keitel soon after; his appreciation was that war with the west was certain – the French army would attack on land while the British fleet blockaded Germany. Hitler's army adjutant Engel caught sight of General Halder, chief of the General Staff, in a state of nervous collapse, sobbing helplessly. The Gestapo surveys found that public morale was also at low ebb, as their dejected reaction to the display of armour in Berlin's streets the previous afternoon had shown. Worse, by midday Berlin knew that the British fleet had mobilized. Hitler undoubtedly realized now that his blackmail would profit him no more: it was this news of the Royal Navy's mobilization, he frankly admitted to Göring later, that tilted the balance for him. (Göring repeated this to Wiedemann.)

The pendulum had however already begun to swing back from war. Late on the twenty-seventh the French ambassador had handed to Ribbentrop's ministry a new Anglo-French plan on Czechoslovakia. And now, early on the twenty-eighth, he asked to see Hitler to bring even wider proposals from Bonnet, of which even the Czechs were still unaware. An interview was arranged for noon. But the Italians were also stirring: shortly before noon Hitler was in conference with Ribbentrop when Göring arrived with word – which his Forschungsamt may have obtained – that Mussolini had telephoned Bernardo Attolico, Italian ambassador in Berlin, a few minutes before eleven to the effect that Chamberlain had just contacted him; Mussolini wanted the Führer to know that he backed him to the hilt, whether or not he went ahead with mobilization at 2 P.M., but would Hitler be willing to postpone mobilization by twenty-four hours?

A heated discussion broke out in Hitler's Cabinet room. Ribbentrop suggested they postpone a decision until they heard Bonnet's new proposals. Göring violently accused Ribbentrop of actually wanting a war. Hitler tersely silenced them both. He was thinking. At noon Monsieur François-Poncet was shown in: the new Bonnet plan offered Germany occupation of all four sides of the Bohemian quadrilateral including the fortifications – but these would continue to be manned by Czech troops. It was an improvement, but not enough. Almost at once an adjutant handed Hitler a folded note – the Italian ambassador was outside. Hitler excused himself, "I'm wanted on the phone," and went out to receive – offically – the Mussolini message he had already learned unofficially from the FA. After pausing twenty seconds, no doubt for effect, he agreed to postpone the deadline by one day. Attolico rushed away to tell Rome. The British were also stirring – the FA is certain to have intercepted Chamberlain's sensational telephone message to his Berlin embassy at 11:30, anouncing that he was ready to come to Germany again.

Hitler returned to François-Poncet, but almost at once the Italian ambassador was back: Mussolini had telephoned that Chamberlain had a proposal to make and it would be such a "grandiose victory" that there was really no point in warring for more. The full text of Chamberlain's proposals was even at this moment being telephoned through from Rome to the Italian embassy. When the neglected French ambassador now pressed for an answer to the Bonnet plan, Hitler therefore replied: "I can't say 'No' – I just can't say now."

At 12:30 P.M., as François-Poncet was leaving, Henderson arrived with Chamberlain's formal proposal for a Five-Power conference: "I am ready", wrote the elderly British prime minister, "to come to Berlin myself. . . ." When Attolico appeared yet again at the door, Hitler showed him the message. He dictated to Attolico a brief summary of his minimum demands for the ambassador to forward to Mussolini, as Germany's discussion basis for such a conference; he also insisted that Mussolini must in person represent Italy there.

Thus peace seemed assured. Over lunch Dr Goebbels belatedly gave voice to thoughts that had been troubling several of those present, shaming the others into silence: the German people, he commented loudly to Hitler, had been very much against this war – as their reaction to the previous day's parade had shown. Hitler was still eating when Attolico returned at 2:40 P.M. He welcomed the Italian with his mouth still full. Attolico made a brave effort to speak German: "*Morgen 11 Uhr München!*" Berlin would be too far for Mussolini. Hitler laughed out loud. During the afternoon invitations were issued to the other two powers. None declined. Czechoslovakia was not invited.

"Munich 11 A.M. tomorrow!" At 8:50 P.M. that 28 September, Hitler's special train hauled out of Berlin's Anhalt station en route to Munich. By 9:30 A.M. he was awaiting Mussolini's train at the small German frontier station. The Italians arrived punctually, and the Duce entered Hitler's saloon car with Count Ciano; both were in black fascist uniform. Hitler greeted his fellow dictator warmly, and – as the train started back towards Munich – he chortled out loud at the way "we two revolutionaries" were managing to set Europe alternately by the ears.

Keitel sketched in the military situation confidentially to the Duce. Mussolini showed interest in the awesome Czech bunker line, but was less impressed by the German strength in the west. Hitler reassured him – the western powers would not intervene. He had cowed the French a month earlier with a phoney display of Luftwaffe strength; and the very fact that Chamberlain and Daladier were coming to Munich showed that the danger of war in the west was over. Mussolini asked for and was given a coloured map showing the language frontiers within the present Czechoslovakia; it had been hastily prepared by the OKW from a 1912 Brockhaus encyclopedia. Hitler explained about the German-speaking areas that he was demanding: but he was not inclined to accept time-consuming plebiscites in the disputed areas. On the other hand, he did not want one Czech village. Mussolini listened attentively.

The events at the Führer Building in Munich itself, bedecked with the flags of the four powers, were inevitably an anti-climax. Chamberlain's plane had arrived during the morning. Hitler waited for him with Mussolini and Daladier in the smoking-room. His major-domo had prepared sandwiches and beer there. Since he was asking publicly only for the German-speaking areas, and the other three powers were agreeing to this, all that remained was to discuss the modes of transfer; and since the draft agreement that he had handed to Attolico yesterday was now being dished up by Mussolini in Italian as though it were his own, the result was a foregone conclusion. The only snag was Hitler's stubborn demand that the Czechs must evacuate the territories immediately, and Chamberlain's equally obstinate defence of the Czech position. Hitler toyed with a watch throughout the morning – he must have borrowed it for the purpose, as he never wore one – as though to hint that he might even now order mobilization at 2 P.M. Between sessions of this languid and untidy conference the ministers sprawled about the squat Teutonic building, or telephoned their capitals; at one time Daladier and Hitler lounged in a deep sofa swapping anecdotes from the World War trenches; at another time Chamberlain was to be seen regaling him with weekend fishing tales.

At 3 P.M. Hitler retired to his apartment for lunch with Himmler and the Italians. Hitler began to betray frustration about the British. He fumed at Chamberlain's obstinacy: "Daladier -- now there's a lawyer who sees things as they are and draws the proper consequences. You can get on with him easily. But that Chamberlain – he has haggled over every village and petty interest like a market-place stallkeeper, far worse than the Czechs would have been! What has he got to lose in Bohemia? What's it to do with him!" What, indeed, had happened to the insignificant man he remembered with affection from Berchtesgaden and Godesberg. Hitler burst out, "I never have weekends – and I hate fishing!" The taste of victory was turning bitter in his mouth. "It's time Britain stopped playing governess to Europe," he complained. "If she can't drop her guardian act, in the long run war can't be avoided. And I'll fight that war as long as you and I are still young, Duce, because this war will be a gigantic test of strength for our two countries, and it will call for men in the prime of life at the head of their respective governments."

The conference resumed later that afternoon, and was again interrupted for dinner at nine. Again Hitler dined with Mussolini; the other heads of government had declined his invitation, as the telephones were busy with Cabinet consultation. In the small hours of the morning, the Munich Agreement was signed by the four weary leaders. Mussolini rejoined his train at Munich station. As the Duce took leave of Hitler, Göring turned to Count Ciano: "Tell the Duce that tomorrow will see a rearmament begin in Germany, the like of which the world has never seen!"

Before he left next day, Chamberlain asked if he could see Hitler. Hitler waited at his apartment with some curiosity – not to say impatience, because the lift at No. 16 Prinz Regenten Platz wheezed to a halt between floors, with Chamberlain and Hitler's adjutants in it, and it took some minutes to start again.

Chamberlain now asked Hitler for an assurance that – if the Czechs were so vainglorious as to reject the Munich Agreement – the German air force would not bomb civilian targets. Hitler gave it. Then Chamberlain produced a sheet of paper containing a typed declaration in English, and asked if Hitler would sign it – this would considerably ease his position in London. Hitler signed it without noticeable enthusiasm. It concluded,

> ... We regard the agreement signed last night and the Anglo-German Naval Agreement as symbolic of the desire of our two peoples never to go to war with one another again.

After the Englishman had left, Ribbentrop came round to the Führer Building. Hitler discussed the strange episode with him. Walking down the long flight of steps afterwards, Ribbentrop mentioned that he was not sure Hitler had been wise to sign such a document. Spitzy overheard Hitler's muttered response: "Ach, don't take it all so seriously. That piece of paper is of no further significance whatever."

One Step along a Long Path

A few days after Munich, Bormann and Lammers circularized all Party and government officials, strictly forbidding them to visit the Berghof unless invited. "The Berghof is the Führer's private residence and household; he stays there when he wants to work in peace and undisturbed. . . ."

But Hitler was not now at the Berghof. He had left Berlin on 2 October 1938 with Brauchitsch, Milch and Todt, for a flying tour of the newly regained Sudeten lands – he was being cheered by tumultuous crowds in the ancient market-places of Asch and Eger, and standing amidst the lines of now-abandoned Czech fortifications: all this his propaganda machine had won for him. Speaking behind closed doors to his editors Hitler would crow, five weeks later: "This was an undreamt-of triumph – one so huge that to this day it is still barely possible to grasp its significance. Its scale was brought home even to me only at the moment I stood for the first time in the midst of the Czech fortress line: it was only then that I realized what it means to have captured a front line of almost two thousand kilometres of fortifications without having fired a single shot in anger."

In fact it had not been a bloodless victory for Hitler. The Party legions – Henlein's Free Corps – had lost a hundred men in their two hundred or so commando raids. As Hitler drove on from Asch and Eger in a column of three-axled cars packed with SS, Henlein's officials and the Party – with Ribbentrop in his new field-grey diplomatic uniform and all his gold-braided finery – some towns looked as though a full-scale war had hit them: buildings were wrecked, telephone lines were down, there was broken glass everywhere, food queues and mobile food-kitchens. The armed Free Corps irregulars they met "looked tough to say the least – not the kind of people to run into on a dark night", a German army officer noted. In the wake of the Wehrmacht came the Reich economic and industrial experts to supervise the immediate restoration of public utilities and the economy, and their exploitation by Berlin.

Hitler's thoughts were never far from the unconquered bulk of Czecho-slovakia, of which Chamberlain and Munich had, he considered, temporarily cheated him. Prague had been the seat of the first German university; Bohemia and Moravia were in the First Reich. "For a thousand years the provinces of Bohemia and Moravia belonged to the Lebensraum of the German peoples," he was to proclaim – from Prague – five months from now. "Brute force and ignorance tore them arbitrarily from their old historic setting and ultimately created a permanent seat of unrest by locking them into the artificial fabric of Czechoslovakia."

As agreed at Munich, an International Commission had begun meeting in Berlin to decide the new boundaries. But the ill-fitting frontiers of Central Europe gave Hitler headaches for some weeks. The Poles not only occupied Tešin against stern Czech resistance but claimed possession of Moravian Ostrau and the important and largely German-speaking towns of Witkowitz and Oderberg as well. Hitler had to use language to Warsaw that was less cordial than for several years.

But the Poles had at least acted in concert with Nazi Germany, while Admiral Horthy's Hungary had hedged her bets until too late. When she now bestirred herself and raised demands not only on Slovakia but on the whole of the Carpatho-Ukraine (Czechoslovakia's easternmost territory) Hitler refused to listen. His governing ambition that winter was to occupy Bohemia and Moravia, as he admitted to Reichenau early in October. Promoting Slovak independence was one cheap way of bringing about the disintegration of Czechoslovakia (nowadays the word would be "devolution"). Having decided this, Hitler was able to use robust language in rebuffing Hungary's demands on Slovakia. When Kolomán Darányi, the former Hungarian premier, brought him a private letter from Horthy appealing for aid on 14 October, Hitler could only say, in effect, "I told you so." Hewel's note of the meeting reads,

> The Führer recalled how strongly he had warned the Hungarians, both on board ship [in August] and when Imrédy and Kánya visited him at the Obersalzberg [in September]: he had told them specifically that he was planning to settle the Czech problem *so oder so* in October. Poland had seen her chance, struck out and got what she wanted. You can solve such problems by negotiation only if you're determined to fight otherwise. It was only this that gained for him, the Führer, everything that he wanted. But Mr Kánya was stricken by doubts, even though the Führer had *told* him that Britain and France weren't going to fight.

Before Munich, significantly, Hitler had scarcely bothered about Slovakia. As recently as April 1938 he had assured the Hungarian envoy that Bratislava, the Slovak capital, would be Hungary's. He was to admit to Voytěch Tuka, the radical Slovak leader, in February 1939: "I always thought the Slovaks' one desire was to return to Hungary." There is no reason to disbelieve this disarming confession of ignorance. He added that it was not until he met the Hungarian premier Imrédy on 20 September that he realized his error. By mid-October he could tell Darányi, "The Slovak leaders of every political shade have been besieging us for days, clamouring that they don't want to join Hungary."

This was also true. On 25 September there was to be seen at Karinhall, Göring's forest mansion, the Slovak engineer Franz Karmasin – leader of the Carpathian German Party. He was now cast to play the "Henlein" role in Slovakia, where there were useful, tightly-knit communities totalling about 150,000 ethnic Germans. The Slovak government had to regard the Reich as their sole protector against Hungary's exorbitant demands, and it was easy for Karmasin to mediate. He arranged for the Slovak deputy prime minister, Dr Ferdinand Ďurčanský, to see Göring on 12 October. Ďurčanský assured him his people never wanted to join Hungary – only the Jews there opted for Hungary. "Slovaks want complete autonomy with strong political, economic and military dependence on Germany." He assured Göring that Slovakia would ban all Communists and deal with the Jewish problem on similar lines to Germany. Göring afterwards noted for the record, "Slovak aspirations to autonomy are to be suitably supported. A Czecho- without the Slovakia will be thrown even more cruelly on to our mercy. Slovakia will be very important to us as an airfield base for operations to the east [i.e. into Russia]."

The Czechs too turned to Hitler for protection. Beneš fled to the United States and moderates replaced his ministers, anxious to salvage what they could of their independence and to curry Hitler's favour. Hitler dismantled "Green" only reluctantly. When armed Czech Communists caused incidents in the German-language enclaves of Iglau and Brünn on 9 October, Hitler had put his troops on immediate stand-by to occupy the towns if German life and limb were threatened; and he seems briefly to have envisaged even wider operations, for although the Wehrmacht's costly mobilization was just ending he raised with his adjutants the possibility of launching "Green" after all. Keitel's adjutant, Captain Eberhard, recorded the subsequent telephone call thus: "Apparently 'Green' is still not settled! – Schmundt inquires how soon 'Green' could be ready for launching again, and how long for 'Red'?" ("Red" was the build-up against France.)

Czechoslovakia's armed forces were still a matter of concern to the OKW; she could still engage up to twenty-five German divisions. But politically she was not the risk she had once been. On 12 October the Czech envoy, Vojtěch Mastny, assured Göring privately that his country had done a "complete about-turn" – Czechoslovakia would realign her foreign policy on Germany, follow the Reich's lead on dealing with Jews and Communists and provide industrial support to Germany. Göring noted, "They have been deeply disappointed by France, Britain and particularly Russia." When the new Czech foreign minister, František Chvalkovsky, visited Hitler two days later, the Führer put on one of his famous acts nonetheless. The Czech's own notes read, "He [Hitler] did not conceal that he was not to be trifled with, and that the final catastrophe would crash down on our state like a clap of thunder if we ever stepped out of line and returned to our old habits. Twenty-four – eight, snapped his fingers." (Hitler threatened to destroy Czechoslovakia in twenty-four or even eight hours – and snapped his fingers to give accent to his point.) "As for a guarantee, he said, the only guarantee worth anything was a guarantee from him: and he was not going to give one [to Czechoslovakia] so long as he saw no point in it."

Hitler had received Darányi and Chvalkovsky on the same day, 14 October 1938. He had returned that morning from a second heavily-publicized tour of the West Wall, which had begun on the ninth at Saarbrücken. Significantly, work had not slackened on the Wall despite Munich: Todt's target was the completion of four to five hundred new bunkers every week, but rail and road transport was already being withdrawn for harvest purposes.

It was at Saarbrücken that Hitler delivered his first blow at the spirit of Munich, in his speech to West Wall workers on 9 October. His temper had been roused by British politicians' attacks on the agreement and on himself – in particular by Mr Duff Cooper, who had resigned as First Lord of the Admiralty over Munich, and by Churchill. Chamberlain was goaded into announcing major British rearmament. Now at Saarbrücken, Hitler bellowed that he did not intend to drop his guard since, in democracies, statesmen who worked sincerely for peace could always be replaced overnight by warmongers: "It only needs for Mr Duff Cooper or Mr Eden or Mr Churchill to come to power in place of Chamberlain, and you can be quite sure that their aim would be to start a new world war. They make no bones about it, they admit it quite openly."

Coming so soon after Munich, the tone of the Saarbrücken speech was a severe setback for the Chamberlain government. Ribbentrop – who first read it in his newspaper next morning – remonstrated with Hitler, but Hitler was unrepentant: "Britain must learn that she cannot rebuke our new Germany without being given a suitable rejoinder." According to the *Daily Express* (Hitler afterwards learned), Lord Nuffield had declared the Führer was quite right to reply sharply to the Churchill and Duff Cooper attacks. Hitler expressed regret to François-Poncet a week later at ever having signed Chamberlain's "piece of paper". Dealing with the French, he flattered the ambassador, you could always expect an honest Yes or No. "With the English, however, it's different. You give them a paper. There's a storm of discussion, then billions for rearmament and you're no better off than before." What was the point of striving for understanding with Britain – like the Naval Agreement of 1935 – if her only reply was to rearm at a furious rate? As soon as Germany had attained the 35 per cent figure in heavy warships, he said, he was minded to revoke the agreement altogether. It would depend on Britain's state of mind by then. François-Poncet spread the word around the other western ambassadors in Berlin – as Hitler no doubt counted on him to do.

For some time Hitler could undertake no further grand adventures anyway. He could not afford to. Germany was gripped by economic difficulties, largely because of the lavish expenditure on arms and the West Wall.

This had not stopped him ordering an immense new arms effort. He explained to Keitel that Britain was merely playing for time. On reading FA wiretaps that suggested that the British and French ambassadors were doing all they could to sabotage the Munich Agreement at the International Commission in Berlin, Hitler mistrustfully hurried back from his Sudeten tour on 4 October and gave François-Poncet a piece of his mind. The wiretaps established that there were factions both at the British embassy and in London bent on war, while Chamberlain's own integrity seemed above suspicion: he even sent a secret message through Henderson to Hitler on 5 October, asking for some words of comfort in the Führer's speech inaugurating the Winter Relief programme that evening (the FA intercepted Chamberlain's instruction to his embassy).*

At Munich, Hitler deduced that he would be at war with Britain by 1942. Even before leaving Munich, on 30 September, Keitel had telephoned instructions to his chief of arms procurement, Colonel Georg Thomas, to act on this assumption. Ammunition enough could be manufactured when the time came: what Hitler needed to stockpile now were new tanks, guns and aircraft. Keitel laid down guidelines at his first staff conference in Berlin.

Hitler personally ordered Göring to launch a "gigantic Wehrmacht rearmament programme", to put all its predecessors in the shade. Göring of course put his Luftwaffe first: it was to be increased fivefold; the army would get more tanks and heavy artillery, the navy more ships, and the munitions industry more fuels, rubber and explosives. On 14 October, Keitel ordered the three services to submit their new plans to him by early December.

The Luftwaffe's plan was approved by Göring late in October 1938. It emphasized the role of the four-engined Heinkel 177 heavy bomber (which

* Such clandestine messages were not published by the British after the war in their volumes of official documents; there also appears to have been a remarkable one in March 1939: see page 191.

had still not flown). The target was to provide four wings – *Geschwader* – of these by 1942, a total of some five hundred Heinkel 177s.

The navy had carried out planning studies all summer, and now had a cautious plan for completing two more battleships, more submarines and various lesser warships by the end of 1943. Admiral Raeder showed the plan to Hitler on 1 November: Hitler tore it to pieces, scathingly criticizing the puny armament and armour of the two new battleships (*Bismarck* and *Tirpitz*), and lost his temper altogether when Raeder calmly advised him that not only these but most of the German navy's other warships were wholly unsuited to naval war with Britain. No longer did Hitler fob him off with glib assurances that "Britain won't fight". He insisted on the strictest adherence to the naval expansion programme laid down, "as a matter of extreme urgency", and warned that he wanted "certain additional ship types of special value and importance for future war operations" incorporated in the programme. In particular, Hitler now ordered that the U-boat fleet be enlarged rapidly to equality with the British submarine fleet. This was provided for under the 1935 agreement – though Hitler had hitherto kept German U-boat construction plans well below parity. The British, he ordered, were to be so informed.

The outcome of this meeting was the startling Z-Plan, under which the navy would build by the end of 1943 six battleships of 35,000 tons, armed with 420-millimetre guns. The Z-plan would inevitably violate the naval agreement: but by 1943 Hitler would long have revoked it, as it had turned out to be a very one-sided concession indeed.

In the solitude of the Obersalzberg that autumn, Hitler had collected his thoughts after Munich. By 17 October 1938 he had mentally drafted his next steps. That evening – according to Fritz Todt's papers – he telephoned Todt in the Sudetenland and "clearly specified how much work was to have been done [on the West Wall] by three target dates: the end of October, 15 December and 20 March". Todt warned him of problems being caused by inclement weather, truck shortages and the harvest transports. Hitler still insisted. That same evening he asked the retiring French ambassador to visit him as soon as possible, and offered to fetch him by plane.

François-Poncet flew to Berchtesgaden next day, 18 October, and reached the Berghof at 3 P.M. From there he was driven up to meet Hitler and Ribbentrop in a small sideroom of the spectacular mountain-top Kehlstein pavilion. Hitler had always confessed to a soft spot for this Frenchman, whose charm and wit were famous in Berlin. Once François-Poncet had silenced speculation as to the identity of a nude of whom the artist had revealed only the lady's rather demure buttocks, by loudly pronouncing, "*Ah, je crois que c'est*

*Madame de Berlichingen!'"** Hitler now startled him by proposing an immediate pact with France whereby each country would recognize their common frontier. On this occasion, François-Poncet felt, it all rang true. "He spoke of our 'white culture' as a common and costly good that had to be defended," wrote François-Poncet. "He seemed genuinely hurt by the antagonism that persists even after Munich, and in his view Britain's attitude had made this abundantly clear. It is obvious that he is preoccupied with the possibility of a coming crisis and general war." The ambassador probably deduced Hitler's intentions correctly:

> We can be sure that despite all this the Führer is sticking to his intention of driving a wedge between the British and French and stabilizing peace in the west, so as to have a free hand in the east. What plan is he already hatching in his soul? Is it to be Poland, or Russia? Or is it the Baltic states at whose cost these plans are to be realized? Does he even know himself?

Hitler's play-acting and bluffing resumed. Two days later, on 20 October, he set off into the Sudeten territories again. He was to be seen leaving the hotel at Linz with his staff – Colonel Schmundt loudly lamenting that Munich had spoilt their plans for a fight. After Hitler had inspected an abandoned Czech bunker site in the Bohemian forests, the whole party descended on an anonymous village inn for lunch – Hitler surrounded by twenty people elbow-to-elbow at the horseshoe table, while the villagers and kitchen-staff gaped through doors and windows. It was like a medieval painting, except for Hitler's Party tunic, Leeb's uniform and the black rig of the SS. Hitler spoke so loudly that everybody heard him. Leeb jotted in his diary, "Huge excitement amongst the population. Führer ill-disposed towards British." A lieutenant-colonel, Helmuth Groscurth, noted in his report, "There was a hail of attacks on the British, the French and above all the Hungarians – who were dismissed as cowards and skunks." Hitler cruelly mimicked the gestures of the Hungarian ministers who had pleaded for his support on the fourteenth, but loudly praised the Poles: Poland was a great nation, and Lipski a fine ambassador.

At Krumau that day the roads were lined with delegations from the brewery town of Budweis. It had a large German population, but would be left stranded in the rump Czech state by the new frontiers. They were waving placards: BUDWEIS WANTS ITS FÜHRER! – but Hitler had not forgotten them. Next day he caused the OKW to issue a directive to the Wehrmacht to stand by and occupy rump Czechoslovakia if Prague should revert to the policies of Beneš after all.

That day, 21 October, the Kehlstein pavilion witnessed its second remarkable

---

* Probably only those familiar with the crude expletive used by Götz von Berlichingen will appreciate the Frenchman's humour.

scene. Frau Magda Goebbels, the beautiful ash-blonde wife of the propaganda minister, had come alone to pour her heart out to Hitler.

There is no doubt that Hitler valued Goebbels highly – as will shortly be seen. Goebbels had captured Berlin from the Communists in the Twenties; and it was he who had created the "Führer" image, and converted the newspaper and film industries into potent instruments of Nazi policy. Hitler had persuaded him to marry Magda, after she had divorced a rich industrialist. In fact he admitted to Otto Wagener and his own secretaries that *he* was attracted to her, and the marriage was one way of ensuring that he did not lose sight of her. He showed a fatherly interest in their family – according to minister Otto Meissner's wife, Magda told her that her son Helmuth was in fact sired by Hitler during a Baltic vacation in 1934.* By 1938, however, Goebbels was in disgrace: among his enemies were Ribbentrop and Himmler, and the SS chief had apparently furnished to Hitler statements collected by the Gestapo from women who claimed they had been forced against their will to have sexual relations with him. "We used to polemicize against Jewish bosses who sexually coerced their employees," sneered Himmler. "Today it is Dr Goebbels."

What upset Magda now was that Goebbels had fallen for a shapely Czech film actress, Lida Baarova. All Germany relished the titbits of the affair, even untrue ones – like the leading man in her first Goebbels movie *Barcarole* having boxed his ears. Hitler knew of it, and had planned to let the affair burn itself out. Not Magda: she told Hitler now she wanted a separation. At their Kehlstein pavilion talk, Hitler persuaded her to stay her action. Two days later he invited both the Goebbels to the pavilion (Martin Bormann listed the visit in his diary, with an exclamation mark!) and persuaded them to persevere if only for their children's sake. Schaub, his ADC, was assigned the delicate job of telling the starlet that the affair was over. She was given a role in a film in Italy, so friendship with Mussolini had produced one concrete advantage for Hitler. Goebbels privately resolved to do something spectacular to retain Hitler's favour: a pogrom against the Jews, in November.

The German army's reactionary behaviour before Munich was a continued source of bitterness to Hitler. At Saarbrücken he had said, "A hard decision had to be taken. Of course, there were those *weaklings* amongst us who failed to appreciate that fact." (Blomberg had once told Hitler, "In the army, obedience stops from generals upwards.") The army retaliated by scorning Hitler's plans and cold-shouldering his favourites. Fritz Todt later complained to Keitel, "When the Führer came to Saarbrücken, the army arranged the seating for the theatre programme afterwards. When the Führer stepped into his box

* Helmuth Goebbels' blood-group did match Hitler's. Until such time as the other candidates for Hitler's paternity will reveal their blood-group, there is no reason to accept their claims.

and looked right-and-left into the rows of saluting people he saw me in the back row of the dress circle, where I had been relegated. Thereupon the Führer sent an adjutant and invited me to come and sit near him."

That the army's hostility should continue even after the triumph of Munich infuriated Hitler, and he decided to act. In mid-October, Keitel's staff drafted a remarkable document designed to bring the Führer's views to the attention of all officers:

> The prerequisite for a state's political and military victory is obedience, loyalty and trust in its leadership. As every officer knows, any body of soldiers without these is useless. Indifference or half-hearted obedience are not good enough. They will not fire enthusiasm or inspire sacrifice and the dedication needed to conquer each successive task. It has always been Germany's lot to fight against unequal odds. Where we have been successful, then abstract forces were at work far more powerfully than any numerical or material superiority over the enemy.
>
> It would be a remarkable thing if an officer's only duty were to weigh his own numerical strength against that of the enemy, while ignoring or under-rating all those other factors that have always decided between defeat and victory in the past.

In an obvious reference to Beck's arguments, the document continued,

> It is unsoldierly and a symptom of poor military upbringing not to credit oneself with what one expects from the enemy as a matter of course, or to minimize one's own strength while inflating that of the enemy. To put the military factors in their proper perspective when deciding the political objective is a task for the statesman alone. Were he to wait until his armed forces were completely ready for war, then he would never act because armed forces are never ready – nor are they ever to be considered ready. I well know that in the past months the broad mass of officers has done its duty in exemplary manner with steadfast confidence in the government, and in a spirit of defiant belief and determination. But I expect this fact and its confirmation by our triumph [i.e. Munich] to be accepted once and for all by my officers, and it is to be adequately emphasized in the training and preparation of new officers.

It was in this mood that Hitler summoned Brauchitsch as C-in-C of the army to Berchtesgaden on 24 October. The frosty interview began at 12:30 P.M. in the Great Hall of the Berghof, and continued after lunch until six up at the Kehlstein pavilion. It culminated in Hitler's demand for the retirement of scores of unreliable senior army officers. Keitel took a detailed note; it has not survived, but the tenor of the interview can be judged from the diary of his adjutant Wolf Eberhard:

> Apropos of the Führer's talk with C-in-C, army, in presence of Chief, OKW, as recorded in Keitel's note. In general: Führer was brutally frank about his

contempt for the military commanders: they need rapid reorganization urgently, show complete lack of confidence in the political leadership and apprehensions about their own weakness. Enemy's strength is exaggerated. A last appeal to the C-in-C, army, to get to grips with his job and act without delay. His historic mission!

Eberhard privately commented, "Let's hope this is the last time that the Führer has to use such language to his soldiers. . . . It is a pity it had to come to this, but in my view an absolutely logical trend in the intellectual attitude of the army, which was accentuated by their Reichswehr upbringing, has thus been brought to an end." (Eberhard himself was a Luftwaffe officer.)

Thus at the Kehlstein pavilion Brauchitsch was given "one last chance" and took it. After laying down a number of technical measures to increase the army's fighting strength Hitler instructed him to retire a number of leading army opponents of his policies. The final list was thrashed out between Brauchitsch and Göring on 28 October and taken by Göring to Hitler two days later. Among those marked with the black spot were these generals: Curt Liebmann and Wilhelm Adam, Hermann Geyer and Wilhelm Ulex – and of course Rundstedt and Beck. On 1 November, Hitler announced this upheaval in the army, and – perhaps tactlessly – coupled it with a wave of promotions in the Luftwaffe.

Early in November 1938, Hitler's uncritical loyalty to his own Party henchmen was put to its most severe test – by the aftermath of an assassination in Paris, committed by a deranged young Polish Jew.

It was symptomatic of racial troubles that had been festering in Central Europe for many decades. Anti-Semitism had plagued these countries for a long time. As a dynamic force in national politics it could not be ignored. In Czechoslovakia, for instance, there were 259,000 Jews, unevenly distributed across the country, and Hitler asked Ribbentrop to investigate whether the 27,000 Jewish settlers in Vienna of Czech origin could be repatriated to Czechoslovakia too. The new Prague regime, aware of its precarious position, steered a gingerly course, anxious to toady to its powerful neighbour: President Emil Hacha, the venerable lawyer who had succeeded Beneš after his flight to America, agreed to retire Jewish officers, to permit the sale of gauleiter Julius Streicher's crude anti-Jewish tabloid *Der Stürmer*, and to oblige Jewish industrialists to resign. The influx of Jewish refugees from the Sudeten territories – where about seven thousand had resided – resulted in fresh anti-Semitism, particularly amongst Czech academics, who publicly demanded the removal of these "immigrants" and other less euphonious epithets. Prague eventually persuaded the British government to lend ten million pounds to finance the further emigration of these hapless people. In Bohemia and Moravia there were about

99,000 Jews; in Slovakia 87,000 and in the tiny Carpatho-Ukraine no fewer than 66,000 – or 12 per cent – most of whom favoured annexation by Hungary, a view which did not endear them to the Slovaks. Slovakia eagerly enacted the anti-Jewish decrees demanded by the Reich: a *numerus clausus* restricted the Jewish intake into schools, Jewish businesses were boycotted, property was confiscated and a wave of deportations began. Those deported were the lucky ones, for no country outside Germany was to apply the grisly Final Solution as enthusiastically as Slovakia when the methodical liquidation programme began in 1942.

Today, after the Holocaust, it is seldom recalled how anti-Semitic the Europe of 1938 tended to be. When Ribbentrop journeyed to Paris with much pomp in December to sign the joint declaration first suggested by Hitler to François-Poncet, Bonnet begged him not to flood France with more German Jews as they already had enough of their own. ("In fact," Ribbentrop informed Hitler, "they are considering Madagascar for this purpose.")

Poland's attitude was hardly more sympathetic. Hitler had confided to ambassador Josef Lipski on 20 September that he was toying with the idea of solving the Jewish problem in unison with Poland, Hungary and perhaps Romania too by emigration "to the colonies". "I replied", Lipski recorded that day, "that we would erect a fine statue to him in Warsaw if he found a Solution." After Hitler's occupation of Austria the Polish government had feared Hitler would repatriate the thousands of Polish Jews from Vienna, and a Law of Expatriation had been enacted in March to deprive these Jews of their Polish citizenship. Munich had now panicked the Polish government into ruling that as from 31 October no expatriate Poles would be allowed back into their country without a special entry visa. The last days of October thus saw frenzied scenes on the frontier: while Polish frontier officials slept, unscheduled trains loaded with Jews under Gestapo guard were quietly shunted across the line and dumped back into Poland. From Hanover alone, 484 Polish Jews were "repatriated" in this demeaning manner.

Among these 484 were the parents and sisters of a Jewish youth of seventeen then living in Paris, Herschel Grynszpan. He had left Germany for France when his residence permit expired in 1937; in August 1938 the Paris authorities had served a deportation order on him, since when he had lived there illegally – an underfed, unemployed and poorly-educated drifter. On 3 November, as Hitler was subsequently told, Grynszpan received a postcard from his sister briefly describing the family's "repatriation" to Poland. He swore revenge – and he decided to murder the German ambassador in Paris, Count von Welczek. Welczek had not been available, so on 7 November Grynszpan allegedly shot Counsellor Ernst vom Rath instead.

At first the incident did not provoke Hitler. He rushed his own surgeon, Dr

Karl Brandt, to Paris to try to save Rath's life; but he made no mention at all of it in his speeches of the next few days.

Hitler was in Munich now for the annual celebration of the Party's 1923 putsch attempt. His speech in the Bürgerbräu beerhall to the Old Guard on 8 November was just a routine compound of warnings against the evil men lurking in Britain and France waiting to do war, and of veiled jeers at his own feeble-hearted generals. On the following day, the March on the Feldherrnhalle was solemnly re-enacted at noon. This time Keitel, Raeder, Brauchitsch and Milch marched at the Führer's side. Wreaths were laid in the temples of honour (where Hitler had decreed that his own body was one day to be laid to rest); and then with splendid ceremony the parade marched to Königlicher Platz and disbanded. After lunch the generals secured private audiences of Hitler in his apartment – there were problems of the SA regiment "Feldherrnhalle", of weapons-training for the Labour Service and of personnel to be attended to.

A word here about Hitler's private Munich home. In May 1920 he had rented a tiny two-room flat in Thiersch Strasse, not far from the *Völkischer Beobachter*'s printing works. But the living-room was too small for his bulging library, so in September 1929 he had rented this gloomy second-floor apartment in a large patrician building on the corner of Prinz Regenten Platz; and over the next years he had gradually enlarged his foothold in the house until it all belonged to him. But he left most of the other apartments in private tenancy. His own Kriminalpolizei guard was in the left-hand ground-floor flat, and his adjutants were on the floor below his; in 1935 he had knocked both second-floor flats into one for himself, as he preferred spacious, lofty rooms. The flat mirrored Hitler as he had been in his years of struggle – and it had an air of mystery: there was a permanently locked room at one end in which Geli Raubal had shot herself in 1931. Hitler's friend and architect Troost had furnished the flat. The furniture was severe and monumental, with tall standard lamps and a dull red carpet. The walls were hung with a few costly paintings by Grützner, Waldmüller and Spitzweg – purchased with the royalties from *Mein Kampf* – and in his study there was an Albrecht Dürer engraving of "The Knight, Death and the Devil" which was a constant source of strength to him. Between the paintings were a few framed prints of Palladian-style architecture.

Goebbels was here with Hitler that evening, 9 November 1938, when word arrived that Counsellor vom Rath had died in Paris. According to Goebbels, he told Hitler there had been anti-Jewish demonstrations in two provinces; Jewish shops had been smashed up and synagogues set on fire; Hitler ruled, said Goebbels, that the Party was not to organize such demonstrations – but nor was it to quell them if they occurred spontaneously. (We have only Goebbels' word for this, spoken to a subsequent Party inquiry.) Goebbels then left Hitler, as he had to speak to an assembly of Party nobility in Munich's old city hall.

It was here that Goebbels did his mischief, believing he would thereby regain the Führer's favour. This is quite clear from the testimony of Ribbentrop – who was present – and Julius Streicher, who had it at first hand from SA General Hanns-Günther von Obernitz, and from the report of the Party Court to Göring in February 1939. Goebbels referred to the demonstrations, and instructed his listeners that further such demonstrations were to be organized forthwith, although the Nazi Party must on no account appear responsible. By the time these surreptitious orders had been disseminated by telephone to propaganda ministry offices, Gau headquarters and the local SA, SS and Party units the message was that the whole of Jewry was to blame for vom Rath's murder. The action report of the leader of SA Group *Nordmark* is eloquent about this chain of command:

> At about 10 P.M. on 9 November the need for the operation was put to a number of gauleiters assembled in the Munich Hotel Schottenhammel by an anonymous member of the Nazi Party's Reich directorate. I thereupon volunteered the services of my SA Group *Nordmark* to the Gauleiter [of Schleswig-Holstein], Hinrich Lohse. About 10:30 P.M. he telephoned his chief of staff in Kiel, "A Jew has fired a shot. A German diplomat is dead. There are in Friedrichstadt, Kiel and Lübeck wholly superfluous places of congregation; and these people are still trading in shops in our midst. We don't need either the one or the other. There's to be no plundering. There's to be no manhandling either. Foreign Jews are not to be molested. If there's any resistance, use your firearms. The whole operation is to be in plain clothes, and is to be over by 5 A.M."

Human nature in its ugliest form had done the rest, and Western Europe witnessed that night the first anti-Jewish pogrom since the Middle Ages. Throughout Germany and Austria an orgy of burning and destruction, of murder and rape, began.

Hitler meanwhile had been preparing to leave his apartment towards midnight for the spectacular SS swearing-in ceremony. Himmler was with him. Himmler's personal chief of staff, Karl Wolff, arrived with an indignant message from Heydrich at the Hotel Vier Jahreszeiten: the local Gestapo HQ had just telephoned that Goebbels' district offices everywhere were whipping-up anti-Jewish demonstrations and ordering the police not to intervene. Himmler turned to Hitler for guidance. Hitler replied that the Gestapo were to protect Jewish property and lives, and that SS units were not to be called in unless things got out of hand. It was clear to Himmler that the whole affair had come out of the blue to Hitler. After the midnight ceremony, Himmler went off on four weeks' leave; the Führer returned to Prinz Regenten Platz, to his apartment.

After 1 A.M., one of Hitler's Wehrmacht adjutants came upstairs to tell him that the Hotel Vier Jahreszeiten had just telephoned asking the adjutants to come and retrieve their baggage, as the synagogue next door was on fire and the hotel might have to be evacuated. Julius Schaub – Hitler's personal ADC – wrote a graphic account of this night of horror. Telephone calls began coming from private citizens reporting fresh outbreaks of fire, and Jewish businesses being looted all over Munich. Hitler angrily sent for SS General Friedrich Karl von Eberstein, the city's police chief, and told him to restore order at once. He telephoned Goebbels and furiously demanded: "What's the game?" He sent out Schaub and other members of his staff to stop the looting and arson. He ordered special protection for the famous antique dealers, Bernheimer's. At 2:56 A.M. a telex was issued by Rudolf Hess's staff as Deputy of the Führer – and was repeated to all gauleiters as Party Ordinance No. 174 – forbidding all such demonstrations: "On express orders issued at the highest level of all there is to be no arson or the like, whatever, under any circumstances, against Jewish businesses." The Gestapo followed suit – thus at 3:45 A.M. the Berlin Gestapo repeated this prohibition. Goebbels, now in no doubt where Hitler's real favour lay, also spent the night on the telephone trying to extinguish the conflagration that his mischievous tongue had ignited.

But the damage had been done, and Ribbentrop left Hitler in no doubt of this.* The German ambassador in London, Herbert von Dirksen, reported a volcano of indignation in Britain – partly genuine but partly, he said, whipped up by the anti-German and Jewish immigrant circles there. Göring, who had been puzzled to see fires reflected from the clouds near Halle as his train steamed back from Munich to Berlin, was speechless with rage and protested to Hitler that German insurance firms would now have to pay the Jews compensation, and that the cost in foreign currency would be huge as the broken glass would have to be replaced with imports from abroad.

Hitler made the best of a bad business, and refused to discipline Goebbels as even the Reichsführer SS, Himmler, demanded – furious that Goebbels had made free with local SS units. Nor, except in the most savage instances, were the humble Party members who had actually committed the outrages brought to book, although ninety-one Jews had been murdered that night. They claimed in the subsequent legal actions that they genuinely believed they were acting in the Führer's favour. Goebbels successfully argued, over lunch with Hitler, that the pogrom had shown international Jewry that the Reich was not

---

* In Ribbentrop's files is a self-congratulatory account of a hostile Berlin press conference addressed by Goebbels at 2:30 P.M. on the eleventh: the frosty reception panicked him into leaving prematurely after repeatedly contradicting himself and betraying a complete lack of inner conviction. The press representatives there privately lauded Ribbentrop for having "stayed aloof from the anti-Jewish demonstrations", and for the moderate tone of his messages after the murder of Counsellor vom Rath.

to be trifled with – that Germans abroad were not fair game for Jewish assassins.

Thus – as on 30 June 1934 – Hitler *post facto* endorsed the excesses of his henchmen. When Göring sent him a sharp letter of protest, Hitler replied that he should drop the matter; but as a sop to him, he appointed Göring to co-ordinate all further moves in the Jewish problem. A collective fine of one billion marks was imposed on the Jewish community for the murder, and the compensation due to them from insurance was effectively confiscated by the Reich. Hitler made no attempt to dissociate himself from Goebbels – indeed he was seen and photographed with him frequently over the next days. Hitler admonished Göring, "You must be more careful. People might get to know of your sympathy for the Jews!"

How can we explain Hitler's tolerance of Goebbels in November 1938? In Hitler's eyes Goebbels was one of the champions of Munich. In a long and astounding secret speech to 400 Nazi editors in Munich on 10 November 1938, he cynically explained to them just how much he owed to psychological warfare. His audience rocked with laughter at his penetrating mimicry of his opponents at Munich. When this cabaret act was over, Hitler moved from table to table to meet the editors in person.

At one table he spoke out loud of his admiration for Ribbentrop – the other champion of Munich. "Even Bismarck had to battle against bureaucracy," he said. "Today's National Socialist government is still stifled by red-tape. It is at its worst in the foreign ministry. Diplomats do not represent their own countries, but an international Society clique. This malady in our foreign ministry can't be rooted out overnight. It will take ten or fifteen years until a new generation of National Socialist-trained diplomats is ready. So far, the first and indeed the only diplomat to do the Third Reich proud overseas has been Ribbentrop. He is the ideal image of what I, as Führer, think a diplomat should be. In these last few months he has shown he has energy, toughness, courage and nerve. In this way he has helped the German public find its feet during the Czech crisis. Ribbentrop", Hitler concluded, "is a new style-diplomat."

With the FA wiretaps of the Beneš telephone conversations still vividly in his memory, Hitler commented: "There's one other good representative of his own country, and that's Jan Masaryk in London. He also put up a brave fight for his country."

His innermost thoughts still revolved around Bohemia and Moravia. Occasionally, these thoughts bubbled like marsh-gas to the surface. Over dinner in Nuremberg on 14 November with a dozen local Party officers, the talk turned to the immense Congress Hall being erected nearby – half as big again as the Colosseum in Rome. Hitler said he needed large slabs of granite, unob-

Nationalſozialiſtiſche 🦅 **Deutſche Arbeiterpartei**

Der Stellvertreter des Führers   München 33,   10.November 1938.
Stab   Braunes Haus

An alle Gauleitungen zur sofortigen Veranlassung:

A n o r d n u n g Nr. 174/38.

(Wiederholung des Fernschreibens vom 10.Nov.1938)

Auf ausdrücklichen Befehl allerhöchster Stelle dürfen Brand-
legungen an jüdischen Geschäften oder dergleichen auf gar
keinen Fall und unter gar keinen Umständen erfolgen.

I.A.

[signature]
(Opdenhoff)

Verteiler:
Gauleiter.

"On express orders issued at the highest level of all there is to be no arson or the like, whatever, under any circumstances, against Jewish businesses." (Party Ordinance No. 174) tainable in Germany. Somebody remarked that the richest quarries were in rump Czecho-Slovakia (now hyphenated, as its provinces fell apart). Hitler chuckled, and commented knowingly: "One more reason! . . ." Two days later Hitler – temporarily residing in Goebbels' villa at Schwanenwerder, while the Chancellery was uninhabitable because of Speer's rebuilding – called Keitel and Brauchitsch for a secret discussion on the continuing problems of Poland, Hungary and the Carpatho-Ukraine. Brauchitsch brought his Intelligence chief, Tippelskirch, to report on Prague's residual military strength: as Hitler said, small and insignificant though Czecho-Slovakia might seem she was still a power factor to be taken into account.

Over their next moves Hitler differed from Ribbentrop's advisers. Weizsäcker definitely advised the foreign minister early in December 1938 to divert Hitler's attention from the south-east to the north-east – let the Reich first acquire Memel and Danzig, and a broad and permanent land-strip across the "Polish Corridor" to East Prussia. Poland, argued Weizsäcker, enjoyed little or no international sympathy at present. Hitler could shrink Poland to a manageable size, and no other country would lift a finger to assist her. Ribbentrop was non-committal, as he did not know Hitler's inner intentions. He allowed his officials to draw up a draft treaty which would bring Czecho-Slovakia under the Reich's economic control without any need for militarily occupying this troublesome area. The document never left the foreign ministry. In Weizsäcker's hearing, Hitler said: "In the spring we are going to take the revenge on the Czechs that we were cheated of last time."

Not that Hitler was planning to seize this rump by war, as he made quite plain during yet another tour of the Czech frontier fortifications early in December 1938. Once again after lunch in a village inn, with forty Luftwaffe and army generals listening, he loudly discoursed on his intention of bringing Bohemia and Moravia into the Reich – but by political processes short of war. He was referring obviously to the subversive labours of his agents in Slovakia. Ten days later, on 17 December, Keitel confirmed Hitler's instructions to the Wehrmacht to prepare unobtrusively for a virtually unopposed occupation of rump Czechoslovakia when the time came.

This instruction was all that remained constant until the spring of 1939. Hitler was manifestly undecided over his next step after that. Could he hold off the western powers by diplomacy and the West Wall long enough, or would he have to deal with them before marching east? On 24 October, at the Kehlstein pavilion, he had again intimated to Ribbentrop that war with the western democracies seemed inevitable within four or five years. In mid-November an English source reported that Chamberlain had just secretly explained to Opposition MPs that the real reason for his Munich "capitulation" was to win three more years for Britain to rearm enough to defeat Germany. Another British source found out that the government and Royal family had plans to emigrate to Canada if necessary, to defend the empire from there.

At Goebbels' villa, Schwanenwerder, Hitler had conjured further with the probability of war in secret talks with Keitel and Brauchitsch on 16 November. His western plans – to which he assigned as yet no code-name – would depend on signing a military alliance with Mussolini. Germany and Italy would then each tackle the western democracies in a different theatre – Italy's being the Mediterranean and North Africa. Hitler would take on France first, by a south-westerly thrust between the Moselle and Rhine. The defeat of France would deny Britain a strategic foothold on the European mainland. Swiss, Belgian and Dutch neutrality would, said Hitler, be respected. He was unimpressed by France's fortifications. "It is quite possible to penetrate her Maginot Line. We have proved that with our firing trials against the Czech fortifications, which were built in the same way as the Maginot Line."

While Hitler's predatory interest was focused on Czechoslovakia, other affairs of state had gone by the board. Many weeks had passed since Dr Lammers had obtained an audience to discuss them with him. At the end of October, Hitler loosely talked of plans for a Cabinet meeting in December, only to abandon the idea and order Göring to convene and speak to the otherwise dormant "Reich Defence Council" instead. Göring did so, for three hours, on 18 November 1938: every Reich minister and state-secretary was present, as were Brauchitsch, Raeder, the service chiefs of staff, Bormann and Heydrich too. There was little new he told them, and much that he withheld. He announced that Hitler had decided to triple the Reich's armaments, but that the events of that summer had placed an intolerable burden on the Reich's economy – in short they were almost bankrupt. Foodstuffs must, for a time, come before armaments – i.e. butter before guns. He added, "The Führer's great architectural projects will still be worked on, as they are of moral and psychological value." Apart from these, however, there would be a strict reduction in building work. The only thing that would tide the Reich budget over this immediate crisis was, ironically, the billion-Reichsmark fine levied on the Jewish community, explained Göring.

In private, as Helmuth Groscurth's diary shows, Reinhard Heydrich referred to the November anti-Jewish pogrom as "the worst setback for the State and the Party since 1934". In their beaver-like work to enforce the Reich's emigration policies on the Jewish community, the SS had hitherto tried hard to keep a low profile, and to avoid any kind of spectacular outrage to international opinion. Göring found himself thus on the side of the SS, in alliance against the radical Goebbels, and on 24 January he formally instructed the Ministry of the

Interior to set up a Central Emigration Office under Heydrich to regulate and organize the deportation of the Jews.

Hitler's personal part in this anti-Jewish programme was one of passive observation. Talking with Colonel Jósef Beck, the Polish foreign minister, on 5 January he rather speciously regretted that the western powers had not entertained Germany's colonial demands: "If they had, I might have helped solve the Jewish problem by making a territory available in Africa for resettlement of not only the German but the Polish Jews as well." On the twenty-first, he uttered to the Czech foreign minister Chvalkovsky these ominous words: "The Jews here are going to be destroyed." The Czech replied sympathetically, and Hitler continued: "Help can only come from the others, like Britain and the United States, who have unlimited areas that they could make available for the Jews." And in a major speech to the Reichstag on 30 January 1939, Hitler uttered an unmistakable threat to any Jews who did choose to remain behind in his Germany:

> I have very often been a prophet in my lifetime and I have usually been laughed at for it. During my struggle for power, it was primarily the Jewish people who just laughed when they heard me prophesy that one day I would become head of state and thereby assume the leadership of the entire people, and that I would then among other things subject the Jewish problem to a solution. I expect that the howls of laughter that rose then from the throats of German Jewry have by now died to a croak.
>
> Today I'm going to turn prophet yet again: if international finance Jewry inside and outside Europe should succeed once more in plunging our peoples into a world war, then the outcome will not be a Bolshevization of the world and therewith the victory of Jewry, but the destruction of the Jewish race in Europe!

When the Nazi national newspaper, the *Völkischer Beobachter*, hit the news-stands next morning, the main headline blazoned:

ONE OF ADOLF HITLER'S GREATEST SPEECHES
PROPHETIC WARNING TO JEWRY

Encouraged by these ugly means, the mass exodus grew throughout 1939: 78,000 German and Austrian Jews (compared with 40,000 in 1938) left during 1939, and 38,000 Czech Jews too. With the outbreak of war the exodus still briefly continued, to stop only in October 1940, by which time Heydrich had successfully evicted about two-thirds of the Jews from the Reich – about 300,000 from Germany, 130,000 from Austria, 30,000 from Bohemia/Moravia; some 70,000 of them reached Palestine, through the unholy alliance of aims that had briefly existed between Heydrich's SD and the Zionists. By that time Europe was enmeshed in Hitler's War. Many times thereafter he recalled his veiled words of prophecy to the Reichstag. On 8

November 1942 he reminded his Nazi Party faithfuls in a Munich speech, "People always used to laugh at me as a prophet. Of those who laughed then, countless already laugh no longer; and those who are still laughing even now probably won't laugh much longer either."

Hitler avoided the Chancellery area in Berlin for many weeks, because it teemed with Speer's construction workers. He dealt with affairs of state by telephone, usually from the Berghof. Lammers and Meissner implored him to attend to at least the more pressing matters, like confirming death sentences on gangsters. (Hitler had a constitutional duty to consider each appeal for clemency and sign the execution warrant.) In bygone times the condemned criminal had had the traditional right to see the Kaiser's signature on the warrant before being led to the scaffold. In Hitler's era, the usages were less picturesque. A telephone call went from Schaub to Lammers in Berlin: "The Führer has turned down the appeal for clemency" – this sufficed to rubberstamp a facsimile of the Führer's signature on the execution warrant. On one occasion the file laid before Hitler stated simply that the Berlin Chancellery would "take the necessary steps" if they had heard no decision from him by 10 P.M. that night. Human life was becoming cheaper in the New Germany. When it was at its cheapest, at the time of Stalingrad, Walther Hewel was to explain to an OKW staff officer, "If you want to understand the way the Führer's mind works, you must look upon the human race as being just a swarm of ants."

However, the problem of inflation faced Hitler all that winter, and obviously shackled his ambitions. Blomberg later stated under interrogation that when he left Germany in January 1938, there had been no restriction on living standards; but now that he had returned from his year's enforced exile in January 1939 he detected a great deterioration, since rearmament had swallowed the foreign currency previously used to import fats and foodstuffs. It was no coincidence that price inflation had begun in May 1938, although the OKW tried to put the blame elsewhere. Dr Hjalmar Schacht, president of the Reichsbank, was openly hostile to Hitler's inflationary policies and saw no way out. By the end of 1938, 8,223 million Reichsmarks were in circulation compared with 5,278 million in March and 3,560 million in 1933. On 7 January 1939, Schacht and seven fellow directors of the Reichsbank signed a stern warning to Hitler about the inflationary pressure resulting from recent "foreign operations": the current tax-burden would not support the "unrestricted public hand-out of funds". Hitler was shocked by this semi-mutiny. In a secret speech to his colonels in February he warned: "There is to be no possibility whatever that anybody at all can even think that there is some institution or other in Germany that has a different opinion from the one expressed by the Führer."

Schacht probably hoped to prove, with his document, that his expert advice was indispensable to Hitler. But he did not. Hitler already suspected Schacht – correctly – of maintaining clandestine contacts with foreign governments.* He summed Schacht to the Chancellery on 19 January, lectured him on the notable lack of sympathy for the Party at the Reichsbank and handed him a document drafted by Lammers announcing his dismissal. The economics minister, Walter Funk, a flabby homosexual, was appointed Schacht's successor. On the same day Hitler also disposed of his personal adjutant, Fritz Wiedemann, whom he suspected of purveying state secrets to the foreign press and – as papers captured in Vienna had proved – to the agents of the Schuschnigg regime. Their final interview was brief and cruelly to the point. "You always wanted to be consul-general in San Francisco," Hitler reminded Wiedemann. "You've got your wish."

It was at about this time that Keitel sent to Franz Halder, chief of the General Staff, a small note that the army would have until 1943 to complete its expansion, and that there would be no mobilizations before then. On OKW advice, Hitler decided to halt all army weapons production during 1939, to enable the Luftwaffe and naval construction programmes to go ahead. This would bring all three services to the same level by about 1944. In a navy-Luftwaffe conference on 24 November, Jeschonnek had outlined Göring's 1942-target Luftwaffe as comprising sixteen fighter wings and fifty-eight bomber wings, primarily operating Heinkel 177s and Junkers 88s (of which thirteen wings would be specializing in naval air war and minelaying).

On 17 January 1939, Admiral Raeder brought the final draft of the navy's Z-Plan to Hitler at the Chancellery. Ten days later Hitler issued a remarkable Führer Order, assigning to this naval expansion programme absolute priority over both other services. Even more remarkably, the air-minded Göring gave it unqualified support as head of the Four Year Plan. Hitler again assured Admiral Raeder he would not be needing the German navy for several years.

But what would even the finest weapons avail Germany if the arms-bearers, the generals, were loath to use them? "The brave will fight whatever the odds," Hitler said on 18 January. "But give the craven whatever weapons you will, they will always find reason enough to lay them down!" This was the damage, Hitler felt, that Beck and his General Staff had inflicted on the officer corps.

* Montagu Norman, governor of the Bank of England 1920–44, told the US ambassador in London that Schacht was his constant informer over sixteen years about Germany's precarious financial position (US ambassador Joseph Kennedy reported this to Washington on 27 February 1939). In 1945, Norman tried to intercede for Schacht at Nuremberg through a fellow freemason on the British prosecuting team, Harry Phillimore (Schacht was also a freemason). The US team flatly rejected Phillimore's advances, but the British judge, Birkett, successfully voted for an acquittal.

Early in 1939, he decided to repair it himself using his greatest gift – his power of oratory.

All his generals and advisers admitted to this power. He could hypnotize them, and destroy their most realistic arguments by flat statements to which they found no ready answer. On one occasion in August 1944 he secured the same effect just by stony silence, until the general concerned – Ferdinand Schörner – himself reversed his stand. He cast the same spell over mass audiences, whether he spoke from a carefully prepared script, which he had polished and trimmed far into the night, or *ex tempore*, timing every gesture and comic pause to ride the mood of his listeners. While Goebbels had a trained and thrilling elocution, Hitler spoke in a rich Austrian vernacular often hard to understand, his speeches were long and his grammar irregular – yet by a different route Hitler arrived at the same hysterical acclaim. Nobody who attended Hitler's speech to newly-commissioned officers in Berlin in February 1942 at the climax of the German army's desperate travails on the frozen Russian front, and witnessed the affection he commanded – a grim-faced Hitler, already leaving the platform hoarse from his oratory about the long struggle still to come, but checked in mid-exit by a sudden undisciplined storm of cheering from the ten thousand army officers, which itself gave way to the spontaneous singing of the national anthem – nobody could doubt that Germany's leader cast a spell that no other had in the past, and certainly none since.

By rare fortune, these three speeches by which Hitler rooted out the Ludwig Beck infection and prepared his officer corps for war have survived.* No brief extract can reproduce their flavour. Held in secret, they are of brutal frankness. Hitler set out the blood-racial basis of the Nazi *Weltanschauung*, the economic reasons obliging him to push further into Central Europe, and the inevitability of war. In this war he would expect his officers to serve him unswervingly, to die honourably and to show true leadership to their men. His contempt for the old Reichswehr spirit was openly expressed, even in the first speech – to 3,600 army lieutenants packed into the Mosaic Hall of Speer's new Chancellery on 18 January 1939, with the three C-in-Cs and Keitel in attendance. "All too frequently," Hitler proclaimed, "we hear the fashionable view that while courage and bravery are commendable virtues in the common soldier, they are of less import in his commanders – that commanders are looked to more for their wisdom and sagacity than courage." He demanded of these young lieutenants that they cultivate optimism, because pessimism was their worst enemy – it bred defeatism and surrender. "What belief do I demand of you?" he challenged them. "I demand of you, my young officers, an unconditional belief that one

---

* The speeches were recorded on disc at the time by German radio engineers, though not for broadcast. Typescripts made from the discs in February 1940 were found in a file of the Party censorship bureau (*PPK*) in a Berlin safe cracked open by Allied authorities in June 1961.

day our Germany, our German Reich will be the dominant power in Europe, that no other power will be in a position to stop us, let alone to break us!" Ten minutes later he went even further: "I'll tell you now what is to be your guiding star your whole life long: It is my unshakeable will that the German Wehrmacht becomes the most powerful force on earth." Finally, he told them: "Above all, my officers, you must be capable and inflexible even in adversity. True soldiers are not recognized by their victories, but after their defeats."

His second speech was more of a lecture, delivered to 217 officers including all Germany's senior generals and admirals after a dinner in the Chancellery on 25 January. He held out the British Empire as an example to them, and the qualities that had gained it.

> All the world empires have been won by deeds of daring and lost through pacifism. If, in all the centuries of its existence, the British Empire had been governed by the forces and trends that it is now claiming to preserve, the empire would never have been won in the first place. The British say the same, they say, "Of course, in those days we were brutal – we admit it, they are the stains on our escutcheon, we were bloodthirsty and vengeful and cruel. But we're not like that at all now. Today we're quite different." If the British really *have* turned over a new leaf, then in the long run they won't be able to hang on to what they won with their *other* qualities.

He conducted his patient audience on a guided tour of German history since Roman times to prove his point – that for a state to survive it must have not just a Leader but an entire leadership-élite, a *Führungsauslese,* such as the Nazi Party had itself acquired by almost Darwinian processes of natural selection in the years of struggle. This was why Germany had failed in 1918: the entire national leadership had collapsed like a pricked balloon.

Hitler held out to them the same fixed and final target – the new Reich as it would be some day. This target would make amends for all past German suffering, and for the suffering yet to come; but Hitler's legions would have one advantage over all the preceding German generations of warriors: "They marched off towards a Dream Land which probably few could visualize and none was ever to see; while we have that target already in sight."

The third speech was one urged on Hitler by Colonel Schmundt. Hitler spoke at 6 P.M. on 10 February 1939 to all the army colonels with active commands, behind closed doors at the Kroll Opera-house in Berlin. Again the Service C-in-Cs were present. This time even Hitler's staff were astounded by his openness on his future intentions and tactics. He described his disappointment at some officers' lack of understanding for his actions in 1938, and he tried to show that Munich was just one of a carefully-planned sequence of events. Some such events had admittedly come earlier than he foresaw – he said he had occupied the Rhineland in 1936 when it was originally timetabled for 1937. He emphasized, "Even though 1938 has ended with perhaps the biggest triumph of our recent history, it is of course only one step along a long path, gentlemen, that stretches out ahead of us."

Some of his arguments were familiar – the need to prevent future German generations from starving, the fact that no future leader would possess the like of his authority, and that though Germany's opponents were numerically superior they were not racial entities. Since 1933, he said, he had struggled to restore Germany's armed strength and world prestige: he was planning to build the mightiest bridge in the world at Hamburg, and skyscrapers to rival those in the USA. Most Germans supported the National Socialist idea now: but his dream was to see a union between nation and Wehrmacht such as there had not been in the era of the Reichswehr, and both must repose their trust blindly in him.

It's probably unique in world history for a man to have embarked as I did on a political career in 1919 – twenty years ago – with my background, and to have achieved what I have these last twenty years. Gentlemen, I did it through the loyalty of the movement that I created. It gave me its blind support not just in good times, but in bad times as well.

Is it too much for me to ask this of the German officer as well? In fact I'm asking even more: I can't be satisfied just with the German officer paying lip-service to my orders – particularly when everything's going well – I must demand of the German officer that even if the whole nation should desert me in my fight for our Weltanschauung, then he must stand at my side, man to man, with the entire officer corps and the German soldier too. For six years now, gentlemen, we had had one good fortune after another. In these six years we have really pulled off miracles.

Gentlemen, things might easily have gone very differently.

Their task now was no less than to repair three centuries of decay. Since the Peace of Westphalia, Hitler argued, the Germans had declined to political impotence. Now, in 1939, Hitler had planted Germany once more on the very threshold of a new age. "It's the duty of all of us to set forth on this new path calmly and courageously, seizing every opportunity we can. Take my word for it, gentlemen, my triumphs these last few years have only resulted from grasping sudden opportunities. Past generations of cowardly leaders and their advisers missed these opportunities by comfortably objecting, 'Militarily speaking we're not quite ready.'. . ."

"I have taken it upon myself to solve the German problem," Hitler declared emphatically. "That is, the German space problem. Take good note of that: as long as I live, this ideal will govern my every action. Take heed too: the moment I believe that I can make a killing, I'll always strike immediately and I won't hesitate to go to the very brink. Because I'm convinced this problem has to be solved *so oder so*, and I'll never shrug my shoulders and say, 'Oh dear, I'll leave that for whoever comes after me.'"

He told these Wehrmacht colonels that he wanted his officers to go into battle with sword and Weltanschauung as once they would have brandished sword and Bible. He himself would never hesitate to show the enemy cold steel.

We can best preserve the respect the prestige that we've already won by seizing every slim opportunity we get to snatch fresh victories. In this way, we'll familiarize ourselves with the enemy and, I dare say, the enemy will gradually get accustomed to Germany's strength too. So don't be surprised if over the coming years every opportunity is taken to attain these German objectives, and please give me your blindest support. Above all, take it from me that I will always have scrutinized these matters from every possible angle first – and that once I announce my decision to take this or that course of action, that decision is irrevocable and I will force it through whatever the odds against us.

Thus spake Adolf Hitler to his Wehrmacht in February 1939.

PART 2

TOWARDS THE PROMISED LAND

In Hitler's Chancellery

When Hitler had returned to Berlin by train on 8 January 1939, Albert Speer's new Reich Chancellery was complete. The long yellow stucco and grey stone frontage dominated a quarter-mile stretch of Voss Strasse. Everything was on an outsize scale. Dwarfed by the tall square columns, the motionless grey-uniformed sentries melted into the buildings, invisible until they presented arms to passing officers. Behind the heavy swing-doors waited messengers liveried in brown, and uniformed guards inspecting all official passes.

The corridors were of polished marble, richly carpeted to deaden the sound. The four hundred rooms of the new Chancellery housed the Civil Service and the Party's organization. To the left were the offices of Hans Lammers, to the right Otto Meissner's Presidial Chancellery. Lift-doors slid open and shut noiselessly. On the top floor was Philip Bouhler's "Chancellery of the Führer of the Nazi Party": initially it dealt with Hitler's incoming and outgoing public correspondence – by 1938 and 1939 it was already controlling more sinister concerns like euthanasia applications by medical practitioners, and in 1941 it effortlessly lent its expertise to the larger liquidation programmes that then began. Everywhere yellow signs pointed to air-raid shelters. It was a strong building, and survived structurally until 1945: now it has vanished, levelled to the post-war ground. No trace of it remains – except the occasional red-marble plancher or tabletop anonymously gracing the home of a former general or member of Hitler's staff.

The State Rooms were on the ground floor. Visitors arrived by limousine at the reception area, and were conducted through a flight of halls of ascending grandeur until the Führer's Study itself was reached. After the entrance hall came the Mosaic Hall, its marble floor and walls embellished with soft patterns of gold and grey mosaics. Then the visitor would pass through immense portals flanked by gilded bronze and stone eagles, each clutching a swastika in its claws – the Reich's emblem – and through a circular domed basilica into a magnificent room of red marble pillars which Hitler had decreed was to be known as the Marble Gallery.

Beyond that was a large hall for state receptions. But from the Marble Gallery itself, the visitor might be ushered into Hitler's Study, a vast room with ponderous chandeliers and an immense pastel-coloured carpet. Three heads adorned the front panels of his great desk: one of them was Medusa, complete with writhing snakes emerging from her hair.

Yet Hitler himself was rarely seen in the new Chancellery. He continued to live and work in the old building, at right angles to Speer's new structure. In the first floor of the old Chancellery he had his Residence. An entrance hall and "garden room" with four more rooms opened on to an old garden of almost monastic solitude. A large dining-room and corridor linked the two Chancelleries. Since Schaub, Brückner and his other personal adjutants also lived here, the house was cramped; and it was old-fashioned, but Hitler liked it. Here was his equestrian statue of Frederick the Great – given him by François-Poncet – and the Lenbach portrait of Bismarck. There was a familiar antique commode with an ancient clock, wall-niches with two statuettes of horses, and four figurines in another niche by some Austrian sculptor. In this building too was Hitler's real study, a thirty-foot-long room with a window behind his desk looking out over the Chancellery garden. Its walls were hung with heavy red velours wallpapers. A sturdy suite of chairs by Troost had replaced the fragile Louis XIV furniture after a misfortune with a bulky Indian maharaja four years before.

That January 1939 only one episode of significance occurred in Speer's new building. It was so slight as to escape all but the most delicate political seismographs at the time. It occurred during the New Year diplomatic reception which – with Göring's official birthday celebration – opened the year for Berlin officialdom. To be precise, it occurred at midday on 12 January 1939.

Wearing his brown Party tunic – unusually for such an occasion – Hitler waited in his Cabinet room for noon. He could hear the diplomats arriving – the drill of the guard of honour and the sounds of protocol: the band played the Present Arms for full ambassadors, mere rolls of drums for envoys (while chargés d'affaires were greeted by dead silence). Hitler had begun to relish this foppery, and to make use of it: as recently as July he had instructed that the Egyptian minister was to be received at the Berghof will a full guard of honour, while the Russian ambassador was to be accorded no honours at all, as the pariah that he was. At noon Hitler now walked through to the great reception hall, where the diplomats had drawn up in self-conscious semi-circle, stationed himself beneath the two crystal chandeliers so that he could read his speech without spectacles, then briefly shook hands with each diplomat in turn. But when he reached the Russian ambassador, Alexei Merekalov, Hitler paused and *began a conversation*. Merekalov's German was still quite inadequate but in the jealous diplomatic world the content was unimportant – it was time elapsed that mattered. Hitler talked to Merekalov for several minutes. In this way he hinted to Moscow that he could easily let bygones by bygones.*

For two decades Russo-German relations had been marked by a mutual distrust if not always enmity. The cautious co-operation launched in 1922 at Rapallo had survived until 1933, as the two outcast countries found they had much in common. Germany looked east for Oswald Spengler's Morgenland, Moscow hoped for a Communist Germany. Germany furnished special equipment and know-how, Russia raw materials and space for the clandestine training activities of the Reichswehr: Heinz Guderian had practised his armoured warfare and tested Krupp tank prototypes on Russian soil, and Hans Jeschonnek, the new Chief of Air Staff, was one of hundreds of Luftwaffe officers who had passed through the German flying-school at Lipetsk near Voronezh in south-central Russia (one of the products of Rapallo). The Reichswehr had supplied the Russians with German training manuals, weapons prototypes and staff college training in Germany. Trade had also flourished, with Russia owing Germany 1,200 million Reichsmarks for imports by the time Hitler came to power.

The Nazi revolution of 1933 thwarted Moscow's immediate aspirations in Germany. Adolf Hitler was, after all, the author of *Mein Kampf*, and Chapter 14 continued to appear unexpurgated in every fresh edition, laying bare his pathological hatred of the Soviet Union and his greedy aims for conquest there. Hitler's bellicose withdrawal from the League of Nations and his pact of non-aggression with Poland in 1934 forced Stalin to adopt a policy of collective security. He joined the League that Hitler had just quit, and concluded mutual-assistance pacts with France and Czecho-Slovakia. Hitler quietly admired how Bolshevism had subjected the Slav sub-humans – as he called them – to "the tyranny of a Jewish ruling clique", precisely the kind of élite leadership that he was struggling to invest Germany with. But each side continued to prepare for war with the other. Stalin reorganized his armed forces in 1935, aiming at a standing army of about 1,600,000 men. In March 1936 he could hear Hitler openly telling the Reichstag about the immense wealth of the Urals, the unending fertile plains of the Ukraine in which the Germans would one day "swim in plenty". Stalin modernized Soviet industry and geared it to war. Strategic highways were built – three parallel roads towards the Latvian frontier and two good highways from Moscow to Minsk and from Kiev to Polish Volhynia.

Until 1939, Hitler had discounted Russian military power. In all his 1938

---

* This is no idle surmise. Hitler bragged to his own generals on 22 August 1939, on the eve of his deal with Stalin, that he had begun working for it at this reception. See page 242 below.

secret speeches, he always referred to the Soviet Union as a *quantité négligible*. But early in 1939, with the realization that Poland was unwilling to become an accessory, it dawned on Hitler that Stalin's aid – one way or the other – might become necessary. Since Munich, Hitler had cautiously stated his first demand on Poland – for the return of Danzig and overland access to East Prussia. Poland had not only rebuffed him, she was entrenching herself more firmly than ever in the Polish Corridor by enlarging the new port of Gdynia to 250,000 inhabitants and inflating the ancient German city of Thorn to 500,000 with Polish settlers.

Hitler could not shelve the Polish problem permanently. East Prussia was vital to his *Ostpolitik* – his future crusade into the east. Its capital, Königsberg,* was German through and through: in its fourteenth-century cathedral were the bones of no less than Immanuel Kant and many a Hohenzollern prince. He had a strategic interest in East Prussia. But the province had an impoverished and declining population, it was over-taxed and under-capitalized (a consequence, he reflected on 12 May 1942, of earlier Prussian governments' folly in regarding it as a penal colony for teachers, civil servants and officers who had failed to make the grade at home). It is significant that Hitler tackled this on 1 February 1939 with a secret decree on the "Reinforcement of the Eastern Borderlands", with economic measures calculated to reverse the drain of manpower and capital from East Prussia. Meanwhile he had long sworn to recover Danzig, the largest port and a "northern Nuremberg" of architecture. Indeed, ever since he had privately sworn that oath, he had worn the Danzig emblem – a silver ship sailing on blue waves – engraved on his cufflinks: to remind him not to forget.

The port of Memel, seized by Lithuania after the World War, would present less difficulty. During the Polish-Lithuanian crisis of March 1938,† Hitler had already ordered Keitel to make contingency plans in case the Poles seemed likely to lay hands on Memel. The port stayed on the slate in each OKW directive after that, coupled in the November 1938 OKW directive with a possible simultaneous coup against Danzig if war with Poland was not involved. Hitler had nurtured the hope since September that he could do a deal with Poland for the bloodless return of Danzig in exchange for the Carpatho-Ukraine coveted by Poland. This idea was aired by Ribbentrop to the Polish ambassador, Josef Lipski, on 24 October – Lipski replied evasively, to the effect that Polish public opinion was not yet ready for such a deal; and he confirmed Warsaw's reluctance to horsedeal in November. Undismayed, Hitler sent for the Polish foreign minister, Colonel Jósef Beck, to come from Monte Carlo in the New Year. Their secret meeting took place at the Berghof on

* Now Kaliningrad, USSR.
† In March 1938, Poland had issued to Lithuania an ultimatum to restore diplomatic relations, broken off in 1920. Ribbentrop persuaded Lithuania that the terms were not dishonourable, and war was thereby avoided.

5 January 1939 – it was to be Hitler's last personal attempt to win the Poles over to an alliance against Russia. Beck would not rise to his bait. Thus Hitler left for Berlin two days later, resolved to play for Stalin's hand instead: his protracted gossip with Merekalov was the first move; a noticeable abstinence from attacking the USSR in his anniversary speech on 30 January was the second.

Until mid-March 1939, Hitler remained in Berlin, except for occasional forays to Linz to discuss the reconstruction of the city, or to Munich for conferences with party officials. The Berghof was under snow: Hitler detested it.

In Berlin he kept relatively regular hours, receiving Cabinet ministers during the morning individually, then lunching as late as three or four. He joked that his dining-room ought to be called "The Cheerful Chancellor's". The placing at the Führer's table was as jealously contested as at any ocean-liner captain's. Women were excluded, here in Berlin. This lunchtable assembly was, in fact, the closest that Hitler came to holding Cabinets after 1938 (though once more, in February 1939, he did agree to Lammers' suggestion that one should be called: but Göring was away in Italy, recovering from a slimming cure, and the project was abandoned). Goebbels and Speer were frequent lunch-guests, as was Karl Bodenschatz, Göring's listening-post in the Chancellery. Todt's diary shows he came nine times (including once, on 27 January 1939, to show Hitler the planning for the immense Hamburg suspension bridge). Other frequent visitors were Rudolf Hess, Martin Bormann and Hitler's photographer, Hoffmann.

After lunch Hitler read newspapers, bought by an aide each day from a kiosk at the nearby Kaiserhof Hotel. Besides these, his press secretary, Otto Dietrich, furnished daily digests of the foreign press. In his library he had every edition of the magazine *Woche*, and bound volumes of the *Leipziger Illustrierte* going back over a hundred years. To Alfred Rosenberg, editor of the stodgy *Völkischer Beobachter*, he would compare these attractive publications with their own Nazi press.

Later in the Berlin afternoon, Hitler liked to receive more visitors or stroll in his Chancellery garden. In earlier years he had taken tea in the Kaiserhof: as he entered, the little orchestra would strike up the "Donkey Serenade" ("clippety-clop"), his favourite Hollywood movie tune. He was, he confessed, a fan of Shirley Temple and Jeannette MacDonald. He saw whatever films he liked, whether censored by Doctor Goebbels' ministry or not, but he kept up a running commentary of invective, unless the movie found his favour right from the first reel: "What filth this is! It should be suppressed." "How can the Doctor permit a film like this! Who directed it?" The Führer's SS adjutants dutifully compiled a list of his pithy one-line reviews and sent them to the propaganda ministry's film division: Hitler's edicts had the weight of law – and woe betide a film that attracted Hitler's ultimate reproof, "broken off in mid-film". *Prairie Hyenas, Tip-Off Girls, King of Arizona, Bluebeard's Eighth Wife, The Great Gambini, Shanghai* – all these movies came to an unscripted end in Hitler's Chancellery. When *Marie Antoinette* was shown, Hitler got up and stalked out.

From these foreign films, of course, he gleaned a fragmentary knowledge of the world outside and a better grasp of English than he cared to admit. The American movies, moreover, largely moulded Hitler's irrational hatred of the USA: the files of the US State Department still hold the acrid correspondence between German and American officialdom about the pernicious anti-German barbs in many a Hollywood screenplay.

At 9:17 A.M., 13 February 1939, Hitler's special train bore him out of Berlin toward Hamburg.

Here the largest Nazi battleship, 35,000 tons of armourplate, was waiting to be launched. But first, in quiet homage, Hitler visited in nearby Friedrichsruh the tomb of Bismarck, the statesman whose name he had selected for the Reich's first super-warship. Next morning, as bands serenaded the fifty thousand spectators, a green Hadag ferry carried the Führer and his invited guests across the Elbe from the Saint-Pauli pier to the Blohm & Voss shipyard. In Hamburg a public holiday had been declared. The bands fell silent as Hitler marched to the tall scaffold and delivered his set speech, praising this great predecessor's works in founding the Second Reich. Hitler had himself positioned every newsreel camera, and forbidden foreign newspaper reporters to attend. After ten minutes of his speech, a small red lamp glowed in his rostrum, warning that the last props were being hammered away and that the colossus was about to móve. The champagne bottle smashed perfectly, and the new battleship *Bismarck* rumbled down into the Elbe, to the strains of the German national anthem.

Hitler's mind was elsewhere. How revealing is Baron von Weizsäcker's private note on the Führer's fireside remarks after an intimate meal at the Bismarck shrine at Friedrichsruh on 13 February – because it clearly proves how far in advance Hitler's occupation of Prague was planned, and how widely known this "secret" was:

> ... In fact [wrote Weizsäcker] the Führer's post-prandial observations, at the fireside, kept on returning to the theme that a statesman's character is far more important than his powers of reason.
>
> For those of us who know that the rest of Czecho-Slovakia will be dealt its death blow in approximately four weeks' time, it was interesting to hear the Führer declare that he himself used to prefer surprise tactics but has now gone off them as he has exhausted their possibilities.

The Führer sketched out the September crisis of last year thus: "I owe my triumph to my unflinching stand, which left the other side with a whiff of war if I felt it necessary."

By this time it was widely rumoured that Hitler was planning to invade the rest of Czecho-Slovakia in the latter half of March 1939; the Vatican knew of it; the new French ambassador, Robert Coulondre, heard it from somebody on Hitler's staff; and a member of the German embassy in London leaked it to the Czechs. The sequence was also laid down, and a formula to make it palatable to the western powers. Baron von Weizsäcker himself noted the likely scenario – the note is undated, and whether they represent his own suggestions or not we cannot say: an artificially-induced squabble should split Slovakia from the Prague government; Slovakia proclaims her unilateral independence; Germany advises Hungary to "restore order" in the Carpatho-Ukraine; Slovak government asks Hitler to guarantee its frontiers; Germans in Bohemia appeal for protection; ultimatum to Prague to sign treaty with the Reich, failing which the Wehrmacht will invade; meanwhile, Germany's "embarrassing situation" is explained in notes to Warsaw, Paris and London, and Goebbels' propaganda machine puts the blame on the Czechs – stressing the mildness of the German action and listing similar episodes in history.

Since Munich, Hitler's agents had burrowed deep into Slovakia's structure, their activities ranging from the open political operations of Franz Karmasin, the fervently pro-Nazi leader of the Carpatho-Germans who was now statesecretary in Father Tiso's government, to the subversion work of the radical fringe groups. Nameless agents of Himmler's SS, Goebbels' ministry, Göring's Four-Year-Plan office and the Nazi Foreign Organization (AO) had fanned out across Slovakia. Without informing anybody else, even the foreign ministry, Hitler in November had directed Wilhelm Keppler, the moustached, stooping economics expert who had masterminded the preliminaries to Austria's union with the Reich, to turn his attention to Slovakia.

By 21 January 1939, when Hitler had a tough interview with the Czech foreign minister Chvalkovsky, it was obvious that his decision had been taken. His language was uncompromising. He demanded absolute Czech neutrality, and a considerable reduction in Czech forces. Chvalkovsky quailed and promised compliance.

Nine days later, Karmasin's party and the radicals formed a new "German-Slovak Association", with Voytěch Tuka as chairman; Tuka was a Slovak agitator who had suffered long years of Czech imprisonment and only recently been amnestied, after the flight of Beneš. Tuka telegraphed to Hitler a fulsome appeal to protect the Slovaks, and accept them as the economic and cultural colleagues of the "illustrious German nation"; Tuka went so far as to offer "a fighting partnership for the defence of European civilization." On about 10

February, Karmasin's men in Bratislava, capital of Slovakia, were confidentially tipped off that Hitler would topple the Prague regime in a month's time. Tuka visited Hitler at the New Chancellery on the twelfth, and formally placed the destiny of Slovakia in Hitler's hands. "My people", he said, "await their total liberation by you." Hitler dropped a series of powerful hints that Slovakia should declare her independence of Prague – the first stage in the scenario outlined (if not actually proposed) by Weizsäcker.

Over the next four weeks, the Nazi pressure on the Slovaks to declare independence increased. Keppler sent his close associate Dr Edmund Veesenmayer to Bratislava to tell them to hurry, as "otherwise Hungary will get our permission to occupy Slovakia at any time after 15 March". And when Ďurčansky and his economics minister visited Göring on 28 February, the field-marshal sinisterly greeted them with: "Now, what's it to be? When are you going to declare independence, so we don't have to turn you over to the Hungarians!" Ribbentrop also received them with a promise to guarantee Slovakia's frontiers, *provided* she proclaimed her independence at a time that suited the Führer.

Up to this point, Hitler had taken the initiative. What happened on 10 March 1939 clearly took him unawares – though by no means unprepared. At 5:20 A.M. Walther Hewel, Ribbentrop's personal liaison officer to Hitler, was telephoned by Seyss-Inquart from Vienna with word that Czech troops had marched into Bratislava, uprooted the Slovak government and arrested Tuka once again. Father Tiso, the prime minister, had taken refuge in a Jesuit college. Hewel's hastily-scribbled telephone notes – hitherto unpublished – list frantic conversations all morning between Ribbentrop, Heydrich, Schmundt and Keppler as they tried to find out more. At 11:50 A.M.: "Keppler telephones: Tuka arrested. Telephones cut off. Martial law. Troops marching in. Karmasin may have been arrested too." 11:55: "I go to the Führer, inform Schaub." 12 noon: "Phoned Chief [Ribbentrop]: is to come to Führer at once." Keitel was also sent for, at 1 P.M.

We are insufficiently informed on the decisions that Hitler now took. But it is clear that he had decided to act. To damp down foreign press alarm, Nazi editors were secretly briefed that morning to devote no more than two columns to the crisis. "Our sympathies for the Slovaks are to be expressed without exaggeration." During the coming night, Hitler's SS Lifeguards regiment (Leibstandarte) – the cream of the SS élite – was alerted and issued with field-grey uniforms; and regional newspapers in Magdeburg and Silesia reported to their Berlin bureaux, as the FA wiretaps show, that extensive troop movements just like those of the previous summer were beginning.

Hitler knew that he was on the brink of leading his Herrenvolk on its next step forward. In a secret – but disc-recorded – speech to staff college graduates late on the eleventh he explained, "In general the structure of a state demands that the Herrenvolk does the organizing, while a somewhat inferior mass of people – or let's call them an *undominating* kind of people – prostrate themselves to that leadership." History, ventured Hitler, afforded more than one example of a relatively thin stratum of dominators organizing a broad mass of slaves. Coming on the eve of the Nazis' first conquest of non-German peoples, this was an interesting disclosure of Hitler's intentions.

For some days there was confusion. The Czech president, Hacha, had appointed Dr Karol Sidor to replace Tiso in Slovakia. Sidor had earlier enjoyed the backing of Seyss-Inquart, but Veesenmayer – sent recently to Bratislava to talent-hunt for a suitable puppet premier of Slovakia – had correctly diagnosed that Sidor was unstable and an opportunist; Veesenmayer recommended that Tiso, as a "modest, sound, healthy, quiet and popular" man, should retain the job instead. Now Hitler sent Keppler in person to Bratislava; there Keppler found groups of Czechs, Slovaks and ethnic Germans confronting each other with weapons looted from arsenals and museums. Keppler salvaged Tiso and flew back to Berlin with him to meet the Führer on 13 March. Without beating around the bush, Hitler told Tiso to proclaim Slovakia's independence of Prague, and to do it now.

The OKW drafted a suitable ultimatum to present to the Czechs. Hitler sent a letter by courier to Göring – still convalescing in San Remo – ordering him back to Berlin, as he had decided to use force against Prague; Göring wrote back at once warning against the use of force, and arguing for the purely economic absorption of Czecho-Slovakia as before. Hitler also sent a courier with the same message to Milch at a ski-hotel in Switzerland.

At noon on 14 March, Keitel reported to Hitler that the Wehrmacht was poised on the Czech frontier, and could invade – as ordered – at 6 A.M. Hundreds of Luftwaffe bombers were standing by. To throttle, if not entirely silence, foreign criticism Hitler informed Prague that it would be to their "great advantage" if Dr Hacha, despite age and infirmity, would travel to Berlin that very day to meet him. At 2:15 P.M. the German legation in Prague reported that Hacha would come to Berlin by train that evening – his heart would not stand the strain of flying. Hitler confidently instructed Keitel to issue orders to the army to invade at 6 A.M., whatever the outcome of the talk with Hacha. Keitel was to return to the Chancellery building at 9 P.M.

Hitler ordered full military honours for the Czech president's arrival. And since Hacha's daughter, Madam Radl, was accompanying him as nurse, Hitler sent an adjutant to fill her room at the Adlon Hotel with yellow roses, and he placed a note there in his own handwriting. Hitler may have been a gangster, but he was a gangster with style.

After dusk, the first German armed units crossed quietly into Czecho-Slovakia – the SS Lifeguards with instructions to infiltrate the region of Moravian Ostrau before the rapacious Poles could lay hands on the modern steelmills at Witkowitz.

After dinner that evening, 14 March 1939, Hitler retired to the music room to watch the latest movie, *Ein Hoffnungsloser Fall* (*A Hopeless Case*). He calmly invited his generals to join him. Shortly, Ribbentrop reported that Hacha's train had arrived at Anhalt station. Hitler examined his fingernails, and softly said that the old fellow should be allowed to rest an hour or two. As the German army was under orders to invade at 6 A.M., his generals were perplexed by Hitler's tactics. They were eager to strike – Colonel Eduard Wagner* voicing the relish of all the General Staff in a private letter that evening: "I don't think much will happen, and the foreign powers have expressed themselves disinterested. End of Czechoslovakia! – And have they been asking for it!"

It was not until about 11 P.M. that Kempka chauffeured Hacha into the New Chancellery's covered courtyard. Hitler was waiting with a guard of honour for Hacha and his foreign minister, Chvalkovsky, to inspect. He had assembled an intimidating host of ministers and generals in his cavernous study. Meissner ushered in the diminutive Czech president. Hacha looked tired and agitated. Hitler ordered everybody else out except Ribbentrop and Hewel, who took a written note of part of their discussion. In a voice trembling with emotion – or was it weariness? – Hacha delivered a long, prepared speech on his own career as a lawyer in the Viennese civil service; he had read of and admired Hitler's ideas, he said, and he was sure that Czecho-Slovakia would be safe in the Führer's hands. But he insisted that the country had a right to a national existence. As Hacha's speech rambled on, Hitler grew uneasy: "The more Hacha laboured on about how hardworking and conscientious the Czechs were, the more I felt I was sitting on red-hot coals – knowing the invasion order had already been issued," he recalled in May 1942. At last Hacha stopped, and Hitler told him: at 6 A.M. the Wehrmacht would invade Bohemia and Moravia; but the country's autonomy was assured. If Hacha would sign on the dotted line, there would be no bloodshed. "I'm almost ashamed to admit that we have one division standing by for each Czech battalion." Twice Keitel came into interrupt him: once with a note that Witkowitz was safely in German hands – Hitler nodded curtly; and again at 2 A.M. with a message that the army was pressing for its orders.

The play-acting had effect. Hacha and his foreign minister retired to another room to consult Prague by that dangerous instrument, the telephone. The line was poor, the old man had to shout and repeat himself, and the strain told on

* Wagner later joined the 20 July 1944 plot, and committed suicide.

him. Between 2 and 3 A.M. he suffered a heart failure, and it took an injection from Hitler's personal physician Professor Morell – about whom more is to be related shortly – to revive him. In fact he recovered so rapidly that Hitler chided Morell afterwards that after the injection Hacha began to dig his heels in all over again. The play-acting resumed, but the minutes were ticking past. Hitler reminded Hacha of the military situation; the Wehrmacht was already moving up. Göring, who had only just arrived that evening from San Remo, interjected that at daybreak his Luftwaffe would appear over the streets of Prague. Finally Hacha caved in, and Keitel drafted a suitably-worded telegram to the Czech garrisons ordering them not to open fire. Göring stood over Hacha at the phone, to ensure that he transmitted its contents correctly.

The main agreement was signed shortly before 4 A.M. In a second document Hacha agreed to surrender all aircraft and weapons immediately to the Germans. But even then there were still problems. Hitler demanded that Chvalkovsky must countersign, which Hacha obstinately opposed. The Führer later recalled having thought to himself, "Look out, this is a lawyer you have facing you. Perhaps there's some law in Czechoslovakia that makes such an agreement as this valid only if it *is* countersigned by the minister concerned!" He would not put any chicanery past a lawyer. Chvalkovsky signed too, and left with Hacha for his hotel. They left Hitler's study by one route, while Father Tiso was ushered in by another and informed of the result.

After that, Hitler must have sent for Wilhelm Keppler, who had masterminded the SS plan to infiltrate subversive agents into Slovakia, because Keppler wrote a few hours later to his boss, Heinrich Himmler: "When we were together with the Führer last night after the agreement had been signed, the Führer paid his particular respects to the men who risked their lives in highly dangerous missions at the front. Whereupon Ribbentrop declared that the whole job had been magnificently performed by the SS alone, and particularly by Dr Veesenmayer and Götsch."

For a few moments after they all left, Hitler was alone in the room. His staff had departed to his Residence, where much beer flowed and the night's events were discussed until long after dawn. The Führer unwound: he was no longer "furious" or "threatening". Keitel looked in briefly to say that the invasion was all set for 6 A.M., and then left him alone again. Hitler turned, opened the invisible door let into the wall behind his monolithic desk and walked into the tiny office where his dutiful secretaries, Christa Schroeder and Gerda Daranowski, had been waiting wearily for the all-night conference to end. His eyes sparkled, and he laughed out loud. "Well, children! Now put one here and one here," he said, and shyly tapped his cheeks: "One peck each!" The startled secretaries complied. Hitler explained, "This is the most wonderful day of my life. I have now accomplished what others strove in vain for centuries to achieve. Bohemia and Moravia are back in the Reich. I will go down as the greatest German of all time."

At 8:02 A.M. Hitler's special train pulled out of Anhalt station. Hacha and his party were still soundly asleep at the Adlon. Lieutenant-Colonel Kurt Zeitzler of Keitel's staff kept Hitler briefed on the army's invasion progress. By 9 A.M. the German armour (Geyr von Schweppenburg's panzer division) was in the streets of Prague. There was no bloodshed – the army suffered only two injuries, and the SS, who became involved in a number of excesses, rather more. One road-bridge was barred by Czech patriots singing the national anthem; the German company commander halted his column until the anthem ended, and ordered the Present Arms – an astute token of respect that had the desired effect. At 2:03 P.M. Hitler's train reached the little Bohemian station of Leipa, where the panzer corps commander General Erich Hoepner awaited him with Colonel Erwin Rommel (who was to command the "Führer HQ" as he had in October 1938).

To the consternation of Himmler and the security staff, Hitler decided to drive on at once to Prague in person. Hoepner said he would vouch for the Führer's safety. Rommel agreed, and Hitler announced: "I'm going in!" At 4 P.M. the frontier barrier was raised for Hitler to cross into Czecho-Slovakia, and in a driving snowstorm his truck convoy headed on to Prague. It was dusk when they arrived. The roads were choked with Wehrmacht transport and troops, and treacherous with ice; one of the trucks of Hitler's convoy rolled over into a ditch. He stood in his open car, returning the salute as he passed his regiments. Fog and snow had grounded the entire Luftwaffe, so it was as well that Hacha had signed the documents.

Nobody knew where Hacha's official residence, the Hradčany Castle, was at first. Hitler's drivers finally entered it through a gate in the rear. The grounds were blanketed in dazzling snow; German troops milled around in the confusion and darkness. A palace flunkey was found to guide them to a wing where these unexpected visitors might sleep, but even so Hitler's adjutants had to sleep on the floor like one of Wallenstein's camps.

Hitler did not sleep yet. He began dictating to his secretaries a law establishing the "Protectorate" of Bohemia and Moravia. He needed neither Ribbentrop nor Brauchitsch for the moment. He boasted shamelessly to his adjutants that once again he had exploited a momentary weakness to snatch a quick victory.

At two in the morning a cold buffet arrived, provided by the German Centre in Prague. There was cold ham and Pilsen beer: Hitler was prevailed on to sample a small glass but he grimaced, did not finish it, and went to bed. The first that the citizens of Prague knew of Hitler's presence in their midst was next morning, when they espied his personal swastika standard beating from a flagpole atop the snow-bedecked palace roofs, against the cloudless morning sky.

Ribbentrop privately advised Hitler that his proclamation of a "Protectorate" would badly damage what little goodwill Germany still had abroad. Weizsäcker initially disagreed, believing that Hacha's 4 A.M. signature on the dotted line gave Hitler sufficient legal basis to stifle foreign criticism.

The first official British reaction was that this was an affair that need not concern them. But the British public, conditioned by now to accepting Hitler's demands provided they had an ethnological justification, refused to swallow his "annexation" of Bohemia and Moravia, and Chamberlain was obliged to deliver a strongly-worded speech in Birmingham, containing the first hints at a new policy – one of encircling the Hitler Reich.* On 18 March, Ribbentrop telephoned Hitler that Britain was recalling her ambassador from Berlin as a protest; Hitler authorized Ribbentrop to recall Dirksen from London in reply.

He was undeterred. He believed that Chamberlain's public utterances were only designed to take the wind out of his more vociferous opponents' sails. Indeed, according to Hitler's own later account, about a week after Prague Chamberlain reassured him through "a third party" that he quite sympathized with Germany's move, even though he was unable to say so in public – as he was being exposed to intemperate attacks by the Churchill clique. Besides, the benefits well outweighed the western powers' opprobrium: control of Prague brought to Hitler the gold reserves to overcome the Reich's financial crisis, airfields to threaten Poland and Russia, and a front line shorter by one thousand miles to defend. It furnished to him Czech tanks, artillery and aircraft of staggering quality and quantity; and more, it put Romania and Yugoslavia in his thrall, because their armed forces were largely equipped by the Škoda arms factory at Pilsen. Hitler's officers marvelled at his fresh accomplishment, and many of the weaker fry, who in harder times would sidle over to the "resistance movement", in March 1939 wrote admiring words in their private diaries and letters to their friends.

Surprisingly, the Berlin agreement brought blessings for the Czechs as well. Their economy was stabilized and unemployment vanished. Their menfolk were not called on to serve in wars in Hitler's coalition. Their armed forces were dissolved, the officers were given state pensions on Hitler's orders (to purchase

---

* Chamberlain said: "Is this in fact a step in the direction of an attempt to dominate the world by force?"

His ministers were being fed alarming – and wholly untrue – reports that Hitler planned to invade Holland next, and to launch a saturation air raid on London. There had been several such war scares since January 1939 in London. The Canadian prime minister, Mackenzie King, was concerned enough to consult with his (deceased) mother at a seance, and on her advice he wrote at length to Hitler reminding him of their 1937 conversation (page 57) and urging him not to imperil his great "constructive achievements" in Germany.

their dependence and complicity). The industrious Czechs settled down, accepted rich contracts from the Reich and in the majority learned even to cherish the *pax teutonica* enforced by Reinhard Heydrich, the brutal Gestapo chief who was appointed Neurath's deputy in 1941. It was the peace of the graveyard, but Heydrich won the affection of the Czech workers to such an extent – for instance, by the first ever Bismarckian social security and pension schemes – that 30,000 Czechs thronged into Wenceslas Square in Prague to demonstrate against his murder in 1942, the womenfolk filing past the cata-falque in mourning clothes and bearing flowers, while bells tolled in the cathedrals and a Requiem Mass was sung. The Czechs had not been called on to sell their souls, and this was what Hitler had promised Hacha in Berlin.

Hacha himself lapsed into virtual obscurity. Humorous stories about him circulated in Berlin. In one, Neurath, Hitler's appointed "Reich Protector" in Prague, was said to have invited Hacha out to dinner; when he showed the Czech the menu, the president fumbled for his fountain-pen and stuttered, "Where do I sign?" But Hacha himself never felt any grievance. His daughter wrote a touching note to Hitler – it is in the files – and Hacha inquired of Morell about the prescription he had been injected with and thereafter obtained a regular supply from Morell's pharmacy. On the Führer's birthday in April, Hacha gave him a particularly valuable painting and was guest of honour on Hitler's podium during the military parade. Buckets of ink had been wept over Hacha's maltreatment by Hitler, in the world's press; he died, forgotten, in a post-war prison in 1945. Tiso and Tuka were both hanged.

On 16 March 1939, as Prague awakened to find Hitler at the Hradčany Castle, his propaganda minister issued a telling confidential notice to Nazi editors: "The use of the term Grossdeutsches Reich is not desired. This term is reserved for later eventualities."

The next items on Hitler's list were, of course, Memel, Danzig and the Polish Corridor. On his instructions Ribbentrop summoned the Polish ambassador, Lipski, on 21 March and restated the offer of October: if Danzig was returned and a secure land-link allowed across the Polish Corridor to East Prussia, Hitler would recognize the Corridor and Poland's western frontier. Ribbentrop even hinted that Slovakia might be the subject of later discussions with Poland – *after* the Danzig issue had been settled. Lipski betook himself to Warsaw to obtain a reply. On the twenty-fifth Hitler privately reassured General von Brauchitsch, C-in-C of the army, that he did not want to resort to force as this would only drive the Poles into the arms of the British. Brauchitsch's ADC noted Hitler as saying, "The possibility of taking Danzig by military action will only be examined if L[ipski] gives us to understand that the Polish government will be unable to explain to its own public any voluntary surrender of Danzig, but that a *fait accompli* by us would help them to a solution." Curiously, Hitler really expected an under-the-counter deal. On 27 March, Raeder initialled plans for Hitler and himself to embark in the cruiser *Deutschland* and appear off Danzig with virtually the entire battle fleet: Hitler would go ashore by torpedo boat and proceed in triumph to the city centre. So much for planning – his actual entry into Danzig six months later looked very different.

Lithuania proved more malleable over Memel. A German ultimatum called for the return of the ancient Teutonic city at the farthest tip of East Prussia. The Lithuanian foreign minister, Juozas Urbsys, hurried to Berlin and signed the necessary papers after Ribbentrop and Weizsäcker had turned the screw. Hitler anchored off Memel aboard the *Deutschland* early on 23 March, symbolically toured the city – with Rommel as HQ commandant, and Milch in lieu of Göring who had returned to San Remo – and then went back to Berlin. The signatories of the Memel Convention looked on passively. After this coup Ribbentrop was viewed by Berlin's foreign press corps in a new – though not flattering – light. One report dubbed him the Führer's "demon adviser", but it admitted that there was no denying the success of these methods.

In the short term, this was true. But for the sake of cheap triumphs Hitler had forfeited the foreign goodwill he really needed for squaring accounts with Poland. The Poles had reacted to Memel by partially mobilizing and moving troops up toward Danzig, as Canaris reported on 25 March. Next day Lipski returned from Warsaw with a brusque rejection of Hitler's offer over Danzig, to which Lipski – and three days later Jósef Beck himself – added the verbal warning that if Hitler persisted in asking for the return of Danzig it would mean war. On 27 March, Weizsäcker summarized in his diary, with evident disquiet:

> It will no longer be possible to solve the Danzig problem, now that we have used up foreign political goodwill over Prague and Memel. A German-Polish conflict now would unleash an avalanche against us. For the time being the only way we can deal with the Poles' insolent attitude and their high-handed rebuff to the offer we made them (over Danzig, extra-territorial transit rights to East Prussia and the recognition of their frontiers) is by breaking the Polish spirit.

At first Hitler could not fathom the origins of Poland's newfound resilience.* Strolling the Obersalzberg mountain he pondered on his next move, just as here in 1938 he had wrestled with the problem "Green". If only the shrewd Marshal Josef Pilsudski were still alive, Poland would surely have conformed. On 25 March, Hitler had assured Brauchitsch that he would not tackle the *Polish* – as distinct from the Danzig – problem yet; while he would like the German army to study a possible war with Poland, he added that for a

---

* Britain had made clandestine overtures to Warsaw. Hitler's armies would have to stand there before he found this out.

settlement to be enforced in the near future, there would first have to be particularly favourable political conditions: "I would then knock Poland so flat that politically speaking she wouldn't have to be taken into account for many decades to come." The Reich would thereby regain its 1914 eastern frontier, from East Prussia to eastern Silesia. He had left Berlin late on the twenty-fifth, telling Brauchitsch: "I don't want to be here when Lipski gets back. Ribbentrop will conduct the negotiations at first."

Lipski's negative response from Warsaw resulted in a distinct shift in Hitler's attitude between Poland and Russia. Late on 30 March, Hitler returned to Berlin in his train – he dubbed it "The Speedy Chancellor's" to his staff. He had now received Stalin's indirect answer to his own oblique overtures. On 10 March, Stalin had delivered a stinging rebuke to the western democracies at a Moscow congress. Hitler studied the newsreel films, scrutinized the great Georgian's features and pronounced that Stalin looked quite "congenial".

In Berlin, however, a rude shock awaited him next morning, 31 March: news arrived from London that Neville Chamberlain was about to announce in Parliament that "in the event of any action which clearly threatened Polish independence and which the Polish government accordingly considered it vital to resist. . . . His Majesty's Government would feel themselves bound at once to lend the Polish Government all support in their power. They have given the Polish Government an assurance to this effect." This was the first of a shower of ill-considered guarantees to be uttered by the British. The effect in Berlin was an immediate lurch towards war: at 12:45 P.M. Hitler sent for Keitel and ordered the OKW to make all due preparations short of actual mobilization for war with Poland, under the code-name "White".

Hitler regarded the startling British guarantee as a blank cheque to Warsaw – as *carte blanche* to thumb its nose at Berlin, whatever the German proposals. It brought to an abrupt end Hitler's short-lived policy of "wait-and-see", as stated to Brauchitsch on the twenty-fifth. In effect it transferred control over British foreign policy from Whitehall to Warsaw – where interest in the well-being of the British Empire can scarcely have been more than academic. From FA intercepts, the guarantee appeared to be the product of the hysteria generated from Berlin by inexperienced journalists and the foreign diplomats accredited there. FA intercept N.114,016 of 31 March, for instance, showed the Bulgarian envoy in London reporting to Sofia that the immediate cause of the British guarantee to Poland was "a report of imminent German action against Poland".* A further factor in London – as the intercept of a Yugoslav despatch showed – was the duplicity of the Romanian envoy, Virgil Tilea, who boasted to

---

* On 29 March 1939 the *News Chronicle's* Berlin correspondent, Ian Colvin ("a nice young man – rather precious"), visited Whitehall, saw Lord Halifax, Sir Alexander Cadogan and then Chamberlain, and gave "hair-raising details of imminent German thrust against Poland" (Cadogan Diary). This was, of course, untrue.

the Yugoslav that he had exploited the endemic hysteria in London to claim – for purely commercial reasons – that Hitler had presented an ultimatum to Romania. Whatever the origins of England's attitude, by the time Hitler left Berlin – that is, by 8:47 P.M. on 31 March – he had given the OKW its orders. At Wilhelmshaven next morning he launched a second 35,000-ton battleship: the *Tirpitz*.

It is to be emphasized that he had still not issued any actual instruction for war. The new OKW directive on "White", issued on 3 April 1939, merely outlined a possible political situation which might make an attack on Poland necessary, on or after 1 September. Meanwhile, the OKW ruled, friction with Poland was to be avoided – a difficult injunction, because few Germans objected to the prospect of punishing the Poles, since the Poles had certainly not behaved kindly toward their own ethnic German minority. As noted earlier, for reasons of diplomacy Hitler had already had to forbid the Nazi press to mention various outrages that had occurred in Poland during the summer of '38; many such edicts to the Nazi editors exist. Hitler knew that the righting of this last injustice of Versailles would be a popular cause in Germany, but during April – and again in May – 1939 explicit fresh directives went out to every Nazi editor not to print reports of the growing stream of German refugees arriving from Poland, or to reply in kind to Polish editorials, let alone to draw acute comparisons between what was happening in Poland and what had happened in 1938 in Czechoslovakia.

Hitler probably hoped that "whetting the blade" alone would force the Poles to think again, particularly if they realized that he was wooing Stalin. As General von Reichenau admiringly commented on 3 October 1938: "If the Führer was a poker player, he'd win hundreds of thousands of Reichsmarks every night. Just look at his form so far!" In April 1939 this poker image also came to Baron von Weizsäcker's mind – the diplomat believed that Hitler was playing a game for high stakes, but would pick up the winnings at just the right moment and stop. In mid-April he forecast privately, "A creeping crisis, but short of war. Every man must do his duty."

Göring's aide, the Luftwaffe general Karl Bodenschatz, dropped a broad hint to the Polish military attaché that if Hitler believed he was being encircled, as the shower of guarantees from London implied, then he would make an alliance with the devil himself. "And you and I are well aware of who that Devil is," threatened Bodenschatz.

A few days later, Mussolini attacked Albania – a thrust into the Balkans that choked Hitler. His entire Ostpolitik depended on keeping the Balkans stable. From FA intercepts, Hitler could see the British at once begin overtures to Turkey to join a defensive coalition in the south-east. He ordered Ribbentrop to rush Franz von Papen, the Reich's most experienced diplomat, to the Turkish capital to assuage fears there that this might be Mussolini's first move towards the Dardanelles Straits. Papen's job would be to do everything possible to prevent Turkey signing an alliiance with the British. Privately, Hitler regarded the Duce's ill-considered action as one inspired by naked jealousy of the Nazi triumphs. "He regrets", noted one adjutant, "that Mussolini didn't consult him over the Albanian operation. But he does see why, because after all he didn't ask the Italians for advice either, thank God! Because if you tell those Italian blabber-mouths anything secret you might as well print it in the daily press."

Curiously, Hitler had not consulted Göring over "White". Göring did not return from his Italian leave until 6 P.M. on 18 April. He appeared at Hitler's dinner table looking bronzed and fit. Hitler told him now of his determination to force a settlement over Danzig. Göring was taken aback: "What am I supposed to understand by that?" The Führer replied that if all else failed to regain Danzig, he was going to use force. Göring was unsettled, and warned that world opinion would not stand for it. Hitler calmed him down, saying he had handled other situations skilfully in the past and Poland would be no exception. Nevertheless, over the next months until 1 September it is noticeable that Göring tried hard to avoid an outright conflict.

Initially, Hitler used his approach to the Kremlin only as a diplomatic lever on Poland. There was no doubting Stalin's interest. Rudolf Likus reported on 1 April that the Soviet war minister, General K. E. Voroshilov, had disparaged the western powers in a social conversation with the wife of the German ambassador, and had suggested that Hitler and Stalin revise their attitude to each other. A week later, Ribbentrop began exploring in Berlin: he asked a member of the Polish Section of his personal staff to brush up his Soviet embassy acquaintances. Shortly, Ribbentrop learned from him that a high embassy official had remarked that Germany and the USSR could pursue a great policy "side by side". Hitler still hesitated to inch out further onto this thin ice, and Ribbentrop instructed his man not to pursue the dialogue. But he and Keitel went in person to see off the Soviet ambassador when he returned to Moscow later that month, and at the end of April, Hitler again omitted all the usual hostile references to the Soviet regime.

A second factor impelling Hitler towards Stalin was the temporary collapse of Ribbentrop's negotiations with Japan on an alliance. So it would hardly matter now if Hitler did put Japanese noses out of joint. Most dramatic of all was the inviting gambit made by Stalin on 3 May – he dismissed Maxim Litvinov, the Jewish foreign minister who would have been an obvious obstacle to any settlement with Nazi Germany. Now Hitler really sat up and took notice.

He ordered key Moscow embassy officials to report to him in Germany. The outcome was an instruction to his ambassador, Count Werner von der Schulenburg, to throw out cautious feelers to Vyacheslav Molotov, the new foreign minister, as to a possible rapprochement and the resumption of trade negotiations. On the fifth Goebbels confidentially instructed all Nazi editors that there were to be no further diatribes against Bolshevism or the Soviet Union "until further notice".

On the following day there was again a curious and sinister hint dropped by Karl Bodenschatz – this time to the French air attaché, Paul Stehlin. Bodenschatz stated that Hitler was determined to regain Danzig and secure Germany's access to East Prussia. "I really can't tell you more," said Bodenschatz,. "but you'll soon find out that something is afoot in the east." And to make himself clearer he added: "When it's a matter of carrying out a plan, then legal and ideological obstacles hardly matter. As you well know, even the most Catholic of kings once had no qualms about making common cause with the Turks. . . ."

Fifty

Most people measure their ages in years expired. Hitler mentally measured his in terms of the years still remaining to him. As he watched the weekly "rushes" of the movie newsreels, in which he often seemed the only figure, he noticed with annoyance that he was ageing and getting paunchy too. If his political pace now seemed to quicken as he moved forward to world domination, this was the cause.

On 20 April 1939, Hitler reached that plateau in life: fifty. Seldom had the world seen such a vulgar display of muscle as Nazi Germany staged to celebrate the Führer's birthday. Reich agencies had been perfecting the plans for weeks. The final programme overflowed backwards on to the nineteenth as well, with 1,600 Party notables crowding into the Mosaic Hall at one moment, and the "Adolf Hitler" Shock Troop and the Wearers of the Blood Insignia – veterans of the 1923 putsch attempt – milling around in the Marble Gallery at another. While the traditional Badenweiler March was played that evening, he drove with Speer along the fine new East-West axis boulevard and opened it as rockets embroidered a huge image of the swastika flag into the sky. At one vantage-point were mustered the surviving ex-soldiers of Germany's nineteenth-century wars – survivors of generations who had marched vainly towards that dreamland that was "now in sight".

When Hitler returned, hundreds of gifts were on display in his Residence's dining-room, including a model of the triumphal arch that he planned to erect on the new North-South axis. The names of all the German and Austrian dead of the Great War would be carved into its stone. Hitler himself had first sketched this monument twenty years before. His secretary, Christa Schroeder, wrote next day:

> The number and value of this year's presents is quite staggering. Paintings by Defregger, Waldmüller, Lenbach and even a magnificent Titian, wonderful Meissen porcelain figurines, silver table-services, precious books, vases,

drawings, carpets, craftwork, globes, radios, clocks, etc., etc., etc. And crates of eggs, huge cakes, boxes of chocolates, fruit juices, liqueurs, a beautiful sailing boat made of flowers (what a pity its beauty will fade so soon). Of course there are model ships and aircraft and other military paraphernalia too – those are the things he's happiest about. He's just like a boy with them.

As midnight approached, a choir of his SS Lifeguards began to sing in the courtyard. From all over Germany units were converging on Berlin for the morrow's parade-spectacular: six army divisions, some 40,000 men with 600 tanks, were to parade past him. By 4 A.M. the marchers were at the capital's outskirts; the railroad stations were packed. At 8 A.M. he was awakened by the Lifeguards band playing a serenade outside his window. The children of the doctors and adjutants shyly came forward to wish him well, and to give him posies of flowers that they had confected with Frau Anneliese Schmundt, his chief adjutant's wife, and to recite poems to him. Hitler wanted these children to have a day they could remember to their grandchildren. (All of them still survive – except the Goebbels children.)

Before the four-hour military parade began, Hitler briefly received his three C-in-Cs – Göring, Raeder and Brauchitsch – with Keitel in his lofty panelled study. It was an occasion their adjutants well recall: Ottomar Hansen, who replaced Keitel's adjutant Eberhard at this time, told his wife that evening that he had attended something that morning which would change their lives, but about which he could not yet say more. Hitler stood with his back to his big desk as the officers were ushered in by Meissner (himself wearing an army colonel's uniform). Keitel stumbled slightly on the thick ochre-coloured carpet as they stationed themselves in line, with their adjutants at a respectful distance behind them. Hitler's speech cannot have lasted more than ten minutes, but when he ended all of this select audience recognized that Germany was heading inevitably toward war with the western powers, not necessarily in 1939 – but soon.

No record survives, unfortunately, but the sense was this: "Gentlemen, the first half-century of my life is now over. Much has been accomplished, but much still has to be done to safeguard the future of our Reich. I am now at the very peak of my vitality and vigour, and no other German will possess the strength or authority to complete what I have set out to achieve. The next years will be crucial for our Reich. Until 1942 or 1943 we shall still have the lead in the arms race with the western powers, but with each passing year this lead narrows. So if anything is to be won, it must be fought for now."

The birthday parade itself gave vivid proof of Hitler's staggering powers of physical endurance. Hour after hour the troops, personnel-carriers, artillery and tanks stomped, rumbled and rattled past his saluting base. Christa Schroeder wrote afterwards, "The birthday was a terrific exertion for him. . . . Yesterday's parade was enormous and dragged on endlessly. . . . I keep wondering where on earth he finds the strength for it all, because to be on your feet for four hours on end, saluting, must be damned exhausting. We got dog-tired just from watching – at least I did."

There is no doubt that Hitler had the physical constitution of a horse.

As seen by his doctors in 1939, Adolf Hitler stood 5 foot 9 inches in his socks and weighed about 155 pounds. His medical files show that until the last months of his life his bodily functions were normal except during brief illnesses. For the record, his veins were filled with group A blood. His skin was pale and fine in texture. On his chest and back the skin was quite white and hairless. The staff doctors noted that the Führer reacted normally to heat and cold, and to sharp and dull touch. His skull was of the kind classified as "slightly delicho-cephalic", with no evidence of mastoid pathology. His hair in 1939 was dark brown with only slight thinning evident. His face was pale and symmetrical, and his expression was regarded as having "an intense quality that subdued and captivated". His large, coarse nose disturbed the fine features, but his "fascinating eyes" compensated for this. The left eye was in fact slightly larger than the right; his eyes were blue faintly tinged with grey. In 1939 they moved in good co-ordination, and his pupillary reflexes were normal. A minimal degree of exophthalmia, a protrusion of the eyeballs, was always present.

When questioned in 1945, the medics who had treated Hitler were unanimous that he had been sane until the very end. One of them, Professor Hanskarl von Hasselbach, has subsequently observed, "The German public would have been lunatic to have given their virtually unanimous support to any man such as Hitler is portrayed today." There were no clinical symptoms of abnormality. He suffered no olfactory, auditory or visual hallucinations; there was no papillo-oedema of the eyes, in 1945 they were still normal in both alignment and movement. During his various examinations of Hitler – referred to in the surviving medical files as "Patient A", "M.F." or "Adolf Müller" – his principal physician, Professor Theo Morell, observed that Hitler could wrinkle his forehead, put out his tongue and shrug his shoulders. His concentration was excellent and he showed no mental faults like euphoria, incontinence, anosmia (loss of smell) or personality changes. Brain examinations disclosed no "sensory aphasia" and no "dream states". Tests on his reflex centres and spinal-root functions revealed no abnormalities either.

Interrogated in 1945 about Hitler's psychiatric condition, Morell described it as "very complex"; the other doctors put on record that his orientation as to time, place and persons was excellent. His memory was so good as to become almost legendary. Their report adds: "He was changeable, at times restless and sometimes peculiar but otherwise co-operative and not easily distracted. Emotionally he was very labile – his likes and dislikes were very pronounced. His flow of thought showed continuity. His speech was neither slow nor fast, and was always relevant." Common symptoms of insanity were absent: his doctors observed neither "globus hystericus" – a ball-in-the-throat sensation – nor phobias or obsessions. They concluded that in Hitler "no hallucinations, illusions or paranoid trends were present." These experts spoke with such unanimity, that all the contrary speculation of post-1945 and more recent writers and "psycho-historians" must be viewed with considerable doubt.

Who were his doctors? By 1939, his principal medics were Morell and Brandt. Dr Karl Brandt had attended him since 1934. A handsome, dark-haired young surgeon with well-proportioned features, Brandt was born in the Alsace but deported by the French as a boy of fifteen when they occupied the province in 1919. He had a grim sense of humour that did not desert him even on his execution in 1947 for his role in Hitler's euthanasia programme: on that grim day's eve he joked with fellow prisoners, "Tomorrow is prize-giving day!" Brandt also had a strict sense of propriety, refusing to discuss Hitler's sex-life with his American interrogators, for instance. He had studied surgery at a Ruhr hospital specializing in mining injuries. His fiancée was the champion swimmer Anni Rehborn, one of the stars in the feminine firmament around Hitler in the Twenties; she introduced him to Hitler in 1932. In 1933 he was on the spot when Wilhelm Brückner was injured in a motor accident, and he operated on the Führer adjutant's fractured skull. Hitler realized that a travelling surgeon might prove useful, and Brandt accompanied him to Venice in 1934. Brandt introduced his Ruhr colleague, Professor Werner Haase, as his stand-in, and in 1936 Hanskarl von Hasselbach was appointed his deputy on Hitler's staff.

By late 1936, Hitler was plagued by a persistent stomach ailment that neither his own nor outside doctors were able to cure: and that was where Morell came in. He was to become the most controversial of Hitler's medicine men. Three years older than Hitler, Dr Theodore Morell was corpulent, with a bald, podgy head and swarthy complexion. His dark-brown eyes blinked myopically through thick-lensed spectacles; his hands were large and hairy. He had established himself by 1935 as a leading doctor in the Kurfürstendamm world of stage and film stars. But his slick black hair and obese figure had made him the archetype of the Jews against whom Streicher polemicized – so the non-Jew Morell had joined the Party to ward off ruin from his practice. The film world introduced him to Hitler's photographer Hoffmann, who needed his specialist attention (he had a venereal disease); Hitler provided a plane to fly him to Munich for the purpose. It was here, in Hoffmann's home, that Morell first met Hitler in May 1936. He found Hitler upset over the death from meningitis of his beloved chauffeur, Julius Schreck, a few days before. Morell gave him the distinct impression that he, Morell, might have saved Schreck's life.

Hitler's stomach pains continued. Professor von Eicken, who had operated on Hitler's throat in 1935,* examined him again on 20 May 1936. His consultation notes survive:

> 20 May. Consultation at the Reich Chancellery in conjunction with Dr Brandt. [Führer suffering from] a roaring in the ears for several days, with high-pitched metallic sound in the left ear at night. Ears: no abnormalities observed. Hearing: more than six metres to each side. Obviously overworked. Preoccupied (chauffeur Schreck!).
>
> Sleeps very little – can't get to sleep. [I recommend:] evening strolls before retiring to bed, hot and cold foot baths, mild sedatives! Time off. Always feels better at Wachenfeld [i.e. the Berghof].
>
> At Christmas 1934, Dr Grawitz treated M.F. [mein Führer] for acute food-poisoning, with Neo-Balestol, which contains fusel-oil. Headaches, giddiness, roaring in the ears.

This was the illustrious patient that Morell took on at Christmas 1936: Hitler had invited the Morells to stay on the Obersalzberg with him. While the house-party was distracted by a noisy contest at the Berghof's basement bowling-alley, Hitler took Morell aside into the winter garden; Bormann and Brandt both tried to follow, but Hitler waved them back. Hitler recounted to Morell his sorry tale – how nobody else could cure his terrible stomach cramps, from the sleek-haired "SS Reich-Doctor", Dr Ernst-Robert Grawitz of Berlin's West End hospital, to the austere Professor Bergmann, the uncrowned king of Berlin's famous Charité hospital: Hitler only had to overhear the drastic cure that Bergmann proposed, for him to flee the consulting rooms. Grawitz's subsequent treatment was no less severe. During 1936, Hitler had grown sicker and thinner. He told Morell: "You are my last hope. If you can get rid of my stomach pains I'll give you a fine house." Morell promised, "I'll have you fit and well again inside a year." The cure worked. Morell got the house, a fine villa on Schwanenwerder Island. And to Morell's subsequent detractors – who were legion – the Führer loyally pointed out: "Morell made me a promise: one year. . . ."

Thus when a young army doctor, horrified at Morell's practices, tried to discourage Hitler's loyalty to his physician in 1944, the Führer replied: "Doctor, you've no idea what I owe Morell. He saved my life in 1936. I was so far gone I could hardly walk. I wasn't being given the right treatment. Grawitz and Bergmann made me starve until I was only eating dry biscuits and tea. I had eczema on my legs so I had to walk swathed in bandages, and it was impossible to wear boots." A small army of dermatologists had anointed him with the grimmest possible lotions, but the eczema just got worse. "I was so weak I could hardly work even at my desk. Then Morell came – and healed me."

Morell's first clinical examination of Hitler was at the Berghof on 3 January

---

* See page 47 above.

1937. He found that the stomach cramps were *not* of hysteric origin. There was a swelling in the pyloric region of the stomach, the left lobe of the liver was extended and there was tenderness near the right kidney. There was severe eczema on the left leg, probably in consequence of Hitler's dietary problems. "Morell", recalled Hitler in 1944, "drew up a healthy daily routine for me, he controlled my diet and above all he permitted me to start eating again. He went right back to first principles. First he examined my intestinal bacteria, then he told me my coli-bacilli would have to be replaced." All this was sound medical practice.

Morell sent an anonymous specimen of Hitler's excreta to Professor A. Nissle, director of a bacteriological research institute at Freiburg. Nissle's report spoke of the presence of dysbacterial flora in the patient's intestinal tract. Nissle had prepared a commercial medicine for treating this condition, called "Mutaflor", an emulsion of a certain strain of *coli communis bacillus* which had the property of colonizing the intestinal tract. "I was given these coli capsules and large quantities of vitamins and extracts of heart and liver," Hitler recounted. He began to feel better. Morell moved in to the Berghof. "After about six months," said Hitler, "the eczema had gone and after nine months I was completely well again." In September 1937, Morell was an honoured guest at the Party rally: Hitler could wear boots again.

Immediately the jealous rumours against Morell began. People said he had never qualified, and that was why he did not claim to be a "Facharzt," a specialist. His technique was anything but antiseptic. He used one cloth to mop the table and to bind an arm after an injection; he used the same needle twice on successive patients without cleaning it; he injected Hitler daily from ampoules unmarked by any kind of label. He began treating Hitler with medicines that he had devised himself and was manufacturing in one of his pharmaceutical companies. Hitler paid him an annual retainer of 36,000 Reichsmarks – not much, considering his previous income had been four times as high – enabling Morell to purchase properties in the largely Jewish coastal resort of Heringsdorf on the Baltic, and to equip a flamboyant surgery in Berlin's West End, in the best part of Kurfürstendamm. Hitler's coterie, however, also rushed to become Morell's patients – Funk, Ley, Speer, Goebbels, Göring, the Ribbentrops, all Hitler's older adjutants, his generals like Kleist, Jodl and Heusinger, and famous theatre names like Richard Tauber and O. E. Hasse too. Morell was the back door to Hitler, people believed. He was too witless to intrigue, but the hostility this situation aroused is easily conceived. The younger adjutants made life uncomfortable for him – Morell was left out of their birthday greeting lists and other invitations. Their wives refused to let him touch them.

It is true that Morell's personal habits were revolting, but Hitler ignored them: this was characteristic of him. Morell rarely washed and was in that sense unapproachable. Hitler defended him thus: "I don,'t retain Morell to sniff at him, but to keep me fit." His eating habits were audible and unpleasant. In July 1939 he was among the guests at Frau Winifred Wagner's house at Bayreuth. When Hitler inquired of Verena, his favourite among the Wagner girls, why she was not eating she pointed to the disturbing spectacle of the fat doctor busily and noisily devouring a whole orange with both hands, sucking its contents through a small window that he had scooped out of its peel.

Morell was the first doctor that Hitler allowed to give him a complete physical examination. As he described it, the Führer's medical history was not unusual. His tonsils had been removed, though he had no recollection of any operation; as a child he had displayed a pulmonary apical pathology, that had disappeared in later years. Morell noticed a scar on Hitler's left thigh, caused by wartime shrapnel. During the 1923 putsch, the dying Scheubner-Richter had pulled Hitler down, resulting in a fracture of Hitler's left shoulder-blade (so that for many years now Hitler had been unable to abduct or rotate his upper left arm more than a limited amount).

In 1938 and 1939, Hitler was unquestionably at the peak of his health. He looked younger than fifty. Major physical exertions like the Birthday Parade were child's play to him. He could still laugh heartily, and was outwardly a very healthy man despite a few private eccentricities like his extreme vegetarianism. The laboratory that periodically ran checks for Morell on the contents of "Patient A's" stomach expressed discreet surprise that these consisted solely of vegetable fibres. A typical Berghof menu for Hitler in the summer of 1937 was this: "Barley soup followed by semolina noodles and an egg and green salad."

From Morell's own records, it is clear that most of his medicines were administered by hypodermic syringe, whether his patients suffered from coughs or cancer. They often felt better afterwards: but Morell was usually just giving shots of harmless dextrose, hormones or vitamins that had very little long-term benefit. He also administered liberal quantities of sulphonamide drugs to treat even the common cold – effective enough, but an irresponsible use of a drug to which the human body rapidly becomes resistant. Hitler certainly was impressed. "Without Morell," he once said, "I would not be able to achieve half as much. I would never be able to endure the mental and physical burden." Three to six Morell-type injections a day soon stopped Hitler's colds almost before they started. The daily injections of 10 cc of glucose and of Morell's own proprietary compound, Vitamultin, containing virtually every vitamin from A to K – it consisted of ascorbic acid, calcium, nicotinic acid amine, and either caffeine or cocoa as a sweetener – left Hitler with a kind of euphoria: and soon Morell was treating Hitler with his "pep" shots of glucose before major speeches and parades. In this way the body's normal built-in powers of resistance were being replaced by injected substitutes – not narcotics, but just as habit-forming.

In fact, Hitler's stomach spasms returned despite the Mutaflor treatment. Morell then prescribed intramuscular injections of "Progynon", a preparation with benzoic acid and dihydro-follicle hormone which tends to prevent spasm of the gastric walls. He also administered "Luizym" enzyme tablets, to make Hitler's vegetable food intake more digestible. From 1938 to 1940 he also occasionally injected 3 cc of "Glyconorm" – the product of another of his associated factories, Nordmark Werke in Hamburg, containing metabolic ferments, vitamins and amino acids. Yet after a while the stomach cramps returned. In 1939, Morell put Hitler on a course of "Euflat" pills that was to last five years, and injections of "Eukodal" and "Eupaverinum".

A modern expert scanning Morell's treatment notes has suggested he was "polypragmatic" – keen to dose Hitler with a bit of everything: not enough to do much harm, but not enough to do much good. Hitler trusted him, and so did most of his staff. In a prison camp in 1945, Brandt rebuked him: "Your behaviour has brought disgrace on the entire medical profession!" Yet Morell cured Goebbels of a skin disease where twenty-two leading dermatologists had failed. And when Rudolf Hess flew to Scotland in 1941, it was Morell's little vitamin pills and energy tablets that he had packed in his luggage. Morell's patient, Hitler, was to outlive both Neville Chamberlain and Franklin D. Roosevelt.

It is to the actions of Chamberlain and Roosevelt in April 1939 that we now return, as – late that month – Europe took another lurch towards war. For domestic political reasons, Chamberlain decided to reintroduce National Service and announced this on the twenty-sixth. Henderson had just returned to Berlin from London, where a strident British press campaign was beginning. He informed the Foreign Office on 25 April – an unpublished telegram, intercepted however by the FA for Hitler – that this rendered his position very unpleasant: "The press is making life very difficult for me." Next day's FA wiretaps showed that the Foreign Office told him to give the Nazi government advance warning of Chamberlain's conscription announcement – Hitler too was due to speak at the Reichstag shortly – and to reassure it that National Service was not to be construed as directed against Germany.

Hitler's speech on 28 April was primarily a diatribe against Roosevelt, however. Hitherto he had felt able to ignore the President's forays into European politics. At the time of Munich, Roosevelt had sent him an open telegram: Neurath took it from Wiedemann's hands and pocketed it with the words, "What business does Roosevelt have poking his nose in here?" That was Hitler's attitude too. He blamed Roosevelt's anti-Reich stance on Jewish influences. The US chargé d'affaires in Budapest had recently advised the new foreign minister there, Count Csáky, that world war was certain in 1939; and on 16 January, Csáky had repeated this to Ribbentrop and quoted the American's remark: "That's why the Americans are exploiting the Jewish issue from Canada right down to the tip of South America."

Hitler believed that the isolationists were still the stronger force in the United States. Fritz Todt had sent to Hewel, for example, a recent letter from a Harvard professor, Arthur Casagrande, reporting, "Roosevelt's attitude to Germany is strongly criticized here among my many acquaintances. There is no doubt the vast majority of Americans are against this meddling in European affairs . . . Roosevelt is trying to distract public attention from his own domestic failures." All this was what Hitler wanted to hear.

Then, in April 1939, Hitler was the bemused recipient of yet another open letter from Roosevelt, appealing to him to give public assurances that he would not attack any of thirty-one specified countries. This unorthodox diplomacy caused embarrassment in London; and wiretaps on the US embassy in Berlin revealed that staff there regarded it as a gaffe. Ribbentrop's staff asked each of the thirty-one countries (except Poland, Russia, Britain and France) whether they felt threatened by Nazi Germany – all replied No (although some negatives were obliquely phrased). Hitler made his reply in his Reichstag speech on the twenty-eighth. The Kroll Opera-house rocked with laughter as he added sardonically his own personal assurance that the Reich was not planning to invade the USA either. A copy of the speech was handed in at the US embassy, betokening Hitler's only reply. The FA wiretaps noted that US embassy staff conceded the Führer had won "the match".

In the same Reichstag speech – delivered as usual without Ribbentrop's prior approval – Hitler revoked the 1934 non-aggression pact with Poland and the 1935 naval agreement with Britain too. Again he notably abstained from attacking the USSR. In private, he justified his stiffer attitude to Britain by the secret documents now found in Prague archives. "One day we'll publish them to all the world, to prove Britain's dishonesty," Bodenschatz told a French diplomat. "All we're asking for is our right to live, and we're not going to let a country that owns three-fifths of the earth deny us this elementary right." But informed Germans still doubted that there would be war. Baron von Weizsäcker commented in one letter on 29 April, "Evidently we are not going to escape a degree of drama. But I don't believe that the Axis powers have any aggressive intentions, any more than that the other side will launch a deliberate preventive war. There is only one danger – and that is the unbridled Polish lesser minions, who are banging and crashing up and down the European keyboard with true Slav megalomania."

On Goebbels' express orders, the newspaper editors continued to soft-pedal their reports on "incidents" in Poland; throughout April, May and June, reporting was restricted to Page 2. But the German army continued its preparations for "White". Late in April, Hitler was shown by Halder a first file of maps and documents setting out the German and Polish strengths, giving a rough invasion timetable and an overall planning timetable beginning in May. The General Staff suggested that troops should be moved up to the Polish frontier under camouflage of an "East Wall" project and of autumn manoeuvres. Further forces could be transferred into the East Prussian enclave, ostensibly for a big military parade to mark the twenty-fifth anniversary of the Battle of Tannenberg – 27 August 1939. Hitler had to admit that under Halder the General Staff was at last improving.

In the third week of May, he set out on a third inspection tour of the army's West Wall and the Luftwaffe's parallel Flak zone, from the Belgian frontier right down to Switzerland. Again hordes of Party notables, press correspondents, adjutants and newsreel cameramen followed. The fortifications had made significant progress, and General Erwin von Witzleben, Adam's successor as western commander, spoke loudly to this effect.

Hitler's contacts with these honest labourers and the local Rhinelanders had a restorative effect on him. He lunched in the village inns, while his adjutant Brückner went out and calmed the milling crowds and assured them that their Führer would shortly reappear. Then he would emerge and stroll freely among them. The women held out their children to him – a simple act that was the greatest mark of respect a leader could be shown, as Hitler remarked to his adjutants. This was the shield that protected Hitler in 1939: he was dictator by consent; an assassin would neither be forgiven nor understood. This monolithic solidarity of Führer and Volk persisted right to his end, despite what subsequent generations have assumed.

On the twentieth he watched an SS exercise with live ammunition at Munsterlager. On his return to Berlin, Hitler decided to speak to his C-in-Cs alone about "White" and its implications soon. His confidence that he could isolate the Danzig issue, and detach Poland from her allies, was growing. A month earlier the USSR had opened talks with Britain and France on a comprehensive alliance, but the secret signs were that the western powers were making slow headway: Stalin knew Hitler had more to offer. And on 25 May wiretaps on *The Times* correspondent in Berlin, Mr James Holburn, showed he had learned privately in London that Chamberlain did not have his heart in an alliance with Stalin – he still hoped one day to resume his direct contacts with Hitler.* While

---

* A wiretap placed by the Secret Service in London early in May 1939 tipped off the Foreign Office that Chamberlain and Sir Horace Wilson *were* talking "appeasement" again. The FO was indignant.

the Forschungsamt provided only patchy data on the Moscow talks, a good source in London was feeding excellent information on the British efforts in Moscow to the German embassy. On 17 May the Soviet chargé in Berlin, Astakhov, hinted that "on present form" the talks were going against the British. Meanwhile, the Russians continued to lure the Germans on. On 20 May, Molotov himself declared to Hitler's ambassador that trade talks with Germany could be resumed just as soon as the necessary "political basis" had been established: Ribbentrop discussed at length with Hitler how this vague remark might be interpreted. The outcome was that Weizsäcker was instructed by Hitler to put this to Astakhov: "You can be our friends or our enemies. The choice is yours."

Hitler delivered his four-hour secret speech to his C-in-Cs on 23 May 1939, in his lofty study. The ulterior object was to put them on their toes that summer. He stood at a lectern and addressed altogether a dozen officers seated in three rows: Raeder, Milch, Brauchitsch and Keitel formed the front row (Göring was out of Berlin), and their chiefs of staff and adjutants the two other rows. In many respects his harangue was no different from the other key speeches of 1938 and 1939 that have since been found: he stated that Danzig was not his ultimate objective – that would be to secure Lebensraum in the east to feed Germany's eighty million inhabitants. He again warned against yearning for colonial possessions overseas: Britain could always blockade these in any war.

"If Fate forces us to fight in the west," Hitler told them, "it will be just as well if first we possess more in the east." To fight a war in the west *first* would be long and arduous, and Poland would then tackle them in the rear. This was why he had decided to "take on Poland at the first suitable opportunity". This time he warned them not to rely on a second Munich or Prague: this time there would be fighting. His immediate purpose now, he explained, would be to isolate Poland. "It is of crucial importance that we succeed in isolating her." The only surviving note is one by Colonel Schmundt, but it is of controversial probative value as it was evidently written much, much later: it lists as present officers – including Göring and Warlimont – who were not there and contains various anachronisms. But Halder, questioned in mid-1945 *before* being shown the Schmundt protocol, well remembered Hitler's assurances that he would keep the western powers out of "White": "I would have to be a complete idiot to slither into a world war – like those nincompoops of 1914 – over the lousy Polish Corridor."

At the end of Hitler's rambling speech, his select audience was little wiser than at its beginning. Admiral Raeder privately reminded him that the navy was not ready for war with Britain. This evoked a further cryptic utterance, according to Raeder's adjutant, Captain Schulte-Mönting. Hitler said, "You'll find I have three kinds of plans. The first we can talk about, man to man, like this. The second I keep secret. And the third are those problems of the future that even I have not had time to think right through to their logical conclusion."

That summer there were few signs that Poland would lie low, as foreign journalists returning from Warsaw privately reported. On 16 May, Rudolf Likus wrote that the Berlin correspondent of *Gazeta Polska*, a personal friend of foreign minister Beck, was telling everybody that Poland was not afraid to fight because now she had mighty allies: and that victory over Hitler would bring the Polish annexation of East Prussia.

Hitler had left Mussolini in the dark about "White". Keitel had not even hinted at it when he met Italian generals at Innsbruck on 23 April. Now the Italians were willing to sign a formal alliance with Germany. On 6 May, Ribbentrop assured the Italian foreign minister Ciano that Italy could assume there would be peace for three more years at least. Ciano came to Berlin to sign the "Pact of Steel" on the twenty-second, and Milch signed a separate air-force pact in Rome two days later. Milch in fact returned to Hitler with a warning that Mussolini had emphasized that Italy would not be ready for war until 1942; in a memorandum to the Führer, the Duce even talked of 1943. So Italy's actions late in August should not have surprised Hitler as they did.

Hitler also briefly courted the Reich's other southern neighbour, Yugoslavia. On 1 June 1939 the Prince Regent Paul and his English wife Olga were welcomed in Berlin with an extravagant military parade on the new East-West axis. A banquet was thrown at Hitler's residence, followed by a gala performance of Wagner's *Meistersinger* at the Prussian State Opera-house. (Here an awkward incident occurred that made Hitler vow to Winifred Wagner that the 31-year-old Herbert von Karajan should never be allowed to conduct at Bayreuth: conducting as usual without a score, Karajan lost his place, the baritone's voice tailed to embarrassed silence and the music died away while the curtain was briefly rung down to restore order. Hitler hoped his visitors had not noticed.) Twice he entertained the royal couple alone – to lunch in his residence, and to tea served in a pavilion in the garden, an honour that even Göring had only enjoyed twice. Later, Hitler showed them the room where the models of new official buildings and monuments were on display.

Yet he was displeased at the outcome, because Paul unexpectedly travelled on to London afterwards without having even hinted at this in Berlin. Hitler did not like being tricked, and raged about it for some days afterwards – Paul was barely suited for a curator's job in the House of Art, while Olga was a typical ice-cold Englishwoman only concerned with high living. The Prince Regent, said Hitler, was slippery as an eel: each time he thought he could extract a firm agreement from him, the Prince had claimed sanctuary behind his Parliament.

Olga for her part had succumbed to Hitler's wiles. The US envoy in Belgrade talked with her and reported,

> Princess Olga quoted Herr Hitler as saying he could not understand why he was so misunderstood in England and that he wished that relations between Great Britain and Germany might be restored. . . . When the conversation turns to children, she said, tears come to his eyes. She described his eyes as being remarkable, clear blue and honest-looking. He told her that he had a dual personality; that his real personality is that of an artist and architect, but that fate had decreed that he should also be a politician, a military man and the builder of a new Germany. . . . Herr Hitler told Princess Olga that he is a man of simple tastes and that he would prefer to live in a small house without any luxury whatever. For the sake of his prestige, however, he was forced to live in a large palace and to be surrounded with a certain amount of pomp and ceremony. She said that he is really musical and that music is his chief relaxation. She described him during the performance of *Die Meistersinger* at Berlin as shutting his eyes as though he were in a trance. . . .

Hitler left Berlin for the summer on 7 June and settled on the Obersalzberg. Once he drove to Vienna, where he paid a furtive visit to Geli Raubal's grave on 12 June. A week later a circular went round all the ministers and gauleiters:

> The Führer will probably spend the summer months of this year also at the Berghof in Obersalzberg. As his main purpose in retiring to the Berghof is to be able to work undisturbed, he has expressed the wish that you should refrain from any manner of visit there unless a firm invitation has been issued by him.

One invitation went to Brauchitsch and Köstring, the military attaché in Moscow. They came on 21 June to discuss planning progress on "White" and the Anglo-Soviet stalemate.

In May a study group under General von Rundstedt – now in Hitler's good graces again – had predicted that the Poles would have to design their defence campaign so as to hold back the Germans long enough for Russian or western aid to come. Poland might even attack first. The Wehrmacht's main strategic problem was to prevent a withdrawal of the Polish army behind the Narev, Vistula and San rivers – but it was felt the Poles would not adopt such a strategy for political reasons. Rundstedt's final plan, dated 15 June, accepted Hitler's demand for surprise attacks to open "White". This would prevent the Poles from mobilizing. The Polish armies west of the Vistula and Narev rivers would be destroyed by concentric attacks from Silesia in the south and from Pomerania and East Prussia in the north; the East Prussian element, a thrust towards Warsaw, was included on Hitler's insistence against General Staff advice. Reinforcements began moving to East Prussia by sea, camouflaged as preparations for the Tannenberg anniversary celebration.

After the generals left that day, 21 June 1939, Hitler relaxed with a sketching pad, deftly drawing a Party Forum that would grace Munich after his death – a vast parade square, Nazi Party office buildings, a bridge across Gabelsberger Strasse, and his own mausoleum, dwarfing the city's famous Frauenkirche and built to "last until the end of time". It was a concrete sign of his optimism about the future.

Hitler's personal household was distinguished by a level-headedness often lacking in his ministers and Party leaders. He liked familiar faces; those adjutants he liked lasted a long time and, oddly, he tolerated the blue-blooded officers like von Below and von Puttkamer the longest. His Chefadjutant, Wilhelm Brückner, aged fifty-four, was a burly ex-machine-gunner who had marched with him in 1923 and served in Landsberg prison: from his private papers, Brückner appears of strongly religious, almost eccentric leanings. Another senior personal adjutant was ex-druggist Julius Schaub, aged forty, an undistinguished cripple but also a Landsberg veteran. Hitler had noticed Schaub painfully hobbling into the Party meetings on his crutches, given him a job and – like most of the household – grown to esteem him. From 1925 to the end there are few photos of Hitler which do not have Schaub hovering in his black SS rig in the background.

Head of Hitler's Private Chancellery was Albert Bormann, a quiet, open-faced Bavarian of thirty-six. His feud with his older brother Martin was notorious: Martin considered Albert had married beneath the family station, and had not spoken to him since. If Martin wanted to tell Albert something an orderly was summoned and a written note was passed. If Albert told a joke, only Martin refused to laugh. Hitler tolerated it as he needed both the brothers.

His favourite secretary was Johanna Wolf, aged thirty-nine, who had worked for him since 1930; but she was often ill, and she alternated with Christa Schroeder, thirty-one, who had worked in various SA and Party offices until 1933 when Hitler took a liking to her. Fräulein Schroeder was stolid and sharp-tongued – her feline comments on the progress of Hitler's war often made her colleagues gasp. Since 1938 the Führer had also enjoyed a third secretary, Gerda Daranowski, aged twenty-five: she was beautiful and bright, and Hitler appreciated both qualities. All the girls stayed with him to the end, proving more loyal than many of Hitler's generals and ministers.

The only other member of Hitler's staff of consequence was Walther Hewel, a handsome Rhinelander bachelor of thirty-five. We have already dipped into the letters he sent home as Hitler's fellow prisoner at Landsberg in 1924.* He had emigrated in 1926 for ten years, working first in Britain and then as a quinine, tea and rubber planter in the Dutch East Indies. He had returned at

* See page *xxii* above.

Hitler's personal request in 1936 – voyaging back via China, Japan, Hawaii and the west and east coasts of the USA. He had a pleasant smile, a Roman profile and a penchant for double-breasted suits and gaudy ties. Hitler frequently ribbed him for his bachelor habits: Hewel had travelled many oceans and broken many ladies' hearts. In March 1937, Ribbentrop had engaged him in his private "foreign office" to advise on British affairs, and he had become Ribbentrop's liaison officer to Hitler in 1938. For twenty years Hewel never lost faith in Hitler, and he died as Hitler did.

Hitler's military Adjutantur was controlled by Rudolf Schmundt, aged forty-two, a jug-eared army colonel born in Metz, Alsace. Schmundt had an impeccable upbringing in a famous Potsdam regiment, and a pronounced sympathy towards National Socialism. He had revered Ludwig Beck until the general's vendetta against the OKW command-concept made reverence no longer possible. Mutilated and burned by the bomb planted by Beck's Hitler-assassins in 1944, Schmundt lingered on to a horrible, slow death some months later. Since June 1937, Hitler's Luftwaffe adjutant had been Captain Nicolaus von Below, aged thirty-one, a quiet Pomeranian who had undergone secret flying training at Lipetsk, USSR, became the Richthofen squadron's adjutant in 1935 and then Staffelkapitän of a fighter squadron in the remilitarized Rhineland. His eyes were grey, his fair hair receded at the temples, he was elegant and slim: Hitler liked him, and trusted him enough to carry his last testaments out of the embattled Berlin bunker six years later. From March 1938, Hitler's army adjutant had been Captain Gerhard Engel, aged thirty-three, whose cheekiness and good humour ingratiated him to lower ranks but not to Hitler (who sent him to the front in 1943).

This left the navy adjutant: and thereby hung a tale. Since Puttkamer had returned to the destroyers in June 1938, Hitler's naval adjutant had been Lieutenant-Commander Alwin Broder Albrecht, aged thirty-five: but in June 1939 the appointment ended abruptly, under circumstances that demand we pay more attention to him than the other adjutants. Once again – as with the Blomberg *mésalliance* of 1938 – a faulty marriage was the cause.

Albrecht had recently married a young schoolmistress of Kiel. But she was well known to the local naval garrison: worse, she had been living in sin with a wealthy man – according to anonymous letters received by the stern and puritanical Grand-Admiral Raeder – who had actually been a witness at the Albrecht wedding. The navy's wives raised a howl of protest. Albrecht was obliged to sue one complainer, and unhappily lost. Raeder sent him on "married leave" and when the commander's absence was noticed and questioned, Raeder called unannounced at the Berghof and insisted on Albrecht's dismissal as adjutant for contracting such a dishonourable marriage.

To Raeder's chagrin, Hitler refused. The argument in the Great Hall raged back and forth for two hours, loud enough for the whole building to hear. Raeder indignantly described it as a new Blomberg affair. Hitler however had been caught before, and demanded *proof*. He sneered, "How many of the navy wives now flaunting their virtue have had affairs of their own in the past! Frau Albrecht's past is the concern of nobody but herself. The Blomberg case was quite different. He deliberately married a woman who committed immoral acts for cash and other considerations." Admiral Raeder, thirteen years Hitler's senior, stiffly announced that he would resign unless Albrecht went. Hitler replied that Raeder might do as he pleased. The admiral returned in a huff to Berlin.

Hitler meanwhile invited Frau Grete Albrecht to present herself on the Obersalzberg for his personal inspection. Strolling with his adjutants he growled, "It looks like there's another typical officers' intrigue afoot. But I've forbidden any attempt at blackening my naval adjutant's name. It's always nasty when people allege things and then can't come up with the proof. But I'm not going to let go. I'm going to get to the bottom of it." Engel collected Frau Albrecht from the Berchtesgadener Hof Hotel next day and smuggled her up to the Bechstein guest-house near the Berghof. Then he drove Hitler alone to the isolated villa, and left them together for ninety minutes. Hitler noticed that the tall blonde schoolmistress had considerable female charm, and he was satisfied that Albrecht had done well to marry her. He showed her every sympathy. Engel drove her back down into the valley, after which he picked up Hitler on the villa steps. Hitler grumbled ominously about the double standards of the officer corps; subsequently he would see that the culprits were found and punished.

All this had an extraordinary consequence. Raeder still insisted, and dismissed Albrecht as Hitler's naval adjutant. Hitler retaliated by making Albrech a personal adjutant (Albrecht's records show he left the navy on 30 June 1939, becoming an Oberführer – Brigadier – in the Nazi Motor Corps next day). Raeder responded by refusing to appoint a new naval adjutant; eventually, on 25 August, Puttkamer was recalled from the destroyers but until October he was formally referred to as Jodl's adjutant, to save Raeder's face. Hitler in turn retaliated by declining to attend the navy's next launching ceremony at Bremen on 1 July. The navy rallied round Raeder: social invitations went to Albrecht – but not to his new wife, Grete. She completed the farce by returning to her other lover, and in 1940 the unfortunate adjutant had to divorce her.* He never forgot Hitler's loyalty to him. He became a convinced National Socialist and put duty above all else, as his moving last letters from Berlin show.

---

* On 8 March 1941 he married again, this time happily. I am indebted to his second wife, Frau Gerta von Radinger, for access to ninety letters that he wrote her as Hitler's adjutant.

Albrecht is believed to have died with a machine-gun in his hands when the Russians took the Reich Chancellery in 1945.

Raeder also never forgot Hitler's June 1939 "insult". He ensconced himself in the admiralty in Berlin and petulantly refused to confer with the Führer any more. He passively attended Hitler's conference of 14 August, and the famous harangue of 22 August 1939; but it took the outbreak of war itself to persuade him to resume personal contact with Hitler again.

Extreme Unction

Adolf Hitler's attitude to the Church was ambivalent. By 1939, the Church was scarcely a power factor in Germany, but even though now absolute dictator, Hitler still hesitated to launch a terminal crusade against it, fearing that he might thereby needlessly lose much of his national support.

The archives reveal several instances of this caution. He had expressly forbidden newspapers to print any reference at all to schisms between the various religions, and transgressors were heavily punished: the entire edition of one newspaper was confiscated in March 1938, its editorial staff dismissed and disciplinary proceedings begun against them; in April of that year all editors had been circularized by the propaganda ministry, "The embargo on polemics against Christianity and the Church is still in force." And when a year later, in 1939, an unseemly squabble broke out between the Reich church ministry, Goebbels, Hess and Heydrich over the desire of the churches to mark the Führer's fiftieth birthday by peals of bells – the Nazi Party was vehemently opposed to this innocent gesture – Hitler ruled, "The churches are not to be prevented from celebrating the event. But nor are they to be compelled to celebrate it." His policy, in short, was still one of *laissez-faire*.

For twenty years, he had tried to keep the Party aloof from all matters of interdenominational conflict. "We must learn to strive for that which unites us, and discard every argument that divides," he had said as a 31-year-old speaker in 1920 in Austria. Admittedly, an element of mischievous cynicism did creep in, over the years. In his speech to Party officials on 23 November 1937 he ruled that the churches were to be left free to portray the Lord in whatever image they wished, since neither they nor the Nazi Party could be certain who was right or wrong: "But let me make one thing quite plain. The churches may decide what happens to Germans in the hereafter – but it is the German nation and its Führer who decide about them now." He argued that while National Socialists might believe in their heart of hearts in God, His image had undergone so many changes over the millenia. Man had this notion of some unseen hand of creation that had elevated him from beast. Man, this "tiny bacillus of the universe", passively accepted that he could at best observe the laws of Nature but that he could not influence them. "There is an immensely wide field for the churches to research and this is why they ought to tolerate each other," Hitler agreed. Then he thundered, "But our nation has not been created by God to be torn asunder by the priesthood."

Hitler's views on life after death were regularly aired in his private conversation, and from the notes taken by Martin Bormann, his adjutant Heinrich Heim, Walther Hewel, Christa Schroeder and Rosenberg's representative, Werner Koeppen, something of the Führer's beliefs and prejudices emerges.

He believed in what he usually referred to as "Providence", to which he attributed the same mystic powers of explaining the inexplicable as Christians do to God. (Thus, "Providence has created each man as an individual, and great is the happiness thereby given.") Hitler's loathing for the clergy was profound. The loathing can probably be traced back to the revolting dress and habits of the religious teacher at his school, about whom Hitler had a fund of distasteful anecdotes. His alert mind thrived on the anomalies of religion. The religious instructors were unable to explain why at 10 A.M. the story of the Creation should be taught from the Old Testament, and at 11 A.M. a wholly different version should be tendered by their science teacher. This was the "barefaced lie" on which Christianity was based and sought to hold the world in its thrall. Admittedly, since the teachings of Charles Darwin the nuances were different, and religious teachers were now permitted explanations for which – Hitler chuckled – they would four hundred years earlier have been roasted "to the chant of pious hymns". His view was simply this: "I know nothing about the hereafter and am honest enough to say so. Others may claim some knowledge about it, but I can't prove that things are otherwise."

In 1939, Hitler regarded the Church as a vast and impersonal corporation of unscrupulous methods, drawing colossal state subsidies at the same time as it viciously attacked the state and strove to divide the people that Hitler had spent six years trying to unite. (In Germany, church taxes were virtually compulsory, and levied directly on workers like trades union dues by deductions from their pay packet; there were nasty sanctions against any person contracting out – not even Goebbels did so.) Hitler privately pilloried the Church's cunning amalgam of hypocrisy and big business. "They allow you to sin at Fasching time – because they know they can't stop you and that from Ash Wednesday onward they can loosen your purse-strings for the Church's benefit by uttering grisly warnings of purgatory!" Or again, "God made man, and man was made to sin – God gave man the liberty to do so. For half a million years God looks on while men tear each other's eyes out, and only then does it occur to him to send his only-begotten Son. Now – that's a devil of a long way round. The whole thing seems colossally ham-handed." And, a few days later:

> How can it be possible for man to be skewered, barbecued and subjected to various other torments in Hell if the human body itself can play no direct part in the resurrection on account of the natural processes of decomposition alone? And how absurd it is to make Heaven seem a temptation, if the Church itself tells us that only those who haven't done so well in life are going to get in – for instance, the mentally retarded and the like. It's not going to be very nice if when we get there we find all those people who – despite the Beatitude: "Blessed are they that are poor of spirit" – have already been a blessed nuisance when they were alive! And what kind of temptation is it supposed to be, if all we're going to find up there are the plain and mentally insipid women!

Hitler argued that the Church failed to live up to its promises. In the World War, Germany had devoutly called for Divine aid – but she had not come out of it very well. And how could the Church respect President Roosevelt as a head of state after he had been photographed in his freemason's regalia along with other worthies of that movement?

As for the Bible, "that Jewish artefact", Hitler regretted that it had ever been translated into German. "Any sane German can only clutch his head in dismay at how this Jewish outpouring, this priestly babble, has persuaded his fellow-Germans to cavort in a manner that we used to ridicule in the whirling dervishes of Turkey and the Negro races."

The churches had a grim history of cruelty behind them, and of "slaying in the name of the Lord". Hitler was to comment in 1942, "We merely enforce the Commandment, 'Thou shalt not kill', by executing the murderer. But the Church – so long as *it* held the reins of government – always put him to death by hideous tortures, by quartering him and the like."

Now that he was in power, the Church problem left Hitler no peace. Christa Schroeder wrote privately on 21 April 1939:

> One evening recently the Chief was very interesting on the Church problem. He made it all seem so clear and logical that I'm sorry I didn't note it all down straight away. He took Gothic architecture as his starting point, a style he rejects as alien and artificial. He said something like, "Why is a beautiful natural arch suddenly interrupted and made to project a wholly unnecessary spire without rhyme, reason or purpose! And why the many spires and turrets that are only there to please the eye, because there is no way up to them and they are all walled up inside?"
>
> It was in this Gothic era that mysticism was born. The gloominess of the buildings fostered it. It was an age of darkness and duplicity. . . . It was in this

age that the occult and mystic made such great strides. Christianity is founded on knowledge two thousand years old – knowledge blurred and confused by mysticism and the occult (like the Bible parables). The question is, why can't Christian ideas be updated using the knowledge of the present day? Luther strove for a Reformation but this has been misunderstood, because reformation is not a once-only affair but a process of constant renovation – not just marking time but keeping up with the developments of the age.

The Chief knows full well that the Church problem is very tricky and if war breaks out it could well rebound on him domestically. My own feeling is that he would be happy if some decent way of solving it could be found.

In earlier years the only way of solving it that occurred to Hitler involved the use of dynamite. But with maturity came a recognition that he might equally let the churches "rot away like a gangrenous arm", until there were only simpletons standing in the pulpits and old maidens sitting in the pews before them: "The healthier youth will be with us," Hitler confidently predicted. Providence, he said, had given man a judgement of his own: "That judgement teaches me that this tyranny of the lie is bound to be smashed. But it also teaches me that that can't be done yet." On 29 June 1941, Hewel noted a conversation with Hitler about religion: "The Party must never aspire to replace religion. One ought not to combat religion but to let it die of its own accord." In August 1941 he assured Goebbels that he had only postponed the settling of the score; and in February 1942, referring to the "seditious parsons", he commented to his circle: "I can't make my reply to these people yet. But it's all going down in my little black book."

What was Hitler's religion, then? He often talked about it. Anneliese Schmundt wrote in her diary on 8 June 1941, "Long conversations in the evening on religion and Christiantiy: cultural retrogression since Greek and Roman art." Hewel wrote a much lengthier note that evening:

Over dinner this evening, a wonderful talk on the Roman empire and its displacement by Christianity. . . . Christianity has been one long act of deceit and self-contradition. It preaches goodness, humility and love-thy-neighbour, but under this slogan it has burned and butchered millions to the accompaniment of pious proverbs. The ancients openly admitted that they killed for self-protection, in revenge or as a punishment. The Christians do so only out of love! . . . Only Christianity has created a vengeful God, one who commits man to Hell the moment he starts using the brains that God gave him.

The Classical was an age of enlightenment. With the onset of Christianity scientific research was halted and there began instead a research into the visions of saints, instead of the things that God gave us. Research into nature became a sin.

The tragedy is that to this very day there are thousands of "educated" people running around believing in all this claptrap – they deny that Nature is all-powerful, they glorify the weak, the sick, the crippled and the simple-minded. In the ideal world of [Pastor Friedrich von] Bodelschwingh the healthy find everlasting life only if they have devoted their lives to the weak, to the idiot and suchlike. the sick are there so that we can do Good Deeds. If this goes on much longer, there will soon be more sick than sound. Today there are already a thousand million of them.

As for cruelty, Christianity holds all world records. Christianity is the revenge of the wandering Jew. Where would we be today if only we had not had Christianity – we would have the same brains, but we would have avoided a hiatus of one-and-a-half thousand years. . . . The terrible thing is that millions of people believe, or act as though they believe, all this: they feign belief in it all. If we had been Mohammedans, today the world would have been ours.

Excerpts from unpublished records like these show that Hitler was inspired by purely Darwinian beliefs – the survival of the fittest, with no use for the moral comfort that sound religious teaching can purvey. "Liberty, equality and fraternity are the grandest nonsense," he had said that evening. "Because Liberty automatically precludes Equality – as liberty leads automatically to the advancement of the healthier, the better, and the more proficient, and thus there is no more equality."

Yet Hitler still prevented the Party from taking its persecution of the Church too far. When Martin Bormann – one of the moving forces of the persecution – demanded in July 1939 that the Wehrmacht should discard its district chaplains, Hitler challenged him to furnish figures from each gauleiter showing how many of their population had actually contracted out of their churches: that proved how little popular support there would be for any persecution campaign. (Not even Hitler himself had contracted out of his Church, the Catholic. And the Church was far too clever to excommunicate him. He for his part had learned much from the tactics, organization and teachings of the Catholic Church.) On another occasion Bormann had the misfortune to order the closure of a convent in which an aunt of Eva Braun was a nun. The nuns were to be evicted. Hitler cancelled the order, and commented to Schaub afterwards that Bormann was "a bit pig-headed" – he hadn't the least idea of the harm such measures did. "Those poor old sisters have spent their entire lives behind convent walls. They're far too remote from reality to make lives now for themselves."

On Papen's advice he had regularized Nazi relations with the Vatican in July 1933 by a concordat defining the rights of church and state in Germany. This, the first international agreement that he signed, brought the Nazi regime great prestige; but it was also the first international covenant that it broke, because the Nazis discouraged Catholic education in schools, the convents and monastries were dissolved and their property was confiscated, and the Jesuits were driven out of influence everywhere. Only the Benedictines enjoyed a certain immunity at first, deriving from Hitler's private affection for the Abbot Albanus Schachleitner: they had met at a demonstration against the French occupation of the Ruhr, on Königs Platz in Munich, and Schachleitner became a supporter – though not a member – of the Party. His church cast him out and he died in penury: Hitler ordered a state funeral in Munich (a benevolence that ensured that the bones were later disinterred and reburied in less hallowed ground when Hitler was no longer able to intercede).

Individual Catholic leaders impressed Hitler by their diplomacy or the courage of their convictions: there was Michael, Cardinal von Faulhaber, Archbishop of Munich, whom he received privately at the Berghof to hear his manly appeal against the series of trials of clergy on homosexual charges – one vile method chosen by the Party to reduce the Church; and there was Theodor, Cardinal Innitzer, of Vienna, whom Hitler had received on his triumphal entry in 1938: the Cardinal had swept into the foyer of Vienna's Imperial Hotel, and when Hitler dutifully kissed his ring he responded with the sign of the cross, struck above the Führer's head with a crucifix. Hitler could not help admiring these Cardinals' panache: he had expected cringing religious worthies to slink in, but Innitzer was a man of self-possession and presence, acting for all the world as though the Catholic Church had not lifted a finger against the Nazis in Austria during the Dollfuss and Schuschnigg regimes.

It was the Lutheran and Reformed Churches in Germany that gave Hitler his biggest headaches. His early years of power were marked by futile attempts to reconcile the thirty warring Protestant factions and bring them under one overriding authority, some loosely constituted council of Churches that would unquestioningly accept the primacy of the state and the Nazi policies it enforced.

In 1932 the Party had already hived off one section of the German Protestant Church and created a body of "German Christians", some three thousand priests strong. A rival faction had formed on the other wing of the Church, the "Confessional Church" led by Pastor Martin Niemöller. Niemöller was an unruly former U-boat commander of the Great War, who had preached since 1931 at Dahlem in Berlin. He was formerly a Nazi, "the first Nazi priest", a fiery and thick-skulled Westphalian. As he had made clear in his 1933 autobiography – *From U-Boat to Pulpit* – Niemöller had welcomed Hitler's rise to power "after the years of darkness". His was among the first telegrams of congratulation to reach the Führer after Germany walked out of the League of Nations in 1933. But he was the eternal Irish-agitator type, a dog-collared Dr Goebbels. Hitler explained to Himmler in January 1939 that the pastor's whole opposition now emanated only from his not getting the promotion that he had hoped for after the Nazis came to power. "After that he began agitating against the state under cover of the word of God."

Niemöller's principal target was the position of Nazi Reich Bishop, appointed for the Protestant Church in Germany. On coming to power, Hitler's first wish had been to see a unified Protestant "Reich Church" established; but throughout the summer of '33 the various Protestant factions had bickered over a suitable Reich Bishop; none of the names they put forward – including that of Bodelschwingh – was acceptable to the ruling Party. Eventually, in September 1933, a synod at Wittenberg largely dominated by the German Christians had elected Ludwig Müller to the position. Müller had been garrison chaplain at Königsberg and was recommended by Blomberg from personal acquaintance. But Müller was both a disappointment to Hitler and a red rag to Niemöller and his friends. Schwerin von Krosigk himself heard Niemöller propose to Bodelschwingh and others one evening that winter that their only solution was to visit Müller one dark night with a few strong-arm boys from his Dahlem congregation and "beat up the Reich Bishop so his own mother wouldn't recognize him".

Tired of the sniping against Müller, Hitler ordered a dozen of the Protestant leaders to assemble in the Chancellery on 25 January 1934. Before that date, Göring began furnishing Hitler with FA wiretaps on Niemöller: one had Niemöller talking insultingly of the Führer on the telephone to President Hindenburg. Another recorded a very recent conversation between Niemöller and a brother clergyman, discussing an audience they had just had with Hindenburg to campaign for Müller's replacement. Niemöller's language about the aged president was less than respectful. "We sure gave the old fellow the extreme unction this time," Niemöller had guffawed. "We ladled so much holy oil over him that he's going to kick that bastard [Müller] out." (There is no doubt about the wording: Hitler used to read the brown-paper wiretap out loud to his dinner guests when the conversation flagged, and he still remembered the words eight years later. His head of chancellery, Hans Lammers – who was present in 1934 – recited them almost identically under interrogation in 1945.)

Now, on 25 January 1934, listening to the dozen bickering Protestant clergy in his study, Hitler's patience left him. He allowed them to make their demand for Müller's resignation – "with mealy mouths and many quotations from the Scriptures", as he described on one occasion, or "with unctuous language" as he put it on another – and then he motioned to Göring to recite out loud from the FA wiretap transcripts. Göring planted his feet astride and relished every minute. Niemöller, challenged on the wiretaps, denied that he had spoken the words concerned. According to Lammers, Hitler expressed much indignation that a man of the cloth should lie. He curtly shook hands with them and indicated that the interview was at an end.

After that, there was open war between Niemöller and the Nazi regime. The pastor's congregations grew in size, and became an open meeting-place for hotheads and dissidents. Disappointed that Müller could not unite the Protestant Church, Hitler lost interest in him. In November 1934, Niemöller's Confessional Church set up a "provisional church directorate" in open competition with Müller; but even within this new body there was friction between the Lutheran and the Reformed Church wings. In July 1935, Hitler made one last attempt to calm these troubled waters, setting up a Reich Church Ministry under Hans Kerrl. Kerrl in turn established a Reich Church Council that October, but again these efforts were frustrated by the squabbling between the German Christians and the Confessional Church, and on 12 February the council resigned. By now Heydrich was involved, for after Kerrl angered Hitler by a speech attacking the churches on the thirteenth, we find (in Bormann's diary) Kerrl, Heydrich, Himmler, Goebbels and Bormann summoned to the Berghof to confer on the growing and divisive religious conflict in Germany. Kerrl was given a dressing down and ordered to prepare elections for a general Protestant synod, which would decide the constitution of the Protestant Church in Germany.

This opened the floodgates of real public disorder. From every Protestant pulpit battle was proclaimed. On 22 February, Kerrl, Himmler and Heydrich were again called to see Hitler to discuss the Church problem. Over the months that followed, a wave of police-raids and arrests befell Niemöller's Confessional Church. He himself was spared at first, but from his pulpit he launched such verbal torpedoes on Kerrl that Franz Gürtner – Hindenburg's and now Hitler's Minister of Justice – warned him to cease fire. But Niemöller, characteristically, refused to listen to his enemies or heed his friends. Hitler came under increasing pressure from the Party, but was loath to make a martyr of the man. Nonetheless he told his ministers, "Niemöller must not mistake liberty for licence." On 1 July 1937, Martin Niemöller was arrested for sedition and for using his pulpit to incite the public against the regime.

The Niemöller trial, in February 1938, was a noisy affair. It embarrassed the legalistic conservatives and seemed wholly superfluous to the radicals who would have preferred him to vanish without fuss into one of Himmler's camps. Brilliantly defended by three lawyers, Niemöller used the witness-box to denounce Hitler and his regime. His lawyers ran rings around Kerrl's church ministry. It was probably because of this case that Hitler groaned, years later, "In future I will allow duelling only between the gentlemen of the clergy and the legal profession!" The court could not acquit Niemöller on the evidence, but they refused to imprison him either: he was sentenced to the seven months already served, and set free. Hitler was speechless at this gesture, but to his pleasure Niemöller refused to give the court the usual assurances to be of good behaviour or to accept its prohibition on further public speeches, and he was rearrested immediately and interned in a concentration camp until such time as he repent.

Here this turbulent priest remained, though comfortably housed and well fed, until 1945. At Munich in September 1938, Mussolini attempted to intercede; Hitler replied with a steely refusal: "That man is dangerous and will never cease to be so. Within the concentration camp he has the maximum of liberty and he is well looked after, but never will he see the outside of it again." Admiral Raeder pleaded for Niemöller's release out of old navy comradeship. Hitler refused to yield. Himmler did release the pastor once on parole to attend his father's funeral, and after the aged Field-Marshal von Mackensen appealed to Hitler, the Reichsführer visited Niemöller in person in January 1939. But Hitler repeated to Himmler: "If there is one man who will never be set free for the rest of his life, it's this clergyman."

In summary, Hitler's religious attitude was best expressed in words he uttered in February 1942: "Life is only granted to him who fights hardest for it. There is only one law of nature: defend yourself!"

The Major Solution

Since the beginning of April 1939, the Wehrmacht had been studying the best way to invade and defeat Poland if Hitler's demands for the return of Danzig were not met.

Overwhelmingly German in history and inclination, the port of Danzig had been put under League of Nations mandate by the Treaty of Versailles. The Poles as protecting power had certain rights, including diplomatic, passport, and military offices – all freely used as a cover for Polish espionage and subversion against East Prussia and the Reich. The railway system, about 120 customs officials and a large post office building were Polish too. In their democratic wisdom, the burghers of Danzig had elected a Nazi senate; both its president and the local gauleiter, Albert Forster, were active Nazis.

If Hitler did launch "White", Danzig would be highly vulnerable for several days, as General Fedor von Bock – commanding Army Group North – warned. The Poles could seize the city and then obstruct his Fourth Army's crossing of the Vistula. His recommendation, stated on 27 May 1939 to the General Staff, was that a secret brigade should be illicitly raised from the 12,000 men with military experience in Danzig – army veterans and reservists, SS and SA men – and from the city police. Bock also suggested that on the actual day of "White" a German naval force might "happen to" be visiting Danzig – it could disembark a battalion of troops to help secure the city.

Hitler approved Bock's outline on 11 June. A few days later he summoned Admiral Raeder to the Berghof and ordered a "friendly visit" to Danzig by two pocket battleships, two cruisers and other warships to be organized, perhaps at the end of July. (Ribbentrop's ministry strongly disapproved, since it would put Germany in the wrong if "White" was launched.) A major-general, Friedrich Georg Eberhardt, was sent in plain clothes to organize a "Free Corps" there. Shiploads of guns and ammunition, ostensibly bound for Königsberg, suffered "engine problems" en route and docked at Danzig for repairs – where Eberhardt's gear, everything from a shoe-nail to a 150-millimetre gun, was unloaded under darkness before the ships went on their way. The SS came from Germany for a sports display in Danzig, but the SS troops stayed on afterwards. By the time of "White", Eberhardt would command two infantry regiments, an artillery battalion and SS irregulars too. Bridges were strengthened, barracks built, pontoon sections stockpiled. This was just the kind of secret war that Hitler relished.

Raeder did warn Hitler against military adventures over Danzig. Hitler retorted, "I was owed 100 Reichsmarks; I've already collected 99 and I'm going to get the last coin too!" He authorized Goebbels to deliver a powerful and provocative speech in Danzig on 17 June, denouncing Polish "ill-treatment" and demanding the city's return to the Reich. Nazi editors were confidentially briefed: "This is to be a first trial-balloon to test the international atmosphere on the settlement of the Danzig question." Ribbentrop learned of Goebbels' intentions only when a tip – evidently based on wiretap sources – reached him from Likus about the confidential briefing of editors.

Berlin began to swelter. On 3 July 1939, Hitler and Göring visited a secret display of new Luftwaffe equipment at Rechlin air experimental station. Hoping to regain Luftwaffe priorities in the fight for scarce labour and raw materials, Göring, Milch and Udet had staged a display of aviation magic that Göring was later to rue, since most of the exhibits were solitary prototypes still many years from squadron service: Hitler was shown an experimental Heinkel rocket-propelled fighter, and a jet fighter only a few days away from its maiden flight; a Heinkel 111 bomber, heavily overloaded, was lifted effortlessly into the air by rocket-assisted take-off units. There was early-warning radar, and pressure-cabins for high-altitude planes; in the laboratory the Führer was shown simple methods of starting motor engines in sub-zero temperatures. The new 30-millimetre cannon was demonstrated to Hitler, installed in a Messerschmitt 110 fighter in the butts: it would be a weapon of devastating firepower. In his closing speech to Luftwaffe engineers, Hitler particularly asked for early mass-production of this formidable air weapon (it was still not available to the squadrons by 1943).

This self-deception in July 1939 had fateful consequences. Hitler decided on a much bigger bite of Poland than just Danzig and the Corridor. In May 1942, when Göring once lost his temper with Luftwaffe engineers, he exclaimed: "The Führer took the most serious decisions on the basis of that display. It was a miracle that things worked out as well as they did, and that the consequences were not far worse." In September 1942, Göring recalled: "I once witnessed a display before the war at Rechlin, and compared with that I can only say – what bunglers all our professional magicians are! Because the world has never before and never will again see the likes of what was conjured up before my – and far worse, the Führer's – eyes at Rechlin!"

As the sun climbed higher, Hitler's ministers fled Berlin. On 9 July, Ribbentrop left to summer at Lake Fuschl, not far from the Berghof. Brauchitsch attended Army Day celebrations at Karlshorst that day, then left for several weeks' furlough. Göring was cruising down the canals in his yacht. Baron von Weizsäcker assessed in his private diary, "The Führer has no desire to pick a fight with the western powers but – so I'm assured – he cannot yet be sure if a war can be confined to Poland. So my own bet is unchanged, that we'll settle for a peaceful general approach."

Hitler could afford to wait. He knew that the Reich had most to offer Stalin, in return for a pact. Stalin wanted a war – all the teachings of Bolshevism showed that the USSR alone would ultimately benefit. Hitler had previously condemned the idea of such a pact. In *Mein Kampf* he had written that he could not represent Bolshevism to his followers as a crime against humanity, if he were to form an alliance with "this offspring of Hell". In 1935 he had said much the same to Rosenberg: "I can't tell the Germans not to steal if I consort with burglars." Now circumstances had changed, however. In mid-June 1939, Moscow had again obliquely hinted – this time through the Bulgarian envoy in Berlin – that they would prefer dealing with the Reich, provided Hitler would sign a non-aggression pact. Ribbentrop had indicated cautious assent two weeks later, only to half-change his mind almost immediately. Of these summer months the British ambassador shrewdly wrote, "The chief impression which I had of Hitler was that of a master chess-player studying the board and waiting for his opponents to make some false move which could be turned to his own immediate advantage."

Meanwhile, Hitler took direct control of every phase, dealing with Heydrich, Goebbels, and – as he lacked a naval adjutant – the admiralty in person. Albert Forster, Gauleiter of Danzig, appeared several times at the Berghof. On 13 July he had what his newspaper *Danziger Vorposten* called "a lengthy discussion" with Hitler; and after another discussion a week later Forster told his own staff,

> The Führer says that . . . for the first time he's making a distinction between his emotions and his common sense: emotionally, he was inclined just to tackle Danzig this summer. But common sense has now dictated that the settlement of this matter should be linked to a solution of the German-Polish problem as a whole, at a suitable time. This shows that the Führer is no longer interested in the "minor" solution.

Forster spelt out the "major" solution now aimed at, thus: regaining the Reich's eastern frontiers as in 1914. (Again Ribbentrop learned of this only from Likus.) On 22 July, Hitler telephoned the admiralty and ordered it to be ready to send the elderly cruiser *Nürnberg* to Danzig at short notice: he would explain the specific purpose later (almost certainly to give artillery support to Eberhardt's brigade, of whose existence the meddling diplomats under Weizsäcker seem to have been totally unaware).

Two days later, on 24 July 1939, Hitler drove to Bayreuth for his annual Wagner pilgrimage. Apart from a brief flight to Berlin and then to Saarbrücken for a fourth look at the West Wall, he stayed with the Wagner clan at "Wahnfried" for the next ten days.

Here he wallowed in a Wagner orgy – *The Flying Dutchman*, *Parsifal* and the whole of the *Ring*. In his youth he had been a chorister at Lambach in Upper Austria (he could still sing the Mozart masses from memory). As a romantic, rootless youth of seventeen he had scraped and saved to visit the opera at Linz, and it was Wagner's early *Rienzi*, seen in 1906, that first stirred Hitler's *alter ego*, the demagogue slumbering within the artist. In a way it was to be Hitler's own story: he recognized this in 1945, and told Schaub the lines from *Rienzi* that he wanted inscribed on his mausoleum. Based on a novel by Bulwer-Lytton which drew on the rapid rise and fall of the real fourteenth-century Roman dictator Cola di Rienzo (1313–1354), *Rienzi* was an opera with thrilling strains of revolution, renaissance and betrayal. It was a story of the Roman plebs suppressed by unscrupulous *nobili* until the young notary Rienzi had risen from their midst, an unknown citizen who rallied and liberated and led them until the very nobili themselves had proclaimed him their master. Rienzi had scorned the modern title "King": "Look back to your ancestors, and call me your people's tribune!" which his Romans had saluted and responded to with full throat: "Rienzi, hail! Hail to you, the people's tribune!" Later the nobili conspired, the faithful deserted him, and the hand that struck him down came from his own ranks.

Hitler was electrified by the Rienzi drama: he left the theatre long after midnight, with a schoolfriend, August Kubizek – whom he charged to keep quiet since he was thinking. They walked the deserted November streets and scaled a hill outside Linz. His eyes blazing with emotion, young Hitler suddenly seized Kubizek's hands and spoke of a compact that the people would one day make with him to lead them out of their subjugation, to the pinnacles of freedom. What subjugation? Which freedom? He sent Kubizek home and spent the night out in the open air. At the moment his friend might well have challenged him: "Rienzi, Hey! What do you plan? / I see you mightily before me – tell/Wherefore needst thou this new might?" At Bayreuth in July 1939 Hitler met August Kubizek again. They dined together at Frau Winifred Wagner's home: the schoolfriend reminded Hitler of that night on the hillside in 1906. To Hitler it was like yesterday – he interrupted, turned to

Frau Wagner and poured out the whole story, ending, "That was the hour it all began."

Hitler patronized the arts as had few of his more recent predecessors, provided that the art was Germanic and in his eyes beautiful. His knowledge of opera was legendary. He had heard *Die Meistersinger* forty times – Schaub believed it was Hitler's favourite because it was a paean to German craftmanship. In Berlin, Goebbels' opera-house at Charlottenburg would stage the lighter works like *Die Fledermaus* or *The Merry Widow*; in Munich, there would be Italian operas like *Aida*. But Bayreuth was Wagner, and "Wahnfried" was like a home from home to Hitler. Frau Wagner, a matronly Englishwoman, widow of the great composer's son, was like a second mother to him. All the most dazzling figures of German cultural life had foregathered at her social evenings in the early Twenties. It was a milieu that Hitler had anxiously sought. From 1925 to 1933 he had kept away from Bayreuth to spare her embarrassment; then he had re-established the friendship, frequently telephoning her under his private nickname of Bandmaster Wolf. This remarkable dowager's admiration for Hitler has not diminished to the present day. Hitler repaid her by granting her favours – sometimes she interceded on behalf of Jews or persecuted musicians. Hitler explained that she was to write to him through Dr Brandt: "If your letters fall into the hands of Reichsleiter Bormann there's no guarantee they'll reach me."

While Hitler stayed at Bayreuth, the foreign clamour mounted: but the initiative was still clearly his.

The British press – as Ambassador Herbert von Dirksen reported from London – had been crying rape ever since the annexation of Austria. Accuracy of reporting varied: the *Sunday Express* of July 1939 was running a sensational series on The Man who Murdered Hitler (the Führer had been assassinated long ago and been replaced by a double!). *The Observer*, *The Times* and *The Daily Telegraph* all stood aloof from this pointless campaign. Individual journalists caused blisters out of all proportion to their importance – like Commander Stephen King-Hall MP, who distributed five tactlessly-phrased newsletters in Germany that summer. On 14 July the FA heard the British ambassador telephoning the wife of the US consul in Hamburg: "The King-Hall letters are damned awkward. It's heartbreaking – what on earth is the use of all my efforts after those!"

What interested Hitler more was that above the raucous Fleet Street editorials, authoritative voices could still be heard from London indicating that Chamberlain even now enjoyed the public's support, and was casting around for ways of divesting himself of the awkward guarantee given to Poland. Hitler had mentioned to Walther Hewel as recently as June – after King George VI had replied warmly to Hitler's condolences on the loss of the submarine *Thetis* – that if only he could meet some upright Englishman of standing, with whom he could talk in German, he could soon settle their countries' remaining differences. He drew optimistic conclusions from the doings of right-wing organizations like the Anglo-German Fellowship and The Link, and from private letters from leading Britons like Lord Rothermere or the chairman of the RAC. At the end of July the well-known British historian Arthur Bryant wrote urging Hewel not to attach too much importance to the anti-German tone of the British press: "Had a general election followed Munich, the majority for his [Chamberlain's] policy – whatever the press might have chosen to say – would have been enormous." Hitler later quoted this view too.

By late July the signs were that Chamberlain and his advisers were preparing for a second Munich. On British initiative, there had been talks between Sir Horace Wilson and one of Göring's economics staff, Dr Helmuth Wohlthat. The Wilson proposal was a sweeping political, economic and military agreement with Hitler, in return for certain assurances. Wohlthat's report quoted Wilson as saying, "Perhaps I'm too much of an optimist, and perhaps the solution I think possible does seem unrealistic to many observers in the present situation. But I've had the opportunity of studying the Führer and I believe that the Führer, acting as a Statesman for Peace, can manage even greater achievements than he has already in his construction of Gross-Deutschland." The usual Foreign Office sources immediately leaked details of these secret talks to the British press; Fleet Street even hinted at a billion-pound loan being offered to Hitler as the price of peace. Hitler would not be bribed: Wilson's colonial proposals were the same as offered by Henderson in March 1938. Besides, the log-jam in German-Soviet negotiations had suddenly cleared: it seems that rumours of the "billion-pound loan" offered by the British had startled Stalin into coming out into the open.

Hitler too had an interest in speeding the talks with Stalin. On 25 July he learned that Britain and France were actually sending military missions to Moscow. And the OKW timetable for "White" would soon come into force: no military decisions of significance were required until 12 August, admittedly, but the General Staff had ruled that the optimum date for attacking Poland would be 25 August, and Hitler was required to rule for or against "White" on the fifteenth. This left barely two weeks for Hitler to obtain Stalin's signature on a pact, and nobody believed that Ribbentrop would manage such a feat in time. "I don't believe the Moscow talks will prove a flop," wrote Weizsäcker on 30 July. "But nor do I believe they can be concluded in the next fourteen days, as we are now attempting. My advice is that we should use blunter language in Moscow about the partition of Poland, but I advise against Ribbentrop's suggestion of talking to Moscow about sharing the Baltic states so that north of the latitude of Riga should be Russia's Lebensraum and south of it ours!"

Hitler stayed at Bayreuth, troubled only by the affairs of his Party henchmen. Magda Goebbels had thrown herself into a sorrowing liaison with the young and handsome propaganda ministry official, Karl Hanke: Hitler angrily forced a reconciliation between the Goebbels couple, and made them share the same room at "Wahnfried". This sent Hanke in tears to his friend Speer. Hitler also made the two Goebbels attend the opera on 26 July; but of all operas, that night was *Tristan und Isolde* and Frau Goebbels openly blubbered while Hitler and his white-faced propaganda minister affected not to notice. Afterwards Hitler told them to leave Bayreuth.

Robert Ley, the Labour Front leader, tormented Hitler in a different way. In Winifred Wagner's exquisite drawing-room he announced that at the coming Nuremberg Rally in September they should dispense with the routine *Aida* fanfare and play instead a little piece which he, Ley, had composed for the occasion. He modestly played a gramophone record of the fanfare. After the last fearsome strains had died away, Hitler tersely announced: "We'll stick to *Aida!*" (He had his own views as to whether there would be a Party rally in September, even if Bormann and the Party were already sending out the official invitations.)

In London there were fewer illusions. Putzi Hanfstaengl, victim of Hitler's 1937 practical joke, became uneasy that he was on the wrong side of the North Sea – once again internment hung over him, but his pride was his undoing. He telephoned from London to Bayreuth, asking for Hitler's promise that nothing would befall him if he now returned. Hitler impatiently told Frau Wagner, who took the call, "Ach Gott – of course he can come back!" But Hanfstaengl asked for Hitler's promise in writing, and the Führer told her to put the phone down. "If he won't take my word for it, a letter won't convince him either."

Bormann wrote to London nonetheless; Hanfstaengl cabled a reply demanding a suitable official post in Germany, and mentioning debts he had incurred. Bormann discussed it with Hitler in mid-August, then wrote back:

> On F's [Führer's] behalf it has been repeatedly made clear to you over the last weeks that the regrettable misunderstandings that led to your going abroad ought not prevent your returning home. It was also made clear that you would be given a suitable position again. Finally, I also cabled you our assurance that we would accept any financial obligations you have incurred there. These repeated assurances should and indeed must suffice. No further assurances can be sent you. We await your early return.

Hanfstaengl's reply burned all boats. It reached the Berghof four days later. "I deeply regret to learn that the only person competent to make amends for the grave insults to my honour on 8, 9 and 10 February 1937 is not willing as a

man and Führer to bear the ultimate consequences." He had therefore postponed his return to Germany *sine die*, he wrote, and he ominously concluded:
"I will take this matter's satisfaction into my own hands."

Alas for Putzi Hanfstaengl, Hitler now had far more pressing matters on his
mind. It was here at Bayreuth that he jovially buttonholed Neurath with the
words, "You're going to be astonished at what I'm going to tell you: what do
you say we come to an agreement with Russia?" Neurath responded favourably. Hitler ventured, "It will probably be hard to reconcile my Party stalwarts
to the move." Neurath flattered him: "The Party is like putty in your hands,
mein Führer."

But Hitler still feared a snub from the Soviet dictator. On 2 August, Ribbentrop, acting on Hitler's instructions, hinted to the Soviet chargé that Moscow and Berlin ought to decide Poland's fate between them – and he added that
there was "no problem between the Baltic and the Black Sea" that could not be
solved. Ribbentrop also emphasized that Germany was in no hurry yet – a
poker-faced utterance that must have been torture to speak, given the rigid
timetable already imposed by the OKW's planning. The clock was already
ticking, but Moscow must not hear it.

Hitler left Bayreuth on 3 August, toured the Nuremberg arena just as though
nothing would prevent the Party rally from opening here in one month's time,
and drove down the autobahn to Munich on the fourth. At his Munich apartment he changed into a dark-blue suit and received Keitel in the drawing-room.
The OKW chief had brought with him the final timetable for "White". Like a
clockwork mechanism, all the wheels and cogs were geared to click into place
on one date and time: the army had put X-day as 25 August, as mid-September
rains would hinder extensive panzer operations in Poland and would also set
the German air force at a disadvantage. By that last week in August 1939,
Hitler would have to reach his decision one way or the other on war with
Poland. To this extent he was tyrannized by the OKW timetable.

Hitler motioned Keitel and his staff officer, Major Bernd von Lossberg, into
easy-chairs, and explained to them in an affable Austrian dialect – which rather
surprised Lossberg – just why the Polish problem had to be settled now. He
blamed Chamberlain's thoughtless guarantee to Poland for stiffening Warsaw's opposition. If, he continued, war with Poland was inevitable, then there
was no time like the present as Britain still lagged far behind Germany in the
arms race. "The gentlemen in London and Paris won't undertake anything
against us this time either," he assured the officers. Then his Austrian dialect
vanished, submerged in a sudden cresting wave of the familiar guttural
Hitler-German: "I will see to that. This Polish conflict will never, never, never
result in a European war."

He drove on that evening to the Berghof. This was to be the scene of the next three weeks' momentous events. His long-term strategy was crystallizing: a rapid war with Poland now, while the west was unready; then a major war against either the western powers or the USSR in 1942 or 1943, while he was still young. From a Likus report of 2 August, it appeared that Britain and France were making heavy going in Moscow. Stalin was indirectly claiming the Polish Ukraine as his price for a pact with the west; some voices in Paris thought that if Poland were offered parts of Germany in compensation, this price could be met. Hitler was, admittedly, uneasy that Stalin could still ostensibly deal with the British and French in Moscow while flirting with Berlin. Outwardly the Führer scoffed at the merry dance that Stalin was leading the western powers; but he was on his guard from now on. His Luftwaffe adjutant, von Below, deduced from his remarks that war with the USSR was on the Führer's mind.

On 6 August we find Hermann Göring conferring with Milch, Udet and Jeschonnek – urgently summoned on the fifth to the stateroom of his yacht *Karin II* in northern Germany – and demanding a vastly enlarged Luftwaffe of attack: Göring was going to activate thirty-two new bomber wings by April 1943 – 4,330 aircraft including 2,460 Junkers 88s.

From London, the signs were again conciliatory. Neville Chamberlain had adjourned Parliament on 4 August 1939 for two months. Simultaneously, he risked a strange, almost illicit move that further convinced Hitler that Britain was not yet ready to fight: Sir Horace Wilson invited Ambassador Herbert von Dirksen to call at his private flat in Chelsea – specifying that he should come on foot so as not to attract attention. Wilson outlined to Dirksen an offer for a "full-bodied political world partnership" between Britain and Germany, as sweeping as the entente with France in 1904 and with Russia in 1907; if Hitler would accept the terms, Wilson-indicated, then Britain would put pressure on Poland to agree to Germany's demands for Danzig and land-access across the Polish Corridor. Thus the awkward British guarantee to Poland would become inoperative. Ribbentrop received Dirksen's astounding telegram on this talk soon after. Weizsäcker noted on the sixth, "Underground feelers from Chamberlain toward a compromise (via Horace Wilson) prove that a dialogue with Britain could be got going, if we so desired."

Hitler was not inclined to bend, however. Secret directives went to the Nazi press on the twelfth, thirteenth and again on the twenty-first, forbidding them even to mention Britain's apparent change of heart. "Britain incited the Poles, now she must pay the price," was the official line to be taken. Editors were commanded to observe "absolute discipline" on this posture.

Hitler was convinced that Britain's talks with Stalin must have reached deadlock. He detailed a Nazi agent to stand by at Croydon airfield, London, as the British chief negotiator flew back from Moscow on 7 August: Strang's dejection betrayed that Hitler's surmise was probably correct. On the ninth, Halifax himself spoke to Dirksen. This time he promised that Britain was willing to go "a long way" toward meeting Germany's desires. But Hitler's central desire now was to have his war with Poland before the month was over. After his Intelligence chief, Canaris, conferred on 10 August with Keitel and Schmundt at Salzburg, and then with Ribbentrop at Fuschl, Lieutenant-Colonel Erwin Lahousen – chief of Abwehr sabotage and subversion – wrote in his diary: "Intimations of a Non-Aggression Pact with R.," meaning Russia.

We shall return shortly to the Abwehr business discussed – routine commando-type operations during "White". Of greater urgency to Hitler was the problem of how to stage a suitable frontier incident to justify his launching "White" on the specified date, on or about the twenty-fifth. After months of deliberate semi-silence in the Nazi press on Polish "atrocities", an immense campaign was about to burst into the front-page headlines. On the sixteenth, editors were secretly circularized: "The time has now come for the German press to abandon its reserve." Real trouble was in fact brewing in Danzig, where reinforcements of Polish customs officials were trying to halt the inflow of arms and ammunition. But Hitler needed a reliable staged "incident" of a given magnitude and at a closely-defined time, place and date – he had a tight OKW schedule to meet.

Here the SS helped him out. Two diabolical schemes had been drafted – independently of Hitler – by Heydrich and Himmler, "following long-standing patterns set by our western neighbours", as Heydrich explained to his SS commanders on about the eleventh. He planned two specific "incidents": in one, his agents would masquerade as Polish insurgents, seize the German transmitter station at Gleiwitz, broadcast a proclamation and escape. In the other, more complex incident a company of rapidly trained Polish-speaking idealists would be recruited from the Upper Silesian work-force, dressed in Polish uniforms on the eve of "White" and ordered to "seize" a German customs post near Hochlinden; a mock battle would be staged with SS troops, while real Polish troops would be lured into the fray from their garrison at Rybnik by a Polish officer who had recently defected to Germany. The Gestapo chief, Heinrich Müller, had also had the macabre idea of strewing fresh corpses – condemned convicts from Dachau – on the "battlefield", equipped with genuine Polish soldiers' passbooks. At the briefing, Heydrich admitted: "Up to now the idea was mine and I've prepared all this without the Führer's knowledge. But", he claimed, "the Führer has endorsed the plan."

Who in London or Paris would sympathize with Warsaw after provocations like these? When Hitler talked with Professor Carl Burckhardt, the League of Nations high commissioner in Danzig, on the eleventh he underlined the point:

"If there's the slightest provocation I will shatter Poland without warning into so many pieces that there'll be nothing left to pick up." He compared the puny Polish air force with Göring's, and cruelly boasted that whereas in 1938 he had had to whip his generals on, this year he was having to hold them back. Hitler also made a point that Burckhardt did not understand at the time, and did not write down: "Everything I'm doing is directed against Russia. If the west is too obtuse to grasp this, then I'll be forced to come to terms with the Russians and turn against the west first, after which I'll direct my entire strength against the USSR. I need the Ukraine, so that nobody can ever starve us out again as they did in the last war." Burckhardt recalled these words years later.

Hitler made much the same point to Count Ciano, Mussolini's foreign minister, next day – that he proposed one day to tread the old Teutonic road toward the east, as he had told the Duce himself aboard the *Conte Cavour* in May 1938.

Hitherto, the Nazi dictator had been far from candid with his fascist allies. They were still in the dark about "White". Throughout July 1939 a meeting had been mooted between the two dictators on the Brenner early in August, but when late in July the Italians proposed a six-power conference their disinclination to shed Italian blood for German war aims came out into the open, relations stiffened, and Mussolini decided to send Ciano instead. On the thirteenth Weizsäcker was to summarize in his diary,

> For the first time we're finding the Italian alliance a nuisance. Because over the last week our [i.e. Hitler's] will to war has become much stronger. Himmler, Ribbentrop and Gauleiter Forster have each been promoting the idea of war in their own spheres. Ribbentrop is guaranteeing that the British and French will remain neutral provided we deal annihilating blows to Poland in the first three days. This he thinks is certain.

Ciano was received at the Berghof on 12 August. The regular house-guests were banished to the lakes and mountainsides around, and Eva Braun was confined upstairs – she later pasted a sequence of snapshots into her album showing the swirl and flourish of limousines arriving, blackshirted fascist leaders greeting Hitler and some of them even glancing up curiously to her window (she girlishly captioned them : "Up there, there's something forbidden to behold – me!").

Hitler had little time or liking for Ciano; he told Schaub the Italian diplomat was "too brilliantined and dandified" to inspire trust. At first they all stood, while Hitler spoke about Germany's strength and Britain's vulnerability to air attack – on her fleet, her aircraft industry and her capital itself. This was all probably meant for English ears, as he regarded the Italians – and Ciano in particular – as the best channel of secret information to the British. (As he said at a conference on 20 May 1943, "Every memorandum I wrote to the Duce reached Britain immediately after: so I only wrote him what I wanted the British to know without fail.") Ciano's own ";'diary" relating to these conferences is not to be trusted. It is pretty clear that Hitler "confidentially" informed him that "White" would start in two weeks' time (because the British foreign office learned of this a few days later*). Ciano was astounded, as Mussolini had always warned that Italy needed two or three more years to complete her arms programme. Hitler assured Ciano that the west would not intervene, but he did not explain why: the Nazi-Soviet pact.

Even as Ciano was uncomfortably remonstrating with Hitler in the Great Hall, a door was flung open and Walther Hewel hurried in. He whispered to Ribbentrop, Ribbentrop took Hitler aside and whispered to him: Molotov had just agreed in principle to receive a German negotiator in Moscow. Stalin seemed therefore to have opted for Germany.

Hitler's mood changed. With a broad grin he invited the fascist guests to accompany him up to his tea-house eyrie, the Eagle's Nest.

Curiously, Baron von Weizsäcker appears to have been left in the dark at first about this news. His diary does not pick it up for some days. (The likely reason was that the FA intercepts now revealed to Hitler that Weizsäcker was communing treacherously closely with the ambassadors of Britain, France and Italy.) On the thirteenth Weizsäcker wrote, "My own formula remains unchanged: if Poland commits a provocation of such effrontery that Paris and London also recognize it as such, then we can set about her. Otherwise we should keep our hands off." On the fourteenth, he recorded:

> As expected, Ciano pulled out just about every organ-stop to keep us from war with Poland. The answer he got was, "As the western powers won't intervene you Italians won't be affected either. We Germans are going to attack!" Does this absolve them from the obligations imposed by the alliance [of May 1939]? . . . Italy has not spoken the last word, anyway, because the way isn't yet clear for her to do a worthwhile double-cross (worthwhile in the long run, that is).

"I am still not quite clear", continued Weizsäcker in some puzzlement, "just what has brought about this somersault at Fuschl [Ribbentrop's home] and the Berghof. A week ago they still inclined to the view that the western powers would not drop Poland, so we couldn't tackle her."

Hitler hesitated several days before responding to Moscow. But the OKW timetable had him in its vice, important decisions were due on the fifteenth and the latest Intelligence reports showed that Britain had offered Poland an

* Late on 18 August 1939, Lord Vansittart called in near-collapse on Cadogan, who noted: "His source has told him H. [Hitler] has chosen war, to begin between 25th and 28th." These were the dates given by Hitler "to the Italian Government", Chamberlain was told.

£8million loan, and that Polish mobilization preparations were far in advance of his own and would in fact be concluded by the twenty-seventh: to keep pace, the Nazi mobilization must begin not later than the twenty-first.

On 14 August, Hitler called his three C-in-Cs to the Berghof and explained why "White" was still on, and why he was sure that the western powers would not actually declare war. General Sir Edmund Ironside had submitted a scathing report on Polish combat readiness – Hitler guessed that Chamberlain would use it as an alibi to ditch the Poles. Were Britain really in earnest, she would have offered Poland more than a measly £8million loan ("The British don't sink money in an unsound business") and the Poles in turn would be more insolent than FA intercepts of late revealed. Hitler said that his only worry was that the British might yet cheat him of "White" by making some last-minute offer; he told Göring, Brauchitsch and Raeder this day that he had hinted to the British that he would approach them again with an offer of his own later – *after* he had dealt with Poland. All he asked of the Wehrmacht was this – the first few days of "White" should convince the world that Poland was doomed (the rest of the operation could take longer, as much as two months). Raeder – still in a huff over the Albrecht affair – did not speak. Canaris wrote in his diary, "C-in-C army [Brauchitsch] didn't get a word in at all." Göring called his generals to see him next day; Milch noted in his diary, "11 A.M. G[öring] informs us of intention! G. on edge."

Now Hitler took the fatal step. At 10:53 P.M. on 14 August, Ribbentrop's dramatic instructions were cabled to the embassy in Moscow: Molotov was to be informed that he, Ribbentrop, was willing to come to Moscow in person. Still Ribbentrop's staff doubted he could pull off this masterstroke in time. Weizsäcker reflected on the twentieth, "If Ribbentrop manages to conclude a pact by the middle of next week, they [the Russians] will thereby be inviting us to attack Poland, presumably without fearing any repetition of 1812."

Next day, 15 August 1939, Hitler authorized all the timetable steps consistent with an attack on Poland on the twenty-fifth. The services were informed, "You are still to assume that "White" will be on." (Two days later he added that he would delay announcing his final decision until the last possible moment.) The navy ordered the pocket battleships *Graf Spee* and *Deutschland* and fourteen submarines to stand by for operations into the Atlantic. The Nuremberg Rally was secretly cancelled, to release railroad capacity for the Wehrmacht (but foreign diplomats were still fed with the impression that the Rally was on).

Less well-documented are the murkier operations now afoot, planned by Abwehr and SS. They had prepared commando-style operations in Polish uniforms or plain clothes to secure vital bridges, tunnels and industrial plants behind the Polish lines on the very eve of "White". Erwin Lahousen's Abwehr Section II had trained a task-force of fifty men to seize the 300-yard-long railroad tunnel at Jablunka, on the main line from Vienna to Warsaw. If the Poles could detonate the demolition charges in the twin tunnel it would bar the entry into southern Poland of Wilhelm List's Fourteenth Army, now massing in Slovakia. Typically, Hitler piously insisted on a clear distinction between these "illegals" and regular German army units: when Manstein asked permission to operate three assault groups in Polish uniforms during Army Group South's attack, Hitler turned him down; Himmler then asked permission for the SS to use Polish uniforms in precisely the same area, and on 17 August Hitler gave him his blessing and ordered the Abwehr to release 150 Polish uniforms from its stocks to Heydrich for the purpose.

At the northern end of the Polish front Hitler personally conceived an adventurous operation to secure the two strategic bridges across the broad river Vistula at Dirschau. Each bridge was nearly a mile long, with its eastern end on Danzig soil and its western end footed on Polish ground, Pomerania. If the Poles destroyed the bridges, it would hamper all military movements into Central Poland. But the Germans could clearly see the demolition charges that the Poles had installed. Hitler became obsessed with the Dirschau bridges, studied air photographs and models and devised plan after plan.

Eventually he agreed with Göring, Himmler and Brauchitsch on a heavy dive-bomber attack on the Polish bridge garrison, the local power station and the demolition fuses themselves, followed up immediately by a ground assault: a goods train would arrive from East Prussia in the last minutes before "White" began, laden with concealed sappers and storm-troops under Lieutenant-Colonel Gerhardt Medem. Hitler briefed him personally. An armoured train would follow, to silence the Polish gun batteries. Timing was crucial, since the attack had to coincide exactly with the Luftwaffe strike against the Polish naval base at Gdynia – the first overt act of "White". Of course, the Dirschau operation might fail: so the army had also moved up pontoons to bridge the Vistula. When the Poles voiced loud protests at all these preparations on Danzig soil, Weizsäcker replied: "Danzig is doing nothing more than defending herself against her 'protector'."

Meanwhile the elderly warship *Schleswig-Holstein* was moved to Danzig. When "White" began, she would immediately bombard the Polish stronghold emplaced (illegally) on the Westerplatte – the sliver of land commanding the entrance to the harbour.

One clandestine operation planned since June 1939 was now dropped. The Abwehr had organized and armed a relatively large Fifth Column organization in the Polish Ukraine, consisting of some 1,300 officers and 12,000 men, under the code-name: "Aid for the Mountain Farmers" (*Bergbauernhilfe*). On 21

August, Ribbentrop telephoned the Abwehr HQ strictly forbidding any Ukrainian uprising after all: the political reason for this will shortly become obvious.

The Poles were aware of the Fifth Column in their midst and intensive security operations began. Blood was spilt. The appeals for help that reached Hitler had a familiar ring – but whether genuine or not their effect *on him* was profound. For instance, there was a telegram on 17 August from the Polish part of Upper Silesia: "For days thousands of German men and women in eastern Upper Silesia have been suffering brutal maltreatment by the Poles. Yesterday and today hundreds were arrested, manhandled and deported. Many of our comrades have been beaten up beyond recognition. In dire distress we appeal to our Führer for protection and relief." Nazi headlines took up the cry: "MASS DEPORTATIONS OF GERMANS TO POLAND'S INTERIOR", screamed the *Völkischer Beobachter*.

But now the Russians began to dither. After Molotov formally proposed – on 16 August – a non-aggression pact, Ribbentrop promptly replied with a suggestion that he should visit Moscow in two or three days' time to sign it. The Russians dragged their feet, and on 18 August Ribbentrop had to telegraph his ambassador urging speed, and mentioning alluringly that he would be authorized to sign a secret additional protocol to the pact, codifying aspects too delicate for public consumption. Even so, Molotov was unwilling to receive him in Moscow before 26 or 27 August. But as Ribbentrop well knew, the OKW timetable was geared to launching "White" on or soon after the twenty-fifth. The political effect of the pact would be nil if it were not signed sooner. In fact the A-movement, the initial movement of 220 trainloads to assemble military equipment and troops in the east, was already beginning. Perhaps the Russians suspected Hitler's motives – perhaps they believed he was just trying to upset their parallel talks with the British and French?

To Hitler it seemed an obvious occasion for grand diplomacy – for taking a personal risk. ("Our enemies still hoped", he bragged two days later, "that Russia would arise as our enemy after we had defeated Poland. But our enemies had not taken my power of decision into account. Our enemies are little worms – I saw them all at Munich!") On 20 August, Hitler took the unprecedented and flattering step of writing a personal note to Stalin, in language incapable of misinterpretation. He asked Stalin to accept Ribbentrop's presence in Moscow not later than three days from now, explaining: "Poland's conduct towards us, a major power, is such that a crisis may blow up any day."

After that, Hitler could not contain his nervousness. For want of a reply and for fear of a rebuff he could not sleep, he telephoned Göring in the small hours, he snarled at Ribbentrop uneasily for having tempted him out onto this trembling limb of high diplomacy. But during the afternoon of 21 August word came from Moscow: his ambassador had been summoned to see Molotov at 3 P.M. More anguished hours passed. Molotov was checking back with Stalin. At last Ribbentrop brought to Hitler and Himmler the ambassador's report. A smile lit up Hitler's face. A photographer was summoned to capture the moment as he read the telegram. Stalin's reply was described as "very conciliatory"; the Kremlin would be happy to receive Herr Ribbentrop in two days' time, as Hitler had requested.

An air of celebration gripped the Berghof, as though a great victory had been won. And in a sense it had, for when German radio interrupted its programmes at 11:15 P.M. to broadcast this chilling news to the world, nobody could doubt that it spelt the end for Poland. "Now," Hitler triumphed to his commanders next morning, "Now I have Poland just where I want her!"

Pact with the Devil

Once again the trump-card in Hitler's hands was his urgent desire for war – not a war to set all Europe alight, but a localized affair that could almost be regarded as an extension of German rearmament itself: the final furnace that tempers the steel of the blade.

To his adjutants he truculently claimed that he wanted only to be allowed his "First Silesian War" and nothing more – to sanctify the German Wehrmacht, put victories on its name and blood on its conscience. He explained to his commanders, "We don't want a general and simultaneous settling of scores – just a squaring of individual accounts one at a time." From now on, he disarmingly added, the German public would just have to get used to fighting. The Polish campaign, "White", would be a good introduction.

He still had no clear notion of the sequence of events after "White" – no doubt the same Goddess of Fortune as had ministered to his needs before would see to that. All that was constant was his long-term goal – the goal that he had set out in *Mein Kampf* in 1924, in secret to his C-in-Cs on 2 February 1933, again on 5 November 1937, 28 May 1938 and most recently in his secret speeches of January and February 1939: in short, "White" was just one more step towards Germany's 300-year-old dream of a Reich dominating Central and Eastern Europe, and thereby the world. Such was the prize he again held out to his commanders. What means were not justified to that end? Britain, he would cajole and win with blandishments: he would offer his Wehrmacht to guarantee and defend her far-flung empire against the Asiatic hordes. Germany's other neighbours, Hitler would cheat, threaten, bribe or deceive. "As a private person I would never break my word," he confided to Walther Hewel in June 1941. "But if it is necessary for Germany – then a thousand times!"

Undoubtedly August 1939 was a most opportune time for Nazi Germany to seize the initiative again. The west lacked leaders – with their politicians and parliamentarians they could only lose, while Germany stood only to gain: so argued Hitler. Neither Britain nor France could aid Poland directly. Göring's

Luftwaffe had 390,000 men – the RAF numbered 120,000, the French air force 72,000 and the Polish only 15,000. Besides, as Hitler was to define it, "This will not be a contest between machines but between men." And the Wehrmacht soldier was disciplined, fanatical, trained and manly – far superior to any of his putative enemies. Above all, for the second year running Providence had favoured Germany with a fine harvest.

Without waiting for Stalin's reply to his letter – since time was now at a premium – Adolf Hitler had already ordained on the nineteenth that on Tuesday 22 August all his senior commanders were to meet him at the Berghof. The invitation issued by the OKW emphasized: "He particularly wants the conference to remain absolutely secret and no word whatever of it to leak to the foreign press." It would therefore be disguised as a harmless tea-party, with half the guests fetched by Hitler's motor pool from Salzburg and half from Munich; all would be in plain clothes. The cynic is entitled to assume that the Führer really wanted to attract attention, for plain clothes would hardly stop the tourists thronging Berchtesgaden from sighting the fleets of limousines bearing sinister and soldierly guests up to the Berghof. (Hitler also began by forbidding his listeners to make notes – with, inevitably, the opposite effect since no less than five unofficial records were privately written that day and several more soon after.)

When he entered the Great Hall at noon on 22 August, with his faithful Ribbentrop at his side, Hitler found about fifty officers arrayed in four or five rows of chairs – army-group and army commanders, their chiefs of staff and their navy and air force equivalents. Prominently to the fore was Field-Marshal Hermann Göring, who had interpreted the "plain clothes" injunction less literally than the others. He was wearing a sleeveless green leather jerkin with thick yellow buttons over a white silk blouse, while his ample lower extremities were sheathed in grey knickerbockers and long grey stockings. A gold dagger dangled nonchalantly from an exotic sword-belt. But the Führer – whose sarcasm over the foreign ministry's gaudy new ceremonial uniform in 1938 had caused even Hewel to leap to Ribbentrop's defence – had a notorious soft spot for Göring and turned a blind, nay bedazzled eye on his latest sartorial excess.

The morning's newspapers were loud with the news from Moscow. It was the main topic of the chatter that still buzzed as Hitler stepped in. His audience was tense. Hitler spread out his outline notes on the grand piano to his right, and launched into his first speech. His argument was simple but persuasive: the Wehrmacht was about to embark on "White", a war they could not lose. He appealed to their martial aspirations. For two hours he set before them the now familiar history of his decision.

In sum, he said this: he had realized since the spring of 1939 that war with

Poland was inevitable, in view of Britain's foolhardy guarantee to her. And there was no time like the present for "White" to be launched – and by "the present" he meant this coming Saturday, 26 August. Neither he nor Mussolini would live for ever: "At any moment I might be struck down by a criminal or lunatic." He had no fears of any second front. There had been no real rearmament in Britain, and so it would remain until 1941 at least. Britain and France might posture menacingly, but they would not really fight. The pact with Russia would ensure that too. Hitler then described how he had set the ball rolling toward rapprochement by his "particularly cordial" welcome for the Russian ambassador at the New Year reception. (Admiral Hermann Boehm, the fleet commander, quoted Hitler in his note as saying: "That same evening the ambassador expressed his thanks to me for this and for not having given him the second-class treatment at the reception.") After further exchanges over the last four days, continued Hitler, he had now established personal contact with Stalin. With a gesture towards Ribbentrop he announced triumphantly that the foreign minister was flying to Moscow immediately to sign the pact. "Now I have Poland just where I want her!"

Now Germany could not be blockaded, because the USSR would supply all the Nazis' cereals, cattle, coal, wood, lead and zinc needs. "I am only afraid that at the last moment some – " and here he paused, searching for the right word – "some *Schweinehund* might put to me a plan for mediation!"

A buffet lunch was served on the Berghof terraces. Afterwards, at 3 P.M., Hitler spoke for another hour as a storm gathered outside the big picture window. He adjured the commanders to display outwardly an iron nerve, even if as was still possible Britain and France did break off diplomatic relations after Saturday, or prepared for war. "Each and every one of you must act as though we have, all along, been longing for a fight with the western powers as well." He hinted that there would *not* be a long period of peace after Poland's defeat – this was why it was vital to crush every living spark in Poland rapidly and, if need be, brutally. "I will provide a propaganda motive for launching this war, whether credible or not: the victor is not challenged afterwards as to whether he has told the truth." Hitler concluded with the appeal, "I have done my duty. Now you do yours!"

At these words Göring rose, importantly mounted three shallow steps and assured the Führer in the name of all present that the Wehrmacht would do its duty. Brauchitsch confidently dismissed his generals with these words: "Gentlemen: to your stations!" The Luftwaffe generals Milch and Kesselring were seen in a broad good-humour. Only Raeder came briefly to remind Hitler of the vulnerability of a sea-cadet ship permanently berthed in the Gulf of Danzig. The Führer was overheard to reply: "What if the old tub does go down!" The Grand-Admiral coldly reminded him that there were several hundred sea-cadets on board. It was the only time he saw the Führer in these last remaining days of peace.

As the Berghof emptied again, Hitler commanded Colonel Schmundt to sniff around for reactions to his speech. Of course the news from Moscow had won the older generals completely – this was the very doctrine Seeckt had always preached. Bock thought it a brilliant speech. Heinz Guderian and his fellow-officers had toasted the previous evening's news in champagne. Probably everybody believed – as had Papen, hearing the news from Hitler the previous day – that the imminent pact had banished the threat of war on two fronts. Ribbentrop set out that afternoon for Moscow, armed with Hitler's private instructions to yield to every Soviet demand: if necessary to secure Molotov's signature Ribbentrop was to deny any German interest in south-eastern Europe, "even down to Constantinople and the Dardanelles Straits".

Hitler detained his C-in-Cs briefly for an operational conference on details – for instance, the Dirschau operation. ("The Führer does not want any trains driven on to the bridge while there is any risk of its being blown up," the OKW directed.)

Hitler was cocksure. He wanted no second Munich. That evening, 22 August, he repeated that his only real fear was that some imbecile might oblige him, by "subtle proposals", to yield ground again. This was no idle fear: since about 16 August the FA had been monitoring furtive phone conversations between Sir Nevile Henderson, the British ambassador in Berlin, and Sir Horace Wilson in London: Wilson – "that swine", in Masaryk's vernacular – was one of the main appeasers among Chamberlain's advisers. Wilson was searching desperately for a formula that would give Danzig back to the Reich, in return for assurances by Hitler. On 20 August he secretly told Fritz Hesse, the German press attaché in London, that he was willing to "come secretly to Germany" if need be; Hesse reported this to Ribbentrop by letter two days later.

Proposals from London arrived almost immediately. Late on 22 August, Henderson phoned Hewel and then Weizsäcker, asking to see the Führer next day. He had a personal letter from the British prime minister to Hitler, he said: "It defines our position exactly," the FA wiretap quoted Henderson as saying. "How we are bound by our obligations to the Poles and how we shall live up to these obligations should Poland be attacked." (This was an unpleasant jolt for Hitler, who had hoped the pact with Russia would see the end of such British intransigence.) According to the wiretap, the Chamberlain letter would propose a cooling-off period while the questions of Danzig and the German minority in Poland were settled: meanwhile London had recommended Warsaw to seek direct consultation with the Reich. But shortly, at 1:10 A.M. on 23

August, Henderson's first secretary, Mr Adrian Holman, was heard asking London not to leak the Chamberlain letter to the British press, as *that* would look like an attempt at *intimidating* the Reich.

By the time Henderson had reached the Berghof at noon on the twenty-third, Hitler had already drafted a reply (since he knew what Chamberlain had written from the FA intercepts). He treated Henderson to a harsh session. Weizsäcker wrote in his diary, "The Führer's purpose was to bully the British government into dropping its guarantee obligations to Poland. The Führer expects Chamberlain's government to collapse on 24 August under the impact of our Moscow coup, and the guarantee concept to be dropped." When Henderson tried to explain that Britain was bound to honour her obligations, Hitler coarsely replied: "Then honour them! If you hand out blank cheques you must expect to have to pay out on them." He asked Henderson to call back later that afternoon to collect his reply to Chamberlain.

Henderson telephoned his Berlin embassy from Salzburg towards 3 P.M. "I hope to be back in Berlin about 8 P.M.," the FA wiretap read.

He [Hitler] is entirely uncompromising and unsatisfactory but I can't say anything further until I've received his written reply. Roughly, the points made by him were: Poland has been warned that any further action against German nationals and any move against Danzig including economic strangulation will be met by immediate German action. If Britain takes further mobilization measures general mobilization will take place in Germany . . . I asked whether this was a threat. His reply was, "No, a measure of protection".

Hitler's written answer was intransigent. In their second conversation Henderson argued that it was proof of Chamberlain's good intentions that he still refused to take Churchill into his Cabinet: the anti-German faction was not representative of the British public – it was mainly Jews and anti-Nazis, said Henderson. Henderson later told the Italian ambassador that his talk with Hitler had been "absolutely unfavourable": the Führer seemed dead set on war – even a general war. He had ordered the British embassy's papers to be transported to London, since he anticipated a German ultimatum to Poland on the twenty-fifth. The FA intercepted Attolico's despatch on this; and another FA wiretap, N125,629 that day, intercepted a report from the Yugoslav envoy in Warsaw to his government that Lord Halifax had written assuring Jósef Beck that the new Stalin Pact would not affect Britain's attitude toward Poland: Britain would honour her guarantee.

Hitler thus had good cause to suspect, after Henderson left the Berghof, that the British might be serious. Weizsäcker caught him briefly alone, and warned that Italy was only lukewarm about war, while the British were the captives of their own foreign policy. "Britain and France are bound to declare war. They aren't people you can take logically or systematically – they're labouring under a psychosis, a kind of whisky-intoxication. . . . Tomorrow Chamberlain will rally the whole Parliament behind him the moment he talks of war." Hitler disagreed, though evidently without conviction because Weizsäcker noted that day: "He still thinks he can localize the war, but he's also talking – today at any rate – of being able to fight a general war as well. Until recently, his view on this was very different."

Impatiently, Hitler waited for word from Ribbentrop in Moscow. Alone or with his adjutants he paced the Berghof terraces. Late that evening Ribbentrop came faintly on the phone from Moscow. Hitler asked what was happening. The foreign minister explained that Stalin was demanding that the tiny but ice-free ports of Libau and Windau in Latvia should be assigned to his sphere of interest. Hitler sent an orderly for an atlas, cursorily glanced at the Baltic coastline and replied that the USSR was welcome to the ports concerned.

Later that evening a paper was handed to him at dinner. Hitler excitedly rapped the table for silence and announced that the pact with Stalin had been signed. After dinner, the whole party strolled out onto the darkened terraces. Across the valley, above the Emperor Barbarossa's mountain, the night sky was lightened by a phenomenon not normally seen in these southern latitudes – an aurora borealis, not shimmering green, but bloody red.

Before seeing Henderson, at noon Hitler had decided that "White" should begin at 4:30 A.M. on the twenty-sixth; he would issue any orders to the contrary by noon on the twenty-fifth. The *A* movement was complete: all units of initial assault-waves were only one or two days' marching distance from the Polish frontier. The second phase, the *Y* movement, had just begun (at 8 P.M.): 1,300 trainloads of *matériel* and troops were moving eastwards, and 1,700 west. Raeder's warships were already at sea. Across the Atlantic a German supply ship, the *Altmark*, was just weighing anchor to rendezvous with the German raider *Graf Spee*.

What could still go wrong? The Poles might concede all his demands: that was most unlikely, knowing them. The Italians could let him down; Hitler frankly admitted concern over this to Weizsäcker on 24 August. The diplomat agreed, and wrote in his diary that evening: "Italy is acting as though the whole affair does not concern her. . . . But the Führer's still banking on a localized war, and won't give up. The thought that he may have to fight the west as well is causing him more concern than I suspected yesterday."

There was a reason for this. At 3:30 P.M. Hitler had flown back to Berlin, to meet Ribbentrop who arrived back at Tempelhof Airport from Moscow at 6:45. In Berlin sober news had awaited him: far from weakening, Chamberlain had just publicly reaffirmed in the reconvened House of Commons that Britain was standing by her guarantee to Poland, despite the Moscow pact. A formal Anglo-Polish treaty was at an advanced stage of preparation. Hitler confided to his chief adjutant, Schmundt, that he was no longer sure that Britain was only bluffing – though he was still loath to pick a quarrel with her.

He analysed the position with Ribbentrop, Göring and Weizsäcker that evening, 24 August. Ribbentrop was full of impressions of Moscow and the Kremlin. Stalin, he said, had toasted each of the very large German delegation in turn (though from a special carafe which may well have contained only water). Hitler's photographer, Hoffmann, had a picture of Stalin toasting even him: he claimed that the Soviet dictator had boasted, "You will see that we have no rich men now" – to which he had replied, "But in our country we have no poor!" "Stalin is just like you, mein Führer," Ribbentrop gushed. "He's extraordinarily mild – not like a dictator at all." In the political discussions, however, Stalin had been less amiable and had not conceded one inch.

More cursorily they discussed Italy. Hitler had ignored every sign that his Axis partner was indisposed toward war – Ciano's negative attitude at the Berghof; the explicit warnings of the Italian military attaché, Mario Roatta, on the fifteenth; and Canaris's information that the King of Italy had vowed never to assent to any mobilization decree that Mussolini submitted. The German finance minister, Krosigk, saw Ciano on the twenty-third and wrote at once warning Ribbentrop that the Italians were insisting they would not be ready for three more years. The only risk that Hitler would admit was that they might bluster that events had taken an "unexpected turn". So in the small hours of 25 August he had Ribbentrop telephone Count Ciano to advise him personally that "White" was now imminent. To Ribbentrop and Hitler it seemed a pure formality: they assured Ciano that the Moscow pact would rule out any western intervention – although even Hitler did not entirely believe that now, because a few hours later he had the admiralty warn all German shipping at sea, some 650 vessels, to steer for friendly ports immediately.

Weizsäcker predicted next day that the Italians would sooner ditch the Axis than find themselves without enough imported coal to cook a bowl of soup in two or three months' time. Ribbentrop heatedly took the opposite view: "Mussolini is far too great a man to leave us in the lurch."

In uncertain mood Hitler retired for the night. When he rose next morning, 25 August 1939, the residence was already crowded. The brown Nazi Party uniform was everywhere. Everyone knew that at 2 P.M. Hitler was due to give the code-word for "White", and none of his followers wanted to miss the historic moment. The photographs show Bormann, Goebbels, Ribbentrop and Himmler all there. In every room the sofas, chair-arms and tables were littered with telephones, the wires snaked across the priceless carpets in tangled profusion.

He knew he had something of a problem: things were not as cut-and-dried as he had hoped. Ribbentrop dictated by telephone a formal letter from the Führer to Mussolini explaining the Moscow pact and hinting that war might come at any hour; Hitler did not even bother to remind his ally of Italy's treaty obligations – he merely asked for an early reply. By noon there was still no reply, so he inquired of the OKW how long he could postpone the attack decision: the General Staff agreed to a one-hour extension of deadline – so Hitler now had to issue the code-word not later than 3 P.M. Meanwhile, Hitler had also decided to throw dust in Britain's eyes: at 12:45 P.M. Ambassador Henderson was invited to come to the Chancellery at 1:30. (Weizsäcker cynically observed in his diary, "Most of the day in the Reich Chancellery. Efforts are still being made to split the British from the Poles.")

Hitler's staff began to swell that day with the midwives of war. At 12:30 P.M. Lieutenant-Colonel Nikolaus von Vormann reported to Hitler, assigned by Brauchitsch as army liaison officer. So did Puttkamer, whom the admiralty had apprehensively recalled from the destroyer force to act as naval adjutant. (Later that day Colonel Erwin Rommel reported as commandant of Führer's HQ: Hitler promoted him to major-general and sent him with the HQ unit to Bad Polzin – a little railroad station in Pomerania, where Bock's Army Group North had also established its HQ.) Characteristically, Hitler waved away the officials pressing him for attention and took Puttkamer aside to talk about his destroyer experiences, until 1:15 when Bormann announced that lunch was served.

In the flower-bedecked room overlooking the Chancellery gardens, white-jacketed SS orderlies began serving the meal. A vegetable platter was put before Hitler, but barely had he settled with his nine-man staff at the round lunch-table when a roll of drums from the courtyard heralded the arrival of Sir Nevile Henderson. Hitler stood up and withdrew with Ribbentrop, excusing himself. For over an hour, speaking with apparent sincerity – at which he was a master – Hitler put to Henderson the folly of Britain's throwing away her Empire for Poland's sake. He followed with an offer: *after* he had settled the Polish problem, he was willing to conclude agreements with Britain which "would not only guarantee the existence of the British Empire in all circumstances as far as Germany is concerned but also if necessary assure the British Empire of German assistance, regardless of where such assistance should be necessary". (In other words, he would help defend the Empire against Japanese expansionism!) He offered partial disarmament as further bait, and even appears to have hinted that if Britain waged a "sham war" to preserve face he would not grudge it. He emphasized that nothing whatever would deter him from dealing with Poland: his mind was made up. But once that was over he would return to his beloved architecture. "I'm not really a politician at all."

It was a shrewd performance, but not shrewd enough. The FA intercepts showed that Henderson was not taken in. He reported in cipher to London that it was plain to him that Hitler was trying to drive a wedge between Britain and Poland. But the Foreign Office agreed he should fly back to London with Hitler's "offer" in writing, promised for that afternoon. Henderson was later heard arranging to fly from Berlin at 8 A.M. next morning. By that time, of course, Hitler hoped "White" would have begun.

There was still no formal reply from Mussolini, but the FA had now intercepted Count Ciano's instructions to the Italian ambassador to see Ribbentrop at once and inform him of the Duce's statement on Italy's position in the event of war: "If Germany attacks Poland and the conflict remains localized, Italy will afford Germany any kind of political and economic aid requested of her." (If the west counter-attacked, Italy was not in a position to take the initiative there, however, as Hitler and Ribbentrop had repeatedly been advised.) To Hitler, this seemed satisfactory enough. When Attolico thereupon asked urgently for an audience, he had been asked to come at 2 P.M. But Attolico had had to wait while Hitler talked with Henderson – and even as he waited he was urgently informed by Rome that his instructions had been *cancelled*. Hitler sent Ribbentrop out impatiently to telephone Ciano. The word from Rome was that Ciano and Mussolini had both left for the beach.

It was now 2:45 P.M. Fifteen minutes to go to the General Staff's deadline. Hitler crossed to the music-room with Ribbentrop and closed the door behind them. We know not what advice Ribbentrop offered: but a possible clue that it was the wrong advice is this – after Hitler's plans began coming badly unstuck that evening, he snubbed Ribbentrop and refused to talk to him for three more days.

At three o'clock Hitler decided he could not wait for the Duce's reply any longer. At 3:02 P.M., pale but otherwise composed, he opened the door and announced to the waiting throng: "Case White".

So the attack would begin next morning. Hitler's special train Amerika was shunted into Anhalt station to await him. The OKW issued Hitler's code-word to every service. Telegrams went out to every Reichstag deputy ordering an emergency session at five next morning. The public telephones to London and Paris were cut off. From Brauchitsch's headquarters the 3:02 P.M. code-word was cabled, teletyped, telephoned and duplicated until it had reached the unit commanders of two million soldiers; camouflage was stripped, engines tested, ammunition cases broken open – for at 8:30 that evening the advance toward the Polish frontier would begin.

Some hours passed. Suddenly one of the many telephones rang, the instrument responsible was identified and tended: a voice said that the British government was going to ratify its pact with Poland that evening – the news had come from the press office. It was typical, in Hitler's view, that this dark news had still not reached Ribbentrop's dandified and ponderous diplomats. At 5:30 P.M. the French ambassador arrived to receivé a lecture on fresh Polish "atrocities": Coulondre now also announced with dignity that France still stood by Poland. Afterwards, Ribbentrop urged Hitler to halt the attack.

But Hitler was no dilettante. He knew that an army is an amorphous and fluid animal, with many brains and many claws – he was not even sure it *could* be stopped. He sent for Colonel Schmundt; Schmundt called for General Keitel; Keitel summoned General von Brauchitsch – but he was nowhere to be found. In growing agitation, Hitler asked Keitel whether the whirring cogs of the OKW timetable had now advanced too far for the machine to be reversed. Schmundt fetched the timetable, the long pages were unfurled and calculations made. It seemed there was still time.

Even as they were talking, at about 6 P.M. the Italian ambassador hurried in, as unceremoniously as ever. He brought a further bombshell – the reply from Rome. In part it repeated the text intercepted by the FA. But it attached such fearful conditions to any Italian aid – for instance, "immediate war material and raw material deliveries from Germany" – and it was couched in such language ("I consider it my absolute duty as a loyal friend to tell you the whole truth . . .") that Hitler could only treat it as a stinging rebuff. He paced through the rooms like a caged tiger, snarling angry comments to the bystanders. He ordered Attolico to quantify Italy's material demands. He instructed Keitel to find out how far they could be met. Now he believed he knew why the British had ratified that pact: Ciano ór the King of Italy must have tipped off their kinsmen in the English Court that Italy would not side with the Reich. To Colonel von Vormann he hissed, "Cunning! That's what we've got to be now. As cunning as foxes!"

He ordered the colonel to summon Brauchitsch and Halder, chief of the General Staff, to the building. But Halder was on the road somewhere with his entire operational staff transferring from the war department in Bendler Strasse to General Staff HQ at Zossen, outside Berlin. Brauchitsch duly arrived at Hitler's residence at 7 P.M. Sober and unexcitable, he agreed that "White" could be postponed. In fact he welcomed the delay, as it would shift the emphasis from a surprise attack to a planned mobilization (the last trainloads of troops would still take some days to move east). He had always opposed Hitler's plan to open "White" with only twenty-seven divisions. He now told Hitler, "Give me a week to complete mobilization as planned, and you'll have over a hundred divisions available. Besides, this way you gain time for your political manoeuvering." He promised: "I can halt the army before it hits the frontier at 4:30 A.M."

Colonel von Vormann's unpublished diary and papers reveal that a thirty-minute drama followed as Hitler tried to reach Halder, still somewhere on the road to Zossen. At 7:45 P.M. Vormann was despatched by car to rush the orders personally to Halder. Keitel meanwhile dictated to one of his staff, Colonel Walter Warlimont, the written Halt order. Both this and the oral versions emphasized that the Wehrmacht's secret mobilization and rail assembly were to go ahead to the existing "White" timetable. When Hitler telephoned Göring, the field-marshal naturally asked him how long he intended to postpone "White". Hitler replied, very significantly, "I'll have to see whether we can eliminate this British intervention." Göring was sceptical: "Do you really think four or five days will change things much?"

For a week the Wehrmacht balanced on the Polish frontier, while the focus of Hitler's activities reverted to the diplomats.

He slept somewhat better and appeared downstairs looking more relaxed at 10 A.M. on 26 August. The news was that the army had managed to halt its attack on Poland virtually in mid-leap. The Halt order had missed out only one army patrol: it had attacked Poland by itself, and suffered accordingly.

The plight of the Abwehr and SS irregular units was more dramatic. A small task-force of Abwehr agents under a Lieutenant Herzner, sent into Poland ahead of zero-hour to hold open the key Jablunka railroad tunnels, could not be recalled. A pathetic message came that they had fulfilled their mission, but for want of the main German army advance they were now being encircled by regular Polish troops. Hitler – his mind still not made up on how long to postpone "White" – ordered the little band of desperadoes to hold out as long as possible. To the Polish authorities, meanwhile, the Germans coolly disowned Herzner's force as an irresponsible Slovakian gang. Heydrich's planned provocations using SS agents in Upper Silesia were called off at the last moment: the "Polish corpses" supplied by Dachau were given a reprieve.

Colonel von Vormann briefed Hitler on the west's preparations for war. Ambassador Henderson was flying to London at that moment to show Hitler's offer to his government; he had written briefly promising not to play for time.

Two curious telegrams had arrived during the night from the German ambassador in Rome. The first described vividly Mussolini's response at 3:20 P.M. the previous day, on reading Hitler's first letter: the Duce had "emphatically stressed" that he would stand unconditionally and with all he had at Hitler's side. That tallied with the first version of his reply as intercepted by the FA. But when Mackensen had handed over Hitler's second letter at 9:30 P.M., asking for details of the materials Italy would need, the tone had changed. Mussolini had indicated that Italy needed flak protection against French air raids, and raw materials like copper, tin, lead, nickel, iron, coal and petrol. A binding list would follow. By now it was 11:15 A.M. of the twenty-sixth, and the list had still not arrived in Berlin.

At 11:52 A.M., however, the Forschungsamt intercepted Ciano's telephone call from Rome to Attolico in Berlin, dictating what he described as Mussolini's demands: Italy demanded from Germany 150 flak batteries, millions of tons of coal, steel, oil and impossible quantities of molybdenum (600 tons!), tungsten, zirconium and titanium. The demands were exorbitant and clearly intended to be so. At noon Keitel, Brauchitsch and Göring came. (Göring had rushed over from Karinhall clad in a memorable outfit of white uniform, shoes and stockings, with a black cravat passed peasant-fashion through a thick gold ring which was set, like the ring on one hand, with three large jewels in red, white and blue.) Keitel confirmed that the OKW saw no prospect whatever of meeting the Italian demands.

At about 1:30 P.M. Attolico brought the list (which Hitler had already seen on the FA's brown-paper intercept). New was Attolico's demand that all the material must reach Italy "before the beginning of hostilities" – an absurd condition that Hitler knew was not contained in the original instructions telephoned to the ambassador. Hitler asked him to enquire whether there might not be some error – perhaps too many noughts had been added? Attolico complacently assured him that all the figures were correct, and left. At 2:30 P.M. Hewel phoned Ambassador von Mackensen in Rome to "verify" the figures direct with Ciano; Ciano also insisted that there was no possibility of error. Mackensen was then instructed to see Mussolini and show him the figures – an instruction he found "puzzling", since the figures were supposed to have emanated from the Duce in the first place.

Controlling his anger, Hitler began drafting yet another letter to Mussolini. He explicitly referred to Attolico's lying addendum and said he would do what he could to meet the Italian demands. Where the Italians had asked only for flak batteries indeed, Hitler proposed in his early draft to promise them flak battalions (*Abteilungen*). Göring was shocked and objected that that was quite out of the question. Hitler cynically replied, "I'm not concerned with actually making the deliveries but with depriving Italy of any excuse to wriggle out of her obligations."

Shortly before lunch General Milch arrived from Karinhall. It was he who candidly suggested that Italy's benevolent neutrality would be far better during "White": Germany could retain her scarce raw materials and obtain more through Italy if need be, and deny the enemy access to the Reich through Italy – which had been her weak spot before. Hitler slapped his thigh and brightened. And the letter that was finally telephoned to Rome at 3 P.M. reflected this change of emphasis: Hitler asked only that Italy should make sufficient military clatter to contain some of the west's forces. Who needed Italian military assistance anyway?

Over lunch he brightened still more. Surely Britain would not really fight? But there was no reply yet from London to his offer, and this was probably why he had still reached no decision on "White" when the C-in-Cs left the building at 4 P.M. He still hoped to isolate Poland somehow, and he called for the precise text of the new Anglo-Polish pact to scrutinize it for possible loopholes.

Mussolini confirmed that evening that since Germany could not supply the materials he had requested, Italy herself could not actively participate. Hitler replied with two lame requests: he asked his friend not to give the world any clue to Italy's disappointing attitude; and he asked for Italian industrial and agricultural workers for the Reich. Mussolini readily agreed.

That day the FA intercepted a report by the Italian embassy in Berlin to General Alberto Pariani, the chief of the Italian General Staff in Rome: Canaris had gleefully described to his crony, the military attaché, how Hitler had revoked "White" on the previous evening. Hitler angrily sent for his devious Intelligence chief and carpeted him for his inexplicable talkativeness which – given the multiplicity of links between Rome and London – had certainly not advanced the Nazi cause.

France's faint-heartedness was apparent in a letter from the prime minister, Edouard Daladier, which the ambassador brought to Hitler at 7 P.M. that evening, 26 August: "You were like me a soldier in the front lines in the last war. You will know as I do what contempt and condemnation the devastations of war aroused in the consciences of nations, regardless of how the war ended. . . ."

Coulondre followed the letter with an emotional forty-minute speech, begging the Führer who had built a whole empire without bloodshed to hesitate before shedding the blood either of his soldiers or of women and children now. Hitler responded with the familiar litany, but the dramatic force of this encounter was not lost on him: he remained silent throughout supper, kicking himself for not having advised Coulondre that, since he would never start the bombing of civilians, he would not be to blame if the blood of "women and children" flowed. Coulondre telephoned to Daladier in Paris that the message had fallen on deaf ears. Daladier responded, "So the German is going to fight? Then I put my trust in God and the strength of the French nation." (The FA recorded the exchange.) Hitler showed the letter to Keitel and commented that if was proof that France wanted to avoid war over the Corridor.

Unlike September 1938, this time the voices in Germany against war were in the minority. The Party liked "White" for a variety of reasons. The army

General Staff anticipated it with barely-disguised relish. Keitel's economics experts did submit a statistical table making unfavourable comparisons between Germany's war potential and that of the western powers; but Hitler retorted that there was no danger of war with the west – the pact with Stalin ruled that out. The only influential voice of warning, that of Göring, was not heeded. He privately warned that the USA would surely intervene; the Forschungsamt had compiled a summary on this very point in mid-August, and concluded that US intervention would come much sooner than in the World War.

Göring was maintaining contacts, wholly independent of Ribbentrop, with high British officials through intermediaries like Wohlthat and a Swedish businessman, Birger Dahlerus. That morning, 26 August, Lord Halifax had given Dahlerus a letter for Göring; Göring showed it to Hitler at about midnight: it confirmed the British desire for a peaceful settlement, but stressed the need for a few days to reach it. Was this again the spirit of appeasement? It required the most cunning cultivation, and Hitler asked Dahlerus to join them. He gave Dahlerus several proposals to convey to London, and sent him back.

Afterwards, he lay awake in the darkness of his Chancellery bedroom, and brooded on whether to take the plunge or postpone war for two years more, until Raeder's Z-Plan of naval construction was complete. All his instincts told him that he must attack now. Otherwise Poland would occupy Danzig that winter, when Germany was prevented by the weather from launching an offensive. Besides, every month saw the balance tilting against the Reich in favour of the western powers. Admittedly, the FA intercepts showed little sign of the western powers ditching Poland yet; but perhaps they were counting on Hitler climbing down again, as he had on the twenty-fifth.

Three times on the twenty-sixth, orders had gone out recalling the Reichstag, which had met only rarely in recent years. But three times the summonses were withdrawn almost immediately. A flak battery mounted guard on the Adlon Hotel where most of the deputies were staying. It was now 27 August. There was no word yet from London, but Hitler felt optimistic. During the day, the Nazi wiretappers heard the absent British ambassador's secretary, Holman, reassuring an American colleague that Henderson was urging London to avoid a war – the Poles should be advised to permit Danzig to return to the Reich and to grant Germany access to East Prussia across the Polish Corridor. Holman predicted that Polish truculence might still be a big obstacle.

Hitler finally met the disgruntled Reichstag deputies briefly at the Chancellery at 5:30 P.M. They recognized that he had spent a sleepless night. His voice was hoarse and his movements and expressions were loose and disjointed. Bormann – who attended with Himmler, Heydrich and Goebbels –

noted in his diary, "For the time being the Reichstag will not sit. After a brief speech the Reichstag deputies were sent home by the Führer."

Hitler told them things looked grave, but he had resolved to settle the eastern problem *so oder so*. He explained that he had made an offer to Henderson, and was still waiting for the British reply. His minimum demand was for the return of Danzig and a solution of the Corridor problem; his maximum demand was for whatever a war would bring him – and he would fight that war "with the most brutal and inhuman methods". Like Frederick the Great he was willing to stake everything on one gamble. Mussolini's attitude was, he suggested, in their best interests. War would be hard, perhaps even hopeless: "But as long as I live there will be no talk of capitulation." He regretted that his pact with Stalin had been so widely misinterpreted. The USSR was no longer a Bolshevik state, he argued, but an authoritarian military dictatorship like their own. He had made a pact with the Devil to drive out Beelzebub. He assured the deputies that Germany need fear no blockade by the western powers, in view of her partial self-sufficiency and the new pact. "If any one of you believes that my actions have not been inspired by my devotion to Germany, I give him the right to shoot me down."

The applause was thin. More than one listener gained the impression that Hitler ultimately intended to turn against the USSR, whatever his formal protestations to the contrary.

Food rationing was introduced on 28 August 1939, without warning. Soap, shoes, clothing and coal were rationed too. Hitler disliked the move; he would have preferred an appeal to the public's honour. The rationing was evident at his own breakfast table that morning: his unhappy staff were served with ersatz coffee and only the smallest portion of butter. But he himself came downstairs in brilliant mood, because he had learned during the night that the Swedish businessman Dahlerus had returned from London with news for Göring that the British were seriously considering Hitler's offer. Hitler boasted to his staff that he had managed to knock Britain out of the game – and thereby France as well. Henderson would surely return that evening to Berlin with the detailed confirmation.

When Brauchitsch reported to the Chancellery, Hitler made no bones about his immediate strategy: he proposed to hustle Poland into an unfavourable bargaining position, then go all out for his "big solution" – the military conquest of all Poland. He would demand Danzig, right of access across the Corridor and a Saar-type plebiscite there. Britain would probably accept these proposals, Poland would reject them, and the split would then be wide open. Hitler instructed the foreign ministry to draft a set of formal proposals along these lines, for the British government to study. The proposals – sixteen in all –

were so moderate that one of his diplomats termed it "a real League of Nations document": its similarity to the plot the Führer had just outlined to Brauchitsch was undeniable – it even proposed allowing the new Polish-built port of Gdynia in the Corridor to remain a Polish enclave. He read them out to Keitel in the conservatory. The general naïvely replied, "I find them astoundingly moderate."

Obviously, the new date for "White" would still depend ultimately on political desiderata; but at 3:22 P.M. Brauchitsch telephoned the General Staff from the Chancellery to the effect that the provisional new date was 1 September. Colonel von Vormann wrote that afternoon: "Hitler is in a brilliant mood. He's confident that we can position Britain so that we only have Poland to deal with. Everybody's guessing at what Henderson is bringing back with him. He took off from London at 4:30 P.M. Not a hint has reached us so far."

At 4:34 P.M. the Forschungsamt did learn that the British reply was now being cabled to the Berlin embassy for translation into German. Henderson was due to come at ten.

Henderson arrived at 10:30 – excusing the half-hour delay by his tiredness (in fact the FA wiretappers reported he had visited his French colleague Coulondre first). Wearing his familiar dark-red carnation, he was received with a roll of drums and a guard of honour at the Chancellery; Meissner and Brückner conducted him to the Führer's study. He handed over the British reply to Hitler's "offer" of the twenty-fifth. It was not what Hitler expected at all: the British announced that they had received "a definite assurance" from the Poles that they were prepared to negotiate. This was just what Hitler did *not* want now. Henderson accompanied the document with a speech, which neither Hitler nor Ribbentrop interrupted. He repeated that Britain could not break her word to Poland. Hitler replied that he was still minded to deal with Poland on a "very reasonable basis" – no doubt thinking of the still-unrevealed sixteen-point proposals. But he evaded Henderson's outright question as to whether he was willing to negotiate directly with the Poles; he merely turned to Ribbentrop and directed him to examine the British reply with Göring's assistance. He told Henderson that he would reply next day. Henderson assured him, "We took two days to formulate our answer. I'm in no hurry." "But I am," said Hitler.*

A rare fragment of Heinrich Himmler's diary casts an unsavoury shaft of light on the tenebrous inner workings of Hitler's mind that evening:

Ambassador Henderson came to see the Führer at 10:30 P.M. and left the Reich Chancellery at 11:45 P.M. Afterwards Göring, Hess, Bodenschatz and

---

* "Henderson", wrote Colonel von Vormann next day, "did not bring what we expected, at least so they say. What follows now lies darkly in the future's womb."

I joined the Führer in the conservatory. The Führer was accompanied by Ribbentrop.

He told us what the British offer contained. It was very courteously phrased, but contained nothing of real substance. Altogether he was in a very good mood and mimicked in his inimitable way what Henderson had put forward – speaking German with a thick English accent.

The Führer then indicated that we now have to aim a document at the British (or Poles) that is little less than a masterpiece of diplomacy. He wants to spend tonight thinking it over; because he always gets most of his best ideas in the small hours between 5 and 6 A.M.

At this Göring inquired, "Mein Gott, don't you get any sleep even now? Or have you got insomnia again?" The Führer replied that he often dozes from three to four o'clock in the morning and then suddenly wakes up to find the problems arrayed in pristine clarity before his eyes. Then he jumps up and jots down a few key words in pencil. He himself doesn't know how it happens – all he does know is that in the wee small hours of the morning everything that might confuse or distract disappears.

Sure enough, by the time Hitler awoke next morning, 29 August 1939, his strategem was clear. He would "accept" the British proposals for negotiations with Poland – under two minor conditions of his own. He particularly enjoyed the British suggestion of an international guarantee: "I like that," he guffawed, "from now on I'll only do things on an international basis. International troops *including Russians* shall go in!" (He knew Warsaw would never swallow that condition.) The other condition was his real brainwave: he would give Warsaw just one day to send a plenipotentiary to Berlin. They would of course refuse: if they accepted, the new scenario would still fit his "White" timetable. On the thirtieth the Pole would have to arrive; next day the talks would break down and cn 1 September "White" could begin, as planned. As an Abwehr colonel noted in his diary: "The Führer has told Ribbentrop, Himmler, Bodenschatz, etc., 'Tonight I'm going to hatch something diabolical for the Poles – something they'll choke on.'" Weizsäcker, equally well informed, wrote soon after 3 A.M. in his diary: "Göring has told the Führer, 'Let's stop trying to break the bank!' to which the Führer retorted, 'It's the only game I've ever played – breaking banks.'"

Hitler still refused to believe that Britain and France were in earnest. The FA wiretaps supported his belief, and other observations too: Britain had not yet embarked troops to France; both countries had assured the Low Countries of their neutrality, but to attack Germany on the West Wall would be sheer suicide. Even if they did declare war to save face, Hitler was sure it would only be a phoney war. "By day," Weizsäcker's diary continued, "the mood here [in Berlin] alternates between extremes of pro-British feeling and war at all costs. Relations with Italy are cooling fast. By late evening the mood is once again all for war: in two months, they say, Poland will be finished and then we'll hold a big peace conference with the western powers."

The reply Hitler handed to the British ambassador at 7 P.M. reflected his new strategem. He said he would approve of direct negotiations with Warsaw – and "counted on the arrival" of a Polish plenipotentiary next day. He would also agree to guarantee Poland's new frontiers – but only in association with the Soviet government. Germany would draft suitable proposals and show them to Britain (a reference to the as yet undisclosed sixteen points). Henderson objected, "This sounds very much like an ultimatum." Hitler retorted that it would only take ninety minutes for a Pole to fly to Berlin from Warsaw. "My soldiers are asking me: Yes or No?" To underline the point, Henderson found Brauchitsch and Keitel outside the study as he left. He ironically asked the OKW chief, "Busy today, Herr Generaloberst?" At 8:28 P.M. the FA heard the British embassy sending a summary of Hitler's reply to London, followed by the full text; this was repeated to the British embassies in Warsaw, Rome and Paris.

Over dinner afterwards, Hitler reminisced on the present crisis and its origins, and commented once more that he was now fit and fifty, and that it was better to tackle these crises now than to postpone them until later. He went over the main stages in the deterioration of German-Polish relations – protesting his own reasonableness and the obstinacy of his opponents. Gradually it dawned on his dinner-guests that Hitler was trying out on them the elements of the Reichstag speech that he would make after "White" began.

The next day, 30 August 1939, was spent in Berlin waiting for a Pole. Hitler conferred all afternoon with his C-in-Cs (except of course Raeder, who was still sulking over the Albrecht affair). His timetable now allowed little leeway; he told Brauchitsch that if absolutely necessary he could still postpone the attack on Poland until 2 September – but no longer, for the well-known weather reasons. Göring was several times telephoned by his contact-man, Dahlerus, from London. The Foreign Office there was describing Hitler's terms as unreasonable. Hitler accordingly was sure that no Polish plenipotentiary would arrive, and the FA wiretaps on the British embassy during the past night revealed that London shared that view. Henderson was heard at 11 A.M. complaining, "You can't just conjure a Polish representative from out of a hat." He added that it would not be easy to talk Warsaw round.

Soon after 5 P.M. a strange FA wiretap report reached Hitler. The Foreign Office had telephoned Henderson that Neville Chamberlain was less impressed than his ambassador by the clamour arising from the Reich Chancellery, "as he's been over there himself" and, by implication, knew these people.

The Voice [speaking from the Foreign Office end] continued that they are really on the right track now: They [the Germans] really mustn't expect to get away with it again by summoning people to them, handing over documents to them and forcing them to sign on the dotted line. All that's a thing of the past now. Berlin must try to realize that just as London does. That said, London is still prepared for that which Henderson has said London is prepared for. London just doesn't want to know about the other matters.*

In plain language, this told Hitler everything: London believed Hitler was bluffing – London certainly was not and was not interested in any proposals that Hitler might have to make.

That did it: Hitler instructed Ribbentrop to read out the sixteen-point proposals to Henderson when the ambassador came that evening, but on no account to hand over the document; at 9:15 P.M. the document was telegraphed to the German embassy in London, but marked secret as it was not to be handed over yet – it would be exploited later for propaganda purposes. At 10:30 P.M. the FA monitored a British embassy official, Sir George Ogilvie-Forbes, telling Attolico that they were all still "twiddling their thumbs" waiting for the telegram of reply from London. The Germans could only – falsely – deduce that the Foreign Office was deliberately stalling until Hitler's midnight deadline had expired.

Precisely at midnight, Henderson arrived at the Chancellery. When he inquired whether the German proposals had now been drafted, Ribbentrop airily replied that they had: but they were now superseded, as Poland had sent no plenipotentiary. Ribbentrop read them out, in German, to show how "reasonable" they were.

Hitler was not obliged by the OKW timetable to reach any binding decision on "White" until three o'clock next afternoon, 31 August. But now he felt his hands were free, and only a few minutes after Henderson left, the Führer sent for Colonel Schmundt, his chief Wehrmacht adjutant. At 12:30 A.M. he issued the code-word once again from his residence: "Case White". Immediately after that he retired to bed.

Throughout the next day, 31 August, Hitler was calm and self-assured – an ominous sign to those who knew him. He had made up his mind and nothing would now induce him to change it.

The activities of the foreign diplomats were only of academic interest to him now – throwing inconclusive and often confusing light on the possible reactions of their governments when "White" began. Henderson had been observed calling on the Polish ambassador, Joseph Lipski, at 1 A.M.; and the FA knew he had advised the Polish embassy to telephone Warsaw for urgent instructions. At 8:30 A.M. Henderson had desperately telephoned the Polish embassy again,

---

* Thus the text of the FA wiretap transcript. A second copy, minus the FA heading, was rushed to the Chancellery by Rudolf Likus. Both are in the files, but they are not reproduced in the published volumes.

warning that an unquestionably reliable source had informed him there would be war if Poland did not undertake some move over the next two or three hours. There was not a moment to lose. Lipski, however, refused even to come to the telephone.

Henderson telephoned the Foreign Office in London about this in code, adding it was just possible that the Germans might be bluffing; but equally, there was every possibility it was no bluff. Henderson telephoned Coulondre in the same agitated vein: Warsaw must be made to see reason. However, the Polish foreign minister, Jósef Beck, had no ambition to emulate Hacha: and soon after midday the FA's intercept of Beck's explicit instructions to Lipski were in Hitler's hands: Lipski was "not to enter into any concrete negotiations" nor to accept any German proposals; he was merely to hand a formal Polish government communication to the Reich government. Thus the Nazis knew that the Poles were merely stalling for time.

Göring called a ministerial conference at his operational HQ outside Potsdam that day. Herbert Backe recorded:

Today again at Göring's operations HQ with ministers Fricke, Funk, Darré, Seldte, state-secretaries as before [Körner, Landfried, Backe, Neumann, Posse], Bormann and Behrens. Waited hour and a half . . . Bormann optimistic. G[öring] said things look good. Poles wanted to prevaricate, we are determined. Decision in 24 to 48 hours. Instead of Mussolini – Stalin. [Göring] mentioned publication of something or other that may just keep Britain out. I don't know if he meant the Führer/Chamberlain correspondence or secret clause of Russian pact. Seems clear now he meant the former. Poland will be defeated. Unfortunately we forfeited surprise element, will cost us a few hundred thousand more [lives]. But then we have the upper hand. [Need only defend] frontier in west and air approaches to coast from Holland to Denmark (in addition to those to the west). Big danger is to the Ruhr. As the new frontier is short, massive demobilization of troops probable after Poland's defeat. And then relentless rearmament against Britain.

There is other evidence of Hitler's beliefs in Colonel von Vormann's notes that day: "The Führer is firmly convinced that France and Britain will just put on an act of waging war." They might raise a martial clatter in the west until Poland was destroyed – but nothing more. In conference with his generals Hitler made one final adjustment to "White" – postponing zero-hour by fifteen minutes to 4:45 A.M. next morning, to meet Luftwaffe requirements. Then, shortly before 1 P.M. on 31 August the OKW issued Hitler's official executive order for war. When Ribbentrop came round soon after, Hitler disclosed to him: "I've given the order. I've set the ball rolling."

To this the foreign minister replied, " – And the best of luck to you!"

The last three days had thus gone as Hitler planned. When the senior civil servant Otto Meissner now handed over papers needing signature, the Führer commented that he was delighted that Warsaw had not taken up his proposals.

He instructed Ribbentrop to "fob off" the Polish ambassador should he try for an interview. During the afternoon Lipski did indeed ask to see either Hitler or Ribbentrop; knowing from the FA the instructions Lipski had from Warsaw – not to enter into negotiations – they saw no urgency in receiving him. In fact all Lipski had was a note stating that his government was favourably considering Britain's proposal for direct talks. Brauchitsch heard through Canaris of Lipski's request for an interview, and told Hitler; the Führer replied at 4 P.M. that he was not going to receive him, and confirmed that "White" was still on.

When Ribbentrop finally deigned to see Lipski at 6 P.M., he merely asked the ambassador whether he was authorized to negotiate (knowing, of course, from the FA's brown pages that Lipski was not). The interview, the first between diplomatic representatives of Poland and Germany since March 1939, was concluded in a matter of minutes. Lipski did not ask for the sixteen-point proposals; nor did Ribbentrop offer them to him. As the ambassador left, all telephone lines to the Polish embassy were cut. (We now know from Polish diplomatic records that Lipski had confidently informed his government that revolution would break out in Germany, hence his misplaced sang-froid.)

Hitler confirmed to the Italian ambassador at 7 P.M. that things had now come to a head. Two hours later, German radio was interrupted with a broadcast of the "ultra-reasonable" sixteen-point offer that Warsaw had refused even to look at. At 10:30 P.M. there were the first radio mentions of serious border incidents, including an armed "Polish" raid on the transmitter at Gleiwitz. Other "provocations by the Poles" were reported near Kreuzburg and at Hochlinden, north-east of Ratibor.

Over two million Germans were now under arms. The final advance on the Polish frontier had already begun: this time it would not be halted. The dedicated and incorruptible civil servants of the Forschungsamt, still eavesdropping on the British and French embassies, could see signs that the western alliance was crumbling. Monsieur Coulondre phoned Henderson about Lipski's visit to Ribbentrop and said that the Pole had merely handed over a Note, without receiving the German proposals (which Henderson had unofficially obtained from Göring during the day). Henderson exploded, "But what's the point of that! It's ludicrous, the whole thing!" In a later conversation Coulondre tried to convince the British ambassador that the German proposals could not properly be accepted by Warsaw if the Poles had no formal knowledge of them. Henderson retorted that Lipski had evidently not even asked to see them; a heated argument broke out, which ended with both ambassadors slamming down their telephones.

On the eve of war, the west was in disarray.

Epilogue: His First Silesian War

By the time Adolf Hitler awoke and rose, his armies had already advanced many miles into Poland. They had stormed the frontier at 4:45 A.M. that morning, 1 September 1939, while the Luftwaffe bombed the enemy airfields and supply-dumps, and Abwehr and SS units moved in to seize vital bridges and military targets before the Poles could destroy them. The Polish navy's three destroyers had escaped to Britain the day before – one of the irritating consequences of Hitler's false start seven days earlier.

In many places Hitler's undercover operations ran into stiff resistance, too. Polish railway officials on Danzig's neutral soil managed to hold up the "goods train" bound from East Prussia for the Dirschau bridge, at nearby Simonsdorf station, for several minutes. By the time the train with its hidden cargo of German sappers and infantry reached the bridge the gates were closed, the lines blocked and a hail of fire met them. The Luftwaffe had attacked the demolition fuses on time, but brave Poles had repaired them and thus the mile-long bridge across the Vistula was blown. (The interfering Polish railwaymen at Simonsdorf were massacred by the SA during the first day of hostilities in reprisal.)

A second bridge at Graudenz had been assigned to a long-range Abwehr holding-squad, operating in plain clothes. These men penetrated into Polish territory, only to be arrested by an officious and trigger-happy German army lieutenant; in the distance they heard that bridge too destroyed. In Danzig itself the Polish post office building held out all day – it was adapted like a fortress inside – while Polish army officers disguised as postmen directed the seige. Thirty-eight Polish "postmen" survived the day: most of them were found to be wearing Polish army underwear, and were executed after army court-martial a month later. It was a rough war for "illegals" on both sides. An Abwehr "army" pulled together by two captains, Ebbinghaus and Fleck, from volunteers, SA guerrillas, the Sudeten German free corps and Polish and German agents, infiltrated Poland at about 3 A.M. to seize railway junctions, coalmines and factories in advance of the invading Wehrmacht: but on this first day alone Ebbinghaus and Fleck lost 174 dead and 133 injured of the 500 cut-throats they had set out with. As for Jablunka, the Poles – forewarned by Hitler's false start on 26 August – now had time to blow up both the railroad tunnels.

Hitler dressed that morning for the first time in a baggy field-grey army uniform, having discarded his Party tunic for the last time the night before.

At ten, he drove with his staff through Berlin's almost deserted streets to the Kroll Opera-house, where he would address the Reichstag. He sensed the same nervous tension as his little convoy of cars negotiated the fifteen-foot-wide approach-passage – one of Berlin's best vantage-points for an assassin. A hundred of the seats in front of him were empty, these deputies having been drafted with millions of others into the Wehrmacht ranks. But the auditorium was packed with Party and Wehrmacht uniforms. Goebbels was animated, Göring resigned, Hess oddly detached.

Hitler's speech was unrepentant, well-rehearsed and noisily received. He formally gave notice that they were at war with Poland: his enemies had misjudged him, he said, they had mistaken his love of peace for lack of courage. He publicly thanked his comrade Mussolini for his understanding attitude and "offer of support" – but, Hitler added, the Italians must understand that he needed no outside aid to fight this war. The speech rang with hollow promises: the West Wall would always remain Germany's frontier in the west; his pact with Russia eliminated every prospect that there might one day be a conflict between them. With a gesture to his uniform, he proclaimed dramatically: "I will never wear another, until victory is ours; not as long as I am alive!"

The deputies applauded frequently; but they applauded with feeling only when Hitler announced that he would fight a chivalrous war. "I will undertake each operation in such a manner that women and children are neither the target nor the victims."

Through still deserted streets he drove back to the Chancellery. But although he had proclaimed himself the "first soldier of the Reich", Hitler stayed on in Berlin, as he believed that the time for diplomacy was not over. The Chancellery telephoned General Rommel that Hitler would not be moving into the Führer's HQ at Bad Polzin yet. The news from London that morning was that the foreign secretary, Lord Halifax, had summoned the German chargé d'affaires, Theo Kordt, and complained that the German action against Poland "created a very serious situation"; this lame remark fell far short of a declaration of war by Britain. Hitler took heart. At 5:36 P.M. the FA did intercept London's instructions to Ambassador Henderson to notify Berlin that Britain would stand by Poland if the Nazi troops were not withdrawn: but no deadline was given. Colonel von Vormann, writing at 6 P.M., observed: "Naturally, everything is not yet clear. The big question – will Britain really stand by Poland? – is quite open. . . . At this moment, 6 P.M., Parliament is in session and the British and French ambassadors have just requested interviews with us in close succession." Henderson handed his Note to Ribbentrop at 9 P.M., but almost at once the Forschungsamt intercepted an incautious remark by a British embassy official that the Note was *not* an ultimatum – just a warning.

Early on 2 September 1939, Mussolini made a vainglorious attempt to halt the avalanche. He proposed to London and Berlin a ceasefire, and an immediate Five-Power peace conference, while the German armies stayed put in Poland. The final settlement, the Italians urged Berlin, was bound to be in Germany's favour. France was said to be in agreement. For some hours Hitler appears to have taken seriously the possibility that Mussolini might oblige him to accept a ceasefire: because in conference this same day Hitler impatiently urged the Wehrmacht to seize as much Polish territory as they could over the next few days, and particularly the whole Polish Corridor. At 9:20 A.M. Captain Engel, his army adjutant, phoned Rommel not to expect the Führer to transfer to his HQ that day either.

Meanwhile the Führer's residence teemed with officials – most of them onlookers, happy to be at the heart of things. Colonel von Vormann jotted in his diary: "Mood is very confident." The towering frame of Wilhelm Brückner moved regularly through the rooms, inquiring each person's business and tactfully easing the idle out into Wilhelm Strasse.

Later it became clear that the Italian bid had failed. In a noisy House of Commons, Neville Chamberlain had insisted that Germany's forces totally withdraw from Poland. The FA monitored this statement being telegraphed to the British embassy at 7:50 P.M. Evidently there had been a Cabinet development since his statement, as there was a postscript: "See my immediately following telegram." Henderson was heard telephoning Coulondre: "I don't know what the next telegram will be, but I can guess." At 8:50 P.M. the Italian ambassador confirmed to Ribbentrop that London was insisting on the complete withdrawal as a pre-condition to any further negotiations.

Ribbentrop had one trick up his sleeve: he phoned Fritz Hesse, his press attaché in London, to take up Sir Horace Wilson's earlier idea of flying secretly to Berlin to meet Hitler and "discuss the whole position, including Poland, heart-to-heart". Hesse saw Wilson at ten: the British diplomat made it plain that the Wehrmacht must first withdraw from Poland. This rebuff reached Ribbentrop at 2 A.M.

Meantime, at half an hour after midnight – it was now Sunday, 3 September – Henderson had received the "immediately following telegram". Its text was as he had feared. "You should ask for an appointment with Minister for Foreign Affairs at 9 A.M., Sunday morning. Instructions will follow." There was no doubt in his mind – or in Hitler's, as he read the FA's brown-page on this intercept – as to what the instructions would be. Britain was about to tender a war ultimatum to the Reich. Hitler's First Silesian War was beginning to spread like a bloodstain across the rest of Europe. At 2 A.M., when news of Hésse's rebuff by Wilson came, Hitler ordered an adjutant to telephone Rommel that the Führer's HQ was to expect him to arrive in twenty-four hours' time. His diplomatic interlude was over. He would now command his armies in person, from the Polish front.

On 3 September 1939, Hitler's reputation for infallibility of judgement suffered a severe setback. Ribbentrop also felt the failure to establish a common ground for negotiation with Britain, and personal abuse was heaped on him by Weizsäcker and others. (Weizsäcker claims to have warned Göring: "Ribbentrop will be the first to hang, but there will be others after him"; and to have admonished Brauchitsch: "The responsibility for actually fighting this war lies nonetheless with the generals, and that means you.") Hitler seems to have feared, to judge from a remark he later made, that the arrogant and touchy foreign minister might document his personal failure to keep Britain out by doing some injury to himself, so he had an adjutant telephone the Kaiserhof Hotel and ask Ribbentrop to spend the next few hours with him at the Chancellery.

It was now 9 A.M. At the foreign ministry, an interpreter was given – in Ribbentrop's absence – the thankless task of receiving the British ultimatum from Henderson. Hitler scanned the hasty translation a few minutes later, without a vestige of consternation. The ultimatum gave him two hours to undertake to withdraw from Poland. He had no intention of complying, and told Luftwaffe adjutant von Below that Britain clearly did not expect him to. He indicated that Keitel and all three C-in-Cs should report to him in person that afternoon. At 11 the ultimatum expired. At 11:30, Henderson saw Ribbentrop and informed him that Britain was now at war with the Reich. Ten minutes later, the FA heard the British embassy report to London that Ribbentrop had handed over an eleven-page reply, refusing to give any assurance as to the withdrawal of German troops and putting the blame squarely on Britain; the embassy had destroyed its ciphers, "The Germans were very polite."

Colonel von Vormann's contemporary account that day, as Hitler's army liaison officer, deserves quoting here:

Last night everybody was in splendid mood, hoping we'd succeeded in putting Britain and France into an at best ambivalent posture.

But now the worst has happened, after all! At 9 A.M. the Englishman came with his ultimatum, expiring 11 A.M.; and at 11 the Frenchman with *his* ultimatum, deadline 5 P.M. I'm not a grouser or defeatist, but the future looks very grim to me. This is just what we didn't want. Until this morning the idea was to play for time somehow and to postpone the decision. Even today the Führer still believes that the western powers are only going to stage a phoney war, so to speak. That's why I've had to transmit an order to the Army at 1:50 P.M. not to commence hostilities [in the West] ourselves.

I can't share his belief. He's got the wrong idea of the British and French psyche.

In the event, Hitler proved right again. It was from the contortions that Britain had gone through to produce even this ultimatum that Hitler deduced her unwillingness to fight yet; he said as much to Grand-Admiral Raeder that afternoon – the first time they had exchanged views since June. Raeder was unconvinced, and penned a sour survey that day beginning: "Today there began a war with Britain and France with which – to judge from all the Führer's utterances hitherto – we should not have had to reckon before about 1944; and a war which he considered until very recently (his speech to the commanders on the Obersalzberg on 22 August) he must avoid at all costs, even if it meant postponing a thoroughgoing solution of the Polish problem until later." In consequence, the German fleet was still only an embryo – it could but show how to die gracefully and thus build a tradition on which to found a new German navy in later years.

Field-Marshal Göring – no admirer of Ribbentrop's – volunteered to fly at once to London. His Junkers plane was already standing by at Berlin's Staaken airfield. Hitler forbade him outright to undertake any such venture. Pacing up and down the room overlooking the garden, oblivious of the audience of officials and ministers, Hitler dictated in rapid succession the proclamations to the German people, to the Nazi Party and to the Wehrmacht in east and west. In them, he branded Britain as the eternal warmonger, whose aim over two hundred years had been to defeat whichever Continental power was strongest, spurning no lies, libels or deceits to that end. Hitler wasted no words on France although Coulondre had tendered an ultimatum too. As Colonel Eduard Wagner, of the General Staff, recorded: "It's now official that France wavered until the last minute, and was only dragged in by Britain. Once again you can only say, *Gott strafe England!*"

The proclamations were hurriedly typed by the faithful secretaries. Hitler picked up his metal-rimmed spectacles from one of the tables, scanned the drafts and released them to the press. Secretary Christa Schroeder wrote that evening to a woman friend: "We're leaving Berlin in a few hours' time. . . . As for me, I'm ready to go through thick and thin with the Chief. If our luck runs out – I'd rather not think about that, but *if* – then my own life doesn't matter to me any more."

In another room, Göring, Raeder, Brauchitsch and Ribbentrop waited for a joint War Cabinet meeting with their Führer such as had never occurred before and would not occur again. Brauchitsch predicted that victory in the Corridor would be complete within two days. In the south, the Warthe river had already been crossed – a first requirement for the encirclement of Warsaw. The Poles had lost the initiative. Everything now depended on whether France actively attacked along the West Wall. Hitler was confident that France would not.

"Almighty God," Hitler had written in *Mein Kampf*, "bless our arms when the time comes, be righteous just as Thou hast always been, judge for Thyself whether we have now merited our freedom. Lord, bless our fight!"

A quarter-century before, Kaiser Wilhelm's armies had marched off to battle through cheering crowds, garlanded with flowers, while bands played. How different was Adolf Hitler's departure for the Polish front that night!

With headlights doused, the column of cars groped through Berlin's blacked-out streets to the almost deserted Anhalt railroad station. A solitary stationmaster waited at the barrier to greet him and his staff. The special train *Amerika* waited on the cordoned-off platform, its locomotive panting steam, while the station's coloured signal-lamps reflected from the metal of the light flak batteries mounted on flat wagons at each end.

At 9 P.M. the long train hauled out of the station, towards the battlefield.

Abbreviations used in Notes

AA   Auswärtiges Amt, German foreign ministry. For a listing of serials against NA microfilm numbers, see George A. Kent, *A Catalog of Files and Microfilms of the German Foreign Ministry Archives 1920–1945*. Vol. III, pages 525 *et seq.*

BA   Bundesarchiv, the German federal archives, based on Koblenz (civil agencies) and Freiburg (military)

BDC   Berlin Document Centre (of US Mission, Berlin)

—C   A Nuremberg Document Series (*e.g.* 100–C)

CCPWE   US Army Interrogation series (now in NA)

CIR   Consolidated Interrogation Report (US army)

CO   Cabinet Office files

CSDIC   Combined Services Detailed Interrogation Centre (these British reports are still top secret)

D—   Nuremberg document series

DIC   Detailed Interrogation Centre (*see* CSDIC)

DIS   Detailed Interrogation Summary (US army)

EC—   A Nuremberg Document series

ED—   An IfZ document series

F—   An IfZ document series

FA   Forschungsamt, literally Research Office: Göring's wiretap agency

FIR   Final Interrogation Report (US Army interrogation)

FO   Foreign Office, London

GRGG   CSDIC document series

II H—   Germany army document, in BA, Freiburg

Ifz   Institut für Zeitgeschichte, Institute of Contemporary History, Munich

IIR   Interim Interrogation Report (US Army interrogation)

IMT   International Military Tribunal: *Trial of the Major German War Criminals at Nuremberg*

kl. Erw.   Kleine Erwerbung, a minor accession by BA, Koblenz

L—   A Nuremberg document series

46—M   Interrogations at Berchtesgaden, 1945, now in library of University of Pennsylvania

MD   Milch Documents, original RLM files recently restituted by British government to BA, Freiburg; microfilms of them are available from Imperial War Museum, London, and soon from NA too. (The citation MD 64/3456 refers to Vol. 64, page 3456.)

MISC   Military Intelligence Service Centre (US Army interrogations)

ML—   NA microfilm series

N   *Nachlass*, the papers of a German military personage, now held by BA, Freiburg
NA   National Archives, Washington, DC
ND   Nuremberg Document
NS—   Collections of Nazi documents in BA, Koblenz
OCMH   Office of the Chief of Military History, Washington, DC
P—   MS series of US Army: post-war writings of German officers in prison camps (complete collection in NA)
PG/   Files of German admiralty, now held by BA, Freiburg
PRO   Public Record Office, London
—PS   A Nuremberg document series
R—   A Nuremberg document series (*e.g.* R–100)
R   Collections of Reich documents in BA, Koblenz (*e.g.* R 4311/606)
RH   German army document in BA, Freiburg
RIR   Reinterrogation Report (US Army)
SAIC   US Seventh Army Interrogation Centre
T   NA microfilm series. (The citation T78/300/1364 refers to Microcopy T78, roll 300, page 1364.)
USFET   US Forces, European Theatre
USSBS   US Strategic Bombing Survey
VfZ   *Vierteljahrshefte für Zeitgeschichte*, quarterly published by IfZ
WR   *Wehrwissenschaftliche Rundschau*, German military science monthly journal
X—   OCMH document series, now in NA
X—P   DIC interrogation series (prisoners' conversations, recorded by hidden microphones, as at CSDIC)
ZS—   *Zeugenschrift*, collection by IfZ of written and oral testimonies
ZSg.—   Zeitungs-Sammlung, newspaper cuttings collection in BA, Koblenz

Notes

p. (*xx*)   Hugh Trevor-Roper emphasized Hitler's singlemindedness in foreign policy, in a paper read to historians in Munich in November 1959 (*VfZ*, 1960, 121ff). See also Karl Bracher's article on Hitler's early foreign policy (*VfZ*, 1957, 63ff), and Hitler, *Das Zweite Buch*, (Stuttgart, 1961).

p. (*xxi*)   The police reports are reproduced in *VfZ*, 1963, 274ff. The speech in Salzburg in August 1930 (pages *xx–xxi*) will be found in BA file NS 11/28. For two more early speeches on the Jews in Vienna, in December 1921 and June 1922, see *VfZ*, 1966, 207f.

p. (*xxii*)   The letters of Walther Hewel from Landsberg are in his widow's possession: microfilm of Hewel's papers is in the Sammlung Irving at IfZ, and may be seen with her permission.

p. (*xxiv*)   The revealing quotation is from Hitler's secret speech to his generals, 22 June 1944 (unpublished, BA file NS 26/51).

p. 4   Blomberg's own surviving accounts of this affair are his manuscript for the US Seventh Army, SAIC/FIR/46 of 13 September 1945, and unpublished jottings in his family's possession, since transcribed by Elke Fröhlich of IfZ. I also used the diaries of Alfred Jodl and Wolf Eberhard; the latter officer was Keitel's adjutant 1936–1939. Microfilm (DJ-74) and a restricted transcript of the Eberhard diary are in the Sammlung Irving, IfZ. Of secondary value were interrogations of Karl Wolff, Meissner, Keitel, Wiedemann, Bodenschatz, Puttkamer, Count von der Goltz, Frau Charlotte von Brauchitsch, Canstein, Siewert, Engel and Lammers; the unpublished memoirs of Hitler's Luftwaffe adjutant Below, written in 1946; and the diaries of Göring's deputy, Erhard Milch (of which I have deposited transcripts and microfilm, DJ 56–59, in the Sammlung Irving, IfZ).

p. 5   The "Buff folder", the police file on Fräulein Gruhn, survives as No. 7079 in the archives of the Berlin public prosecutor. It contains no evidence whatever of a criminal record or of morals charges. From the testimonies of Miklas and Löwinger in the file, it is possible to reconstruct how she was entrapped. I traced her to West Berlin in 1970, but she was not willing to be interviewed.

p. 7   Fritsch's personal handwritten notes written between February 1938 and 27 September 1938 were removed to Moscow in 1945 from the Potsdam army archives, and were kindly made available to me by a Soviet source. I have deposited restricted transcripts of them with the BA for their Fritsch collection, N33, and the Sammlung Irving, IfZ. Their authenticity was confirmed to me by Fritsch's adjutant, Colonel Otto-Heinz Grosskreutz. Of supporting interest were Fritsch's private letters to the Baroness Margot von Schutzbar – of which the originals are now (1977) in an Oxford

University basement – and the February 1939 manuscripts of Fritz Wiedemann, Hitler's ex-adjutant, in the Library of Congress, Box 604 (see my transcript in the Sammlung Irving, IfZ).

p. 12 Fritsch was interrogated by the Gestapo's Dr Werner Best and Franz Josef Huber on 27 January 1938. The 83-page verbatim record – on NA microfilm T82/272 – quotes the Fritsch dossier extensively, as do his own notes.

p. 15 My predecessors have without exception dated this speech by Hitler on 4 February 1938: but Fritsch's notes, the diaries of Milch, Eberhard and the later Field-Marshal von Leeb are clear that it was the fifth. The best summaries are those by Liebmann (IfZ, ED1), Felmy, Adam, Weichs, Hoth and Guderian.

p. 16 Heitz described his meeting with Hitler and Himmler on various occasions, e.g. to Weichs, Viebahn and von der Goltz; he himself died in Soviet captivity.

p. 18 I base my account of Hitler's speech of 13 June 1938 winding-up the Fritsch affair, on Fritsch's notes, on the letters written by Halder and Karl-Heinrich von Stülpnagel to Beck on 14 and 15 June (N28/3), on the diaries of Milch and Eberhard and the written recollections of Liebmann, Below, Adam, Felmy, Judge-Advocate Rosenberg and General von Sodenstern.

p. 21 The OCMH team under Georg Shuster conducted a series of perceptive interrogations of leading Germans including Schacht, Dönitz, Schwerin von Krosigk and Ribbentrop in 1945: these give much frank information on these early years. (Copies in Sammlung Irving, IfZ.)

p. 22 Robert Ley wrote several manuscripts in his Nuremberg cell before committing suicide in October 1945. The Nuremberg authorities ordered them destroyed, but they fortunately became lodged in Robert H. Jackson's files instead (NA, RG-238, Jackson files, Box 181). My microfilm of them, DJ-79, is in Sammlung Irving, IfZ. See also Ley's interrogation on 29 May 1945 (SAIC/30) and an East German's view in *VfZ*, 1970, 443ff.

p. 23 On the history of the autobahn, I was fortunate to obtain access to the Fritz Todt family papers and diaries (still restricted); and I used Shuster's interrogation of Dorsch. See too Dorsch's paper of 8 March 1950, in BA Kl.Erw. 529/2.

p. 24 Oron J. Hale, in *The Captive Press in the Third Reich* (Princeton University Press, 1964) wrote the definitive history of Nazi press monopoly. I also used the Cabinet records (BA, R43 I/1459), Shuster's interrogation of Eugen Maier and Max Amann, and Seventh Army interrogations of Amann and Hans Heinrich Hinkel. For the loan from Epp, see his papers (T84/24/9692).

p. 25 The birth of the SS and police state: see Shuster's interrogations of Frick and Göring, July 1945. Himmler's letter of 18 May 1937 is on T175/40/0962f; Heydrich's letter to Himmler, 23 May 1939, is in BDC file 238/I. My transcript of Himmler's notes is in the Sammlung Irving, IfZ.

p. 26 Historians are only slowly waking to the huge importance of Göring's Forschungsamt wiretapping agency. It was controlled formally by Göring's state-secretary Paul ("Pili") Koerner, but apart from its budget had no connection with the Reich air ministry, which was used only as cover. For a history of the FA, see my publication *Breach of Security*, (London, 1968) and manuscript ZS-1734 in IfZ files, by Ulrich Kittel, a senior FA official. The FA is also mentioned in CCPWE-32 interrogations of Göring, Steengracht and Ribbentrop, June–July 1945.

p. 27 Hitler's relationship to Hindenburg is described by Lammers under SAIC and USFET interrogation. See also Hitler's letter to the president, 5 April 1933 (T81/80/2044f).

p. 28 Hitler's secret speech of 3 February 1933 is the most important proof that his foreign policy remained constant from 1933 to 1941. Mellenthin's record is in IfZ files; I also used Liebmann's notes and Raeder's version, in his manuscript on Hitler and the Party (in Robert H. Jackson's files).

p. 30   On the founding of the secret Luftwaffe, I used Milch's papers and diaries and Cabinet records. See my book, *The Rise and Fall of the Luftwaffe* (London & New York, 1973); and the German official histories by Karl-Heinz Völker, *Die deutsche Luftwaffe 1933–1939* (Stuttgart, 1967) and *Dokumente und Dokumentarfotos zur Geschichte der deutschen Luftwaffe* (Stuttgart, 1968).

p. 30   Raeder's study on German naval policy 1933–1945 is in Jackson's files (NA); see also his Nuremberg interrogation, 9 November 1945, and particularly the wartime German studies by navy historian Dr Treue (BA files PG/33965a and 33966a); these quote many pre-war documents no longer traceable. A good guide to the documentation is James Hine Belota's 1954 Ph.D. thesis, University of California: my microfilm of this, DJ-47, is in Sammlung Irving, IfZ.

p. 31   Hitler's command is quoted in Fritz Todt's letter to Oberbaurat Koester, 14 November 1936 (Todt papers).

p. 33   On the growing tension between SA and regular army, I used Fritsch's and Liebmann's papers, and referred to documents published by Klaus-Jürgen Müller in *Das Heer und Hitler* (Stuttgart, 1969); also to Weichs' manuscript (N 19/6) – he had been Fritsch's chief of staff for one year, earlier. Papers in Krüger's files (T580/265) have a March 1934 marginal note by Kr[üger] indicating that he believed the Abwehr was conniving against the SA.

p. 35   This is from Vormann's manuscript (IfZ, F34). Keitel and many other army generals have testified that the SA was stockpiling illegal weapons; and see the evidence in Wehrkreis VII file 1652 (BA).

p. 36n   Notes on Raeder's discussions with Hitler in June 1934 are in his files (BA, Raeder 3) and file PG/36794.

p. 37   The most important items from Wehrkreis VII file 1652 (BA) have been published and analysed by Klaus-Jürgen Müller in *Militärgeschichtliche Mitteilungen*. 1968, 107ff. I also used Milch's diary, notebook and unpublished memoirs; papers from the "Röhm Trial", Munich, May 1957; Shuster's interrogations of Göring and Frick, July 1945, and of Walter Buch by CCPWE-32.

p. 38   On Schleicher's murder, see Theodor Eschenburg's paper in *VfZ*. 1953, 71ff.

p. 39   Hitler's anger at the unnecessary murders is described in Julius Schaub's private papers – still in the family's possession; a restricted copy is in the Sammlung Irving, IfZ. Wilhelm Brückner also described this in several affidavits and drafts for the Traunstein police in 1952 (ditto). For the report of Lutze's "drunken meanderings" see Himmler's files, T175/33/1892ff. Lutze's version is credibly supported by Ley in a long typescript, "Thoughts on the. Führer", written in summer 1945 (Jackson papers, copy in Sammlung Irving, IfZ). For a list of 83 victims, see T81/80/3456ff.

p. 40   Hinderburg's sympathetic comment was known by Kempka (Shuster interrogation), by Funk (see Henry Picker, *Hitlers Tischgespräche*, Stuttgart, 1963, 405) and by Brückner (a memo dated May 1949).

p. 41   Adam relates this significant Hitler boast in his own secret memoirs (IfZ, ED109) which vanished in 1945 into a monastery, and after a long odyssey only recently reached the IfZ. On the Dollfuss murder, see Helmuth Auerbach's article in *VfZ*, 1964, 201ff; I also used Papen's (monitored) conversation on 7 May 1945 (X-P3) and Shuster interrogations of Seyss-Inquart in July 1945. The Austrian historian Dr Ludwig Jedlicka has also published important documents of the SS, dredged up from Lake Schwarzensee in Czechoslovakia in 1964, in *Der 25. Juli 1934 im Bundeskanzleramt in Wien* (Vienna, 1965).

p. 44   On relations between the Wehrmacht and SS, Walther Huppenkothen – a Gestapo official – wrote quite illuminating studies, which are in the BDC's special Canaris file. I also used Fritsch's papers and a manuscript by General Edgar Röhricht on Himmler's fight for military power, dated March 1946 (IfZ).

p. 44   There is reference to Hitler's speech of 3 January 1935 in the diaries of Leeb and Milch; the best recollections of it are those of Raeder (August 1945), Admiral Hermann Boehm (IfZ: ZS12) and Dr Werner Best (March 1949, IfZ).

p. 45   The most recent biography of Beck is by Dr Nicholas Reynolds: *When Treason was no Crime* (London, 1976). He and I draw heavily on Beck's papers (N28).

p. 46   Blomberg's important directive of 10 July 1935 is not found, but adequately paraphrased in Fritsch's order of 3 March 1936 (naval files, AA Serial 9944, page E695952ff). See Donald Watt's convincing argument on this in *Journal of Contemporary History*, October 1966, 193ff.

p. 47   Hitler's remark on 25 May 1935 is reported by Raeder's adjutant, Captain Schulte-Mönting, IMT, xiv, 337; see also Shuster's interrogations of Dönitz and Raeder, and Wolfgang Malanowski's paper in *WR*, 1955, 408ff. For a history of the German admiralty, 1935–1941, see Michael Salewski, *Die deutsche Seekriegsleitung 1935–1945*, Bd.I (Frankfurt/M, 1970), and – specifically from Hitler's viewpoint – the little manuscript published by his naval adjutant, Rear-Admiral Karl-Jesco von Puttkamer, *Die Unheimliche See* (Munich, 1952).

p. 47   Eichen's medical notes were microfilmed: NA special film ML/131, I also used a British interrogation of Eicken, and papers by Schaub.

p. 50   Koerner's letter was to State-Secretary Herbert Backe. Frau Ursula Backe, the latter's widow, made her husband's letters and papers available to me. As for Hitler's August 1936 memorandum, see Professor Wilhelm Treue's excellent study, printing this document, in *VfZ*, 1955, 184ff. Hitler briefly referred to it in his Table Talk on 24 January 1942. For the Cabinet (Ministerrat) of 4 September 1936 see ND, 416-EC.

p. 51   Milch's records are important for the origins of the Legion Condor. I also used Shuster's interrogations of Warlimont and Göring.

p. 51   For Göring's comments (to Milch, Bodenschatz, etc.) see ND, 3474-PS.

p. 52   Several authentic accounts of the Hanfstaengl affair exist, by Schaub, Brückner and Bodenschatz, and an interrogation of Göring dated 15 August 1945. In July 1937, Bormann confidentially banned all printed references to Hanfstaengl throughout Germany (NS 11/19).

p. 53   Re *Who's Who*, see the Chancellery file, "Personal Affairs of Adolf Hitler" (R 43 II/960); the quotation is from his speech to field-marshals and generals on 27 January 1944 (BA, Schumacher collection, 365).

p. 56   Below describes Hitler's growing interest in Japan, in his manuscript. A first-rate source is Shuster's interrogation of Dr Werner von Schmieden, who headed the Far East division of the AA.

p. 56   For Hitler's early warmth of feeling toward Britain, see e.g. G. Schubert, *Anfänge nationalsozialistischer Aussenpolitik* (Cologne, 1963) for the period 1922–1923; and the little-known article by Hitler in the monthly, *Deutschlands Erneuerung*, 1924, 199ff (on which cf. Wolfgang Horn, in *VfZ*, 1968, 280ff). Ribbentrop dwelt at length on his endeavours to cement Anglo-German friendship, in his interrogations and manuscripts: of particular interest is his manuscript of 2 August 1945, found among Robert Jackson's papers (NA), of which I have placed a transcript in Sammlung Irving, IfZ. Ribbentrop frequently referred to his 1936 offer of an alliance to Britain: and so did Hitler, e.g. on 31 August 1944 (Helmut Heiber, *Hitlers Lagebesprechungen 1942–1945* [Stuttgart, 1962], 614).

p. 57   For Hitler' references to Lloyd George's remark, see his speeches of 30 May 1942 (Picker, *op. cit.*, 503) and 27 January 1944, and Table Talk of 18 July 1942.

p. 59   See Ribbentrop's discourse on the Duke of Windsor to the Bulgarian regents on 19 October 1943.

p. 60   The quotation is from Hitler's secret speech to Nazi editors on 10 November 1938 (transcribed, February 1940, in BA file NS 11/28; a different transcript was published in *VfZ*, 1958, 175ff and the speech is summarized by Rudolf Likus in Ribbentrop's files, AA serial 43, 29044ff).

p. 60   Hitler's agents like Keppler and his assistant Dr Edmund Veesenmayer demand much closer attention than they have been afforded by historians; they exercised greater immediate influence on foreign policy and events than Neurath, Ribbentrop, and the diplomats. I obtained all possible interrogations of them (US State department, OCMH, Shuster, and Nuremberg) and studied their BDC personnel files too.

p. 62   There is material on the iron and steel shortage of 1937 in Milch's and naval staff files and the Jodl diary. For the raw-materials origin of the Hossbach Conference, see Milch files, MD 53/867, 53/849, 65/7510.

p. 63   François-Poncet reported on the Hossbach Conference in two *télégrammes chiffrés*, numbers 4409–10, on 6 November 1937 (unpublished); that these were decoded by the FA is evident from correspondence between Blomberg, Raeder, Puttkamer and Wangenheim in naval staff files (PG/33272).

p. 63   An authentic but evidently incomplete note of the Hossbach Conference of 5 November 1937 exists, written on 10 November 1937 (ND, 386–PS). Controversy raged over its genuineness: e.g. Walter Bussmann in *VfZ*, 1968, 373ff. I am satisfied with it, as Hitler's adjutants (Below, Puttkamer) told me they saw it at the time; it is also mentioned in Jodl's diary, and in Beck's horrified commentary of 12 November (BA, N28/4), and indirectly in the Wehrmacht directive of 7 December 1937. Other useful arguments on it: Kielmansegg, in *VfZ*, 1960, 268ff; and Hermann Gackenholz, *Reichskanzlei 5 November 1937* (Berlin, 1958), 459ff. It is to be noted that there is no acceptable evidence of any opposition by Fritsch either at this conference or later. He did not even mention the conference in his private papers. Alan Bullock, in *Hitler, a Study in Tyranny*, describes a dramatic row between Hitler and Fritsch on 9 November: it must have been a loud one, because Fritsch spent the day in Berlin and Hitler was in Munich.

p. 64   The letter from the naval commandant, Captain Schüssler, to Raeder is dated 26 June 1937 (BA, PG/33273). On 10 January 1944, the Admiral speculated that Hitler had decided quite early to square accounts with the USSR, primarily for Weltanschauung reasons. "In 1937 or 1938 he did hint that he intended to eliminate the Russians as a Baltic power; they would then have to be diverted toward the Persian Gulf." (PG/33954b).

p. 65   The speech of 23 November 1937 is on BA discs F5/EW.68 368–68 400.

p. 66   Ribbentrop's long letter to Hitler, A.5522 dated 27 December 1937, is in the British FO library; it seems to have been handed by Ribbentrop as a carbon copy to Montgomery in May 1945 to ensure it was brought immediately to public attention. Quite the reverse happened: it vanished from sight until recently. I have supplied transcripts to the AA, the IfZ and BA.

p. 67   A misdated and unsigned summary of Hitler's speech on 21 January 1938 is in BA file RH26–10/255. Milch noted in his diary, "Three-hour speech by Führer to Reich War Ministry. Tremendous!" And Jodl, "At the end of the National-Political course the Führer speaks 2½ hours to the generals on his views on history, politics, the nation and its unity, religion and the future of the German people."

p. 69   Todt's remark is in a letter to Dietrich, 15 July 1937 (family papers).

p. 71   Letters listing films shown to Hitler and his comments are in his personal office (Adjutantur) files, e.g. NS 10/48.   ·

p. 72   *Finis Austriae*: The events leading up to the Führer's meeting with Schuschnigg were exhaustively examined in *Der Hochverratsprozess gegen Dr Guido Schmidt* (Vienna, 1947), which contains documents and illuminating testimony from Schmidt, Hornbostel, Tauschitz and others. Apart from the countless interrogations of Papen (e.g. X-P 3), Keppler, Veesenmayer and Dirksen, I found the important unpublished file of Austrian documents captured in 1938 by the Nazis invaluable: AA, serial 2935.

p. 73   In his interrogations, e.g. by the US State department and at Nuremberg, Neurath gave specious reasons for his dismissal as foreign minister.

p. 73   Ribbentrop was described by Stülpnagel thus to Vormann (IfZ, F34). He attracted few friends, but in private some diplomats still speak kindly of him – for instance Hasso von Etzdorf, who mentioned several positive qualities to me. In view of Weizsäcker's bitter hostility to him, as a professional diplomat, the references in Weizsäcker's diary need taking with a pinch of salt: I strongly suspect that some such entries – which were on loose sheets – were interpolated by Weizsäcker years later. Ribbentrop told Shuster in July 1945, "It was my sole function as foreign minister to execute the Führer's foreign policy by diplomatic means." He wrote the same to Himmler on 6 September 1942 (T175/117/2473).

p. 74   Reinhard Spitzy, Ribbentrop's secretary, gave me an eyewitness account of the Berghof meeting. Minister Guido Zernatto's account of these events, published in *Candide* as "The Last Days of Austria", will be found usefully in Ambassador von Mackensen's papers (AA, serial 100, 65372ff).

p. 75   On the Hamburg suspension bridge project, there is an informative letter in Todt's papers from him to Major-General Hermann von Hanneken, 1 April 1939 ("The Führer has expressed the wish that work should begin this year"). Test drilling was complete, but a petrol wharf would have to be moved to make way for the southern pylon and bridge pier.

p. 77   Schuschnigg's memoirs, *Ein Requiem in Rot-Weiss-Rot*, (Zürich, 1947), are not to be trusted. The extract he quoted from Hitler's speech of 20 February ("The German people is no longer inclined to put up with the oppression of ten million Germans on her frontiers") is his own invention.

p. 77   Further evidence that Hitler planned no *immediate* action on Austria is implicit in a letter from his special agent Keppler to Himmler, dated 7 March 1938 (the day after both had met Ribbentrop): ". . . May I remind you that you were going to submit proposals as to which officers you considered best suited for the exchange with Austria." (Himmler files. T175/32).

p. 78   When Winston Churchill's attention was directed to the secret British files on this offer of colonies to Germany, he wrote in July 1943: "I think it is a pity that Mr Eden's name should be mixed up directly with the policy of appeasement." On his instructions, the papers were never published. (See PRO files.)

p. 79   The OKH study of 7 March 1938, drafted by Beck but signed by Brauchitsch, is in naval file PG/33311. Hitler's reaction is in Keitel's memoirs.

p. 81   The FA intercepts of the French telegrams were dictated by telephone to Bodenschatz on 13 March 1938 (ND, 2949–PS).

p. 82   The 1945 interrogations of Glaise-Horstenau, and above all his conversation with Ribbentrop's aide Likus on 20 April 1938 (AA files, serial 43, 28926ff) provide most of the narrative. My timing of events is based on the diaries of Bormann, Eberhard and Jodl, on the FA reports (2949–PS) and post-war interrogations of Göring, Papen, Keppler, Wiedemann and the police general von Grolmann.

p. 85   Hitler's anxiety about Mussolini's reaction is plain from the FA's record of his phone conversation with Prince Philipp of Hesse, his courier to Rome, on 11 March 1938 (2949–PS). On 12 March, Jodl noted in his diary, "Schörner [commanding a Mountain Corps] is pushed forward to the Italian frontier." In a letter to the OKH on 28 March, Keitel mentioned that Hitler was asking whether the three mountain divisions "are adequate for an initial defence of our southern frontier and to what extent they are to be reinforced by frontier guards" (PG/33274). I have put a transcript of Jodl's unpublished diary 11–18 March 1938 in the Sammlung Irving, IfZ.

p. 85   On the nocturnal phone calls to Hitler, see Weizsäcker's letter to his mother, 13 March 1938: "The last days were pretty hectic. Even at night – i.e. on 11–12 March – Marianne got little sleep as my phone never stopped ringing." Most of the calls came from Vienna, as Weizsäcker recalled on 26 March: "After Seyss-Inquart was successfully installed, he represented that it would be superfluous and undesirable for German troops to march in. During the night of 11–12 March I passed on these representations, in part, supported by our chargé d'affaires [in Vienna] von Stein, by General Muff [the military attaché] and by the C-in-C of the army, General von Brauchitsch; but nobody in the Reich Chancellery would listen." Since I wrote this work, the Weizsäcker papers have now been published by Professor Leonidas Hill (Berlin, 1974). There is no excuse for past historians (A. J. P. Taylor, Alan Bullock, Joachim Fest, John Toland) to have ignored them.

p. 86 Viebahn's nervous breakdown is described in Jodl's unpublished diary, and the unpublished part of Keitel's memoirs too.

p. 87 That Hitler only decided on Anschluss when actually in Linz is proven by entries in the diaries of Weizsäcker (26 March 1938) and Milch, and by the testimony of Keitel, Keppler, Milch and the secretary of the Austrian legation in Berlin, Johannes Schwarzenberg; both Ribbentrop and Göring were astounded by Hitler's decision.

p. 88 Wolf Eberhard described the finger-and-thumb episode to me; after Prague in March 1939, Keitel actually reminded Eberhard of it!

p. 89 In addition to published and unpublished British, French, German, Czech, Polish and American documents I drew extensively on interrogations of Ribbentrop, Andor Hencke (the Secretary of the Prague Legation), General von Wietersheim, General von Salmuth, Halder, General Kalman Hardy (the Hungarian military attaché), Nicolaus von Horthy, Brauchitsch and Blaskowitz, and on the written testimonies of Below, Engel, Adam and Henlein's Berlin agent, Fritz Bürger, for the chapters that follow.

Besides the Weizsäcker, Jodl and Eberhard diaries two more are now of importance: that kept by Hitler's ADC Max Wünsche from 16 June to 20 November 1938 (NS 10/125) listing the Führer's appointments and decisions; and the diary of Helmuth Groscurth, published as *Tagebücher eines Abwehroffiziers 1938–1940* (Stuttgart, 1970).

p. 91 For Keitel's instruction of 28 March 1938, see file PG/33274.

p. 92 Hitler's private remarks were in his Table Talk, 21–22 October 1941. See also the post-war interrogations of Albert Speer and – with due caution – his books, and the fine (but unpublished) dissertation by Dr Armand Dehlinger on Nazi reconstruction plans for Munich and Nuremberg (IfZ, MS 8/1).

Schmundt recorded Keitel's and his own secret conferences with Hitler several times between April and October 1938, and filed the notes with telegrams and directives on "Green". The original file (ND, 388–PS) was microfilmed by NA at my request (their film T77/1810). A formal war diary was also begun shortly by Helmuth Greiner for the OKW's National Defence branch (L.), as an entry in Eberhard's diary on 22 November 1938, on Keitel's daily conference records: "Greiner: goes on leave, after completion of War Diary for period from 21 May 1938 to conclusion of Czech crisis: valuable material compiled daily, largely from handwritten notes of Chief of OKW [Keitel]. Wehrmacht adjutant, Lieutenant-Colonel Schmundt, suggests note to effect that further complementary documents are in his files." (The Greiner war diary has not been seen since.)

p. 94 Likus reported, on 26 April, Hitler's remarks to Sztójay (AA serial 43, 28929).

p. 95 Hitler's visit to Rome is described in many sources – notably in Julius Schaub's manuscripts, in Engel's notes and Wiedemann's San Francisco manuscript of 28 March (1939?).

p. 97 Hitler's remark aboard *Conte Cavour* was recalled to Ciano on 13 August 1939: it is clearer from the draft (Loesch film, F5 or T120/610) than from the final typescript that this was Hitler's, not Mussolini's, remark.

p. 97 Speer and Schaub both confirmed Hitler's gratitude to the Social Democrats for abolishing the monarchy; and see Dr Werner Koeppen's note on his supper Table Talk on 18 September 1941 (T84/387).

p. 98 Jeschonnek's report is in naval file PG/33272.

p. 100 In Reich Justice Ministry files is a note on the fate of the two Czech policemen (Koranda and Kriegl) who gunned down the two Sudeten German farmers. On 20 October 1940 the minister ruled that they had no case to answer; but Himmler nonetheless committed them to life imprisonment (BA, R22/4087).

p. 101 In view of their importance, I completely deciphered Beck's pencilled notes written during Hitler's speech on 28 May 1938 (N28/3); my transcript is in Sammlung Irving, IfZ. Wiedemann also described the speech in his 1939 and 1940 manuscripts (film DJ-19, Sammlung Irving) and in various interrogations. In his diary Weizsäcker observed on 31 May 1938: "On 28 May the Führer briefed his intimates in a three-hour speech to the effect that preparations for the later settlement of the Czech problem are to be forced ahead. He named . . . ? [*sic*] as the date."

p. 102 Hitler's order for the West Wall – popularly dubbed the Siegfried Line – is mentioned in Fritz Todt's diaries and papers (in family possession), in Adam's memoirs, and in records of the General Staff's fortifications branch (T78/300).

p. 102 Puttkamer cabled Raeder on 24 May 1938 about Hitler's prediction that Britain and France would now be the Reich's enemies: see naval files PG/36794, 33535 and 34162 for the telegram, together with the flurry of conferences Hitler's prophecy instigated at naval staff level.

p. 103 Raeder's stipulation appears again in the naval staff's study of 25 October 1938 (PG/34181): "The objective of land operations [in the west] must be to occupy the Channel coast as far as the western approaches (Brest etc)", because to occupy this coastline would be "of overriding importance for the navy and Luftwaffe in the event of war with Britain/France". Raeder doubtless made this plain to Hitler on 27 May, because in his secret speech next day Hitler confirmed (according to Beck's cryptic notes), "Objective of a war in west (France and Britain) is enlarging our coastal baseline (Belgium, Holland). Danger of Belgian and Czech neutrality. Therefore eliminate Czechs." Wolfgang Foerster's interpretation of these lines in *Ein General Kämpft gegen den Krieg* (Munich, 1949) is wrong: he expands them to suggest that the enlarging of the baseline (Belgium and Holland) would be the objective of war with the western powers; in fact it was the *prerequisite*, as Beck's original note shows.

p. 105 Wünsche's diary has lain – unrecognized – in Adjutantur des Führers files since 1945: now in BA file NS 10/125; and see NS 10/116. Fan-mail on the Schmeling fight: NS 10/13 and NS 10/88.

p. 106 For Hitler's directive on pornographic interrogations, as quoted, see Lammers' file R 43 II/1536 and Justice Ministry file R 22/1085.

p. 107 The quotation on Kempka is from his RuSHA dossier (BDC).

p. 108 My account of Hitler's relations with women is based on Wiedemann's February 1939 manuscript; Schaub's papers; a manuscript by Henriette Hoffmann; and an interrogation summary of Dr Karl Brandt titled "Women around Hitler", 6 August 1945. Specifically on Geli Raubal, I interviewed her brother Leo Raubal in Linz, and used too the interrogation of their mother, the later Frau Angela Hammitzsch (46M-13) and of the housekeeper Anni Winter (IfZ, ZS-494).

p. 108 Maurice discussed his role with one of Hitler's secretaries, who is my source (but desires not to be named).

p. 111 The Eva Braun diary, 6 February to 28 May 1935, is periodically "rediscovered" – most recently by Dr Werner Maser in *Jasmin*. Its faking by Eva herself is testified to by one of her friends at the time, Frau Marion Schönmann.

p. 113 Speer's memorandum is in Party Chancellery files (T580/871).

p. 114 Todt's letter to Thorak is in Todt family papers.

p. 116 A transcript of Hitler's secret speech is in BA file NS 26/51.

p. 117   The quotation is from his secret speech to Nazi editors on 10 November 1938. See my note to page 60.

p. 119   Adolf Hitler's "Study on the Problem of our Works of Fortification" is dated Berchtesgaden 1 July 1938 (ND, 1801–PS). Warlimont stated under interrogation, "It is one of the best examples of Hitler's military talent." And General Kurt Zeitzler agreed in a 1961 lecture (N 63/96) that Hitler had enormous sympathy with the hardships of combat troops – it was Hitler who pointed to the need for fortified latrines in the West Wall. One sketch of a command post by Hitler will be found in BA file 75134/38.

p. 120   Todt refers to his visit to the Berghof, in a letter to Ministerialrat Schönleben on 12 August 1938 (Todt papers).

p. 121   "Put the wind up them" – the quotation is from Eberhard's diary, 15 August 1938. Eszterházy's report to the Hungarian General Staff is in the Budapest national archives. See Professor Jörg Hoensch's standard work, *Der ungarische Revisionismus und die Zerschlagung der Tschechoslowakei* (Tübingen, 1967). Winston Churchill, who had seen Henlein in London on 13 May 1938, was clearly completely taken in by his reasonableness and apparent independence of Hitler's will. (See Martin Gilbert, *Winston S. Churchill*, vol. V, 939ff.)

p. 121   For this visit, see Wiedemann's papers. Sir Alexander Cadogan, Chamberlain's adviser, wrote in his diary on 18 July 1938, "He [Wiedemann] said he was Hitler's adjutant when H. was a 'despatch bearer' during war, had to confess he never suspected his possibilities – thought him just a brave, reliable soldier." As for Forster's meeting with Churchill, the Soviet government published Churchill's account of it as found in German files (*Dokumente und Materialien aus der Vorgeschichte des Zweiten Weltkrieges, 1937–1938*, Bd.I [Moscow], 144).

p. 122   Jodl's diary has the best account of Hitler's Berghof speech (of 10 August). Wietersheim, Keitel, Adam and Halder rendered later descriptions, as did Salmuth in a manuscript dated 2 February 1946 in my possession.

p. 123   Eberhard glued a four-page note on Hitler's secret speech of 15 August into his diary. Some months later Liebmann also wrote an account (IfZ, ED 1).

p. 126   Post-war publications by the exile Hungarians are coy about how far they agreed to aid the Nazis, but the contemporary records seem plain enough – especially the Hungarian notes on their talks with Hitler, Göring, Keitel, Beck(!), and Brauchitsch 22–26 August 1938, in which the Hungarian position was stated at one stage as: "Hungary has every intention of squaring accounts with Czechoslovakia in her own interest, but cannot be precise as to a date" (T973/15/0326ff); see also the 1941 report by the German general attached to Hungarian forces (T78/458/5349). I used in addition Weizsäcker's private papers, interrogations of Hardy and Horthy, and interviews of Spitzy and Raeder's adjutant, Captain Herbert Friedrichs.

p. 126–7   Hitler's conferences with the West Wall generals are recorded in General Staff files (T78/300/1364ff) and Adam's memoirs (IfZ, ED 109/2) as well as Jodl's diary.

p. 131   The letter, dated 1 September 1938, is in Schwerin von Krosigk's files (T178/300/1302ff).

p. 136   The complete file of FA "brown pages", 14–26 September 1938, reporting Beneš's telephone conversations with Masaryk and others, was handed to the British ambassador in Berlin by the Nazis on the twenty-sixth (PRO, FO 371/21742). In Prague and London the Czechs (Hodza and Masaryk) indignantly denied them at the time; but one of Masaryk's staff later admitted to British author Laurence Thompson – who did not see the actual wiretaps – that the conversations had taken place (See *The Greatest Treason* [London], 121). Kittel and Spitzy confirm this.

p. 137   Chamberlain's visit to the Berghof is reported in his own notes, in Wünsche's diary and the diary of former ambassador Ulrich von Hassell, *Vom andern Deutschland*,

(Frankfurt, 1964), 17 September 1938, and in the British Cabinet minutes. On 16 September, Weizsäcker wrote to his mother, "For about an hour yesterday the Führer related to Ribbentrop and me how his talks went. Both from an objective and from a psychological point of view it was perhaps the most interesting thing I've heard for a long time."

p. 138 On the Sudeten Free Corps, see Dr Martin Broszat's excellent study in *VfZ*, 1961, 30ff; and Köchling's own report dated 11 October 1938 (ND, EC–366–1).

p. 142 Churchill's sneak visit to France raised hackles on both sides of the Channel. Sir Maurice Hankey wrote in his diary on 2 October, "Winston Churchill's sudden visit to France by aeroplane, accompanied by General [E.L.] Spears, and his visit only to the members of the French Government like Mandel, who is opposed to the policy of peace, was most improper – Bonnet, the French foreign minister, has complained about it, asking what we would say if our prominent French statesmen did the same."

p. 149 The events of 28 September 1938 are chronicled in Hassell's, Eberhard's, Jodl's and Weizsäcker's diaries and in the telegram of the American chargé d'affaires to the US State department on 21 October 1938 (*The Foreign Relations of the United States, 1938, I*, 727ff). I also used Likus' report to Ribbentrop, 3 October (AA, serial 43, 28993). According to Wiedemann under interrogation in 1945, Hitler admitted to Göring that the British fleet mobilization was the reason for his change of heart: "You see, Göring," Hitler said a month later, "at the last moment I thought the British fleet would shoot."

p. 150 The Luftwaffe lieutenant who acted as interpreter at Hitler's private meetings with the Italians that day, 29 September, was Peterpaul von Donat: see *Deutsches Adelsblatt*, 15 June 1971, for his account.

p. 151 The "piece of paper" went into the AA archives with a Top State Secret classification. In a private letter that day, 30 September, Fritz Todt wrote: "The last few weeks have been tough going. But in four months we have poured the same amount of concrete along our frontier as the French managed in four years. This fact was not without its effect on the [Munich] conference."

p. 153 For a published work on Nazi subversion in Slovakia that winter, see Jörg Hoensch, *Die Slowakei und Hitlers Ostpolitik* (Cologne–Graz, 1965). Notes on the Nazis' talks with Slovak leaders are on Loesch film F18 (T120/625). For the Czech documentation, see *Das Abkommen von München, Tschechoslowakische diplomatische Dokumente 1937–1939* (Prague, 1968).

p. 156 For these FA wiretaps, see the FA's vitally significant summary "On British Policy from Munich to the Outbreak of War" (N.140098) in Woermann's AA file, "Documents: Outbreak of War" (serial 1132). It seems surprising that every historian who has written on that subject (including A. J. P. Taylor, Walther Hofer, Joachim Fest) overlooked this file. I published the entire document in translation in *Breach of Security* (London, 1968), with supporting materials.

p. 156 Thomas described Keitel's telephone call from Munich in several post-war interrogations, and in a speech to his Armaments Inspectors on 29 March 1940 (see the BA publication, *Geschichte der deutschen Wehr- und Rüstungswirtschaft 1918–1945*, Appendix III).

p. 159 Goebbels' scandalous behaviour is noted in the private diaries of Groscurth, 30 December 1938, and Hassell, 22 January 1939. Rudolf Likus minuted his chief, Ribbentrop, on 3 November 1938: "There has been uproar at the Gloria Palace cinema from Friday to Sunday during showing of the film *Spieler*. Lida Baarova was jeered. As from Monday the film has been dropped." (AA, serial 43, 29042). Hitler's desire for Magda Goebbels arose, as he admitted to a secretary, from her personal likeness to Geli Raubal.

p. 159 Fritz Todt's complaint is in a long letter to Keitel dated 21 October 1939 (family papers).

p. 160 The quotation is from Jodl's draft of 19 October 1938 (T77/775/0629).

***p.** 161* For the Jewish problem in Czechoslovakia after Munich, see Heinrich Bodensieck's analysis in *VfZ*, 1961, 249ff. Helmut Heiber wrote a brilliant study of the unusual Grynszpan case in *VfZ*, 1957, 134ff. Here is not the place to explore the extraordinary manner in which the alleged assassin's adroit French lawyer obliged the Nazis to drop their plans (in 1942) to try the case: suffice to say that Grynszpan survived the war in a concentration camp and was last known living in Paris in the '50s.

***p.** 164* The action report is in BDC file 240/I.

***p.** 164* The "igniting" function of Goebbels' speech that evening is clear from a Nuremberg interrogation of Ribbentrop on 13 September 1945, and of Julius Streicher (who had it at first hand from SA General Hanns-Günther von Obernitz); and from the report of the Party Court to Göring, 13 February 1939 (ND, 3063–PS).

The telexes issued that night also tell their own story: at 11:55 P.M. an "igniting" signal by the Gestapo, Berlin (374–PS); at 1:20 A.M. a further one by Heydrich from Munich (3052–PS); at 2:10 A.M. one by Eberstein (BDC file 240/I) to his subsidiary police commanders at Augsburg, Nuremberg, etc., expanding on 374–PS – no doubt before Eberstein's bawling out by Hitler; and then at 2:56 A.M. the "extinguishing" telex was sent out as quoted (3063–PS), and repeated to all gauleiters (BDC file 240/I). At 3:45 A.M. the Berlin Gestapo came into line (copy in Groscurth's papers).

***p.** 165* The fury of Hitler, Göring, Himmler and even Heydrich at Goebbels' arbitrary act is borne out in varying degree by numerous contemporary sources: Groscurth's and Hassell's diaries, Wiedemann's 1939 manuscript on the pogrom, the unpublished memoirs of the Luftwaffe's chief judge-advocate Christian von Hammerstein, Engel's notes, and Likus' report of 30 November (AA serial 43, 29067).

***p.** 165* The principal witnesses of events in Hitler's apartment are Below and Schaub, the adjutants. I also used the IfZ testimonies of Karl Wolff, Max Jüttner, Wiedemann, Brückner and Engel, and Schallermeier (Wolff's aide: see IMT, vol. xlii, 511ff.).

***p.** 166* For Hitler's attitude on the Jews at this time, see his talk with the South African minister Pirow on 24 November 1938 and especially with Colonel Jósef Beck, the Polish foreign minister, on 5 January 1939. He said, "If the western powers had summoned up a little more understanding for Germany's colonial demands I might have made available a territory in Africa as a solution for the Jewish problem, which could have been used to settle not only the German but also the Polish Jews. . . ."

***p.** 166* The speech of 10 November: see my reference to page 60, and Bruno Werner's novel *Die Galeere* (Frankfurt, 1949), 157.

***p.** 168* SS Brigadier Dr Benno Martin, the Nuremberg police president, was present when Hitler made the remark at dinner on 14 November. Weizsäcker refers to Hitler's "revenge" remark several times in his diaries – in February, on 16 March 1939, on 28 January 1940 and in his October 1939 survey of events leading to the war.

***p.** 169* Hitler's thoughts in November are set out by Keitel in a brief dated 26 November, sent by him to the services on 1 December 1938 (PG/33316 and Loesch film F19 or T120/624).

***p.** 169* One record of the Reich Defence Council session of 18 November is in naval files, PG/33272; a better one is Woermann's note, on Loesch film F19 (T120/624).

***p.** 172* As Krosigk emphasizes (IfZ, ZS A/20), Schacht was dismissed – he did not resign. For Chancellery records leading up to Schacht's dismissal, see the Allied compilation DE 482/DIS 202 of 26 October 1945, and 3520–PS.

***p.** 173* Hitler's three secret speeches – of 18 and 25 January, and 10 February 1939 – will be found with the transcript of his speeches of 10 November 1938 and 11 March (page 187) in BA file NS 11/28. For different transcripts of two of them see IfZ files F 19/10 and ED 57, together with the diaries of Groscurth, Hassell, Milch and Eberhard, and Likus' report of 2 February 1939.

***p.** 181* On Hitler's changing posture towards the USSR: interrogations of Gustav

Hilger, and his memoirs *Wir und der Kreml* (Frankfurt, 1955); of General Ernst Köstring, the former military attaché there; of Friedrich Gaus, Ribbentrop's legal expert; and E. M. Robertson's early but authoritative Cabinet Office monograph, "Barbarossa, the Origins and Development of Hitler's Plan to Attack Russia" (March 1952).

p. 183 Film buffs will find Hitler's views on the current movies in his Adjutantur files (BA, NS 10/44 and 45).

p. 186 I found Hewel's note of events on 10 March 1939 among his family papers.

p. 187 General Josef (Beppo) Schmid, who carried Hitler's letter to Göring, recalled under interrogation the field-marshal's horror when he read its contents.

p. 188 Elisabeth Wagner, the general's widow, lent to me about 2,000 pages of his letters – only the more innocuous parts of which she published in her book *Der Generalquartiermeister*.

p. 189 For my account of Hitler's controversial all-night session with Hacha, I relied – apart from Hewel's protocol – on the testimony of Keitel, Warlimont, interpreter Paul Schmidt, Keppler, Göring, Werner Kiewitz and Schaub.

p. 190 "I'm going in!" – The scene was witnessed by Keitel and Schweppenburg, who later commented that Hitler had obvious personal courage: "On the afternoon of 16 March 1939, Prague was anything but a safe place for the German head of state to be." In a private letter Eduard Wagner – one of the 1944 plotters! – also expressed his "uneasiness over the Führer's personal safety" that day; and see Rommel's private letter of that day (T84/R275/0015).

p. 192 For the letter from Hacha's daughter, thanking Hitler for his courtesy, see the Adjutantur file NS 10/18. Propaganda directives to editors are in BA file ZSg 101.

p. 192 Colonel Curt Siewert's note on Hitler's discussion with Brauchitsch, 25 March 1939, is ND, R–100. Referring to Stalin's speech of 10 March, Molotov was to remark on 31 August 1939: "It is now evident that in Germany they understood these statements of comrade Stalin correctly on the whole and drew practical conclusions from them [*Laughter*]." Friedrich Gaus also testified in a Nuremberg affidavit that when Ribbentrop related to Stalin on 23 August how the Führer had interpreted the March speech as a Soviet overture, Stalin replied: "That was the intention" (Jackson papers).

p. 194 The evidence that it was on 31 March – i.e. after the British guarantee was announced – that Hitler asked for an OKW directive on "White", is to be found in the diaries of Eberhard, Bormann and Major Wilhelm Deyhle, Jodl's adjutant (ND, 1796–PS), and an interrogation of Warlimont. On 30 March, Colonel Wagner wrote, "Tomorrow the C-in-C [Brauchitsch] and the Führer get back and all our briefing notes must be ready by then"; and on 1 April, Wagner used the phrase, ". . . yesterday, when the Führer took the decision . . ." (*gestern bei der Führerentscheidung*).

p. 201 Except for Grawitz and Stumpfegger, Hitler's medical staff survived the war; but Haase's widow tells me that he was beaten to death in a Soviet prison camp in 1945. Morell, Giesing, Brandt and Hasselbach were extensively interrogated (e.g. USFET MISC reports OI-CIR/ and /4) as was dentist Blaschke (OI-FIR/31). Unhappily, the US army lost all Morell's records on Hitler; the rest are on NA microcopy T253. I interviewed Giesing and Hasselbach and obtained Morell's private papers from the widow's collection. The ENT specialist Eicken's treatment records on Hitler are on NA special films ML/125 and /131. A surprising number of Hitler's staff found Morell quite satisfactory; Brandt wrote an essay on him in September 1945 strongly expressing the opposite view (BA, K1. Erw. 441–3). Finally, I closely examined the personnel files of each doctor in the BDC and had Morell's prescriptions assessed by the medical expert Professor Ernst-Günther Schenck.

p. 208 The only note on Hitler's 23 May 1939 conference is by Rudolf Schmundt (ND, L–079) but there are grounds, too numerous to elicit here, for believing that the note was written much later, probably for OKW historical branch files. At least five passages appear anachronistic, and I have therefore ignored them. Halder's earliest description of it is in USSBS interrogation, 25 June 1945. See also his study OKH-OKW dated 7 August 1945 (CSDIC report GRGG 3326C).

p. 209   Prince Paul's visit was described to me by Frau Winifred Wagner, Frau Schmundt and Engel; Schaub, Below and the interpreter Schmidt wrote about it, and the planning is in file NS 10/126.

p. 211   Brückner's son lent me his father's papers (restricted copy in Sammlung Irving, IfZ). Schaub's papers are voluminous but honest, and reward patient study (ditto). Colonel von Below allowed me access to his unpublished memoirs.

p. 212   The extraordinary Albrecht affair took place in June 1939, not July as the Engel "diary" suggests; see Albrecht's BDC file. By 8 July, Below was already performing some of his duties (see e.g. Weizsäcker's files, serial 97, 108413). I also drew on statements of Puttkamer, Admiral Gerhard Wagner, Karl Brandt, Vormann and Raeder's two adjutants, Friedrichs and Kurt Freiwald, and on the Groscurth diary. Christa Schroeder recalls telling Hitler of public criticism of the way the older Party figures were loosely divorcing their wives in favour of younger women. Hitler replied, "The hardest fighters deserve only the finest women!" This enabled her to reply: "Oh, mein Führer, then what a beauty *you* ought to have!"

p. 215   Hitler's attitude to the Church establishment and to religious doctrines is well illustrated in the Table Talk notes written by Heim and Bormann, and by Rosenberg's liaison officer Koeppen in 1941 (T84/387), and the Hewel diary entries that I quote. An official circular of 10 December 1935 formulated, "The Reich Chancellor [Hitler] was born a Catholic; he still adheres to the Catholic religion, but makes no use of its amenities, e.g. regular churchgoing or religious services" (BA file R 43 II/961). According to his doctor, Hasselbach, Hitler paid Church Tax dues to the very end (quoted in *Frankenpost*, 12 March 1947).

p. 220   Niemöller roused strong passions even in 1945. The material on him includes vivid OCMH interrogations of Meissner, Krosigk and Lammers; Engel's notes; Likus' reports to Ribbentrop; Hans Buchheim's study on the Niemöller trial in *VfZ*, 1956, 307ff, and Krosigk's papers in the IfZ (ZS A/20).

p. 221   I unearthed a delightful wealth of sources on the FA wiretaps and Hitler's confrontation with Niemöller on 25 January 1934, including a Göring interrogation and a handwritten account by Lammers in July 1945 (OCMH). Rosenberg recorded in his diary six years later, on 19 January 1940: "The Führer then described the reception of the church leaders at which the Confessionals and the German Christians almost came to blows in his presence over who got the allowances. He mimicked Niemöller's sanctimonious phraseology and then ordered the man's earlier telephone conversation – which was conducted in the crudest matelot's jargon – to be read out loud to them. Result: embarrassed collapse of stout brethren!"

p. 223   Many moderates considered Niemöller's internment well deserved, among them Dönitz – the pastor's former crewmate at naval academy – Lammers and Krosigk (OCMH): Niemöller was after all preaching open sedition from his pulpit. The Allied interrogators also minuted that Niemöller's personality was "a matter of concern to AMG [Allied Military Government] officers". As late as 28 July 1943, Field-Marshal Wolfram von Richthofen recorded in his diary Göring's reflection that "the Führer tried just about everything to establish one Reich Church along Lutheran lines; but the obstinacy of the Church leaders thwarted every attempt".

p. 224   The surreptitious preparations in Danzig are referred to in the war diaries of the Military Commander of Danzig (BA, RH 53–20/v.25) and the divisional surgeon of Eberhardt's Kampfgruppe (BA, P.1355). See also the diary kept by Field-Marshal Fedor von Bock (N22/1), and his formal operational proposal submitted on 27 May 1939 to Brauchitsch (BA, II–H.821) Himmler also outlined the role of the SS Heim-wehr in Danzig in his speech of 3 August 1944 in *VfZ*, 1953, 357ff. See too *Danziger Vorposten* (the local Nazi Newspaper).

p. 225 The Rechlin display is extensively covered by the Milch documents: see my reference to page 4, and especially MD 51/5667ff, MD 62/5293 and 5470, MD 65/7326 and 7347 and MD 56/2678.

p. 227 August Kubizek related the 1906 episode in his book, *Adolf Hitler mein Jugendfreund* (Göttingen, 1953); it was confirmed by his widow Paula in Eferding (Austria) and by Winifred Wagner in interviews with me.

p. 229 Wohlthat's report of 24 July 1939 is on NA special film ML/123; see also Dirksen's report of 21 July. The secret talks were leaked by *The Daily Telegraph* and *News Chronicle* on 22 and 23 July. The best study so far is by Helmut Metzmacher in *VfZ*, 1966, 370ff.

p. 230 The hilarious Bormann/Hanfstaengl correspondence is in Bormann's files, NS 19/171. Winifred Wagner told me the rest.

p. 231 I rely on Lossberg's unpublished manuscript, rather than his later book *Im Wehrmachtführungsstab* (Hamburg, 1949).

p. 232 Hitler afterwards bragged of the agent he had placed at Croydon: see Captain Wolf Junge's unpublished manuscript (restricted, Sammlung Irving, IfZ).

p. 233 This fragment of the Lahousen diary is ND, 3047–PS.

p. 234 Heydrich first put the scheme to manufacture "border incidents" to SS Colonel Trummler, SS Brigadier Otto Rasch and SS General Heinrich Müller – of the Gestapo – in a Berlin conference on 8 August 1939. The later police general Otto Hellwig was present and wrote a manuscript which is in my possession. The famous Gleiwitz operation was first adumbrated at the second conference, on or about 11 August. See also the Hassell diary, 15 August, and Dr Jürgen Runzheimer's study in *VfZ*, 1962, 408ff (he also supplied me with further unpublished material).

p. 235 The interpreter Eugen Dollmann described the scene as Hewel hurried in, in a (monitored) conversation of 4 June 1945 (CSDIC report CMF/X 173).

p. 236 Hitler's Berghof conference of 14 August 1939 is referred to in the diaries of Halder, Bormann and Milch. For the pages that follow I also drew heavily on naval staff files PG/33984, PG/33979, PG/32201 and the AA files on Poland, Danzig and the outbreak of the war.

p. 236 For the deception methods, see the papers on *Die Meistersinger* (BA, Schumacher Sammlung, 368) and on the Tannenberg ceremony (MD 65/7323). The US envoy was completely hoodwinked, cabling Washington on 8 August that it was "unlikely that any action requiring extensive use of railroad and other transportation will be launched by Germany from the latter part of August to middle of September" (NA, 740.00/2026); and see Meissner's letter to Brückner, 15 August (NS 10/12).

p. 237 The Jablunka tunnel and Dirschau bridge operations are well narrated in the official German monograph by Herbert Schindler, *Mosty und Dirschau* 1939 (Freiburg, 1971). I also used Lahousen's diary 17 August *et seq.*, and his post-war testimony, Canaris's note on a talk with Keitel on 17 August (ND, 795–PS), Halder's diary of that date and – with caution – Groscurth's second-hand version in his diary of 24 August; and the War Diary of the Eighth Army, 31 August 1939. together with an Abwehr file in the BA, OKW-74.

p. 241 Hitler often stressed the influence of the harvest on his strategic planning: see Liebmann's November 1939 manuscript (IfZ, ED 1); Eberhard's diary, 15 August 1938; Admiral Albrecht's diary of 22 August 1939, and Table Talk, 10 May 1942, midday.

p. 241 The OKW invitation dated 19 August is in naval file PG/33984. Five versions were written of Hitler's speech on 22 August: by Halder, Albrecht, Boehm (ND, Raeder–27), Bock and Canaris (ND, 789–PS and 1014–PS); see also Groscurth's diary, 24 August 1939. The speech is briefly mentioned in the diaries of Milch, Leeb and

Felber (the Eighth Army's chief of staff, N 67/2). Other versions exist, but they are of only secondary value; the lurid script played into the enemy's hands by the Canaris/Oster circle (ND, 003–L) is quite worthless. See Winfried Baumgart's scholarly investigation in *VfZ*, 1968, 120ff.

p. 242 Hitler did not deny that the western powers might declare war (but he believed that they would not actually fight). Bock later quoted him as having said: "I don't know whether the British will join in against us or not." Vormann was briefed by Keitel on 24 August that Hitler still hoped to face Poland alone; but the Führer realized that Britain and France would be hostile and might even break off diplomatic relations and start economic warfare against the Reich.

p. 242 The reference to crushing "every living spark" – *die lebendigen Kräfte* – in Poland was misinterpreted by the Allied prosecutors at Nuremberg. In fact Hitler was just stating the basic military fact that the strategic objective was to destroy the enemy, not attain some line on a map. The professional soldiers present understood this perfectly (see, e.g., Bock's diary). Note that Hitler used precisely the same turn of phrase in his harangue to the generals before the Battle of the Ardennes, on 12 December 1944 (Heiber, *op. cit.*, 721).

p. 244 It was probably on the next day, 23 August 1939, that Göring called an important conference with the leading Reich ministers, about which Dr Herbert Backe – state-secretary in the food ministry – wrote privately on the thirty-first: "I came to Berlin on Sunday [20 August]. On ... [23 August?] we were asked round to Karinhall. Göring, Funk, Darré, Körner, Landfried, myself, Behrens, Neumann and Posse. Göring disclosed in strictest confidence to us that it has been decided to attack Poland. He asked each of us about our own war preparations. Ration cards. We have managed to keep bread and potatoes ration-free for the first four weeks because of the good supply postion. Fortunately, Göring reluctantly agreed. To safeguard the element of surprise, Göring has insisted on the strictest security. Everybody's mood was very optimistic. The attack has been set down for Friday the twenty-fifth.... After Karinhall, it was obvious to me that we would only be up against Poland – i.e. there would not be a world war – and that this risk could be accepted."

p. 248 For the text of Mussolini's first letter to Hitler on 25 August (later cancelled), see Ciano's letter to the King in Mussolini's personal papers (T586/405/0237).

p. 248 The time – 3:02 P.M. – is recorded in the private diaries of four people present: Vormann, Weizsäcker, Halder and Wagner. See also the war diary of Führer's HQ (T77/858/4392ff) and Rommel's excited letters to his wife (T84/R273a), and the naval staff war diary, 3:30 P.M.

p. 249 Many observers thought that after this fiasco of 25 August 1939, Hitler would be forced to call off "White" altogether. Eduard Wagner, representative of feelings in the General Staff, wrote to his wife next day: "Couldn't write last night as evening very hectic. You can calm down – as far as I can see nothing's going to happen!" Vormann's letter of 26 August also gives a vivid picture of the previous day's events (transcripts in Sammlung Irving, IfZ).

p. 250 Lieutenant Herzner's handwritten account of the desperate Jablunka operation is in Günter Peis's possession in Munich, as is Hellwig's narrative of the last-minute cancellation of fake "Polish" incidents in Upper Silesia.

p. 251 The FA "brown pages" on Ciano's phone call to Attolico, numbers N.125,894 and N.125,910, will be found in an OKW file (T77/545). See also Mackensen's papers, AA serial 100. On Italy's posture, Göring was surprisingly sympathetic. Backe's letter of 31 August continues ". . . On Sunday [27 August] at his operational HQ in Wild Park [Potsdam]. . . . G. [Göring] disclosed to us in strict confidence that Italy's not going to join in. This is why the attack was cancelled.... Now we've got to see how we can get out of the mess. He says that besides the Russian Pact we also signed a secret deal (he told us that already once at Karinhall: it evidently partitions

Poland, with Warsaw allocated to us). Göring spoke up stoutly for Mussolini and his predicament, but added that if he was a real man he would have overthrown the monarchy. A tight spot for us. War unthinkable. If we get Danzig out of it, we'll be happy enough. Perhaps a slice of the Corridor too. Conference (Funk) concluded that new situation has a silver lining for us too, as now we won't have any bones to pick with France, while Italy has; so if we drop Italy we have a good chance of keeping France out. . . . We must avoid war and try to save face."

p. 252 At midnight – 26/27 August – Goebbels sent for Backe, ostensibly to rebuke him for the low fruit and tea rations proposed. Backe wrote, "Goebbels heaps exceptionally bitter criticism on the foreign ministry for over-secretiveness. Everybody knows Henderson and Coulondre have been to see the Führer, only the German radio isn't reporting it. The upshot is that the German public is forced to listen to foreign radios. I informed him of our grim food situation. . . . Goebbels made a brilliant impression: objective, serious, determined. He has asked [his state-secretary] Gutterer to brief the Führer on the difficulties with the foreign ministry, which rather leaves the impression that he himself is being given the cold shoulder."

p. 253 Keitel's economics expert Georg Thomas referred, in a speech on 29 March 1940, to two unfavourable reports he had submitted: one warned of fuel and ammunition shortages, and called for economic mobilization in view of the possibility of war with the western powers (possibly the document dated 9 August 1939 on film T77/312/4349); Hitler however responded there would be "no western war, just war with Poland". On 26 August 1939, Thomas submitted to Keitel a second report, which Keitel reluctantly forwarded to Hitler. Hitler rebuked him, "Won't you ever stop pestering me about your 'western war'!"

p. 253 As before, the FA wiretaps were all printed in my book *Breach of Security*. For another FA wiretap, see Halder's diary, 28 August: "Enemy knows old date (26th) and postponement. Britain and France feel unable to give way so long as our troops on frontier. Henderson working to gain time. Chamberlain shocked at personal insults."

Among other wiretaps shown to Hitler now was one resulting from the tap on the Crown Prince's telephone at the Cecilienhof Chateau outside Potsdam. General Joachim von Stülpnagel, freshly appointed commander of the 740,000-strong reserve army, telephoned to announce his new appointment and to promise an early visit "to ascertain your Majesty's orders"! Hitler sacked him that same day and replaced him with General Fritz Fromm.

p. 254 No transcript of his speech to the Reichstag deputies exists, but it is outlined adequately in the diaries of Halder, Groscurth, Hassell and Weizsäcker and mentioned in Backe's letter of 31 August. See also Rudolf Likus' report of 27 August (AA serial 43, 29617). As for Hitler's private intentions towards the USSR, the Gestapo official Dr Werner Best recalled later, "After the Moscow pact was signed on 23 August, word was passed round 'internally' that we were not to be deceived by it – in two years at most the war against Russia would begin (IfZ, ZS-207). Hassell, too, commented on 11 October 1939, "It's highly possible – indeed quite probable since Hitler's speech to the Reichstag deputies – that deep down he's saving himself up for an attack on the Soviet Union."

p. 255 The date of the sixteen-point proposals is not clear. The copy in Ribbentrop's office file is marked 28 August 1939. Other sources suggest it originated next day.

p. 257 I publish this FA intercept in *Breach of Security*. Shorn of its minatory FA heading, the transcript is in Ribbentrop's office file (serial 43, 29636) also.

p. 261 The war of the "illegals" is highlighted in the war diaries of the Military Commander of Danzig, and of Frontier Defence Command (Sector 3), in BA file E.271/1. For the role of the SA brownshirts, see Viktor Lutze's letter to Brauchitsch, 13 October 1939 (RH 1/v.58) and his successor Schepmann's speech, 6 October 1943 (T175/119/5023ff).

Index